A CRUEL LOVE

Other books by Carol Ann Lee

One of Your Own: The Life and Death of Myra Hindley

Evil Relations: The Man Who Bore Witness Against the Moors Murderers
(originally published as *Witness*)

*Somebody's Mother, Somebody's Daughter: True Stories
from the Victims and Survivors of the Yorkshire Ripper*

*The Pottery Cottage Murders: The terrifying true story of
an escaped prisoner and the family he held hostage*

A Passion for Poison: The Extraordinary Crimes of Graham Young

Something Wicked: The Lives, Crimes and Deaths of the Pendle Witches

A Cruel Love

The Ruth Ellis Story

CAROL ANN LEE

MAINSTREAM
PUBLISHING

EDINBURGH AND LONDON

TRANSWORLD PUBLISHERS

UK | USA | Canada | Ireland | Australia
India | New Zealand | South Africa

Transworld is part of the Penguin Random House group of companies
whose addresses can be found at global.penguinrandomhouse.com.

Penguin Random House UK, One Embassy Gardens,
8 Viaduct Gardens, London SW11 7BW

penguin.co.uk

Penguin
Random House
UK

First published in Great Britain in 2012 as *A Fine Day for a Hanging* by
Mainstream Publishing Company (Edinburgh) Ltd, a division of Penguin Random House
Mainstream paperback edition published 2013
Mainstream paperback edition reissued as *A Cruel Love* 2025

002

Copyright © Carol Ann Lee 2012

The moral right of the author has been asserted

Printed and bound in Great Britain by Clays Ltd, Elcograf S.p.A.

The authorized representative in the EEA is Penguin Random House Ireland,
Morrison Chambers, 32 Nassau Street, Dublin D02 YH68.

A CIP catalogue record for this book is available from the British Library

ISBN: 9781910948316

Contents

Preface to original edition, published in 2012
as *A Fine Day for a Hanging*   7

Acknowledgements   9

Part I: La Vie en rose   13

Part II: West End Girl   29

Part III: A Poor, Twisted Boy   97

Part IV: Table of Drops   195

Part V: The Loss-ness of Everything   339

Part VI: Worms in the Carnations: Appendices   387

Notes   406

Bibliography   443

Preface to original edition, published in 2012 as *A Fine Day for a Hanging*

At the age of sixteen, I was mesmerised by Miranda Richardson's portrayal of Ruth Ellis in *Dance with a Stranger*. Named after Ruth's favourite song, the film was directed by Mike Newell, with a screenplay by *A Taste of Honey* author Shelagh Delaney, and focused on the relationship between Ruth Ellis and David Blakely (played by Rupert Everett). Released in 1985, it made far more of an impact on people of my generation than any of the books about the case, despite the narrative ending with David's shooting in Hampstead. The dramatic story of Ruth's arrest, trial and execution remained untold, together with her troubled childhood and life before she became manageress of the Little Club. Although sublimely acted and beautifully shot, with Delaney's trademark incisive dialogue bringing the script shimmering to life, *Dance with a Stranger* unfortunately fixed the character of Ruth Ellis in the public mind as a screeching mass of neuroses.

In the quarter century since then, and for the past thirty-five years, there has been no in-depth, objective study of this infamous but distinctly oversimplified case. Its central themes – passion, class, gender and politics – are as relevant now as they were at the time of Ruth's execution. In addition, capital punishment has recently been fiercely debated again in the UK, with most broadcast discussions referring specifically to Ruth. Yet, unlike Derek Bentley and Timothy Evans, who were executed in 1953 and 1950 respectively for crimes they did not commit (and for which both have been posthumously pardoned), Ruth *was* guilty of shooting David Blakely that Easter Sunday evening in 1955. Nonetheless, it was her death on the scaffold that gave the campaign for abolition its greatest emotional spur. 'By their decision to execute Ruth Ellis,' wrote Rupert Furneaux within a short while of her hanging, 'the Home Office have abolished the death penalty.'[1] There were other legal ramifications besides: the defence of diminished responsibility was introduced in the Homicide Act of 1957, a plea which might have saved Ruth from her appointment with the hangman. Thus this most notorious of British crimes of passion had the effect of bringing compassion into murder law.

A Fine Day for a Hanging explores Ruth Ellis's life and death from a new perspective, aiming to describe all the tumultuous twists and turns of a short but very intensely lived life without making value judgements; it is, as ever, for the reader to make up his or her own mind about the events of almost sixty years ago (as of 2025 now seventy years ago). When Ruth stood in the dock to answer for her crime, the manifold prejudices of the period were as discernible as the fresh peroxide in her hair. From a modern viewpoint, this makes her case extremely poignant and challenging to evaluate, acting as a mirror to that era, in whose reflection we see our own ethics and moralities. Past studies have concentrated, like *Dance with a Stranger*, on the affair between Ruth and David, but *A Fine Day for a Hanging* is a biography which seeks to illuminate Ruth's life and the time in which she lived; it also aspires to provide a much fuller picture of the aftermath of her arrest, to look at what happened to the other protagonists, and to explain the wider implications her execution had on our society.

In a recent private email to Laurence Marks, co-author of *Ruth Ellis: A Case of Diminished Responsibility?*, criminal barrister Edward Henry posited:

> It was an open and shut case, you are right; but there is an enduring sense of injustice because of the background of profound physical abuse, and the unexplained acquisition of the gun. There remains the suspicion that Ruth was hanged on moral grounds, because she was 'undeserving' (hostess/escort at the Little Club) or partly to do with class. Could you see a deranged daughter of the shires being hanged for this? Convicted, yes, but reprieved surely? So what is acceptable after a decanter of whisky on a grouse moor is outrageous in a city ... Ruth's case is all too easy to explain but the society in which she lived was not ready to hear it.[2]

Are we ready now?

Acknowledgements

A great many people helped in the research for this book. I must first of all thank author and historian Keith Skinner, whose assistance in areas too numerous to mention enriched my experience of writing about Ruth and without which the book would be much poorer. Keith also facilitated a visit to the Crime Museum, whose curator Paul Bickley I would also like to thank, and to Hampstead Police Station and the now defunct Hampstead Magistrates' Court, where we were shown around by Sergeant Philip Hewetson, an extremely knowledgeable and patient guide.

I am grateful to Francesca Findlater for answering my questions about her parents, and to John Riley, who introduced me to Georgina Ellis's widower, Mike Blackburn, in my quest to learn more about Ruth's daughter. I learned much about Ruth's son Andre by speaking to his fellow pupils at St Michael's College, Hitchin, some of whom have very painful memories of their time there. I would like to single out for particular thanks Andre's best friend, Brian Jacobs, for his insight and suggestions for further research. The following Old Michaelians provided vital information about Andre and school life in general: Tony Caruana, Michael Craigen, Nic Szeremeta, Tony Stansfield, Peter Bodle, Michael McCartney, Bob Ashurst, Terry Simpson, Jim Hoare and Christopher Hoefkens. I am extremely grateful to all of them and also to Simon Curtis, who runs the St Michael's College website. The school photograph of Andre was passed to me by Mr C. de la Salle and I thank him for that.

Next I should like to thank Laurence Marks for his considerable knowledge about Ruth Ellis, and for his kindness, good humour and endless patience. I thank too writer Peta Steel, daughter of Laurence's co-author Tony Van den Bergh, and would like to take this opportunity to set straight a matter raised in *Ruth Ellis: My Sister's Secret Life*. In her book, Ruth's elder sister, Muriel Jakubait, claims that Tony passed Ruth's very distinctive compact and handbag to his daughter and that he had something of a vendetta against Ruth after she rebuffed his advances. Unaware of these comments at the time, Peta explains that this was not so:

> My father was an award-winning journalist with an excellent reputation. He was a brilliant raconteur who would have enjoyed telling everyone that Ruth had rejected him because he could always take a joke against himself. He certainly never owned any of her possessions and therefore I would never have seen – and never did see – Ruth's compact or her handbag at any point. Both Laurence and my father were very protective of Muriel and did their best by her – and Ruth.

Dr Mike Morrogh, Shrewsbury School archivist and historian, helpfully provided David Blakely's school reports; Tony Cox, former headmaster at Sherborne St John Primary School was able to add to my knowledge of Ruth's school years; Paul Sullivan, who runs Diana Dors's official website, answered my questions patiently and expertly; author Michelangelo Capua was equally helpful regarding Deborah Kerr; and author Douglas Thompson very kindly put several questions to Christine Keeler on my behalf – I am grateful to both him and to Miss Keeler, as I am to Olivia Temple, whose aunt Gwen Nockolds managed the Steering Wheel Club during its heyday.

I am indebted to the staff of several archives, including the National Archives in Kew; Sheffield historian Chris Hobbs, who runs a website under his own name dedicated to unearthing Sheffield's forgotten past; the Tameside Local Studies and Archives Centre; Janet Warr at the Fairfield Moravian Church in Manchester; Robin Wiltshire at the Sheffield City Archives; Manchester City Library; Colin S. Gale at the archives and museum at Bethlehem Royal Hospital; the South London and Maudsley Trust; Alison Gill at the Manchester Room and County Record Office; Adam Shaw at the Co-operative College; June Wailling at the Centre for Buckinghamshire Studies; Andrew Stoodley at Hampshire Archives and Local Studies; Helen Roberts at the Royal Northern College of Music; Buckinghamshire County Council; Colonel Bobby Steele, Regimental Secretary of the Royal Highland Fusiliers Museum; Jim Devine, Secretary of the Highland Light

Infantry Association; Andrew Hudson of Folkestone Library; Michael G. Speers, Smith & Wesson Collectors' Association administrator; Smith & Wesson historian Roy Jinks; Phil Barnes-Warden of the Metropolitan Police Heritage Centre; Neil Paterson of the Metropolitan Police Heritage Centre; and Sioban Clark, chairman of the Friends of the Metropolitan Police Historical Collection. I am grateful too to the staff of the Magdala in Hampstead, for answering my questions. I would like to single out for particular thanks author Margaret Drinkall, an expert on Yorkshire history, who took time out from her own work to conduct research into the Blakely family for me. I extend the same gratitude to author and crime historian Stewart P. Evans, who very kindly clarified a number of facts concerning the execution process.

Thanks too, to Corinne Wiseman at the *Jersey Evening Post*, and a special thank you to Alex Henwood of Fremantle Media for promptly sending me a copy of the terrific Thames Television documentary *The Story of Ruth Ellis*, produced by Peter Williams in 1977. It is a lost gem and deserves to be broadcast again; I found it incredibly useful during the writing of this book and returned to it many times. I would also like to thank Nigel Hulme in the UK and Julian Messent of LMB Racing in Belgium for information on David Blakely's beloved Emperor, which now resides in Belgium, having been expertly restored.

I must also thank the following: Bruce Robinson, Martin Fido, Sean O'Connor, solicitor Bruce MacGregor, Chief Superintendent Simon Ovens and Aysha St Giles. There are several other people who do not wish to be named but whose memories and suggestions for further research were extremely helpful. I thank them all and apologise if I have forgotten anyone here, but am truly grateful to everyone whom I contacted during the writing of this book.

My agent Jan Michael and all the staff at Mainstream Publishing have given staunch support to this book from its inception to its end and I owe them a huge debt of gratitude for that. As always, the support of my partner Alan, my son River and that of my other family and friends has meant everything to me.

Between the 2012 and 2013 editions of *A Fine Day for a Hanging*, I have made some very minor amendments and included further information about David Blakely as a result of reading Nicola Beauman's excellent biography, *The Other Elizabeth Taylor*.

*

11

There are two previous biographies of Ruth Ellis: Robert Hancock's *Ruth Ellis: The Last Woman to be Hanged* (Weidenfeld & Nicolson, 1963; an updated edition was published by Orion in 2000) and Laurence Marks and Tony Van den Bergh's *Ruth Ellis: A Case of Diminished Responsibility?* (Penguin, 1977). Hancock's biography occasionally tips into misogyny but, nonetheless, his interviews with those involved in the case who are no longer living are a useful source. Marks and Van den Bergh's impeccably researched book likewise provides much that is invaluable for anyone either interested in reading or writing about the case. Muriel Jakubait's *Ruth Ellis: My Sister's Secret Life* (Constable & Robinson, 2005), ghostwritten by Monica Weller, is a fascinating memoir which presented a new theory about the death of David Blakely; I refer to this specifically in Appendix I. Georgie Ellis's *Ruth Ellis: My Mother* (Smith Gryphon, 1995) is a personal account from a very different but equally interesting viewpoint. Jonathan Goodman and Patrick Pringle's *The Trial of Ruth Ellis* (David & Charles, 1974) is an excellent reference book, and Victoria Blake's *Ruth Ellis* (National Archives, 2008) in the Crime Archive series is a superb compact biography.

*

I always felt that the horror of David Blakely's death was frequently skimmed over in discussions about the case, and he is too often seen as someone who may well have deserved what happened to him. Similarly, very little was known about David Blakely, and one of my aims with this book was to restore his character to him. In a letter to the *Evening Standard* shortly before Ruth's execution, crime writer F. Tennyson Jesse remarked that we are 'too apt to forget the first corpse' – that is, the victim. I hope that *A Fine Day for a Hanging* will go some way towards correcting that.

I

La Vie en rose

Holloway Gaol N7, the Thirteenth Day of July in the
Year of Our Lord Nineteen Hundred and Fifty-Five

1

'Today Ruth Ellis was hanged,' began a letter sent in to the *Islington Gazette* by a teacher at a school close to Holloway Gaol:

Not only myself, but many of my colleagues were faced with the effect of this upon the boys and girls we teach. The school was in a ferment. There were some children who had waited outside the prison gates; some claimed to have seen the execution from their windows; others spoke with a fascinated horror about the technique of hanging a female. My colleagues and I agree that if there is any argument which weighs above all others for the abolition of capital punishment, then it is this . . . For not only was Ruth Ellis hanged today, hundreds of children were a little corrupted.[1]

But the children did not see what happened to Ruth Ellis that hot, sooty morning. Nor did Gladys Langford, another local teacher and keen diarist, who recorded: 'There are still agitations to obtain a reprieve for Ruth Ellis. She has been in my mind all day; worthless as she is, it is a grim thought that she is to be hurled into eternity in this gold weather.'[2] Neither did celebrated journalist William Connor, whose 'Cassandra' column in the *Daily Mirror* raged against the Home Secretary's decision to refuse a pardon:

It's a fine day for haymaking. A fine day for fishing. A fine day for lolling in the sunshine. And if you feel that way – and I mourn to say that millions of you do – it's a fine day for a hanging . . . In this case I have been reviled as being a sucker for a pretty face. Well, I am a sucker for all human faces because I am a sucker for all humanity, good or bad. But I prefer them not to be lolling because of a judicially broken neck.[3]

And nor did the crowds who gathered, bare-headed and perspiring, outside the prison gates to give vent to their feelings about what was being done in their name.

No one saw and no one heard, apart from a select few. For while England sweltered, a thick veil of secrecy was drawn over the end of 28-year-old Ruth Ellis's life. Deep within the prison walls, past the stone griffins with their keys and shackles held aloft the massive gatehouse, and beyond the foundation stone inscribed '*May God preserve the City of London and make this place a terror to evil doers*', the circumstances of her death were as measured and suppressed as the rules that had governed her last three weeks of life.

On a winter morning more than 30 years before, another young woman had stirred inside Holloway and risen to meet an identical fate. Edith Thompson, executed in January 1923, had resigned herself to the shadow of the rope: 'It is an existence, that's all, just a "passing through" . . . eventually being submerged and facing Death, that thing there is no escaping – no hope of defeating.'[4]

*

At 6 a.m. on that summer's day, the executioner and his assistant awoke in a room near the condemned cell. Their arrival the previous afternoon had caused great unrest among the assembled protestors but passed without incident, giving them no reason to suspect that their long-established routine should go awry. A warder brought them hot tea, which tasted like straw, and left them to prepare.

The older man was tall and spruce, smoothing his salt-and-pepper hair with a manicured hand, the picture of efficiency in his trademark double-breasted suit. Born in 1905 in Clayton, Bradford, Albert Pierrepoint was the son of a hangman and the nephew of one. Between them, the three Pierrepoints put to death more than eight hundred people.

Albert's assistant that morning was 36-year-old Royston Lawrence Rickard of Maidstone, Kent. Royston's first assignment had been with Albert in 1953 at Armley Gaol in Leeds, when they hanged 25-year-old Philip Henry for the rape, battery and murder of 76-year-old spinster Flora Gilligan. The two men found further common ground by virtue of the fact that they each worked as pub landlords to earn a regular income.

Tea supped, they made their way to the execution chamber. The entrance doors were in a narrow cell separating the chamber from the room where the condemned prisoner awoke to the strange torment of knowing the precise hour and means by which she would die that day. Albert and Royston worked with practised aptitude. The sandbag they had attached to the noose the evening before to remove any stretch on the rope was drawn up, detached and lowered into the pit below the gallows. Royston went quietly down the stairs and cast the sandbag into a corner of the dark space; it was empty but for a stretcher to one side, placed there in readiness for the expelled body. He then secured the trapdoors and climbed the stairs.

In the execution chamber, Albert turned his attention to the lever that would activate the process of death. He slid the bolt and plugged in the cotter pin and its guard at the base of the lever, which acted as a safety catch. Then, with a ladder against the upper beam and Royston holding a tape-measure, Albert adjusted the fall of the rope to the last half-inch of his rigorous calculations, allowing for the overnight stretch. The two men spoke only when necessary and then very softly, aware that their 'client' moved about her cell a mere fifteen feet away.

Albert measured the rope and made an official note of it. The noose lay on the trapdoors. He coiled the spare rope until the noose was at shoulder height and held the coil where he judged it best, above the noose. Royston wrapped a piece of twine around the coil and the rope, then passed the ends of the twine to Albert, who tied it, securing the loops to the rope itself. When the time came, the sharp strain of the woman's plunging body would break the twine and cause the rope to unroll for the length of the drop.

Albert glanced about the execution chamber, checking there was nothing untoward. Using a stub of chalk he went over the 'T' mark under the noose on the front drop where the prisoner's toes would be aligned, the arches of her feet directly over the shallow gap in the trapdoors. Albert shifted the cross-planks slightly on either side of the 'T' and made another adjustment before crossing to the lever and releasing a split pin that held the cotter pin fast. He eased out the cotter pin for half its length; while resisting an untimely push, the end of it was now flush with the side of the lever, poised for action.

He straightened up and gave Royston the nod. Together they left the execution chamber and returned to their room for breakfast.

*

Along Camden Road, traffic was beginning to build. There were more motorcars than on an ordinary day, and the red buses turning in at the junction with Parkhurst Road trundled at a slower pace, as if allowing passengers time to look out at the scenes by the prison walls.

A huge press of people lined the wide pavement: women in twinsets and cotton dresses, men in light suits or shirtsleeves, some with their thumbs tucked into their braces, and children with school satchels slung and forgotten at their shoulders. Young men on bicycles weaved in and out of the throng, bells ringing. In the hot, gritty draught of the passing traffic, policemen braced themselves against the crowd, eyeing those who waited impatiently at the road crossing.

The horde was at its deepest near the secured entrance to the prison, where mounted police kept order. Occasionally there was a surge as newcomers strained for a glimpse of yesterday's notice pinned to the gates; it announced that Ruth Ellis, found guilty of murder, 'will be carried into execution at 9 a.m. tomorrow'.[5] The first signature below the proclamation belonged to the acting Under Sheriff of London, Harold Gedge, who was at that moment preparing to leave his mews home on Philpot Lane in order to witness the execution.

The notice was also signed by Dr Charity Taylor, in her tenth year as Holloway's first female Governor. A former medical officer at the prison, Dr Taylor had declared upon her appointment in 1945 that she intended 'to give some of these people the hope that they will become decent citizens again. Severe punishment is not always the way to prevent an individual doing something wrong.'[6] In a handful of cases, such as that of Ruth Ellis, the law overrode the Governor's beliefs and the 'terrible responsibility' of overseeing a judicial death weighed heavily upon her.[7] She had read the detailed memorandum sent in by the Establishment Officer ('prisoners will be scattered over the prison at their respective tasks . . . Their minds will be occupied, any noise caused by the trap doors should pass unnoticed'), but wrote for further guidance, determined that the event would be as swift and straightforward as possible.[8] The prison commissioners replied a fortnight before the date set, clarifying a number of points: 'If the execution is to take place at 09.00 a.m. . . . . the prison clock chime should be disconnected for the hour of nine . . . the executioners should be lodged so that they neither have to enter the prison or cross the yards . . . ' and so on.[9] Each detail, from the stopped clocks to the copra mats laid outside the condemned cell to muffle the approach of the execution party, encapsulated an almost theatrical need to conceal this most final of acts.

Outside the prison, in the oppressive air between crowd and high wall, a group of schoolboys squeezed into a gap, earning a restricted view of the castellated gatehouse. 'Gruesome curiosity about what they were doing just up the road prompted a small gang of us to visit the prison on our way to school,' one boy admitted years later.

> When we arrived at about eight o'clock, apprehensive and unsure about what we were doing there, about 1,000 people were standing outside the main gate at Holloway, some praying, some holding up placards protesting the execution and some just curious as we were. There was a muted fury in the air and a dreadful awareness that an awful thing was about to happen and there was absolutely nothing that could be done about it. There was a lot of jostling as journalists and photographers arrived to join the crowd. In the middle of this grim frenzy a policeman came across and asked us what we were doing. As we 'ummed' and 'aaahed' an answer, he squatted down to our eye level. 'Back to school, lads,' he said. 'There's nothing for you here. Go on. Hop it!'[10]

Griping about their dismissal, the schoolboys dawdled on in the sunlight, speculating about what might be happening inside the condemned cell. Their imaginations ran riot, but the truth was somewhat less melodramatic.

*

The long corridors inside Holloway were painted in shades of cream and green. They radiated out from the central tower, a London landmark whose purpose was to ventilate and heat the entire prison complex. A constant thrum of activity echoed about the labyrinth: clanking pails, shoes clattering on iron staircases, the low vibrations of speech pierced by screams and shouts, and a ceaseless jangle of keys. Then there was the peculiarity of light within the prison: a permanent bright yellow fog bathed the edifice from ceiling to floor.

But the condemned cell was a place apart. Down the corridors with their distinctive smell of boiled food, disinfectant and despair, through the blurred artificial glow into CC wing and then up a flight of stairs worn semi-hollow by decades of tramping feet, the cell stank of its own segregation. In that 15 ft by 14 ft room, with its pink and brown walls and long window fitted with glass that allowed the occupant to look out without being seen, the last vestiges of normal life vanished. Isolated and yet never alone, the condemned woman moved between the bed, wardrobe, table and chairs of the main room and the wash basin, bath and lavatory of the adjoining room. Another door led from the bathroom to the visitor cell, where a partition precluded physical contact.

A Home Office memorandum set out Ruth Ellis's existence in stark terms:

> Immediately a prisoner sentenced to death returns from court, she is placed in a cell for condemned prisoners and is watched night and day by two officers. Amenities such as cards, chess, dominoes etc., are provided in the cell ... Newspapers and books are also provided. Food is supplied from the main prison kitchen, the prisoner being placed on hospital diet ... ten cigarettes or half an ounce of pipe tobacco are allowed ... The prisoner may smoke in her cell as well as at exercise. It is the practice for the Governor, medical officer and chief officer to visit a prisoner under sentence of death twice daily, and the chaplain or minister of any other denomination has free access ... She may be visited by such of her relations, friends and legal advisers as she desires to see and as are authorised to visit her by the Visiting Committee and the commissioners, and she is given special facilities to write and receive letters.[11]

The wardresses working shifts in the condemned cell expected their charge to be a hard, vulgar young woman, deceitful and brassy; that was how the popular press had portrayed her, after all. Durham-born Evelyn Galilee, employed at Holloway since 1951, was surprised by the reality:

> In came this fragile girl, a Dresden doll. She was my age and tiny – no more than 5 ft – and so very slim. Her skin was like porcelain. They had taken away her false nails, eyelashes and glamorous clothes and put her in baggy prison issue clothes. But they could not strip her of her dignity. Not once did she break down, scream or cry. Ruth had this

acceptance of what she'd done and felt the punishment fitted the crime. Her eyes . . . were bewitching, the most beautiful violet-blue, the colour of forget-me-nots.[12]

Officer Galilee and Principal Officer Griffin were the two wardresses who came to know Ruth best. She did not ask for any of the 'special privileges' granted to the condemned prisoner, other than cigarettes. Her sole complaint was that she could not sleep: the naked bulb overhead had to remain lit day and night. The two officers fashioned a cardboard lampshade to dim the glare – a small gesture, against prison rules, but the Governor said nothing about it. Each day, they witnessed Ruth submerging her fears about the execution by reading, writing letters, doing jigsaws and making dolls from the materials brought in by her mother. Even then, she was inexorably drawn to the green, 6 ft-high screen that almost ran the length of one wall.[13] 'She kept asking me what was behind the screen,' Officer Galilee recalled. 'I think she knew what it was, but she kept badgering me to have a look.'[14]

Officer Galilee had checked the roster for that last morning, praying her name would not be on it. When she saw that it was, an overwhelming guilt descended; shortly before her own death half a century later, she still spoke of it.

Slowly, Ruth rose from the iron bed with its creaking springs. Officer Galilee helped her dress: prisoners wore their own clothing on the day of execution, and Ruth abandoned the regulation blue smock with its tiny bows, choosing instead a skirt and blouse. She cleaned her face, brushed out her hair and used the lavatory. Then she applied a minimum of make-up, clicking open the powder compact that played a faint, tinkling tune: 'La Vie en rose'. The music seemed to come from afar, drifting up from a barrel organ on the glittering, dusty streets. When she lit a cigarette, Officer Galilee held the flame steady on the small, expensive gas lighter that Ruth had brought in to the prison; it was a running joke among Ruth's friends that she never could light a cigarette first time.

Before breakfast, Revd John Williams visited. Ruth knew and liked the deeply compassionate Welshman in his mid-30s who had arrived at his post as chaplain in Holloway in 1951. After his departure, she asked to write a letter. Putting on her spectacles, she adjusted the blue diamante frames with a quick push of her index fingers, and accepted the pen and paper passed to her. In a neat, looping hand she addressed her solicitor:

> Dear Mr Simmons
> Just to let you know I am still feeling all right.
> The time is 7 o'clock am – everyone (staff) is simply wonderful in Holloway. This is just for you to console my family with the thought that I did not change my way of thinking at the last moment.
> Or break my promise to David's mother.
> Well, Mr Simmons, I have told you the truth and that's all I can do.
> Thanks once again,
> Goodbye.
> Ruth Ellis.[15]

At the top of the sheet were printed instructions: 'In replying to this letter, please write on the envelope' followed by blank spaces for the name, number and prison whereabouts of the correspondent. This time there would be no reply.

The cell door opened at eight o'clock and four male prison officers entered. The wardresses who had worked the night shift departed, leaving only Officer Galilee to remain until the hour of execution. The law dictated that women might hang, but only a female Governor or deputy Governor was to witness the death.

The door opened again, admitting a warder with Ruth's breakfast. She ate the scrambled egg delicately, observed by the guards and her only other constant companions in the cell: a pair of goldfish in a bowl. Outrage rose in Officer Galilee's chest: 'Even on that last day she wasn't allowed the dignity of eating with proper cutlery or plates. She had to use plastic because they thought she might use the crockery as a weapon. The breakfast tray was taken away.'[16]

The wardress steeled herself for the coming necessity: she was to escort her charge to the lavatory and exchange Ruth's own underwear for the padded calico knickers that all condemned women were required to wear. The edict followed Edith Thompson's execution in 1923, when rumours of how 'her insides fell out' caused revulsion among the populace.[17] The evident trauma of those who witnessed Mrs Thompson's death and the doctor's failure to fill in the internal examination section of the post-mortem report did little to expunge the story, which was never resolved. She was thought to have suffered a severe haemorrhage or miscarriage on the scaffold, and shortly thereafter it became mandatory for women facing the gallows to wear thick, wadded underwear.

In the cramped bathroom, Officer Galilee presented Ruth with the garment. 'I'm sorry, Ruth, but I've got to do this,' she said, looking away.[18]

Ruth put on the unsightly knickers, fumbling with the tapes attached to the front and back of the fabric to keep them firmly in place. 'Is that all right?' she asked. 'Would you pull these tapes, Evelyn, I'll pull the others.'[19] The wardress secured the tapes tightly, as she had been told to do, but when Ruth asked what the change of underwear was for she couldn't bring herself to answer.

They returned to the stifling main room. Sun on the sealed window revealed a thick cake of dirt. The noise of the crowd at the gates penetrated faintly: a low, persistent hum of outrage. Officer Galilee stood by the door, gripping the redundant heating pipes. Ruth sat silently at the table. Behind her, just inches away, loomed the high green screen.

At quarter to nine, the door to the corridor opened. The deputy Governor entered with Revd John Williams and they took a seat at either end of the table. While they spoke quietly with Ruth, the door opened again. A nursing sister walked in, carrying a kidney tray on which stood a small bottle and a phial. She set the tray down on the table, poured some liquid into the phial and passed it to Ruth, who refused it. The sister hesitated, then said, 'It will calm you,' but again Ruth politely declined the sedative. The sister tried one more time before giving up. Balancing the tray with its unused medication in the crook of her arm, she left the cell.[20]

For a moment no one spoke. Then Ruth slowly removed her glasses, the diamante flecks catching the sunlight, and handed them to the deputy Governor. 'I won't need these any more,' she said. 'Thank you.'[21]

The silence fell again and no one seemed able to break it. The hour was almost upon them.

*

Some distance away in the prison, a telephone rang with loud, insistent peals. It startled several people, resonating as it did in the Governor's office, just as Dr Taylor was about to lead the Under Sheriff and Principal Medical Officer on the final journey to Ruth's cell.

The Governor took the call, listening in astonishment to the voice on the other end of the receiver: a Miss Holmes, private secretary to Major Lloyd George, was ringing to inform her that a stay of execution was on its way for Ruth Ellis. Temporarily thrown, Dr Taylor replied that she would have to verify the matter and call back to confirm the message. She cut short their conversation, then dialled the Home Office number. She spoke urgently to a number of people, but no one was able to trace a Miss or Mrs Holmes, no one could corroborate the information she had offered. Dr Taylor persisted, dialling the number of the private secretary whose assistant told her that he was not yet in the office. Hope rapidly diminishing, she then telephoned Mrs Forbes, the other private secretary, but she was not available either.

Defeated, the Governor replaced the receiver. She looked at Harold Gedge, the Under Sheriff, and asked what he thought they should do. Later she recalled grimly how 'in view of the unsatisfactory source of the message . . . it was decided to carry on with the execution'.[22]

Outside, the sun shone brighter than ever. The temperature on the Air Ministry roof in London read 75 degrees and the crowds gathered along Camden Road wilted like unwatered plants as they struggled to keep up the chant of '*Evans–Bentley–Ellis!*' But in Holloway prison there was a deed to be done, and no amount of bellowing, broiling heat or hoax calls could stop it.

Along the cream and green corridors they walked: the Governor, the Under Sheriff and the Principal Medical Officer. Dr Mervyn Ralph Penry Williams knew Ruth best, having examined her physical and mental health on many occasions. She had impressed him with her rationality and pleasant manner, and shocked him by declaring that she felt no remorse for her crime, which she said was a result of being 'unfairly treated by the deceased to whom she had shown much kindness in the past'.[23] There was far more to it than that, as the doctor well knew.

They climbed the stone stairwell to the corridor where Albert and Royston were waiting with the warders who had been detailed to conduct Ruth to her death. An overpowering sense of finality struck them all as the Governor entered the condemned cell. Harold Gedge and Dr Penry Williams followed her in, shutting the door on the group in the corridor. 'The next minutes of waiting were the worst, not only then but on every occasion,' Albert recalled afterwards. 'It is impossible not to feel apprehension and even fear at the prospect of the responsibility of the moment, but with me the frailty passed as soon as there was action.'[24]

It came in the form of a signal: Harold Gedge opened the door and silently raised a finger, letting Albert Pierrepoint and his assistant pass like ghosts into the condemned cell.

*

Upon her first sight of the executioner, Ruth sprang to her feet, knocking over the chair. From her position against the wall, Officer Galilee gripped the heating pipes so tightly that her arms were rigid. The tall, dapper man's confidence both repelled and relieved her: 'Pierrepoint was very reassuring, if you can say that of a hangman. He said to her, "It's all right, lass. It's all right." He kept to the back of her so she wouldn't see his face, picked up the chair and told her to sit down again. He said, "Put your arms behind the chair."'[25]

Deftly, Albert bound Ruth's wrists with the soft leather calf strap he kept for certain prisoners. A warder pushed the screen away from the wall and the door to the execution chamber slid into view. Albert straightened and Ruth stood; he walked in front and she followed, a warder at each elbow, holding her firmly. She turned swiftly to glance at Officer Galilee, who remembered, 'It was a look of pity – she felt sorry for me. She looked at me and mouthed, "Thank you", and she went out.'[26]

Through the door and straight ahead, suspended at chest height above the trap, was the noose.

Ruth walked calmly with Albert, not even flinching at the apparatus of execution. In that stark yet claustrophobic chamber, Charity Taylor, Revd John Williams, Harold Gedge and Dr Penry Williams stood with their backs to a wall. The escorting officers mounted the cross-planks beneath the great beam, guiding Ruth to the 'T' mark Albert had chalked there at daybreak. She stepped in her black court shoes onto the fissure in the trapdoors.

Royston stooped behind Ruth, fastening her legs together with the ankle strap. Albert moved nimbly into position, extracting the white hood from his breast pocket, where it was tucked in meticulous folds.

The hood had to be put in place before the noose to prevent the sudden draught caused by the drop lifting it from her face. Albert shook out the white cowl like a gentleman flourishing a silk handkerchief. When his fingers reached for Ruth's long, loosely combed hair, she looked at him and lifted the corners of her mouth in a faint smile.[27]

He drew the hood down until it covered her face.

Averting his eyes from the small square of white cloth convulsing against Ruth's mouth, he reached for the rope. In a seamless movement he lowered the noose over her head, tightened it to one side of her chin and pulled a rubber washer along the rope to secure it. Then he darted to his left. Crouching like an athlete at the start of a race, with one hand he pulled the cotter pin and with the other he pushed the lever, hard.

The trapdoors banged open and Ruth plummeted through the cavity into eternal darkness. The length of twine used to keep the noose in place spiralled down after her. A brief eddy of dust gusted up from below and then all was silent, save for the soft creak of the rope in the pit.

*

All over London, people stood to reflect upon what had taken place in the name of British justice that morning. The *Evening News* reported outside Holloway:

> As the chimes of Big Ben striking nine o'clock echoed from a radio in a house nearby, the crowd of more than eight hundred stood bareheaded. The only sound came from the moving traffic and from a violinist playing in a side street. It was Bach's *Be Thou With Me When I Die*.[28]

The Times observed:

> The crowd remained silent, with some people praying, as the execution hour of 9 a.m. passed. Eighteen minutes later the notices of execution were posted and the crowd rushed forward, blocking the road and halting the traffic. Police moved them back into two orderly queues and they filed past the notices on the prison gates.[29]

At the same hour in a school in Middlesex, the headmaster noticed four boys standing utterly still in the playground. He frowned, curious and then appalled, as one boy held up a watch: 'Only four more minutes,' the child said in a hush, 'One . . . two . . . three . . . four – she's had it, boys!'[30] Elsewhere another teacher noted: 'The entire episode had a profound effect on the children. Their initial curiosity became a morbid and fearful obsession . . . It is something they will never forget.'[31]

*

In Holloway, Albert descended the stairs to the pit. Ruth's body turned imperceptibly on the rope, but there was no movement of breath now to make the white hood twitch. He undid the first buttons of her blouse for the immediate medical inspection. Then he returned to the execution chamber and nodded at Dr Penry Williams.

The medical officer went below. It was cool and fairly dark in the pit as he placed the stethoscope against Ruth's heart. He knew what to expect: after hanging, the palpitations would speed, then fall and, within a few minutes, weaken to nothing. When he was satisfied he could hear only his own heart beating as it should in the gloom, he removed his stethoscope and climbed the stairs. The prison staff dispersed from the execution chamber while Albert and Royston went about the last stages of their work.

In the condemned cell the overhead bulb was extinguished for the first time in three weeks.

It would never be lit again.

II

West End Girl

Rhyl, 9 October 1926 – Knightsbridge, summer 1953

> I was born in Rhyl, Wales, in the same circumstances as millions of
> you. I came from a happy home, with a sister and brother, and my
> parents were loving and understanding. My father was a musician with
> all the loveable qualities that music gives a man . . . My father travelled
> a lot and mother was the greater influence in my upbringing.[1]

This apparently autobiographical account of Ruth's early years
appeared in the *Woman's Sunday Mirror* shortly before her execution.
Serialised across four issues, it was ghostwritten by reporter Robert
Hancock, whose editor had struck the usual deal under the
circumstances: in return for exclusive rights to her story, the newspaper
paid for Ruth's defence. There was no question of the money reaching
her ten-year-old son as Ruth had intended; the ink on the negotiations
was already dry. In 1963 Hancock admitted that 'like all newspaper
stories of this kind it was an occasionally obscure and sometimes
misleading account [but] also contained enough truth to make it
interesting'.[2]

There was little reality in those opening sentences. Ruth's
background was not the demonstrative and vaguely bohemian
childhood portrayed in the press. The facts of her upbringing were
obscured for the purpose of a less controversial, libel-free read. Like
most seemingly well-known stories, it had been manipulated,
fictionalised and suppressed – by Ruth herself, among others.
Retrieving the truth even now is a matter of unpicking infinite strands
from the material of a short but calamitous life.

Contrary to popular belief, Ruth's background was not poverty
stricken. Her paternal great-grandfather, Charles Hornby, was a
prosperous boot and shoemaker who employed several men in his
business and could afford to have his children privately educated. The

family home was in Droylsden, then 'a township-chapelry in Manchester parish, Lancashire, on the Rochdale canal and the Manchester and Sheffield railway, four miles east of Manchester'.[3] During the latter half of the Industrial Revolution, Droylsden thrived as people left the farmsteads of the countryside to labour in the large factories and cotton mills; one of the major employers in the district was Robertson's jam factory on the banks of Ashton Canal. Schools sprang up, churches flourished and sport became a common pastime. Ruth's grandfather, Walter William Hornby, was a professor of music and much-respected lecturer on singing. He became organist at Drolysden parish church in 1888, at the age of 21; his older sister Jane Elizabeth was a teacher. Walter listed his hobbies in a guidebook to organists as literature and tennis, but he never took his privileged position for granted. In addition to his duties at the local church, he was equally involved in the community elsewhere, serving as conductor of the Droylsden and District Philharmonic Society and Droylsden Co-operative Society.

In 1893, Walter married Jane Louise Davies. Their son Douglas Geiah was born a year later, quickly followed by a daughter, Marjorie Mariel. In 1897, Jane gave birth to twin boys: Charles Granville and Arthur Nelson – Ruth's father. The 1901 census shows the family living at 304 Fairfield Street in Droylsden with their young domestic servant, Agnes. The close-knit township dispersed as more people moved to the nearby city, although one section continued to expand: the Moravian community (a Protestant denomination which began in Eastern Europe), who lived by the maxim: 'In essentials, unity; in nonessentials, liberty; and in all things, love.' The Moravians settled in the area in 1785 and built their own inn, shop, bakery, farm and other amenities. The heart of this self-contained village was at Fairfield Square, where Ruth's father and his family lived at Number 13A.

The extent of the Hornbys' involvement with the Moravian community is unknown, but Walter's passion for bringing music to society remained strong. He passed his enthusiasm on to Ruth's father, Arthur, who became a gifted cellist. When the Great War began, Arthur cut short his studies and enlisted in the army on 15 July 1915, giving his profession as 'musician'. Walter signed his papers as next of kin and bade farewell to his 19-year-old son, now Private Nelson Hornby of the 2nd Manchester Regiment of Infantry. After basic training at Fulwood Barracks in Preston, in December that year

Arthur was posted to France as bandsman in the 2nd Manchester Battalion Machine Gun Corps. His duties included assisting in burial parties. He committed one offence during his time as a soldier, and then only after the war ended: his records of service disclose that while on leave in December 1918 he failed to arrive as commanded at Manchester's Victoria Station and was docked three days' pay. On 21 February 1919 he was demobbed and awarded the 1914–15 Star, presented to those individuals who served in France, Flanders and any other operational theatre during the first year of conflict.[4]

Arthur returned to Manchester and a new life following the death of his father. He began courting a local Belgian refugee, Elisa Bertha Goethals, then a 20-year-old single mother working as a domestic maid. They married on 9 August 1920, at Chorlton-upon-Medlock Register Office, in unconventional circumstances: Bertha was six months pregnant, and she and Arthur were already living together. The wedding certificate lists them as Arthur Nelson Hornby, aged 23, a bachelor and 'bass fiddle' musician, resident at 103 Rusholme Road, and Elisa Bertha Goethals of the same address, a spinster of 21 with 'no profession' and the daughter of Julius Arthur Goethals, a labourer.[5]

General confusion surrounds Bertha's background. From the available sources – none of which are in complete agreement – a hazy picture of Ruth's mother emerges. Bertha was born in Belgium at the turn of the century into a middle-class Jewish family of girls. One died tragically young and Bertha grew up with her sisters Charmaine, Rachel and Olga. Their father Julius was in the Belgian army and stationed in India when his wife died, leaving the four young sisters alone. The army arranged for their care in a convent in Bruges, where the girls apparently converted to Roman Catholicism. Bertha later told her own children that in 1914 she had watched from a window in the convent as the Germans invaded and ransacked the Stadhuis (town hall). The nuns hastily destroyed the birth certificates of the children under their roof and smuggled Bertha and her sisters onto a boat bound for England. The girls had no possessions apart from clothes in which they travelled and a blanket each.

The British government had already offered 'victims of war the hospitality of the British nation' but left the actual responsibility of housing and welfare to local authorities. Manchester was one of the main reception points. Cheering, flag-waving crowds greeted the refugees after the hazardous journey by sea; the bewildered new arrivals were then driven to lavish receptions with city dignitaries. They were assigned temporary accommodation but had to find work, learn the language and adjust to life in a new country themselves, although the Belgian Relief Committee provided assistance. During Christmas 1914 the *Manchester Guardian* reported: 'The majority of the refugees are living in houses provided by local committees or by congregations of churches and chapels. Many women and children have found hospitality in Roman Catholic convents in the neighbourhood.'[6] This was true of the young Goethals sisters, who remained in a convent until they each reached the age of 18. Bertha was not an especially devout Roman Catholic, but took solace in her religion and would encourage her sons and daughters to do the same. She was a fine seamstress and particularly skilled at embroidery and lacemaking. After leaving the convent, Bertha went into service in a large house and lost touch with her sisters, but renewed her relationship with her father when he settled in Manchester during the war.

According to Ruth's sister Muriel, Bertha's experience of domestic service was harrowing: she was one of several servants raped by the son of the household and in 1918 gave birth to a boy, whom she named after her father. Life as a penniless single mother in the aftermath of the Great War was a daunting prospect, but by the summer of 1920 Bertha was stepping out with Arthur Hornby. Together with her son (whose name they anglicised to Julian), the couple embarked on married life in a modest terraced house on Chorlton's Rusholme Road.

Much of those early months of marriage were spent apart, since Arthur played cello in an orchestra onboard the ocean liner *Kaiserin Auguste Victoria*, once the largest ship in the world. When his daughter Irma Muriel Hornby was born on 11 November 1920, Arthur was en route to New York. He made several crossings on the same liner, using Nelson Hornby as his professional name. If Bertha was lonely in Manchester – her mother-in-law disapproved of Arthur's marriage to a Belgian-born Jewess with a child out of wedlock – she could count on her growing family to keep her occupied. Bertha was 'Mammur' to her children, the name a concoction of her own broken English and the Flemish of her youth. Bertha's pregnancy in 1921 resulted in a stillborn daughter whom she and Arthur called Lilian. In August 1922, a son was born and named Granville after Arthur's beloved twin brother. There was another stillbirth in 1925; again the child was a girl, whom they called Marion.[7]

In spring 1926, while living at 45 Nelson Street in Chorlton, Bertha found herself pregnant again, but the child would not be born in Manchester. Four-year-old Granville had contracted encephalitis lethargica ('sleepy sickness'), a serious illness that afflicted millions between 1915 and 1926, with sufferers experiencing a sore throat, then tremors, double vision, hallucinations and increased drowsiness, with some victims ending up comatose.[8] There was no known cure, but the doctor advised a move to the coast.

Arthur and Bertha chose Rhyl, a seaside town in north-east Wales and a popular tourist resort since the 1830s. Their home on the promenade at 74 West Parade was a handsome yellow-brick villa with a white porch, overlooking an endless vista of sea and sand. The house was divided into two flats, with an outside toilet. The Hornbys had the use of four bedrooms, a sitting-room, front room and large kitchen, and Bertha let out the attic for extra income. Arthur found work as principal cellist in Rhyl's Cinema Royal orchestra, then in its sixth year.[9] He changed his surname by deed poll and the family adopted Neilson (a slight variation on Arthur's middle name) as their moniker.

Ruth was born in the house overlooking the bay on Saturday, 9 October 1926. There was no ominous violent sandstorm racing across the sands as reporters later gleefully claimed; it had been a dry autumn but a light rain fell that day, quickly replaced by fair weather. Ruth's birth, like her death, occurred behind a screen – in this case, a white sheet draped across a corner of the room to provide Bertha with some privacy. The birth certificate names the parents 'Arthur Neilson, musician' and 'Bertha Neilson, formerly Goodall', a curious error. The new baby, named after the nurse who helped to bring her into the world, became her mother's favourite. In a 1955 letter to the Home Office, Bertha described Ruth in poignantly simple terms: 'Ruth grew up a sweet and lovely child. She never gave me any trouble of any kind.'[10]

Before Ruth was two, the family moved again, within the area to a house near the railway line. Arthur left the Cinema Royal to join the house orchestra at Colwyn Bay Theatre. If domesticity was not especially exciting, it was not disruptive either, and Arthur enjoyed his work, which brought in a decent wage, and followed in his father's footsteps by conducting a choir and writing music. As a special treat he would put Ruth and her siblings in his three-wheeled car and drive them across the undulating rope-and-plank bridge over the River Clwyd.

Then all at once, life began to unravel.

*

In September 1928, Arthur's twin brother was killed in a horrific road accident when his bicycle collided with a steamroller. Married four years earlier, Charles Granville was only 31 years old when he died. Arthur returned to Manchester for the funeral in Southern Cemetery, where his twin was laid to rest in the family plot.

If the birth of another son that same year helped Arthur to come to terms with his loss, then the consolation was painfully brief and doubly heartbreaking; in March 1929, John Neilson – whom everyone affectionately called Jacques – died before his first birthday. Perhaps hoping to start a new chapter in their lives, shortly after burying their infant son Ruth's parents left Rhyl for Bramley, a quiet village between Basingstoke and Reading. Arthur found work in the cinema orchestra at the Grand Theatre in Basingstoke, but his job was not so well-paid as before and it was precarious: 'talkies' were on the horizon and the days of in-house music were numbered.

Bertha had another loss to contend with in the early 1930s when her father, Julius Goethals, died at his home in Manchester. She was shunned in the village too, by locals who viewed her with suspicion; in Germany the Nazi party was on the rise and Bertha's foreign accent led to angry taunts. Home offered little respite, since Arthur had begun drinking heavily and lashing out with his fists. Money grew scarce, and Bertha found work as a cook in a large house in nearby Baughurst. She and Arthur fell behind with their rent nonetheless, ricocheting from one Hampshire village to another in a futile attempt to outrun their debts. Muriel recalls that her father's violence spread like an ugly stain: he frequently attacked his children, who learned to avoid him whenever possible. 'You have to understand how Ruth and I were brought up,' she told an interviewer years later. 'Our father was a strict and frightening man. We were cowed, kept down. Made to feel insignificant.'[11]

In September 1932, one month before her sixth birthday, Ruth began attending Sherborne St John School with her elder sister and brother Granville. The family had moved again, to a rented cottage in Monk Sherborne, a tiny, ancient village four miles from Basingstoke. The old Victorian school accommodated about one hundred pupils aged four to fourteen. Ruth did not stand out: she was a fragile, plain little girl with a light brown bob and spectacles, eager to please but without friends. Muriel claims that other children ostracised them and called them ragamuffins because of the extreme poverty into which the family had fallen; she remembers the threadbare clothing they had to wear and how they drank from jam-jars at home and used orange boxes in place of furniture. She maintains that the headmaster was sufficiently concerned about their welfare to call in the school nurse in January 1933, although Tony Cox, former headmaster of Sherborne St John, explains:

> The entry [in the school log books] on 11th January 1933 indicates that the School Nurse issued a note to four pupils including R. Neilson [Ruth]. There are no other details. Notes were sent home by the nurse for a variety of reasons including lack of cleanliness, vermin, dirty heads and other skin complaints but there is nothing to indicate what this particular note was appertaining to. There do not appear to be any other references.[12]

The three Neilson children left Sherborne St John in 1934. Ruth joined Worting village school, where she remained unassertive and without any discernible academic strengths. Muriel finished her education the following year and worked as a seamstress until her father insisted that she was needed at home to care for the younger children. By then, their 16-year-old half-brother Julian had disappeared from their lives, following an explosive fight with Arthur. He travelled across North America and did not return until several years later.

Just as he had feared, Arthur was made redundant when talking pictures arrived at Basingstoke's Grand Theatre. The family moved to a one-bedroom chalet-style building in Park Prewett, where after many months of unemployment Arthur found clerical work at Park Prewett Mental Hospital, then the largest psychiatric hospital in the district, with 1,400 patients and its own railway station.[13] The staff remembered Ruth visiting the hospital with other children to see the film shows that were staged to encourage outside interaction and 'as a child in her summer dresses at Hospital Sports Days'.[14] Ruth's memoirs for the *Woman's Sunday Mirror* also recall a fancy dress ball which she and Granville attended with their father – Granville as an ancient Briton, Arthur as the back end of a horse, and Ruth as an angel in a white dress with a silver halo. 'I felt ready to ascend into Heaven at any moment,' she remembered dreamily.[15]

In contrast, her elder sister's memories of that time are hellish in the extreme. Muriel writes in *Ruth Ellis: My Sister's Secret Life* that Arthur began sexually abusing her in the wake of his twin brother's death and explicitly details his incestuous violence, which she states culminated in the birth of a child in August 1936, when she was 16. She is frank about her mother's role in the situation, claiming that Bertha was not only aware of the abuse, but also attempted to bring on a miscarriage. When this failed and Muriel's son Robert William Neilson was born, Bertha pretended to be the child's mother. It is unclear how Granville, Ruth and family acquaintances were successfully deceived, but Muriel writes that the matron where she gave birth was not fooled; police questioned Arthur about the child's parentage but took no action. Later, when Bertha ceased masquerading as Robert's mother, Muriel admitted that he was her son and told most family and friends that Robert's father had been killed in the air force. In her memoir, Muriel is blunt about her hatred for Arthur but remarks that Bertha 'on the whole . . . was a good mother'.[16] She maintains that Arthur turned his attention to Ruth when she reached puberty; she writes of hearing her young sister screaming as he attempted to rape her. Afterwards she warned Ruth to stay away from home if their mother was absent. Ruth reacted to the abuse by fighting back, telling Muriel, 'I'm not letting him do to me what he's done to you.'[17] Decades later, Muriel reflected: 'Ruth was terribly frightened of him. Poor little thing, she was as thin as a rake in those days . . . She never went through what I did, but what she did go through was bad enough.'[18]

Neither Arthur Neilson nor his wife is alive to answer their elder daughter's allegations, and Ruth never spoke of it to anyone but Muriel, who writes that she was sworn to secrecy. But the Neilson household was undoubtedly in turmoil. There was a marked change in Ruth's own behaviour as she reached her teens: she grew impertinent and prone to running off unexpectedly, refusing to explain her disappearances when asked. Muriel bore the brunt of Arthur's inability to bend his younger daughter to his will.

In 1937, Bertha gave birth to another daughter, Elizabeth – Betty to everyone. Money was in shorter supply than ever and matters deteriorated further when Arthur was made redundant again. The family moved to a timbered cottage in Sherfield-on-Lodden, a picturesque village six miles north of Basingstoke. Nearby was Bramley army training camp. Spurred by its proximity, Granville gave up his job at the barbershop in 1938 and joined the Hampshire Regiment, later transferring to the Lancashire Fusiliers. His was not the only absence from home: Bertha left abruptly after finding work at the Red Lion in Basingstoke. She returned six months later, without a word to her children about her departure.

During this time, Ruth briefly attended the village school before transferring to Fairfields Senior Girls' School in Basingstoke. She was hopelessly myopic and in her own words, 'skinny as a rabbit and plain as hell'.[19] No teacher was able to inspire her; she was an atrocious speller whose lack of purpose in lessons extended to the sports field and gym. An epiphany of sorts came when she discovered a passion for dancing and realised how much she enjoyed socialising. She badgered Muriel into accompanying her to local dances, fobbing their father off with some plausible excuse. Arthur had been offered the job of caretaker at a printing firm in Reading, which necessitated yet another move, to a house on Southampton Street in the town centre. Ruth was cheerful about relocating to Reading; although living under her father's roof meant a barrage of questions whenever she left the house, she felt much less isolated than in the backwaters of the past.

Bertha once described her favourite daughter as a bird with beautiful feathers. The description was accurate enough, for Ruth was blossoming into an eye-catching young woman, poised to fly the unhappy nest of her childhood.

3

When war broke out on 3 September 1939, London was imbued with an excessive, artificial hedonism. As thousands of children from the boroughs were evacuated to the countryside, and blackouts, rationing and disruption to public transport became a grim reality, the city boomed. Bars, theatres and West End nightclubs were crammed to the full regardless of restrictions. Ruth already sensed that she belonged there; London was both tantalisingly close yet unreachable – although not for long.

In 1940, she left school at the age of 14 without qualifications. Even so, Ruth made it clear that she had no intention of letting her circumstances or lack of education hold her back. In a 1955 interview with the *Sunday Dispatch*, Bertha recalled:

> Ruth hated us to be poor. She hated boys too at that time. That seems so strange now. But she always liked clothes and she would borrow mine and dress up in them. She wasn't like my other children. She was so very ambitious for herself. She used to say, 'Mum, I'm going to make something of my life.'[1]

Holloway's medical officer noted the same drive from his interview with Ruth's parents: 'As a child she was excitable. She was very ambitious. Father states she was very independent . . . She hoped to get away above their station and was succeeding.'[2]

Ruth's first job was as a waitress in a Reading cinema cafe. 'Men liked me,' she recalled:

> but I was too shy to go out with anyone who asked me for a date. For the first time I had money of my own, and I got lots of tips. I put them higgledy-piggledy in my handbag, then I would hurry home and turn

them all out on the table. It was such fun counting the money. I gave most of it to Mother.[3]

Ironically, it was Arthur who provided Ruth with a foothold in London. He was offered the live-in position of caretaker/chauffeur at Porn & Dunwoody, lift manufacturers at Southwark's Union Works. He promptly left for London, leaving his family behind in Reading, but Ruth followed him – with an unlikely companion in tow. Her half-brother Julian had returned from North America with a girlfriend; Edna Turvey was an unconventional woman in her 30s whom he had met while on leave from the navy. The romance didn't last, but Edna struck up an improbable friendship with fourteen-year-old Ruth and the two of them pitched up one day at Arthur's flat in Southwark.

Muriel admits she cannot explain why Ruth should have willingly moved in with their abusive father, particularly when he continued to mistreat her, as Muriel claims. But the perennially black-clad Edna provided a diversion for Arthur, and when Bertha called at the flat unexpectedly she found her husband in bed with her son's former girlfriend. For once, Bertha seized control of the situation, heaving Edna's suitcase through a window and forcing her to leave. Equally uncharacteristically, Arthur allowed the drama to unfold without resorting to violence and accepted his wife's insistence that they should live as a family again.

By then, Ruth had begun dating a young apprentice engineer named Joe Jakubait, who switched his attentions to Muriel when she arrived in London. Ruth shrugged it off; she was emerging from her shell, refusing to wear the spectacles that spoiled her fine-boned, animated face, and growing wise to men's interest. She remained slim and coltish, and learned how to make the most of her heavy auburn hair. Throughout her teens, she kept it natural, and the deep, rich hues enhanced her flawless complexion. It was years yet before she discovered the peroxide that helped define the tabloid image of her as a common, cold-hearted murderess.

*

On 7 September 1940, the Luftwaffe launched an unrelenting assault on London, with Southwark as a main target. By mid-October, civilian casualties were mounting and thousands of homes had been destroyed. Along with the majority of Londoners, Ruth was determined not to let the Blitz dictate her life, but when the air-raid warning wailed and searchlights panned the sky, there was no sensible alternative other than to run to the nearest shelter – often a converted railway arch. She had little option but to sit tight while the foundations of the capital shook under falling bombs. Returning home from a dance often meant threading her way through burning streets in the blackout, avoiding careering ambulances and fire engines as the long, high peal of the All Clear sounded. By the end of November, an estimated 3,000 unexploded bombs were waiting to be defused in London.

Christmas Day saw a temporary lull in the attacks, but on 27 December the Luftwaffe resumed their pounding of the city. Near Ruth's home in Southwark, 50 people were killed when a public shelter received a direct hit. Two days later, the worst raid yet wreaked devastation across the capital: 22,000 incendiaries were dropped on the city, setting countless buildings alight. When morning came, bringing with it a chill wind and breath of snow, hundreds lay dead or seriously injured. A heavy air raid on 17 February 1941 brought destruction closer still; 34 incidents occurred in Southwark that night.

Displaying typical dark humour, Ruth borrowed a line from a British Pathé newsreel about Christmas turkeys to use as her mantra: 'A short life and a gay one.'[4] While their upbringing left Muriel cowed and nervous of men, Ruth responded by throwing herself into London nightlife, visiting cafes and dance clubs alone if she couldn't persuade her sister to join her, and necking with boys in unlit doorways. When Muriel tried to remonstrate with her, Ruth laughed: 'You may be my elder sister, but I'm ten bloody years older than you in experience.'[5] The two girls worked alongside each other at the now iconic OXO building across the road from the flat. Originally a power station, in the 1920s it became a meatpacking factory and was known as Stamford Wharf when Ruth was a machine minder there. It was a distinctly unglamorous job, but she heard about dances from the other girls and took to wearing curlers beneath her headscarf, ready to polish her appearance as soon as her shift was over. 'The excitement of wartime London began to grip me,' she recalled. 'Slowly I drifted away from family life . . . I heard other girls talking of their dates. I did not go on any risky dates – my parents saw to that – but I began to grow restless at their control.'[6]

When the building was hit in an air raid, she and Muriel found work at Marconi's munitions factory, but Ruth craved something that would bring a little glitz into her life and was delighted to secure a job as a waitress at Lyons Corner House Restaurant near Trafalgar Square. A famous chain of art deco-style eateries, Lyons Corner Houses were set out over several opulent floors comprising food halls, hairdressing salons, theatre booking agencies and telephone booths. The restaurants provided the centrepiece, each decorated to a different theme and with its own orchestra. Corner House waitresses were renowned for their efficiency, hence the nickname 'nippies'. Wearing the distinctive black uniform with white apron and cap, Ruth learned how to offer prompt service with an ever-present smile and the ability to make customers feel special – a useful grounding for the future nightclub hostess. Working at Lyons briefly inspired her with a different ambition, which she confided in her brother Granville: 'One day *I'll* have a chain of restaurants.'[7]

But if Ruth struck those who didn't know her well as flighty, an incident during the Blitz proved that there was more to her than met the eye.

*

The Auxiliary Fire Service was formed in 1938 as part of Civil Defence Air Raid Precautions. Unpaid volunteers – mostly men unable to join the military for any number of reasons – were recruited to support the beleaguered London Fire Brigade. Ruth's father was among them, and wore his steel helmet and insignia with pride. He was on duty during the evening of 10 May 1941, when the air-raid siren sounded just after 11 p.m. An hour later, the sky filled with German bombers prepped to carry out the most desolating raid of the Blitz. Incendiaries rained on the city, exploding in a sizzle of white-blue fire at the point of impact. Bombs hurtled down in the north at Islington, east at Wapping, west at Notting Hill and south at Southwark, where a landmine exploded on a row of houses owned by R. White's Lemonade company, killing 14 people.

Ruth was with her father that night, battling alongside him. Granville recalled: 'The whole street was ablaze and Dad told me that Ruth . . . stuck by him, fighting the fires.'[8] When a sudden series of explosions tore up the ground, hurling rubble skywards, something struck Arthur hard, knocking him unconscious. Ruth dropped to her knees and clawed through the debris, digging until she had uncovered her father. An ambulance took him to hospital that night, where he was found to have a cerebral thrombosis.

The raid was the last major assault on London until the summer of 1944. As the sun rose, almost 1,500 people lay dead and a further 1,800 were seriously injured. The asphalt at Waterloo Station melted from the fires in the vaults below; the Chamber of the House of Commons, the House of Lords, Westminster Abbey, Westminster Hall, St James's Palace and Lambeth Palace were all damaged, along with most major railway stations, 14 hospitals, the British Museum and the Old Bailey, where 14 years later Ruth would be sentenced to hang.

Arthur's injury left him partially disabled and unable to work for some time. He lost his job and the flat that went with it, and, although he eventually found employment as a caretaker in a garage on Lambeth's Herne Hill Road, he suffered a stroke soon afterwards. Bertha visited him every week at the hospital on Poplar Road in Leatherhead, where he received specialist treatment for months until he was finally discharged to the family flat at 19 Farmers Road, Camberwell. Muriel dates this as the end of his abuse, writing that despite her father's attempts to continue as before, she found the strength to refuse him, largely due to her deepening relationship with Joe Jakubait.

In mid-March 1942, Ruth herself was admitted to hospital. She awoke in the night, crying from severe pain in her left hand. Muriel sat with her until she had to go to work, but the pain still hadn't lessened and Bertha ran for a doctor, leaving Ruth weeping on the window seat in the lounge. An ambulance took her to St Giles Hospital, where she was diagnosed with acute rheumatic fever.

Although Ruth said nothing to her family, for the past three weeks she had been in agony, with swelling and redness in her left knee, pains in her ribs, left wrist, thumb and ring finger. An X-ray on 4 April revealed that she had acute infective arthritis in a joint in her left hand 'destroying the bone on each side of one of the first inter phalangeal joints and periostitis of the first phalanx'.[9] Ruth described the affliction as 'a crippled ring finger' and complained of pain in the balls of her feet.[10] She remained hospitalised until 3 May, not quite the length of time claimed in her story in the *Woman's Sunday's Mirror*: 'For a year I lay on my back in St Giles Hospital, Camberwell, with rheumatic fever. For a year I ate nothing but boiled fish.'[11] In reality, after several weeks in hospital, Ruth returned home eager to follow the medical advice she had been given: to use dancing as a form of therapeutic exercise. Bertha wrote to inform Granville, then serving overseas with the army, that his young sister was 'dance mad'.[12]

By late 1942, the Neilsons were living in a three-storey Victorian villa on Brixton's Bengeworth Road, which they rented from an elderly Italian woman. Arthur and Bertha occupied the ground floor with five-year-old Betty, Muriel was on the first floor with her son Robert, and Ruth had the top flat. Julian was still in the navy and Granville remained overseas for the duration of the war; he was shot in one eye and held in a German prisoner-of-war camp. Betty, the youngest member of the family, contracted asthma as a result of being lifted too often from a semi-warm bed to be carried down to the damp Anderson shelter.

Ruth's first serious relationship was long thought to have begun while she was working in a dance hall, but Muriel demolishes this story in her memoir. According to her, at Ruth's suggestion the two sisters visited a dive bar one night, which Muriel describes as similar to an air-raid shelter: a dark, underground spot where couples drank and canoodled. Dive bars were particularly popular with Canadian and US servicemen, and one khaki-clad soldier in his mid-20s approached Muriel. Already involved with Joe, she introduced him to Ruth, who was immediately drawn to 'his soft Canadian drawl and the warm way he said, "Hello, honey" . . . He looked wonderful in Army uniform. By the end of the evening I was in love – hopelessly in love for the first time.'[13] They spent the rest of the evening together and afterwards the three of them wandered around the dark streets, eating chips and chatting. The soldier, whose name was Clare Andrea McCallum, insisted on seeing the two girls safely to the tube. When he asked Ruth if he could meet her again, she said yes.[14]

Very little is known about Clare, a French Canadian serviceman from Quebec. When he and Ruth met in 1943, the 1st Canadian Army had been scattered throughout Britain for two years, based largely in southern England. A number of Canadian units sailed for Sicily at the end of June 1943 but many stayed in Britain to prepare for D-Day. In all probability Clare was stationed at Aldershot and, like many young servicemen, headed regularly into London on nights out. For Ruth, the attraction was instant: he was dark-haired, of average height and build, ten years her senior and generous to a fault, while his occupation and accent imbued him with distinct appeal. There was just one detail he failed to mention: at home in Quebec were his wife and three children.

From the outset, Clare was exceptionally attentive to Ruth and shared her flat on Bengeworth Road while on leave. She recalled 'weeks of rapture . . . [he] loved me devotedly and when he was not with his unit he would write not once but often twice a day'.[15] To Ruth's surprise, her parents encouraged the relationship, which Muriel claims was motivated not so much by a wish for their daughter's happiness as by an avaricious interest in the well-stocked haversack Clare carried, usually filled to bursting with tinned food and cigarettes. Ruth was genuinely besotted by him. When she discovered she was pregnant in early 1944, Clare asked to marry her – still retaining the pretence that he was a bachelor – and she began excitedly preparing for the birth and wedding. According to Muriel, the pregnancy caused Bertha and Arthur to withdraw their approval entirely; they stopped speaking to Ruth. But not even their lack of support and Clare's posting overseas failed to dim her happiness. She worried only over his welfare: 'I felt that while he was in England I could protect him in some way, but once he was sent abroad I felt lost. I read and re-read his letters – I felt that nothing could happen to him while I read them.'[16]

Ruth continued to work at Lyons until a few weeks before her due date when, under the care of King's College Hospital, she was dispatched north to Gilsland Nursing Home. Set in rolling grounds and woods high above a village spanning the border between Cumbria and Northumberland, the home was originally a luxury spa hotel. In the early 1940s Newcastle Corporation appropriated it as a maternity home for Tyneside mothers-to-be and gradually women from other areas were sent there to give birth away from the air raids. Staffed by Roman Catholic nuns, the home provided care at a cost of five shillings per day; those carrying illegitimate babies had to perform light work for their keep. Ration books were surrendered upon admission: pregnant women were entitled to extra rations of one pint of milk a day, cod liver oil, orange juice, more meat and cheese, and further coupons for clothing. Rations were fairly shared among residents, who were well fed and fussed over, with the extra milk used for evening cocoa. The camp beds were the only drawback; they were uncomfortable and creaked dreadfully, especially while giving birth.

But the camaraderie between residents compensated, and there was even a piano available for anyone who could play, with impromptu dances held for expectant mothers, who led each other bump-to-bump about the rooms. The older and more experienced women offered advice to the younger ones and would often comfort them during labour.

Ruth spent the summer of 1944 at the home, hundreds of miles from the flying bombs and rockets that had begun to fall on London. The V1s – Doodlebugs – came first, killing and injuring thousands. The V2s followed in a swarm, travelling silently at colossal speed, each carrying a one-ton warhead that brought carnage on a vast scale.

On 15 September 1944, after a difficult labour for which she needed 'a lot of stitches', Ruth gave birth to a healthy, dark-haired boy.[17] She registered his birth a fortnight later in the nearby market town of Brampton, giving her occupation as 'cafe cashier' and her new address in London: 20 Padfield Road, Camberwell. A single line was drawn through the column for the father of Ruth's child, but she named her son after him: Clare Andria Neilson.

Thus, Ruth joined the 20,000 or so British women, many of them unmarried, whose children were fathered by Canadian servicemen. For some, the stigma of an illegitimate child was too great and the baby was surrendered for adoption. Many women tried to trace their vanished partners after giving birth only to find that his regiment denied he existed; others married their Canadian boyfriends and discovered that their union was bigamous. Predictably, there was a significant increase in illegitimate births during the war years: in 1939, 32,000 babies were born out of wedlock in England and Wales; in 1945 that figure had leapt to 73,000. For extremely young, impoverished women like Ruth, defying the social prejudices that focused condemnation on unmarried mothers but not the men involved required a significant amount of courage.

Ruth wrote to ask Muriel if she and Joe would meet her from the train in London. Her sister, who had recently married, replied that they would and sent her a shawl for 'Andre', as Ruth had taken to calling the baby. A few days later, Muriel and Joe made their way across the concourse at Waterloo, where Ruth – still a small, slight girl of 17 – waited beneath the station clock with a suitcase at her feet, clutching her sleeping baby in his new shawl.

4

When the war ended in 1945, it took with it any notions Ruth might have held onto about a happy-ever-after with Clare. Her mother had written to his commanding officer, dissatisfied with his inability to set a date for the wedding, and was duly informed that Clare already had a wife and children in Canada. Granville recalled: 'I must say this of him, he wanted to stand by Ruth and divorce his wife but Mum told him to do no such thing.'[1] Ruth was more distraught than anyone had ever seen her; Muriel declares that her sister was heartbroken and changed forever by the revelation. Ruth's natural resilience enabled her to withstand Clare's deception, but it came at a price: she vowed not to put her faith in relationships from then on. 'I no longer felt any emotion about men,' she recalled ten years later. 'Outwardly I was cheerful and gay. Inwardly I was cold and spent.'[2] She blamed herself for failing to recognise that Clare's promises were hollow and swore never to make the same mistake again: in future, she would be more vigilant.

Clare returned from France with a beautiful white pram for the baby and continued to send Ruth maintenance money for some time. When the day came for his departure to Canada, he wrote to Ruth from the ship and sent a vast spray of red carnations to the Neilson house in Padfield Road, where Ruth shared the rooms Muriel occupied with Joe and their children.[3] She kept the bouquet, but Clare's letter went unanswered. As he sailed out of her life, Ruth borrowed a story from her sister to tell anyone who asked about Andre's father: he was an American pilot who had been killed in action.

Britain's VE Day celebrations were in full swing: jubilant crowds converged on Trafalgar Square for days and danced a conga down the middle of bunting-frothed Piccadilly to the sound of military bands. Ruth returned to work at Lyons, entrusting Andre to Muriel and

Bertha's shared care; her parents had acknowledged their grandson and were no longer shunning her. She moved in with them again and learned how to look after Andre while working as many hours as possible to keep them afloat. But serving in the restaurant had lost its allure and she handed in her notice, having secured a job as a photographer's assistant at Streatham Locarno.[4] Dominating Streatham High Street, the Locarno was the first purpose-built dance hall in Britain, opened in 1929 by bandleader Billy Cotton.[5] The interior was stylish and opulent, with balconies overlooking the enormous dance floor where *Miss World* and *Come Dancing* were launched. The photographer snapped couples whirling, waltzing and jitterbugging about the place and Ruth's task was to persuade them to buy the pictures. The hours meant she was able to spend more time at home but there were so many arguments between Ruth and her parents that she was forever moving from their flat to Muriel's and back again.

While Ruth was at the Locarno, her elder sister tended to look after Andre. Muriel was now taking care of several children: Andre, her nine-year-old sister Betty (whom she writes was being regularly beaten by their father) and Christopher and Joey, her own sons with Joe. Soon after Christopher was born, Muriel's husband and parents insisted on her first child, Robert, being sent away to Darrenth Park, a boarding school in Kent for people with learning difficulties. Muriel visited him there occasionally at weekends. She and her family then moved in with Joe's parents in New Eltham, while Bertha and Arthur found a flat in a three-storey house in Herne Hill Road.

Ruth sought to gain control of her life and find her niche, leaving Streatham Locarno for a succession of jobs elsewhere, including singer with a big band. She even toyed with the idea of becoming an actress and at one point enrolled in a drama school in Richmond but lost interest after a couple of months, her enthusiasm dented by the course fees. Single motherhood had consolidated rather than deflated her ambitions; she paid her mother to look after Andre while she strove to find work that would engage her interest and play to her strengths, as well as ensuring she left behind the acute poverty of her childhood. Those episodes in her past that might have felled a less spirited person – the shambolic upbringing, her father's violence and abuse, and the pain caused by Clare's dishonesty – only served to make her keener to succeed.

Post-war Britain was not the easiest place for a young woman like Ruth to rise above her circumstances. Austerity held the country in its grip: as the new Labour government struggled to pay off the debts accumulated during the war, former servicemen returned to a drab homeland where rationing was still in force and people queued for everything only to be told there was nothing. Crime and unemployment were on the up, young couples embarked on married life in squalid rented rooms or lived with their in-laws, and nearly everyone suffered from chilblains. One visitor to London described it as 'a decaying, decrepit, sagging, rotten city' where public buildings were 'filthy and pitted with shrapnel scars running with pigeon dung. Bus tickets and torn newspapers blew down the streets: whole suburbs of private houses were peeling, cracking, their windows unwashed, their steps unswept, their gardens untended.'[6]

Ruth pursued work that might bring a touch of sparkle to her life, with modelling the obvious choice. She was not conventionally beautiful, but she had that indefinable something that made people look at her twice, and took pride in her appearance. The unflattering spectacles were sequestered in their case unless absolutely necessary; Ruth preferred to squint instead. She would not set foot outside unless fully made up, and relied on Max Factor's panstick, rouge and lipstick to give her some definition – mascara was expensive and therefore to be used sparingly. She looked after her skin with a little cold cream rubbed into her face and neck, and washed her hair with soft green soap bought for a few pence from the chemist, using pipe cleaners or fire-heated tongs to give it bounce. With the bit of money she saved from her wages, she was eventually able to put away the hand-me-downs and bought clothes from a Brixton arcade, growing fastidious about the pieces she could afford.

Rather than approach a modelling agency, however, Ruth answered an advert for evening work at the Camera Club, where no experience was necessary for nude 'but artistic' poses. She went along for an interview at the Camera Club's premises in Manchester Square, a short walk from Bond Street tube, and was engaged immediately. 'At first I felt frightfully embarrassed,' she recalled, 'but I soon got used to it.'[7] In her memoir, Muriel is at pains to disprove earlier claims that the work her sister undertook at the Camera Club was tawdry and semi-pornographic, and aims to banish the notion (repeated in the 1985 biopic *Dance with a Stranger*) that Ruth abandoned her clothes before groups of up to 20 amateur cameramen, some of whom didn't even trouble to load their cameras with film. Muriel describes how her father showed her some of Ruth's photographs, which he said he had found in a cupboard, that were not seedy at all; Ruth was naked or semi-undressed but the shots had an accomplished originality to them. Terry Turner, the longest-serving member of the Camera Club, confirms that Ruth wasn't officially on their books but would have modelled for a private individual who paid for the studio – certainly not a whole group of idly lecherous men. Turner described the place as very much in the style of a gentleman's club, with strong connections to the RAF. Muriel's protestations are convincing: Ruth was still auburn-haired while she modelled at the Camera Club and the only well-known photographs of her that might be judged sleazy or obviously pornographic show her as a blonde, which would date them as 1953 at the earliest.

The Camera Club was a useful stepping stone in the careers of a number of actresses and professional models, including Diana Dors. Britain's favourite 1950s pin-up worked there regularly from 1946 until 1951, mostly in the evenings:

> for the princely sum of one guinea an hour . . . It was a rule among these amateur photographers never to touch the models, and, as some of them posed in the nude, it must have been quite an achievement for the men who rushed along there, armed with their cameras, for an evening away from their wives. Eventually, I, too was asked if, with the strictest propriety, I'd be prepared to remove my swimsuit and allow the photographers to snap me in my birthday suit . . . the extra money from posing nude came in most handy.[8]

Ruth viewed her own work at the Camera Club as a means to an end, hoping it would lead to more prestigious assignments and introduce her to influential people. She socialised with the photographers and their associates, one of whom invited her for a drink at the Court Club on Duke Street, where she found herself 'monopolised' by the club owner.[9] Far from handsome and many years her senior, his portly flashiness intrigued Ruth nonetheless – as did his guarantee of a proposition that would be to their mutual advantage.

Eighteen years later, while awaiting execution in Holloway, Ruth traced her downfall to the owner of the Court Club. The prison doctor noted: '[She] came under "influence" then of Conley ... and graduated to the type of life she was leading.'[10] He added at Ruth's prompting: 'Conley is one of the worst characters in the West End.'[11]

*

Morris Conley was memorably described by crime reporter Duncan Webb as 'the monster with the Mayfair touch'.[12] In his December 1955 exposé, Webb declared: 'Right in the centre of corruption in the West End of London stands the figure of Morris Conley. I hereby name him as Britain's biggest vice boss and the chief source of the tainted money that nourishes the evils of London night life.'[13]

Born into an impoverished Jewish family, by the 1930s Conley was running his own West End furriers, Caplan & Conley Costumiers. Following a gambling scam in 1934, he falsely declared himself bankrupt and closed the company down, netting £10,000 in the process. His inability to resist boasting about it alerted the trustees of his bankruptcy case, who launched a seven-month investigation into his activities and brought charges against him in February 1935.[14] The jury at Conley's trial were twice unable to reach a verdict, but in the third instance he was found guilty of fraud and sentenced to two years in prison. After his release he set up a business supplying gaming machines and opened an amusement arcade on the Harrow Road. In August 1939, *The Times* reported that a man had been sentenced to 21 days' imprisonment with hard labour for smashing up a pin table at the arcade. Conley appeared as a witness on that occasion, but he was soon in the dock again, listening to Chief Inspector Bye informing West London magistrate's court that his one-arm bandits were 'so rigged that the jackpot could never be won if the machines were played on for a hundred years'.[15]

After serving a second prison term of four months, Conley returned home with his next business venture already planned: to reign in London's lucrative nightclub world. Shrewdly, he identified a gap in the market. Men regarded as heroes during their time in the forces found it difficult to adjust to mundane post-war occupations such as travelling salesmen, and the corresponding decline in female attention was equally dispiriting. Conley sensed that ex-servicemen would dig deep in their pockets for the opportunity to relive their exploits – real or exaggerated – in an environment that offered a little ersatz luxury, alcohol, light dining and the company of desirable young women.

The crime wave that engulfed London immediately after the war made his dream easier to achieve. Lorry hijackings and warehouse raids were frequent, as one writer commented in December 1945:

> Armed robberies of the most violent and vicious kind feature daily in the newspapers. Even the pettiest crimes are, it seems, conducted with a loaded revolver in hand ... Hold-ups of cinemas, post offices and railway booking offices have become so commonplace that the newspapers scarcely bother to report them.[16]

The black market mushroomed in the capital's back streets, disgorging umpteen gambling clubs, afternoon drinking dens and nightclubs. Notorious criminals and their cohorts – Billy Hill, Jack Spot, the Whites – fought for control of the West End, making nightclubs a breeding ground for gangland turmoil. At the same time, Soho and the West End became notorious for

> louche, loose, licentious living. Here was everything that was being frowned out of everyday England, in particular sex, glamour, jazz, unusual drugs and weird people. Here one could behave outrageously, promiscuously, bibulously and guiltlessly. Here was an entire community geared not just to pleasure, but to pleasure with an intellectual, continental, bohemian edge.[17]

Strict licensing laws ensured that pubs closed at 3 p.m., but by the mid-1950s there were hundreds of afternoon drinking clubs in the West End, varying from the very basic (an upstairs flat accommodating a few chairs and a bar) to the more sophisticated, replete with subdued lighting and haughty staff. For the serious reveller, it was then but a short stagger to one of the nightspots radiating out from Leicester Square where alcohol could be served until 12.30 a.m. provided it was accompanied by food.

Morris Conley was keen to impress Ruth as a respectable businessman running four well-placed nightclubs. If at first she considered him the pudgy, genial uncle type, generous with his compliments and cash, she quickly discovered the truth: Conley was a pimp and gangster, using his underworld connections to exploit demoralised ex-servicemen and disadvantaged young women alike. There was no shortage of anything in Conley's clubs, thanks to his long-established black market contacts. Gratuities clattered into the tills as salesmen, socialites, gangsters, aristocrats, Members of Parliament, actors and the odd peripheral royal also jostled for the chance of sympathetic feminine attention – just as Conley had predicted. His nemesis-in-waiting, crime reporter Duncan Webb, observed how young women like Ruth, eager to see a bit of life and earn a decent wage, flocked to 'drink from the troublesome cup of sophistication in London's West End'.[18] In the bogus glitter of pubs, nightclubs and hotel bars, vivacious girls sometimes no more than 16 and stylish women rarely older than 30 concealed

> the sordidness which lies behind the glittering veneer of Mayfair and Soho . . . They are there to make the men feel at home, to listen to their silly stories or boastful adventures, to subscribe to their ego and encourage them to spend money. They are there also to earn a livelihood, which many of them do. The main object of most of them is to have a good time, as well as give it, to get from the men of their acquaintance whatever they can in the way of cash or kind.[19]

Lust was the inevitable common denominator among the clientele. Between the wars, the West End had been the nucleus of prostitution, with Shepherd Market and Piccadilly the main red-light districts. After 1945, women were still soliciting on the streets around Piccadilly Circus, despite the threat of police intervention. Magistrates began cracking down on those caught living off immoral earnings, particularly brothel-keepers. Occasionally a case hit the headlines: the ubiquitous Duncan Webb unmasked the Messinas, five brothers who ran a prostitution racket and ruled the West End through violence and intimidation.

Morris Conley devised a subtler route to being crowned London's vice king. He personally arranged any sexual transactions between his hostesses and the club clientele, and demanded that the girls should also be available to him – 'Morrie', as he preferred to be called – and his friends, at any hour. This proved such a money-spinner that he decided to employ a middle-aged woman at each of his clubs to cater specifically to the clients' preferences, if necessary calling girls in from other clubs. The 'madams' earned commission, but the bulk of the profits landed in Morrie's wallet, leaving the girls themselves precious little cash for their efforts. Another profitable sideline emerged as a solution to the problem of customers not always finding it convenient to be 'looked after' in their hotel rooms or at home; Morrie set his girls up in flats, becoming a property developer in the process. Post-war London was a deeply scored map of ruined houses, bombsites and fractured working-class districts, with blanket plans in place for high-rise blocks of flats to overcome the acute housing shortage. As the regeneration of the capital got under way, Morrie bought up flats and renovated derelict buildings to rent out at extortionate rates. Most of the properties were registered in his wife Hannah's name and let to the club hostesses, girls with no other income who frequently found the rent impossible to meet. Again Morrie had a remedy, accepting sexual favours for himself and his gangland associates in temporary lieu of payment. If a girl refused – which he found incomprehensible, considering himself a skilful lover whose status compensated for his dearth of physical charm – then she was either evicted or paid a visit by one of his minders.

When Ruth first encountered Morrie, he was enjoying extraordinary prosperity as landlord, pimp, nightclub boss and black marketeer. Brandishing one of his ever-present cigars, he welcomed her into his club at 58 Duke Street near Grosvenor Square. Despite its reputation as a fashionable nightspot, the Court Club was 'the next thing to a brothel', populated by 'a mix of the English upper class and racketeers'.[20] Upon meeting Ruth, Morrie put on his most affable expression and assured her that as a hostess she would earn twice as much as in a factory or shop, plus 10 per cent commission on the food and drink she sold. Her basic duty was simply to sit and chat with a customer for a flat fee of £5, provided he bought a bottle of champagne for £3. The hours were 3 p.m. until 11 p.m., although she could expect to work another shift at the Hollywood Club on Welbeck Street occasionally, which was open until the early hours. Perks included keeping her own tips, free eveningwear and the option of a flat.

Ruth accepted on the spot. Soon she was picking up predictable habits and mannerisms from the other hostesses: she began smoking, developed a taste for gin and tonic, and worked to improve her naturally high-pitched voice until it was all stilted vowels punctuated by a laugh like falling water. Her wages went almost entirely to her parents, who cared for Andre while Ruth was at the club. Together with the rest of her family, they knew nothing of the world into which she had been inescapably drawn. The extra duties Morrie had hinted at during their first meeting swiftly became apparent. Having relinquished her earnings to her parents, the most consistent means of making ends meet was to sleep with the customers occasionally – and Morrie himself. Ruth suspected he had fallen in love with her, but more probably he was gratified by how good she was at her job. In turn, his belief that Ruth had deeper feelings for him was very much mistaken. As events would prove beyond doubt, she found him physically repugnant and never regarded him as a close friend.

Ruth learned to view sex as part of business, giving customer satisfaction while shutting her emotions off. Otherwise, she appreciated the trappings being a hostess brought: socialising with a wealthy, fast and eclectic crowd; wearing glamorous clothes and being told she was desirable; and, not least, the capacity to earn a decent income. Rather more touchingly, for the first time she had real, laugh-out-loud fun with girls her own age and discovered an essential element that had long been missing from her life: a best friend. That role was fulfilled by captivating Vicki Martin, whose life would be as quick, tangled and tragic as Ruth's own.

5

Born Valerie Mewes on 2 August 1931 in Staines, Middlesex, Vicki Martin had an unhappy, lower middle-class upbringing. Her parents divorced during her childhood and she was deeply unsettled at home, turning to her beloved grandmother, Alice, for comfort. Like Ruth, Vicki began working at the age of fourteen, moving from one job to another and unable to find anything – even nursing, which she had expected to like – that interested her. She told everyone that what she really wanted was to be a film star, a dream shared by most of her contemporaries who had no idea how to fulfil it. Vicki's friend Joyce Edmonds, who lived in the house opposite Alice's bungalow, recalled, 'She was one of our gang. We all used to talk about leaving home, living in London, becoming film stars, meeting famous people, and marrying a prince. No one ever thought [Vicki] would actually do it.'[1]

In October 1949, 17-year-old Vicki set out to realise her dream, leaving her grandmother's bungalow in Egham with a bag stuffed full of film magazines, make-up, clothing and her radio. She caught the 701 bus to London, 18 miles from home, and disembarked at Park Lane without knowing where she would spend the night. For a while, she stood clutching her bag, gazing at the well-dressed people passing through the doors of the Dorchester and Grosvenor House hotels, then turned and headed left out of Park Lane, walking until she reached the neon signs and poised arrow of Eros in Piccadilly Circus. She approached several clubs for work and advice on where to stay; someone directed her to Duke Street, where the convivial owner of the Court Club offered her a job and accommodation on sight. Vicki could scarcely believe her good fortune.

Twenty-three-year-old Ruth immediately took Vicki (then still known as Valerie) under her wing. She was more cynical than Vicki, who lived in the moment; Ruth kept her grounded, while Vicki encouraged her to lighten up a little. Their friendship became the bedrock of their lives and eventually, as well as working together, they shared a flat in Tooting Bec. Five-year-old Andre remained with Ruth's parents, where she visited him most Sundays and during the week when not working. She rarely saw Muriel, but they kept in touch by telephone. Ruth's life revolved around the club, where the work was hard and anything but pleasant at times; she had toughened up considerably and was determined that if men were going to expect something from her, then they would pay well for it. Wealthier club members often asked her to spend the weekend at their country homes, and she agreed on the understanding that the invite was extended to Vicki. Together they learned how to manipulate their hosts, particularly the older men, into expensive shows of appreciation. Ruth devoured society columns to gain insight into the lives of her more affluent acquaintances and she took an avid interest in the news in order to converse knowledgeably about current affairs at dinner parties.

In 1950 Ruth became pregnant by one of the regular, well-off members of the Court Club. There was no question of keeping the baby but abortion was illegal, punishable by a custodial sentence for both parties. However, around 12,000 lawful abortions were performed annually on the grounds that the expectant mother would suffer a mental or physical collapse if the pregnancy was taken to full term. Ruth secretly visited an obliging doctor in north London, recommended to her by one of the other hostesses at the Court Club; her pregnancy was terminated in its third month with none of the life-threatening infections or ill-health that often followed an abortion. She returned to work within days.

*

Society was static during the early 1950s. Hoardings across London carried adverts proclaiming, 'Top People Read *The Times*'; the royal family was revered as an unassailable ideal. The need to cling to conventional values and tradition appeared to be a reaction not only to the horrors of the recent war, but also to underline comradeship and the glory of victory. Even entertainment and fashion were slow to change. Dance halls were not licensed to sell alcohol and bands had to stop playing at 11 p.m. prompt, while the continuing popularity of crooners and big-band music saw ballroom dancing dominating until mid-decade and sartorial codes enforced. Cinema reigned supreme; at the time of the coronation in 1953, there were still only two million television sets, mostly dotted around the bigger cities, and hours of broadcast were rigidly restricted.

In *The Plough Boy* (1965), Tony Parker's account of the 1953 Clapham Common murder, there is a description of how the ongoing obsession with the war made many young adults feel marginalised:

> It seemed to be somehow the war was over and we'd missed out on it, and yet it was still going on, if you know what I mean. It was in the atmosphere all the time, there was a kind of perpetual carry-over from it. The best-selling books were war books and the most popular films at the cinemas were war films. People didn't seem able to have enough of it, somehow they didn't want to let it go . . . That went on for quite a long time after the war, you know, the feeling was in the air you breathed, you could sense it all round you – older people looking back on it with excitement and pleasure, almost, as something to be enjoyed.[2]

One of the least welcome facets of life on the Home Front lingered on dismally: rationing of meat, bacon, butter, cheese, tea, sugar and sweets was more severe than in 1945. Coal shortages battered train services, steel shortages shut down car factories, and the housing shortage saw large numbers of families cramped together in prefab homes with asbestos walls. For most working-class people, automobiles and white goods were a luxury; hardly anyone owned a car or a refrigerator. Utility furniture stood spindly and plain in radiator-free rooms, and housewives bought from door-to-door salesmen or the corner shop. Income tax was high and people were cautioned to be thrifty, to save their pennies and reject self-indulgence of any kind.

Yet although most commodities – be it grey, scratchy toilet paper or rationed tobacco – were scarce, the sense of 'all being in it together' compensated to some extent. People flocked to the cinema, to pubs, to allotments, to church and on day trips en masse; they joined societies and had hobbies, and looked forward to a week at Butlin's or Pontins, or at a seaside lodging house or static caravan. Winning the Football Pools would solve everything but until then communities gathered to celebrate holidays and festivals: Wakes Week, Whitsun, Bonfire Night and Christmas.

Neither Ruth nor Vicki were interested in such an existence. Ruth was 24 in 1950 and Vicki 18; both were fiercely ambitious at a time when the majority of young women didn't think in career terms but looked forward to marriage and a family. By far the most paradoxical aspect of the era was the role of women:

> After sharing the camaraderie of the fighting services or the hardships of civilian bombing on equal terms, surely women would not go meekly back home to wife-and-motherhood? But they did, with a fervor that would have amazed the feminists of their grandmothers' generation . . . In the early years the baby boom carried almost all women before it. Women gave up their jobs in droves and went home to have children in hordes . . . The Happy Housewife beamed at the world from countless advertisements.[3]

Aims outside the home were rarely fostered, with *Women's Weekly* telling its readers in 1951: 'To make a man feel happy and comfortable and to make a child feel cherished. No Woman's Work is more important than these.'[4]

Ruth's situation, in which she not only needed but also wanted to work, even if that meant leaving Andre with her parents, was fairly unusual. Most children below school age stayed home with their mothers, who were the voice of authority. There were a number of best-selling books on childcare, with psychoanalyst John Bowlby warning single mothers like Ruth that failing to remain at home resulted in 'deprived children [who are] the delinquents of tomorrow'.[5] There was no mention of the absent fathers.

But while virtuous motherhood was the peak of achievement, women were presented with another dichotomy: fetishised 'blonde bombshells' were everywhere in 1950s cinema. Marilyn Monroe, Brigitte Bardot, Diana Dors and Jayne Mansfield were blonde, busty and sexually confident (on screen at least), embodying what it meant to be an attractive woman, the importance of which could not be underestimated. In the early 1950s, *Everywoman* ran a series titled *How to Dress to Please Men*, gravely explaining the importance of personal grooming because 'he likes you to be soft and silky'.[6] *Woman's Own* agreed, admonishing a case in point: 'She won't get far without polishing up her good points and disguising her bad ones so that he's completely befogged by glamour! It's at this stage that the romantic compliments are paid and the diamond engagement rings get shopped for!'[7] Yet women continued to dress like their mothers, most of whom still favoured the pre-war staples of hats, suits, gloves and cigarette holders. Hair was carefully tucked and set, burnt-smelling from curling tongs heated in the fireplace, or reeking of the pungent setting lotion used in perms.

Ruth was less confused and more honest than many of her contemporaries; sex was a commodity, financial security the goal, and along the way she intended to enjoy life. The last thing she wanted was to open herself to emotional hurt again. Her attitude was uncommon, as Mass Observation's 1949 survey showed:

> Generally it seems fairly clear that people's approach to sex tends to be limited not only by their intentness on doing what they regard as socially 'correct', but also by anxiety and fears, particularly fears of transgressing the bounds of 'normality' and which may be all the stronger for their vagueness.[8]

Children growing up in post-war Britain were not told about sex by their parents; when Ruth had her first period, she told Muriel that she had one of those 'political' things. The act of sex was subtly alluded to in fiction and film, where censorship was strict, and a government campaign against all things obscene resulted in the prosecution of seaside postcard artist Donald McGill for his rendering of a large, upright stick of rock.

Women were expected to act as the guardians of the nation's sexuality. An early 1950s survey found that 55 per cent of men and 73 per cent of women disapproved of girls having intercourse before marriage, which remained the 'unassailable norm'.[9] The lack of effective contraceptives was undeniably part of the no-sex-before-marriage equation; even condoms, which were only slightly more readily available, had to be bought discreetly and therefore were not used as often as they should, and even then there was a 'widespread superstition that the Catholic church made sure that one in twenty was faulty, as a sort of divine vengeance'.[10]

Ruth and Vicki were far more worldly young women than most, but not nearly so sophisticated and sceptical as they liked to pretend. They had a catchphrase that was used as liberally as the swear words that now peppered their vocabulary: 'Gosh dear, now you've done it.'[11] Although both would have laughed at the idea that they couldn't spot trouble from a mile away, they were each about to meet men who in very different ways were exactly that.

*

Vicki's life was the first to change. One afternoon in April 1950, she was window-shopping on Oxford Street when a cloudburst forced her to dash for shelter in a doorway. While she stood there, shivering and waiting for the rain to stop, she was joined by a tall, slim and suavely handsome man in his late 30s. They smiled at each other: 'It was a smile you could never forget,' the man raved to his friends later, 'spontaneous, uninhibited and genuine.'[12] The man was Stephen Ward. Then a society osteopath and sought-after portrait artist, he became infamous in 1963 as one of the key players in the Profumo affair that brought down the Macmillan government.

Journalist Frederic Mullally, who came to know both Vicki and Stephen well, reflected:

> Stephen saw ... the cheekbones, the clear, opaque skin, the superbly-turned legs inside the laddered hose. And he must have seen something else, something most of us would have missed. [Vicki] was about 18, of poor parents, uneducated, out of work. Her accent was plain working class, but she was an original.[13]

In his memoir, Stephen Ward remembered that first encounter with something akin to wonderment, despite the many beautiful women who passed through his life before and after:

> I met Vicki in a shower of rain at Marble Arch. Blonde with large eyes set wide apart, and with probably the most exquisite smile you have ever seen, revealing perfect teeth. I used to try to keep her laughing just to see it.[14]

Ward suggested that they take a taxi to his flat in Cavendish Square, where they could have coffee and dry out. Vicki agreed, talking animatedly throughout the journey. In his smart flat, Ward handed her a towel and a change of clothes, explaining that they belonged to his ex-wife. Vicki swapped her damp clothes for the ones he offered and dried her hair before the fire, curling up while he made coffee. When Ward returned to the room, he asked if he might sketch her, with her hair piled on top of her head. He told her she should be a model, and said he could introduce her to the right people, if she were interested. When he asked her if she wanted to stay the night, indicating that she could sleep on his sofa, Vicki agreed. During the night, she climbed into Ward's bed, murmuring that she was lonely. He responded by kissing her forehead and telling her that he understood. They passed the entire night in conversation. Vicki told him that she had fallen out with her boyfriend and shared a flat with her best friend Ruth, who worked with her at the Court Club on Duke Street.

Ward listened, fascinated by Vicki's chatter and beauty. Although she did not know it then, her new friend was a collector of exquisite young women, not especially for his own sexual interests but more to 'ingratiate himself socially' by presenting them to his wealthy, influential friends.[15] Ward supplied girls for the sex parties he attended, at which he was usually a voyeur. At the height of the Profumo scandal years later he was accused of living off immoral earnings, but he had no need to do so, since his work as an artist and osteopath to some of the country's most well-known political, society and media figures provided him with a very generous income. Ward's friend Michael Pertwee described him succinctly as 'a man who knew a lot of pretty girls. He was a snob and a social climber, and this was a passport into the kind of circle he liked . . . He was, if you like, a social pimp.'[16]

One of Ward's habits was to take an outstandingly pretty working-class girl and shape her into a chic young woman of manners and charm who then took London society by storm. In exchange for the transformation, she slept with the men to whom he introduced her. Ward began playing Pygmalion to Vicki by suggesting that she discard her old name and thereafter spent months schooling her. She adored him for it and he exulted in watching her change before his eyes. '[Vicki] was a born optimist,' Ward recalled:

> She never showed her unhappiness although it was evident she had no one to turn to. And her talk was constantly punctuated by her smile . . . I never got tired of her laughter. She bubbled over with the sheer love of life.[17]

Aware that Vicki missed her grandmother, with whom she had lost contact, he drove her to Egham for a visit, earning the devotion of both women.

While Vicki prepared for her society debut, Ruth also met a man who would change the course of her life. Initially it seemed as if she, too, had climbed several rungs of the social ladder, albeit on a smaller scale. But within months the ladder had become a snake, depositing Ruth even further back than where she began.

Forty-eight-year-old George Johnston Ellis was known as 'the mad dentist' in the nightclubs of the West End. Born on 2 October 1909 in Chorlton-upon-Medlock, Manchester, he was the elder of two boys; his brother James arrived in 1916. Their mother Ella pushed her sons into excelling at school. George remained slightly fearful of her throughout his life and felt he could never meet the high standards she set him. After school and at weekends the boys worked for their father. James Edward Ellis came from humble Irish beginnings but had built up a successful business as a 'fish, game and poultry merchant', with two retail outlets on Oxford Road and Wilmslow Road in Manchester. The family was comfortably middle class and lived on Palatine Road in the leafy, well-to-do suburb of Didsbury.

Neither George nor James followed their father into the business. Both eventually became dentists, although George was a gifted piano player who could play any tune by ear and might easily have made a living from music. Instead he was accepted into the Manchester University School of Dentistry in 1929 and graduated in 1933. Following his father's death in 1936, George moved to Surrey and set up his own dental practice in Sanderstead. In September 1938 he married Vera Hume, an upper middle-class girl who spent much of her time in amateur dramatic productions, hoping to succeed as a professional actress.

George joined the air force but spent the greater part of the war years building up his dental practice. He and Vera became parents to two boys: John, born in 1945, and Richard, born in 1947. Around 1946 George took over directorship of Crystal Palace Football Club, when the Football League resumed after its wartime hiatus. He didn't hold the position for long, possibly due to his excessive drinking, which eventually destroyed his marriage. Two years later, George's doctor at Warlingham Hospital recorded a few details of this unhappy period:

> His troubles began in December 1948, when his wife to whom he had been married 10 years left him. He came home one day and found that she had cleared out and removed as much of the furniture and moveable possessions as she could . . . His general attitude is that he had done everything for her, had women in the house to do the domestic work, and the mending of the clothes, and this is what she does. The marriage had never been satisfactory . . . She waited until he started earning £6,000 a year on the health service and then left him in order to get alimony. She obtained a divorce against him on grounds of physical and mental cruelty. He says the allegation was quite untrue but he did not contend it, owing to the effect this would have had on his children and his professional standing.[1]

George refused to shoulder any responsibility for the failure of his marriage. His doctor noted that since his wife left:

> He has been in a very bitter and destructive mood. He has contemplated suicide but never had the courage. He has been drinking more than a bottle of spirit a day, but less in the last two weeks. He has had blackouts lasting for some time in which he does things he has no knowledge of, finds himself in Paris or on an airfield about to get to Dublin to get a steak. He does not blame his wife, he blames her mother, who influences her . . . His wife has the custody of his two children.[2]

In this frame of mind, George abandoned his dental work in March 1950, preferring the bars and nightclubs of London. At the Court Club he became infatuated with Ruth, who had no knowledge of his troubled past but was wary of him nonetheless:

> I thought he was rather pathetic. He told such wild tales I think he really believed them. He used to spend a lot of money and was good for champagne. He seemed to have taken a liking to me. I found it easy to make him buy me champagne.[3]

George persistently asked her to go out with him, but she always refused until one disastrous evening in June.

Ruth recounted:

> Vicki, Pat [another hostess] and I were in company with some members and George Ellis walked in, he wanted me to join him but I did not want to, he used to frighten me with his wild ravings. Vicki and I had planned to go out that night to a party. George Ellis kept pestering me so to get rid of him I said, 'You go to the Hollywood and I will meet you there later.' I had no intention of going there. So Vicki and I went to our party.[4]

At seven o'clock George arrived at the Hollywood Club, where he knew the manageress, Beth, and spent some time talking to her. He then began dancing with another girl. When it became obvious Ruth had stood him up, he asked the girl if she would join him at the Astor Club in Berkeley Square and she agreed. He later told Ruth that he and the girl were about to climb into his chauffeur-driven car when he was attacked by a man he had never seen before; his assailant slashed at him with a razor and kicked the girl on the pavement. Afterwards, Ruth stated that the man (a notorious criminal) was the girl's boyfriend and was sentenced to four years' imprisonment.[5] George was equally insistent months later that the man was part of a gang dispatched by Ruth to the club for the purpose of causing him harm. However, his claims were made during the breakdown of their relationship and at the time of the attack he did not suspect Ruth of any involvement.

Whatever the true circumstances, George was admitted to St Mary's Hospital in Paddington, where he received eight stitches for the deep wound on the left side of his face. In her account, Ruth wrote that she was so shocked by what had happened that she finally agreed to a date with him:

> Next day I got to work at three o'clock – I was a bit late in getting in – and Vicki, Pat and I were sitting on the side and the door was wide open. It was a very hot day. The first thing Vicki said was, 'Guess what happened last night?' I said, 'Tell me slowly, I don't feel so good today.' Vicki said, 'George Ellis was razor slashed outside the Hollywood last night.' I said, 'Oh Lord, was he? I feel dreadful, I sent him there.' Vicki said, 'Don't be

silly, he always goes there, whether you told him or not he would have gone anyway, he likes Beth.' Later on, early in the evening, George Ellis walked in wearing dark glasses and a most ugly red gash across his cheek. I felt like crying. He was looking in the mirror at the back of the bar at me. I did not know what to do, whether to go up and say I was sorry for not keeping the appointment with him. He bought some champagne and sent me a glass . . . I couldn't do enough for him. He asked the Manager if he could take me out to dinner. Ronnie asked me if I could stand it. I said, 'I think I ought to go.' I was given permission as long as I was back at a certain time.[6]

George asked his chauffeur to drive the two of them to Purley Downs Golf Club, where he was a member. They watched his friends playing a few rounds and then had dinner, admiring the sweeping views of London from the club. By the time they returned to the Court Club, it was late. Ruth recalled:

Ronnie was annoyed. George Ellis spent the rest of the night at the club. I had been drinking quite a lot . . . We went to the Astor after this and I was very drunk. I woke up next morning at Elmwood, Sanderstead, George's house. That day I heard the story of his wife leaving him – he told me he had gone to play golf at Purley Downs Golf Club. When he returned, his wife and children had gone. I really felt sorry for him. He was very much in love with her.[7]

In fact, George was *still* in love with Vera and hoped to win his wife and sons back, feeling that his life was on hold until they returned to him. But he liked Ruth and was attracted to her; she helped ease his loneliness and was a lively drinking companion. Ruth in turn enjoyed the unpredictability of being with George, who was 17 years her senior and generous with money, gifts and time. 'He took me out shopping, bought me lots of expensive things,' she recalled. 'We ate at the best places; in fact he showered me with everything . . . I did not get fond of him, only to the extent of what he could spend on me.'[8] George's extravagances included a lengthy holiday in Newquay, one of Britain's most popular seaside resorts, described in a 1951 issue of *Reynolds News* as 'bright, breezy, and clean' where 'on every side one hears the accents of Scotland, the Midlands and London'.[9] Ruth deliberately waited until the last moment to ask Morrie for the time off, knowing he would be annoyed to lose both his favourite hostess and a loyal customer for several weeks. It was not a child-friendly holiday despite the location, and Andre remained at home with his grandparents. He would not have enjoyed the day trip George had arranged by boat, during which he and the skipper proceeded to get 'well and truly tight', as Ruth phrased it.[10] Night fell and they remained far from shore, then one of the engines broke down. While the skipper tried to mend it, an inebriated George tried to steer the boat. 'I was frozen,' Ruth remembered.

> The little boat seemed to toss up and down and the waves seemed to be so high – the boat was leaking badly, I was bailing water out. Then the skipper discovered that he had not got any more fuel on board, also we had not got any navigation lights or compass ... I was disgusted to think that they could start a journey like this without all the necessary things ... Then it started to rain, I wrapped myself in oilskins I found in the boat and hoped for the best – the sea can be very frightening when you are not on any course and you haven't got a compass.[11]

In the distance, Ruth saw a lighthouse beam. George told her to start praying because the boat was in bad shape. 'So am I!' Ruth replied. By a miracle, they managed to pull up alongside a French trawler, who gave them enough fuel to reach land and, with the engine fixed, they sailed into St Ives, 'frozen, sick and wet'.[12] They spent the night in the first hotel they found, had hot baths and fell asleep. 'We slept all through the day,' Ruth recalled.

> I got up first. George was ill so I arranged hot milk for him and aspirins ... I had to make a call to Newquay to our driver and get him to put some clothes in a case and bring the car. George intended to go back by road [but] the boat had to be taken back to Newquay.[13]

Against Ruth's better judgement, they returned to Newquay by sea: 'When we got back to the hotel everyone knew of our adventures and it was the talk of the town for a few days ... I don't think Newquay would have forgotten us in a hurry.'[14]

Vicki Martin visited Ruth and George while they were on holiday, staying for several days and bringing all the gossip from London. She had made her debut at Siegi Sessler's new club, the Fine Arts in Charles Street. Journalist Frederic Mullally was there:

> The euphoria hadn't quite mounted to its heady pre-dinner peak when Stephen and Vicki made their entrance. There were girls in the room far lovelier than Vicki, and all of them were more expensively and elaborately dressed. It just didn't matter. They all lost their escorts for as long as they stayed in the bar, to a girl-of-the-people with short-cropped hair the texture of hemp, a laughing, unguardedly-avid face, and a body you would commit crimes for.[15]

Vicki was thus launched with all the success Ward had intended:

> She was seen at expensive restaurants, film premieres, first nights at the theatre, and at a seemingly endless round of cocktail parties. The smart young men of London liked her because she was different . . . After a night out in Mayfair, she would order her titled escort to Covent Garden where she would spend the early hours talking to market workers. Or instead of a lavish dinner in the West End, she would take her escort to a pub in Whitechapel where she would stand on the table and lead the community singing.[16]

Vicki was now the darling of London, taken to royal meetings at Ascot and a regular in the gossip columns as the 'Golden Girl', the 'Girl from Nowhere', the 'Girl with No Past'.

When Vicki left, Ruth's spirits sank; she missed London and the other girls at the Court Club. Morose and drinking heavily, George was poor company. Aware that he was proving something of a disappointment, he booked the two of them into Selsdon Park Hotel in Surrey, a vast Elizabethan house with suits of armour and tapestries in the lobby, and a golf course in the grounds. Hoping to impress Ruth, he hired a biplane at nearby Croydon airport in order to demonstrate his piloting skills. Ruth enjoyed the flight until he suddenly flipped the plane upside down and began performing 'crazy aerobatics'. She declared: 'I have never been so scared in my life. I don't know what was wrong with him but I thanked God when I landed.'[17]

A surprise awaited them at Elmwood, George's large house in Sanderstead Hill: Ella Ellis greeted them from the kitchen. George was so unnerved to see his mother that he introduced Ruth as his wife, even calling in his chauffeur to confirm the story. Ella then berated her son for marrying in secret. Ruth kept a tactful silence, and did the same when he repeated the tale to his neighbours. But it led to a serious discussion about marriage. George believed that Ruth was in love with him and felt that with her help he could help re-establish himself professionally, while Ruth was unexpectedly 'tiring of the bright lights' and wanted stability.[18] He had a decent lifestyle which appealed to her, his own home and business, and was sociable but quiet when sober. Her feelings for him had genuinely deepened, and she was certain that with a few adjustments he could be a decent husband and potentially a good stepfather to Andre. Her son was now six years old and had lived with his grandparents for some time; he had recently been knocked down by a car, leaving him with a head injury that rendered him excessively clumsy. Marrying George meant she could give up her job at the club and bring Andre to live with her. She convinced herself that if George could refrain from drinking, their relationship might stand a chance; she failed to see that he was a chronic alcoholic obsessed with his ex-wife.

Ruth agreed to marry George on one condition: that he sought professional help for his problems. Courageously – for he had never discussed his excessive drinking with anyone in the past, not even his brother, who was also troubled by it – George agreed to make an appointment at Warlingham Park Psychiatric Hospital. He came under the care of Dr Thomas Percy Rees, a kind and benevolent Welshman in his 50s who was made medical superintendent at Warlingham in 1935 and received an OBE in 1949 for his work. Dr Rees disagreed with the locks and keys approach of psychiatric care and asked for respect, dignity and civility to be extended to all patients with mental health problems.

George was admitted to Warlingham on 23 September 1950. His hospital case notes describe his condition:

He is a moderately well-built man with slender limbs. His breath smells slightly of alcohol . . . he looks unwell and is shaky in his posture . . . He appears in a generally agitated and distressed state and his conversations sometimes deviate from the point and become unclear. But he is cooperative and gives a fair account of himself. He appears fairly well educated . . . He has been living with a girl [Ruth] who loves him but he desperately wants his wife and children back, feeling that nothing will ever come right until that happens. He has come in here of his own volition.[19]

After a period of emotional unrest requiring special treatment and conditions, George began responding to therapy. By mid-October he was enjoying working with a group and was deemed 'fairly sociable and cheerful. He says he has cut out alcohol and does not miss it.'[20] By the end of the month, he was confident enough to discharge himself, declaring that he was recovered, although the doctor noted: 'He is suffering from chronic alcoholism and there is no doubt that his personality was unstable in view of the separation and divorce from his wife.'[21]

Rather than adjust quietly to life outside the hospital, away from the temptations of drink, he and Ruth then departed for the market town of Westerham in Kent, where they stayed at the Kings' Arms Hotel, an elegant coaching inn, for a week before their wedding. It was a place Ruth knew well, having visited the pub often with Vicki on weekend jaunts from the Court Club. In preparation for the wedding, Vicki joined them there again, accompanied by other friends from London. Almost inevitably George began drinking again; gin was his favourite tipple. He and Ruth were already having problems and approached the marriage with differing degrees of ambivalence. Some time after the event, George insisted that Ruth had threatened him with another razor attack if he didn't marry her, while she claimed that he only wanted a wife to give him a veneer of respectability. Nevertheless, on 8 November 1950, Ruth and George were married at Tonbridge Register Office. When the groom tried to fit the wedding ring on the bride's finger, it would not fit; the bone was deformed by the arthritis she had suffered in her teens, and she wore the ring on an adjacent finger instead.[22]

She was Ruth Neilson no more, but Ruth Ellis.

*

George entered Warlingham again the day after the wedding. Ruth maintained that she had visited Dr Rees beforehand for a discussion about George and only agreed to the marriage if he returned for further treatment. George's hospital case notes show that he was still drinking and upon admission

> smelt of alcohol . . . Patient stated that he had had a lot to drink today and that he felt low . . . he has difficulty concentrating and says he was the man who had risen so high and had fallen on his face in a dramatic way. He was married yesterday to Ruth, the nightclub hostess whom he married because she threatened to get a gang on him to slash his face. Coincidentally, the left side of his face was cut by this gang, seriously.[23]

A less auspicious beginning to a marriage would be difficult to imagine. George told the doctor that he had begun drinking again because he was unable to find work abroad as he and Ruth had hoped; patients and new visitors to the surgery were alarmed by his scar and he believed they viewed him as a gangster because of it. His alcoholism was so severe that during his consultation with the doctor he kept asking for a drink. He was placed in a special unit where he was observed to be 'very sensitive and bewildered'.[24]

Ruth remained at the house in Sanderstead, visiting George regularly. He spiralled into an intense depression and was thought to be in the early stages of temporal arteritis, complaining of headaches and passing out while working on the farm attached to the hospital. By the beginning of December he had rallied sufficiently enough to seek work, keeping his whereabouts confidential. Ronald Morgan, who had a number of surgeries in Southampton, invited him to join his practice in the New Year. Euphoric, George discharged himself shortly after Christmas, but the hospital case notes were condemning: 'He is a chronic alcoholic with a narcissistic personality in which the "mother element" is a large problem. There is a significant and persistent degree of hypertension . . . The outlook is not too good.'[25]

Until George started his new job, he and Ruth registered their address as 7 Herne Hill Road, implying that they moved in with her parents and Andre, although Muriel remembers 'much family hostility towards the union', especially from Ruth's brother Granville.[26] Certainly her parents did not know George well, and Muriel claims to have been kept in ignorance of the marriage for some time; she arrived at her parents' flat one evening to find the table laid out nicely in preparation for Ruth introducing George over dinner. Muriel judged him too old and shifty for her sister, and the meal was oppressively awkward, with no one knowing quite what to say. She left as soon as possible.

In early 1951, Ruth, George and Andre moved into a four-bedroom house at Oak Bank in Warsash that accompanied the job in Southampton. To cover his long absence from working, George told the Morgans that he had suffered a nervous breakdown following overwork during the war, and that he and Ruth had only recently returned from honeymoon. Ruth was frank about having worked as a nightclub hostess, and George explained his scar as a result of rushing to Ruth's aid when thugs attacked her in the club. Much of George's work for Ronald Morgan was conducted at Warsash, but he occasionally took surgeries in Southampton's Bitterne Road and at Botley. Ruth, wearing fewer cosmetics than usual and her hair in a smart up-do, did her best to settle into life as a housewife and stay-at-home mother. She kept the house spotless and became friendly with Mrs Morgan, but otherwise did little socialising.

Her husband was a different matter. Within weeks of their arrival in Warsash, George had taken to the bottle again and was soon a regular in the town's Rising Sun pub. His attitude towards Ruth was increasingly antagonistic, particularly under the influence of alcohol. One night they attended a dinner dance, hosted by the Southampton branch of the British Dental Association, at the Polygon Hotel with the Morgans. George spent the evening propping up the bar until Ruth, tired of sitting alone with the Morgans, decided to dance. Wearing an asymmetric chiffon dress, she was whirled about the floor by a number of men, and then began chatting animatedly to a group of male admirers. George pried himself from the bar and told her they were leaving. Borrowing the Morgan's car, they had a furious row on the drive home. Suddenly George stopped the Fiat and told Ruth to get out, despite rain lashing down on the unlit country lane. Aghast, she did so, still wearing only her dress and black satin shoes. George sped away but returned a short while later to collect Ruth, who was apoplectic with rage. At home Ruth threw some clothes into a suitcase and caught the train back to London early the next day with Andre, who had not taken to his stepfather at all. But staying with her parents didn't agree with her either and she wanted to make her marriage work; within days she and Andre had returned to Warsash.

Unfortunately, George's incessant drinking, coupled with Ruth's isolation and boredom, money problems and George's ongoing fixation with his ex-wife, eroded the little stability within the relationship. Ruth's earlier biographers describe her as unreasonably jealous of her erratic husband, but like all alcoholics he became devious and unreliable in his efforts to drink surreptitiously. Ruth is said to have suspected George of making secret assignations to meet female patients or of having an affair with one of his assistants, even hiring cars to trail him on his travels. She is reputed to have driven to confront a patient with whom she believed George to have been involved, but the woman in question was not at home. Such stories mirror her behaviour with David in time to come, but equally George could have given Ruth good reason to be jealous.

Far more disturbing was the violence George began inflicting on Ruth, taking out his self-hatred and resentment of life in general on her. In the fortnight before Ruth's execution, Bertha gave a statement to her daughter's solicitor in which she recalled George's aggression (the grammatical errors are Bertha's own):

[George] was an alcoholic drinker and turned out to be a cruel man. They went to live in Warsash near Southampton. It was a lonely house, my daughter sitting by herself night after night, her husband coming home in a taxi because he was unable to stand he was so drunk. On one of these occasions he told my Daughter to go into the kitchen. Once she was there he locked the door. He pulled her hair and banged her head against the Wall six or seven times. After that seen she started bleeding from the nose. Losing pints of blood. She suffered from terrible head ages for a long time. On another occasion he ill-treaded her by knocking her on the floor and kicking her. She was black and blue all over. She ran into the garden and stayed behind a bush all night. She was terrified of him and ran away from him the next day. She stayed home with me for three days. Her husband asked her to return to him, he would phone her two or three times a day. She went back to him. But within a fortnight she was back home again. This time for good. Both her eyes were swollen. She had a bald patch on the left side of her head. Her legs were bruised. She was a very sick girl. I put her to bed and kept her there for several days. I refused to let her return to this Brute of a man. She told me she was pregnant. I feared for this unborn child.[27]

Ruth's father had also given a statement to the police about his daughter's marriage, declaring: 'Ellis treated her cruelly and assaulted her on numerous occasions. In the end she had to apply for police protection and was advised by the police to leave him and apply for a separation which was granted.'[28]

Muriel recalls her mother telling her that on one occasion George locked Ruth in a bedroom; she climbed out wearing only a white dental coat and was found by a lorry driver. When Ruth sought refuge at Muriel's home a few weeks later, the bald patch her mother had mentioned seeing was still visible. Bertha refused to allow George access to his wife, and Muriel remembers Ruth being in a terrible state, running out to use a public telephone box and clearly in great fear of something (presumably her violent husband). Any vestiges of mutual respect had vanished: George addressed his pregnant wife as a bloody bitch from Brixton and she retaliated that he was a drunken old has-been from a lunatic asylum.

George's conduct outside the marriage became increasingly volatile. He would disappear to the Astor Club in London and remained away from home for days. By April 1951 he was absent more than he was present at the surgery, and prone to vanishing when he did put in an appearance. One afternoon Mr Morgan received a call from George's receptionist; he had promised to be back by 2.30 p.m. – two hours earlier – and there were seven patients in the waiting room. Half an hour later George called from the Isle of Wight, cheerily instructing his receptionist to cancel all his appointments because it was such a beautiful day he had popped over to Cowes. He left Ronald Morgan little choice but to dismiss him, although he insisted he had handed in his notice.

Improbably, after George had sent out the usual enquiry letters for work, he and Ruth departed for a holiday in Bettws-y-Coed, where Ella Ellis owned a cottage. They had not been away long when George learned that a W.J. Littleton was willing to offer him a position at his practice on Cliff Road in Newquay. He left for Cornwall while Ruth travelled back to her parents and Andre in London. She eventually joined her husband at Beachcroft Hotel, where he had taken a room, but their time together was spoiled by further blistering rows, all fuelled by alcohol. Typical of these was the occasion when George told Ruth he was leaving to visit the inspector of taxes in Southampton. For whatever reason, she would not hear of him travelling alone on the overnight train to Paddington. Arriving at Waterloo, Ruth asked George for her tube fare and he watched her head down to the Underground before he went for his train. As he rose for the dining car, Ruth appeared in the corridor and said she had decided to accompany him to Southampton. George visited the tax inspector as arranged but proceeded to get roaring drunk afterwards. In London, the couple made their way to the Court Club, where they both drank heavily and squabbled until they had to leave for the night train from Paddington to Penzance. Within days there was another altercation in Newquay, this time at the cliff-top Great Western Hotel, where George yelled that he had married beneath him and Ruth retaliated by throwing a glass of orange juice in his face.

Again Ruth returned to London, certain that her marriage was finished. She had no money, one child to support and another due in October. Out of the blue, a lucky break presented itself, seemingly offering the glamour she had craved for so long. Unfortunately, like much else in Ruth's life, the golden opportunity turned out to be made of gilt and disintegrated almost as soon as she reached for it.

When Ruth returned to London in spring 1951, the city was preparing for the Festival of Britain. Although the country remained stuck in an austerity rut, the Labour government planned a celebration of British arts, science and design that summer to commemorate the centenary of the Great Exhibition. The South Bank, one of the largest derelict areas in the capital, was chosen as the principal site for the event, already heralded as a show of optimism in the nation's brilliant future.

Ruth's own future was less assured, but London offered a welcome respite from the marital discord in Cornwall. She began socialising again and, according to her story in the *Woman's Sunday Mirror*, one of her admirers from the club even presented her with a racehorse as a gift. It didn't win any races and was reluctantly handed back to her benefactor. Ruth savoured her time in London and the more stimulating company there. Her husband, too, had returned to the city's bars and nightclubs, but she avoided him wherever possible.

One upshot of Ruth's arrival in London was the offer of an uncredited role in a new film. *Lady Godiva Rides Again* (*Bikini Baby* in America) was a comedy about beauty contests and the British film industry. The cast list was impressive: Diana Dors, Alastair Sim, Kay Kendall, Sid James, George Cole, Dennis Price, Stanley Holloway, Dora Bryan, Jean Marsh and Joan Collins in her movie debut. The making of the film was given a great deal of press attention since Diana Dors was one of Britain's fastest-rising stars, although her part in *Lady Godiva* was relatively minor. During filming she married Dennis Hamilton at Caxton Hall, generating further acres of newsprint.

It was Muriel who made the remarkable discovery decades later that Ruth had a walk-on role in the film. However, in *Ruth Ellis: My Sister's Secret Life* she makes several leaps of faith when discussing the subject, asserting that Ruth was a close friend of Diana Dors and that Stephen Ward supplied many of the girls for the beauty parade scenes. While Vicki's mentor was undoubtedly present about the set, this was due to his romance with one of the actresses, as Dors recalls in her autobiography:

> I commenced filming on location at Folkestone, where I met a beautiful young girl named Jane Hart who was playing a small role. We became good friends, and on the day we were due to return to London she offered me a lift with her boyfriend, who was coming to fetch her . . . But when the boyfriend arrived at our hotel I did not take to him at all: he looked devious and was something of a show-off. Before lunch he insisted that I go for a quick ride in his new sports car, and he drove around the country lanes at such speeds that I was terrified. Just as we prepared to leave for London, he turned to Jane and announced that he couldn't possibly give me a lift back. There just was not enough room for three of us. So off they went, leaving me virtually in tears, high and dry at the hotel with no more trains going to London for several hours.[1]

She makes no mention of Ward supplying the girls for *Lady Godiva*. Kay Kendall and Joan Collins were both acquainted with Ward, but Kendall was given her role after producer Frank Lauder had seen her television work and Collins won a part as an extra when her agent put her forward for the lead. The local press explained that the other, uncredited girls were chosen from modelling agencies in London, where Ruth had done some forgettable advertising work as well as posing at the Camera Club.

Nor does Dors ever refer to a friendship with Ruth – and the actress was notoriously indiscreet. When writing about her role as a murderess sentenced to hang in *Yield to the Night*, Dors openly discusses the parallels with Ruth's case and recalls at length her own encounter with Albert Pierrepoint shortly after filming *Lady Godiva*, yet there is no mention of meeting Ruth. Paul Sullivan, author of Diana Dors's official website, confirms:

> I can only remember Diana talking about Ruth Ellis on a chat show once, and I think it was clear that they were not close

friends. It seems that Ruth got a bit part in the movie and I guess Diana being one of the stars they just shared the scenes and maybe polite conversation.[2]

The beauty parade scenes in which Ruth appears were filmed during the first weekend in May 1951. Four months' pregnant and almost unrecognisable with her hair in a sophisticated black bob, Ruth is only fleetingly visible, but several still shots of her were published in the local newspapers. The *Folkestone Herald* reported: 'Yesterday afternoon local people formed the audience at the Leas Cliff Hall, for the scene of the beauty contest. Thirteen professional mannequins came down from London for the dress parade, one of the features in the contest.'[3] Joan Collins recalls spending 'three freezing days in a black, boned suit shivering in Folkestone Town Hall'.[4] *Lady Godiva Rides Again* was set for release in November 1951. If Ruth hoped it would lead her to greater things, she was to be severely disappointed; her only film role was forgotten until Muriel unearthed it half a century later.

Ruth decided to make one last, desperate attempt to save her marriage after filming wrapped in Folkestone, but on 20 June George was readmitted to Warlingham. His dependence on alcohol was destroying him, as his hospital case notes report:

> He is tremulous and shaking and his breath smells of stale drink, a smell like formaldehyde. There are rashes on his lower legs . . . He is in an agitated and slightly confused state. He has sought admission here because he is desperate and feels at the end of his tether again. He has been drinking heavily for the last few months.[5]

George was in the best place to beat his addiction; that year a new unit opened at Warlingham to treat alcoholics under the direction of Dr Max Glatt, a former inmate of Dachau concentration camp. Inspired by Alcoholics Anonymous, a new self-help group in America, Glatt established Britain's first regional treatment centre for alcoholics in Pinel House, a villa in the hospital grounds.

Ruth's visits to Warlingham were not a success. There are several references to her in George's case notes, largely based on the patient's confidences:

He says he is in such a state that he doesn't know whether he's mad or his wife is ... Latterly he has been adrift again in London, going round the hotels and clubs drinking. His wife followed him to the hospital gates trying to stop him coming in. She refused, however, to enter the hospital to discuss things with the doctor. It is these marital problems which have been driving him to drink.[6]

Ruth did agree to speak to George's doctor after her husband was admitted. The hospital case notes go on:

His wife states that he has been drinking almost continuously since he left hospital and that he has frequently been violent towards her. Patient himself states that his wife has been trying to make trouble since their marriage, and declares that he only recommenced drinking two weeks before admission. He is adopting a very hostile attitude towards his wife and he gives the impression of being in the early stages of paranoid alcoholic dementia.[7]

There are further notes on 3 July:

He is fairly cooperative in the ward but although he chose to work in the gardens, he has not started to work there yet. He seems very hostile towards his wife and tells other patients all about her behaviour.[8]

The following month the notes observe: 'His wife, he says, is still making accusations that he is carrying on with women here. There is no evidence that he is.'[9] By September, George's doctor noted that he was 'making plans to leave hospital and not tell his wife where he is working. He is seeking a job at the moment.'[10] George was determined that Ruth should sign a document, which he insisted was legally binding, apologising for her behaviour and retracting all allegations of misconduct and adultery. When she refused, he informed his doctors that he didn't wish to see her unless someone else was present.

George told anyone who would listen that Ruth was pathologically jealous. Many years after her execution, his accusations were supported by psychiatrist William Sargant, who worked at Warlingham with Dr Rees:

> There is a sworn statement by a male nurse of nineteen years duration – in other words he's a very competent man – saying this: It was common knowledge among the staff at the hospital, including myself, that Mrs Ellis appeared to be on constant watch and enquiry, and continually checking up with the staff, patients and even visitors on the bus serving the hospital as to every movement of Mr Ellis.[11]

Ruth's earlier biographers claim that she accused George of having an affair with a female doctor and said of a patient, 'So that's the old bag you're getting it on with here.'[12] She is said to have told George that she was going to inform the Dental Board that he was 'plotting' to bring up 'that bag from Newquay'.[13] Marks and Van den Burgh, authors of *Ruth Ellis: A Case of Diminished Responsibility?*, write that Ruth had to be physically restrained after she marched into Warlingham yelling that George was 'a fucking adulterer' and that, to calm her, Dr Rees administered the sedatives on which she was to be reliant for the remainder of her life – with grave implications in the murder of David Blakely four years later.[14]

*

Ruth returned to London heavily pregnant, having finally admitted that her marriage was finished. The mood of the city did not match hers: London was transformed during the Festival of Britain. The slender steel tower of the Skylon, brilliantly illuminated at night, rehabilitated the capital's fragmented skyline. Crowds flocked to the exhibitions within the Dome of Discovery and welcomed the Festival Hall, Britain's first new public building since the war. Above all, they loved the colour and dynamism which, after years of utility shades and make-do-and-mend, 'could hardly have struck a brighter, more optimistic note'.[15] The Conservatives won the general election that October, ousting Labour and making Churchill Prime Minister again as a more prosperous Britain was promised for all. Harold Macmillan was appointed Minister of Housing, vowing to replace the railway carriages and prefabs that were home to thousands of families. Old city slums would be demolished and bombsites cleared throughout the country, with vast suburban estates providing new homes and amenities. But, despite the assurances and general sense that change was in the air, financial limitations delayed the redevelopment of Britain and rationing remained in place. 'Emotional claustrophobia' blanketed the country.[16]

On 2 October 1951, Ruth gave birth to a daughter, Georgina Jayne, who shared a birthday with her father, still a patient at Warlingham. There were complications during labour and delivery; Ruth's Holloway case notes describe how the baby was put in an oxygen tent while Ruth required 'heavy sedation' afterwards and was 'kept asleep for days'.[17] She was distressed beforehand 'over domestic affairs' and 'rather confused because of drugs'.[18] When Muriel visited mother and child in hospital, Ruth was listless and hardly spoke. She may have been suffering postnatal depression and admitted some time later that 'for a long time I had no interest in the future'.[19]

Ruth stayed with her parents after leaving the maternity ward, introducing Andre to his new sister, a quiet baby with her mother's startling blue eyes. In her 1995 memoir, Georgina recalled:

> The first two years of my life I was cared for by my grandmother and Aunt Muriel. Since Muriel had a large family of her own, I probably spent most of my time with Bertha, and from her correspondence in later years, she had forged a strong attachment to me. Furthermore, from the letters I have, it appears she bore no bitterness towards my father even after Ruth's death and wrote to him too, never missing our shared birthday.[20]

George provided a layette for his daughter and gave Ruth an allowance of £4 a week. He discharged himself from hospital on 27 October, with his doctor noting: 'Summary: a case of psychoneurosis and alcoholism, precipitated by his inability to manage his relationship with his wife.'[21] George wasted no time in attempting to legally end his marriage; on 7 November, the day before his first wedding anniversary to Ruth, he made an application to the High Court to file a petition for divorce. During the early 1950s, only two marriages in a thousand ended in divorce, which was regarded as something shameful, particularly for the woman concerned. The judge refused George's application on the grounds that the statutory three years had not yet passed and advised both parties to seek reconciliation.

Although Ruth was willing, George was not and she was forced to seek legal representation.

Ruth approached Victor Mishcon & Co. Founded in 1937 as a one-man practice in south London, the company eventually became a tremendously successful law firm with a long list of famous clients. Ruth would turn to Victor Mishcon in the last days of her life, but during the winter of 1951 she needed assistance in dealing with George, who was determined their daughter should be adopted without explaining his reasons. Leon Simmons, legal executive with the company, took on Ruth's case and recalled in a 1955 letter to the Home Office:

> I have no doubt at all that Mrs Ellis suffered considerably both mentally and physically at the hands of her husband . . . following the birth of Georgina, Mrs Ellis was in a hopeless financial position and I recall that at one stage she was in fact walking the street with Georgina in a pram looking for accommodation.[22]

Ruth returned to the only fiscally stable life she had ever known: she spruced herself up, dressed in the best outfit she had – a black tailor-made suit, which she wore with a white silk blouse – and headed for Duke Street, where a new sign hung outside No. 58. Morrie welcomed her back with pleasure, and showed her round his refurbished palace, now known as Carroll's and boasting a restaurant, cabaret and dancing until 3 a.m. When Ruth baulked at the late hours, which meant she would be unable to travel back to her parents' flat, he offered her a room at Gilbert Court off Oxford Street, where several of his girls lived. Ruth visited Flat 4 and decided to take it, repeating the prestigious telephone number in her best BBC voice: Mayfair 8534.

The long shifts at Carroll's went against her doctor's advice; Ruth remained in lacklustre health for months after Georgina's birth and . had regular examinations at the gynaecological clinic until June the following year. She was told she needed treatment but failed to arrive for her appointment and never returned to the clinic. Each weekend she visited Andre and Georgina but otherwise immersed herself in work, disguising the anguish of her broken marriage behind an arch expression and effervescent persona. Ruth's high, tinkling laugh echoed around Carroll's, where her admirers included a Persian banker, a Norwegian industrialist, a Canadian oil tycoon and a Swiss businessman who inundated her with notes signed 'naughty Norbert'. Outside, the city was grey and choked with smog, buses thundered through the streets with headlights blurred and there was a bitter chill in the leaden air, but inside Carroll's was a bright, synthetically exuberant world, with Ruth at its centre.

Vicki's star continued to rise, but she and Ruth remained firm friends. 'At the end of 1951 London was filled with northern manufacturers loaded with money,' Ruth recalled:

> Vicki and I were ready, willing and able to help them spend it . . . we went to the best parties that Mayfair could offer. At weekends we toured the exclusive country clubs and hotels in a fleet of Rolls Royces . . . Like Vicki, I never kept any of the money I earned.[23]

When the other hostesses teasingly asked Ruth if she missed life in Warsash, she replied with a derisive hoot: 'Do you know that in that bloody hick dump you can't even buy a pair of nylons?'[24] Unbeknown to her, George had begun a new chapter in Warrington, where he found work as a dental officer and tried to forget the recent past.

*

On 6 February 1952, Britain woke up to the news that the King had been found dead in his bed. All radio services other than weather forecasts and the news were suspended. On 11 February, the King's coffin was placed in the cold, shadowy surroundings of Westminster Hall, where over 300,000 mourners paid their respects. Four days later the coffin was conveyed on a gun carriage to Paddington Station for the funeral in Windsor.

It was not the most auspicious beginning to 1952. Although the much-loathed identity cards were torn up that year, rationing was still in place and there were rumblings about the 'immigration problem'. The slow trickle of West Indian workers arriving in the country saw the initials 'KBW' ('Keep Britain White') appearing on walls, bridges and doors. When political theorist Hannah Arendt visited England, she observed:

> A dull blanket of fear lies over the country, which is softened though, by the fact that they've been eating too little for such a long time that they barely notice the difference anymore. And

yet it's almost unbelievable. Not just what the shops look like – groceries and so on, everything scarce, everything of bad quality (which is quite new for this country), but also their genius to make life uncomfortable. Everything set up as if expressly to make life difficult, or at least to challenge you to muster so much cheerfulness that everything can be overcome.[25]

Ruth was one of the fortunate few able to enjoy a holiday; on 19 March 1952, she was issued her first passport and explained in her published life story that one of her customers not only paid for her to accompany him on a trip but also gave her a considerable sum afterwards, for what must be obvious reasons. That same year Vicki made her film debut with a role in the Rank Organisation's *It Started in Paradise*. Marketed as the fashion world's *All About Eve* (1950), the film starred Jane Hylton as a ruthless designer, with Kay Kendall as her muse and Vicki playing a model. Producer Kenneth Harper, who went on to have major successes with *The Young Ones* (1961) and *Summer Holiday* (1963), mused that Vicki 'always lived too close to the wind. One had the feeling that something had to happen to her.'[26] In tandem with Ruth's venture into movies, *It Started in Paradise* bombed at the box office. Vicki was less upset than she might have been due to her romance with the Maharaja of Cooch Behar, an archetypal international playboy prince. Educated at Harrow and Cambridge, Cooch Behar was divorced from film star Nancy Valentine and a close friend of Aly Kahn, Clark Gable, Errol Flynn and Prince Philip's cousin the Marquess of Milford Haven. Aged thirty-four, with a vast tax-free allowance, palaces in India and flats in London, he was regarded as one of the world's most eligible bachelors when he asked his friend Stephen Ward to introduce him to Vicki. Shortly before their first dinner date, he bought every bouquet in the Dorchester Hotel's floristry department and had them sent to Vicki at Ward's flat.

Ruth enjoyed the high life vicariously through Vicki's tales but otherwise 1952 passed uneventfully for her. December brought the Great Smog: Ruth was used to the perpetual greenish, shifting fog that stung her throat and deadened all sound, but on 4 December 1952 a lid of warm air trapped the cold air beneath it, causing an impenetrable fog that reduced visibility to no more than a few yards. Apart from the underground trains, all public transport was suspended as the polluted air seeped into cinemas, schools, dance halls and sporting venues. By the time it lifted on 9 December, an estimated 4,000 people had died and thousands more had fallen ill. The smog and its after effects led to the introduction of the Clean Air Act in 1956.

That same month saw the Craig and Bentley trial held at the Old Bailey. Several weeks earlier, 19-year-old Derek Bentley, who suffered from epilepsy and had learning difficulties, broke into a warehouse in West Croydon with 16-year-old Christopher Craig. The younger boy was armed, and when police arrived Derek allegedly shouted: 'Let him have it, Chris!' Craig fired, killing a policeman. The trial took place in a blaze of publicity, much of it focused on the question of whether capital punishment should be abolished. A verdict of guilty was reached: Craig was too young to be executed but Derek was sentenced to death, despite the jury's recommendation of mercy.

At the tail end of the year, Muriel and her family moved into the large villa on Franciscan Road in Tooting that was already occupied by her parents and Ruth's children. Andre began attending school with Muriel's sons and she and Ruth saw more of each other than they had in recent years; Muriel recalls watching her glamorous sister playing whist with their parents and lugging a huge Christmas tree by herself through the streets. Ruth could afford to buy everyone presents that year; she even went on a spending spree on Bond Street and loaned Vicki a small sum.

Shortly before Christmas Ruth fell ill with what she thought was gastric flu. After doubling up with pain in the bathroom at her parents' flat, Ruth's doctor was called. He sent her immediately to Middlesex Hospital, where she was diagnosed with an ectopic pregnancy and had an emergency operation. She remained in hospital for a fortnight, but the other hostesses came to see her – Vicki, Betty, Michele, Cathy, Jacqueline and Kitty – causing a stir with their looks, laughter and the flowers with which they filled the ward. Ruth missed out on the New Year celebrations but looked forward to 1953 nonetheless, hoping her luck would change. It was undoubtedly the year when Britain finally began to escape the shackles of austerity and inch towards a better quality of life and even affluence for some.

It was also the year that Ruth Ellis met David Blakely.

8

'We're Buying More Now!' announced the *News Chronicle* in 1953. Although rationing remained in force and regeneration was slow, food was more plentiful in the shops and city councils gave the green light to overspill estates, new towns and innumerable tower blocks. A new food appeared on British high streets: the Wimpy Burger, a 'square meal in a round bun', and Italian actress Gina Lollobrigida opened the Moka espresso bar in Soho's Frith Street, ushering in cafe culture.

On Monday, 26 January 1953 Derek Bentley's parents were informed that there would be no reprieve for their 19-year-old son. Twelve thousand people signed a petition in protest and two hundred MPs called for a pardon, but the Home Secretary was not to be swayed. The *Daily Mirror* supported his decision: 'The fate of Bentley must be read as a warning that there will not be leniency towards anyone who goes along with a man who carries a gun.'[1] Two days after his family had been told he would hang, Derek Bentley was executed by Albert Pierrepoint at Wandsworth prison. Housewife Nella Last, whose diaries were made famous through Victoria Wood's acclaimed drama *Housewife, 49*, wrote: '"Emotional" people cannot be let rule – or override wise if terrible decisions.'[2]

The debate concerning the future of capital punishment simmered again in March, with the revelation that three bodies had been found walled up in a house where two previous murders were known to have been carried out. The house was 10 Rillington Place, whose former occupant, Timothy Evans, had been hanged by Albert Pierrepoint at Pentonville in 1950 after being found guilty of killing his wife and child. The integrity of that verdict was immediately put in question when John Christie, another tenant at the address and a witness at the Evans trial, was arrested on 31 March and confessed to seven murders.

Ruth would have been aware of the Bentley and Evans cases, particularly since she took a firm interest in the news, but obviously she had no idea that her name would one day be joined with theirs. In early 1953 she was still recovering from her operation and unable to work for some time. At the house on Franciscan Road there were fresh difficulties when her half-brother Julian appeared after a long absence and Bertha decided that Muriel and her family should find alternative accommodation. Ruth's elder sister was pregnant again; she and Joe already had two more children by then, daughters Pauline and Marlene. They left for a halfway house and were eventually allocated a council maisonette in St Paul's Cray. In the summer of 1953, Muriel was astonished when she saw Ruth after months apart; her sister visited with Georgina and had not only lost weight but her hair was platinum blonde. Muriel told Ruth that it suited her: she wore it shorter than ever, cropped into Monroe-esque waves that framed her small, delicate face. Afterwards, Ruth said the decision to go blonde was done 'on impulse. You know how it is – you look in the mirror one morning and decide that you must do something to change that drab old hairstyle.'[3]

That summer was memorable for the street parties, concerts and pageants in celebration of Queen Elizabeth II's coronation. The headlines were also filled with the trial of John Christie, who was hanged at Pentonville on 15 July 1953 by Albert Pierrepoint. The controversy over the execution of Timothy Evans in the wake of Christie's conviction led to a motion to suspend capital punishment for five years. The Bill was defeated in Parliament.

*

Ruth's return to Carroll's Club was nothing short of triumphant in terms of her popularity. Author Robert Hancock describes the 'business cards' she handed out to club members: 'Why women over 40 are preferred: THEY DONT YELL! THEY DONT TELL! THEY DONT SWELL! And they are as GRATEFUL AS HELL!'[4] He claims that she earned commission for a company specialising in handmade rainwear for customers who could only be aroused by 'memories of the rubber sheeting of their nursery days' and that she kept a collection of erotic sketches for other clients.[5] Ruth herself posed for risqué photographs; there are several of her in existence, all dating from 1953 and afterwards, in which she appears with blonde hair.

At the same time, she began socialising with a different crowd. Mayfair had long been a gathering place for motor sports enthusiasts. Their favourite watering hole was the Steering Wheel Club at 2a Brick Street, just off Park Lane, which opened in the late 1940s. An advert in the 1956 *BARC Yearbook* states that 'members of any recognised motor club' were welcome to join 'this small and attractive Social Club [where] the leading personalities in motor sport meet'.[6] Thursday nights had a reputation for rowdiness, but on any day of the week members of the racing set could be found in the bar. Young, loud and boisterous, being part of their clique involved hard drinking and horseplay in London and champagne picnics and parties in glitzy locations elsewhere.

Most working-class people couldn't afford to own a car and those who did were seen as getting above themselves; transport in general was all about speed, from the new passenger jets to the motor-racing circuit. When it came to the latter, letting off steam afterwards was virtually a requirement, and the Steering Wheel Club played host to some infamous parties, often led by blond Ferrari driver Mike Hawthorn, dynamic, tall and with a smile as wide as the racetrack. He and his fellow drivers – Sterling Moss, Peter Collins, Roy Salvadori, Alberto Ascari and Innes Ireland among others – would congregate in the club as often as they met at the starting line.

Gwen Nockolds managed the Steering Wheel; most members of the family were involved in the motor world in some way. Gwen's niece, Olivia Temple, recalls:

> My father, Harold Nockolds, was the motoring correspondent of *The Times*, and later editor of *Motor* magazine and his brother, Roy Nockolds was a well known motoring and aviation artist whose work hung in the Club. Their brother, Conrad 'Twinkie' was a photographer and they all frequented the Club. Apart from the young motor racing men there were all sorts of other characters, among them Peter Ustinov. People connected to motoring Guilds and racetracks all over the world would head for the Steering Wheel when in London. There was a small dining room, the Bar was always open and the atmosphere was somewhat evening-like. Once you opened the door and went straight up the stairs the world of Mayfair and Hyde Park seemed a long way off.[7]

Other visitors to the club included Stephen Ward, who introduced Vicki to the place, Douglas Fairbanks Jnr, several MI5 officers and – on the very fringes of the racing set – Desmond Cussen, who was destined to be known as Ruth Ellis's 'alternative lover'.

Born in Epsom, Surrey, in March 1923, Desmond Edward Cussen was the younger son of middle-class couple William David Cussen and Mary Williams; his brother William was four years older. Like George Ellis, Desmond remained in awe of his forceful mother throughout his life. After completing a solid boarding-school education, he returned to the family home at Dapdune, a large detached property on Garlands Road in Leatherhead. During the war he became a pilot officer in the RAF, training to fly Lancasters from a base in South Africa. After being demobbed, he dabbled in automobile sales and worked briefly as an accountant until joining the board of the family business in 1946. Cussen & Co. were wholesale and retail tobacconists with outlets throughout London; Desmond worked from their head office at 93 Peckham High Street and had a two-bedroom flat at 20 Goodwood Court, a private mansion block on Devonshire Street in Marylebone. His brother William lived in Westminster and had his own successful business that required him to make frequent trips to America.

Although he never raced professionally, Desmond was a motor sports enthusiast and zipped about town in a glossy black Ford Zodiac. He was a shy, extremely well-mannered man with a ready smile, who despite being a familiar figure in many of the city's bars did not make friends easily. In his early 30s, with thickly Brylcreemed hair and a clipped moustache, he was too quiet and self-effacing to appeal to Ruth when they met that year at Carroll's Club. In some respects he quite closely resembled George Ellis: the two men were not unalike physically, both had comfortable upbringings with a father who had his own business and a mother who was the dominant parent, both had served in some capacity in the air force during the war, and neither were the usual rowdy men to frequent the clubs they joined in London. They shared a love of alcohol but reacted to it differently – Desmond was never violent, although he had a tendency to become morose when drunk. Their affairs with Ruth were an obvious parallel: George married her and Desmond fell for her, but was unable to persuade her to become his wife. He might have stood a better chance had he not met her that summer of 1953, within days of her first encounter with David Blakely.

*

When the Steering Wheel Club closed during the afternoon, members often carried on drinking in other venues nearby, one of which was Carroll's. Vicki was involved with the racing set before Ruth became acquainted with them; then living on Upper Berkeley Street, she was known to have a 'dangerous love of speed' and even gained a reputation in the press for it, with gossip columnists referring to her as 'the unluckiest girl who ever rode in a car'.[8] Vicki's boyfriend, Cooch Behar, owned a midnight blue Bentley, and on 16 July 1953 the couple were driving near Baldock in Hertfordshire when the Bentley clipped the kerb and spun into the air, landing on its roof. Cooch Behar suffered a broken collarbone and five broken ribs while Vicki had concussion, a black eye and injuries to her legs. She held an impromptu press conference in Hitchin's Lister Hospital, where her boyfriend was in a nearby ward. Reporters working on the story of the crash headlined their articles: 'London Model to Wed Prince' and 'Vicki's Romance with the Maharajah'.

But when Cooch Behar left to convalesce with his cousin in the distinctly un-exotic location of East Grinstead, Vicki turned to Stephen Ward for advice about their relationship. Wearing her boyfriend's gift of a gold Cartier tiger brooch, she explained that he might lose his royal allowance if they married. Ward agreed it was difficult, and asked if she had also considered what it would mean to sacrifice her independence for the realities of life in an Indian palace. When Cooch Behar returned to London, Vicki told him there could be no wedding. Their relationship continued on the understanding that he would ask her again to marry him if their problems could be resolved. The couple spent an idyllic summer at various sporting events and called on Vicki's grandmother on the way to Windsor for the polo; Joyce Edmonds spotted a blue Bentley whose beautiful blonde passenger waved at her and shouted hello: 'It was only later that I realised that the Vicki Martin I kept reading about in the newspapers was my old friend Valerie Mewes.'[9]

If Ruth was envious of Vicki's luxurious lifestyle and glittering romance, and there is nothing to suggest she was, then August 1953 brought two distractions, one business, the other personal. The first was Morrie's suggestion that she should take over the Little Club in Knightsbridge as manageress. The second came in the form of a young, brash and deeply insecure aspiring racing driver: 24-year-old David Blakely.[10]

Ruth was at Carroll's Club as a guest with the motor-racing boys – including Desmond Cussen, whom she had only recently met – when she noticed a 'handsome young man in an old sports coat and flannel trousers' leaning against the bar.[11] He deliberately turned his back on her and was offhand in accepting a drink from someone in Ruth's company, then made derogatory comments about the club and its hostesses, calling the place a den of vice. Ruth recalled:

> Slowly and offensively he turned to the girls, looked them up and down and said, 'I suppose you are the hostesses?' I said to my friends, 'Who is that pompous little ass?' My party was composed mainly of motor racing drivers. Somebody said, 'Oh, that's David Blakely. He's a driver too.' Mr Blakely was really mad with me. He said, 'I suppose you're another of these hostesses?' I smiled politely and said, 'No, as a matter of fact, I'm an old has-been.'[12]

As David's lean build disappeared through the door, Ruth turned to a friend and commented disdainfully, 'I hope never to see that little shit again.'[13]

Morrie was serious in wanting her to manage the Little Club and Ruth leapt at the opportunity, moving into the flat above the bar with Andre and Georgina. The sought-after location alone thrilled her: 37 Brompton Road was in the heart of Knightsbridge, with the opulent Hyde Park Hotel across the junction to the right and Harrods only a two-minute walk to the left. During the day, chauffeur-driven automobiles and the distinctive green and gold Harrods vans streamed past Ruth's door, while immaculately dressed women clipped to and fro, patronising the expensive stores whose window displays gleamed temptingly.

The Little Club itself was in a narrow, five-storey Dutch-style building near the traffic junction. On the ground floor was a shop selling exclusive handbags and, next door, a chic hairdressing salon. The bar was on the first floor with a large, bow-fronted window overlooking the main road. The decor was gold and pastel throughout, with little electric candelabras softly lighting the narrow bar where bottles of optics hung from ornate plaster alcoves. There was an upright piano in another alcove for the in-house pianist but, when she left, Ruth preferred to keep a radiogram playing in the background while her staff of three served expensive cocktails during opening hours, which were 3–11 p.m. She employed Alexander Engleman, a flamboyant artist in his 50s, as doorman-commissionaire; although his main duty was to check members as they came in, his sketches of clients and their guests proved hugely popular. The club's membership book has been lost, but, as with all such places in the area, a wide range of people tripped up the stairs from the street: actors, politicians, journalists and, of course, those Steering Wheel and Carroll's Club regulars who knew Ruth well. As ever, the core clientele consisted mainly of demobbed servicemen but the Little, as it was known, was also a safe place for gay men, then actively targeted and prosecuted on the instructions of Tory Home Secretary Sir David Maxwell Fyfe. Ruth would invite them to sit with her at the hostess's table and one older man would bring along his latest 'chicken' for Ruth to get the measure of him. Her Holloway hospital case notes record that she was 'proud that she was the youngest manager of a club in London' who 'did all work herself' and had 'an expensive French cook to prepare the food'.[14] As soon as Ruth took over the running of the place, she had new business cards printed up; a gold embossed knight on horseback stood against a pale blue background with '*The Little Club*' picked out in maroon lettering.

Above the club were two flats. Ruth's was on the second floor and initially she lived there rent-free. There was a large sitting-room diner with a bed-settee for Bertha to sleep on whenever she stayed overnight to look after the children (for which Ruth paid her generously), an electric fire, modern furniture and slatted blinds throughout. In Ruth's bedroom, everything was Hollywood-starlet-style white. Her signature scent, Miss Dior, lingered in the flat whether she was there or in the club. The basic salary of £15 per week plus commission on bar sales, with an entertainment allowance of £10 a week, gave Ruth money to spend on herself and her home. When Muriel visited, she was impressed to be served tea in a bone china cup and saucer and given sardine sandwiches.

Authors Marks and Van den Burgh assert that Ruth's boss didn't trouble to install a madam at the Little because he was able to leave that side of the business to Ruth, who was well-acquainted with the system from his other clubs. According to Marks and Van den Burgh, Ruth entertained clients herself occasionally but otherwise Morrie's girls would look after them in the flats above hers. Morrie demanded a cut of the profits and kept a key to Ruth's flat, where she was still expected to take care of his sexual needs despite managing the club. When Muriel called one afternoon, she was shocked to hear the unmistakable sounds of copulation from the flat upstairs, although she claims not to have realised what the noises were. Ruth banged on the ceiling with a stick and yelled, 'Be quiet you dirty bastards!' before turning up the volume on the radio. When Muriel asked her what was going on, she replied pithily, 'Well, if you don't know, I'm not telling you.'[15] Ruth had already set her sister straight when Muriel remarked that she envied her, warning that it would knock ten years off anyone's life. But the Little Club was a roaring success in its first year with Ruth at the helm:

> Many of these clubs were sordid, but the Little Club, in the expert hands of Ruth Ellis, was a superior establishment which attracted the rich racing set and generated a good cash flow [in] a peculiarly unsavoury era of lust and brutality, masked beneath dinner suits and cocktail frocks.[16]

Ruth was painfully aware that the club was a far from ideal environment for two young children, but she was assured of an income, a roof over their heads and was able to have Georgina and Andre living with her properly for the first time. It was a livelihood she knew and trusted, however different the reality was to the mask. Andre, who lived there longest with his mother, was able to recall the flat clearly in later years, while Georgina retained only fleeting impressions:

> A vague recollection of [Andre] or someone else often frightening me with some hideous wooden doll. [Andre] admitted he had delighted in terrifying me with one of his Christmas presents, a model of the radio dummy Archie Andrews ... my other immovable memory is the perfume my mother used [and] a sketchy recall that my mother was blonde.[17]

Prompted by a reporter in the mid-1980s, Georgina said, 'My mother was bubbly, bright and smelled delicious. She did love me. I can remember it. I remember her feeding me with a spoon. She laughed and told me not to eat the spoon too.'[18]

After settling in at the flat above the club, Ruth arranged her staff for opening night, dimmed the lights in the bar, turned on the radiogram and prepared to meet her public. Her very first customer was David Blakely, already a member of the Little. They looked at each other. 'I've seen you before, haven't I?' Ruth said, knowing perfectly well who he was and where they had met. 'I was rude to you, wasn't I?'

He smiled, 'Well, we must improve on that at any rate. Have a drink?'[19]

David Blakely remained in the bar all evening, downing gin and tonics. 'I was not exactly stirred by him, but faintly interested,' Ruth mused afterwards:

> I had seen him playing 'hard to get' with other girls in the clubs, and I was wondering how I would make out. We talked about racing cars and about friends we had in that world. He was – as he could be when he wished – completely charming, almost shy. Perhaps it was because he was on his own. He was certainly better dressed this time. A neat pinstripe suit had replaced the old sports coat and flannels. I noticed he had dark brown eyes and curly eyelashes . . . When he left at closing time, I wondered if he would ever return.[20]

She did not have long to wait to find out; the next afternoon he came bounding up the stairs at opening time and stayed until the bar closed again. He appeared most afternoons during the next few days, until one night just after last orders Ruth invited one of the barmaids up to her flat for a drink. She knew David was within earshot and pretended to be blasé when he leaned forward to ask if he might join them.

'Would you care to, Mr Blakely?' Ruth asked coolly.

He grinned at her, 'I'd be delighted.'[21]

Long after the barmaid had gone, David remained in Ruth's flat drinking, and eventually they went to bed. Despite Ruth's protestations that she was 'not in love with David. I felt that I could like men but not love them. I had learnt my lesson with the father of my first child,' within a fortnight David was living with her in the flat above the Little.[22]

III

A Poor, Twisted Boy

Knightsbridge, summer 1953 – the Magdala Tavern,
Hampstead, 10 April 1955

By unhappy coincidence, the Blakely family had their lives blighted by murder even before David's death in 1955. In the first instance it was one of their number who was accused of murder, rather than being the victim. The suspect was David's own father.

To the outside world, the family appeared to have a charmed life, but in, truth David's parents' marriage was deeply troubled. His mother Annie and father John were from very different backgrounds, although both had Irish roots. John Blakely was born in Glasgow in October 1884; five years after graduating from Glasgow University as a Bachelor of Medicine in July 1908, he married twenty-year-old Annie Moffett from the small market town of Ballynahinch, County Down. Annie's father was a horse dealer; she and her brothers were brought up as members of the Christian Brethren, a conservative evangelical Christian movement. How Annie came to meet the newly qualified Dr Blakely is not known, but after their marriage in 1913 the couple settled in Sheffield, where he opened a medical practice at 203 School Road in the Crookes district. The large house also served as the family home.

In June 1916, Annie gave birth to a stillborn daughter, whom she and Dr Blakely named Mary. A healthy son, Derek Andrew Gustav, followed in 1918. Two years later a second son came along, John Brian (always known as Brian) and then a daughter, Anne Maureen Maud, who was also called by her second name. On 17 June 1929, Annie gave birth to her last child at Oakvale private nursing home on Collegiate Crescent in Broomhill. The baby was named in honour of his mother's Irish background: David Moffett Drummond Blakely.

They were the archetypal doctor's family. Tall, dark and debonair, John Blakely liked his golf and was a fond father; he was without doubt the most popular physician in the area. Prior to the formation of the National Health Service, all doctors' visits incurred a fee, but Dr Blakely never turned away those who could not afford to pay him. His reputation in that respect was unquestioned. In contrast to her quiet husband, Annie was regarded by her neighbours as having a few airs and graces; she dressed very smartly and was keen on socialising. A nanny was employed to care for the children and they adored her to such an extent that she remained an integral part of their lives even in adulthood. The boys and their sister were all educated at boarding school, where Derek and Brian excelled. David struck those who knew him then as a happy child and was especially close to his sister Maureen. On the surface, it was perfect. But in a statement Ruth gave after her arrest in April 1955, she said that once, when she walked out on David, she asked him why his mother left his father. He replied, 'For the same reason as you, he knocked her about.'[1] If that was true, then John and Annie Blakely's marriage was a chilling precursor of David's relationship with Ruth, marred by violence and unfaithfulness – and eventually torn apart by murder.

*

The affair began in 1932, when 47-year-old Dr Blakely met Phyllis Staton, an unemployed waitress almost exactly half his age. She lived with her parents in a modest terraced house at 91 Cresswell Road in the Darnell district of Sheffield. Dr Blakely later admitted he had quickly become infatuated with Phyllis, seeing her on an almost daily basis for two years. Her father knew that she was involved with a married man and made plain his disapproval, although he had no idea it was Dr Blakely. After discovering she was pregnant, on 15 January 1934 Phyllis left home without telling her family about her predicament. In a note to her mother she said she had found work and promised to write soon.

Dr Blakely confessed in his police statement that he had driven Phyllis to her friend Gladys Bailey's house on Holme Lane, where she was given a room to share with one of two female lodgers. Phyllis visited home once to reassure her mother and kept in touch through letters. Dr Blakely called on her three times a day, bringing food. On Saturday, 27 January, he arrived at 2 p.m. Gladys and one of her lodgers went out to the pictures and when they came back early that evening Dr Blakely had gone. Later that night Phyllis showed Gladys a mark just above her elbow. 'It was like a pinprick and was red,'

Gladys recalled.[2] The following morning Phyllis did not get out of bed. She remained in her room for the rest of the week and Dr Blakley called twice a day, carrying an attaché case. 'I spoke to him and asked him why Phyllis was staying in bed,' Gladys later told the court. 'He said, "She has got a temperature," so I asked him if I could give her some hot milk but he said she must have everything cold.'[3] Gladys noticed that on one occasion when he left he was carrying both his attaché case and a brown paper parcel, although she had not seen him arrive with the parcel.

In his statement to police, Dr Blakely said Phyllis had suffered a miscarriage that week but when he urged Gladys to call in another doctor, she replied that if Phyllis was ill then she should go home. On Saturday, Phyllis rose and dressed; she looked pale but seemed calm and made no complaint when Dr Blakely suggested that it was time for her to go home. He promised to call for her after he had watched a local football match. When he arrived that evening Gladys heard him ask, 'Are you ready for your sherry, Phyllis?'[4] She watched him pour the girl a drink and Gladys herself added milk to it. After drinking the concoction, Phyllis left with Dr Blakely.

Shortly after 6 p.m., there was a knock at the back door of 91 Cresswell Road. Elizabeth Staton opened the door and was horrified when her sister collapsed in her arms, crying, 'Oh mother, I shall die!'[5] The girls' father rushed outside and glimpsed a car driving off; he recognised it as one he had seen at the house before. In court Elizabeth recalled: 'I could see that [Phyllis] was very ill and could not walk, and I asked who had brought her there. She said, "The doc." At the time I did not know who she meant.'[6] She put her sister to bed and sent for Dr Gilmore; the girls' mother was in such a state that she too collapsed. Phyllis was acutely ill and feverish. She was admitted to hospital the next day where Dr James Clark diagnosed septicaemia. Phyllis vehemently denied that anyone had interfered with her, telling Dr Clark that a few days ago she had been going down some steps with 'her boy' when one of the heels came off her shoe and she fell.[7]

Within hours, Phyllis Staton was dead.

Dr Clark performed a post-mortem the following day, estimating that she had been over four months pregnant and had suffered a miscarriage between five to ten days earlier. He suspected foul play and performed a further examination with Dr Webster, the police surgeon. They found no natural cause for the miscarriage but neither was there any evidence of an illegal operation or the use of drugs. The coroner was notified of the death and contacted the police.

Two days later, on the evening of Wednesday, 7 February 1934, the head of Sheffield CID, Detective Superintendent Bristow, accompanied by Chief Inspector Flint, set out to find Dr Blakely. Bristow recalled:

> I saw the defendant in Tudor Street. After making known our identity, I told him that we desired to have a talk with him, either at his house or at the police office. He agreed to attend at the police office and came there at 10.35 the same day. I cautioned him and said, 'We are making inquiries into a very serious and delicate matter concerning the death of a girl named Phyllis Staton, whom I think you know, and our object in seeing you is to give you, if you care, an opportunity of saying anything you wish.' He said, 'I will tell you anything you want to know.'[8]

At the Central Police Office in Sheffield, Dr Blakely made a statement admitting his association with the dead girl, whom he said had known he was married from the start. About six months previously she had confided that she was pregnant and asked if something could be done. He claimed that she had slept with three other married men but 'apparently picked on me because I was fairly well off and I told her I was willing to take my share'.[9] He advised her to let the 'thing go through' and showed her a newspaper cutting about a London doctor who had been prosecuted for procuring an abortion. Dr Blakely continued:

> She asked me to take her to the house in Holme Lane. She thought she was going to have a miscarriage and did not wish to have it at home. On Tuesday 30 January she told me she had had the miscarriage. I did not examine her or treat her for her condition. I made it perfectly plain that I would not under any circumstances treat her as a patient.[10]

He admitted depositing her on the doorstep of her home but said he was 'surprised' to learn that she had died.[11] The next day, police searched Phyllis's bedroom and found a diary containing a timetable in Dr Blakely's handwriting for inducing labour. They also recovered a small box containing some capsules and a phial of liquid, which upon analysis was found to be pituitrin, a drug used to bring on labour.

On Sunday, 10 February 1934, a small news item appeared in the *Daily Herald*: 'DYING WAITRESS RIDDLE – DRIVEN HOME THEN CAR VANISHED'. The following day Dr Blakely was arrested on suspicion of murder. On entering the police station he announced, 'I may be morally responsible. I certainly have no criminal responsibility towards her.'[12] He was shown the box containing the capsules and phial found in Phyllis's bedroom and declared, 'I don't know anything about them,' before adding, 'she may have got those pills . . . from somewhere at Woodseats'.[13] He was charged with Phyllis's murder, to which he replied, 'Not guilty to that.'[14]

On Tuesday, 12 February, Dr Blakely was brought before city magistrates. DS Bristow's request for him to be remanded in custody for eight days while inquiries continued was granted. A small news item on the case appeared in the *Manchester Guardian*. The *Sheffield Independent* and the *Sheffield Star* reported proceedings in full and the city buzzed with the scandal of the respected doctor who had been having an affair with a young waitress and was now accused of her murder. When Dr Blakely's trial began at Sheffield Police Court on 20 February 1934, the press and public were out in force to hear him answer the charge of wilfully murdering Phyllis Staton by supplying 'a certain noxious thing called "pituitrin", well knowing it to be intended to be unlawfully used'.[15] Prosecutor Mr J.W. Chant outlined the case, beginning:

> The medical evidence of the post-mortem examination which is very material, is that [Phyllis Staton] died from acute septicaemia following an abortion . . . In the submission of the prosecution this abortion was procured by Dr Blakely in such a way, with his knowledge of medicine, that it was extremely unlikely that anything would be found to implicate him.[16]

He explained that pituitrin was impossible to detect because everyone has certain quantities of the drug occurring naturally in their bodies. He then pointed out that a curious feature of the case was that no trace had been found of the dead child, adding that the girl could not have disposed of it and the two women in the house would say that they had not seen it. The prosecution submitted that Dr Blakely had taken the child's body away with him on a visit to the house – very probably this was the brown paper parcel Gladys had seen.

Doctors Gilmore and Clark, Gladys Bailey and Detective Superintendent Bristow were the principal prosecution witnesses. DS Bristow spoke about his interviews with Dr Blakely and his visits to the Staton home before reading the accused's statement in which he admitted having given the girl some of the drug, but denied having carried out an illegal operation. In cross-examination DS Bristow said he could find no evidence to support any allegations about the deceased's relations with other men. When Dr Clark was cross-examined, he stated that there were no indications of an illegal operation or the taking of drugs, but asked if it was possible for an experienced medical man to procure an abortion without leaving any evidence, the doctor replied, 'Yes, it is.' Asked, 'Would you give a phial of pituitrin to a pregnant woman?' Dr Clarke replied emphatically, 'I would not.'[17]

The trial continued the following day amid sensational headlines but proceedings were brought to an abrupt end when Dr Blakely's defence counsel submitted that there was no case to answer, since there was not the slightest evidence on which a charge of murder could be brought and no evidence that the dead girl's miscarriage was not perfectly natural. After a retirement the judge agreed, pronouncing: 'I have carefully considered this case, and have come to the conclusion that the evidence on both charges is so weak that no jury would convict. The prisoner is therefore dismissed.'[18] There were gasps within the court.

The *Sheffield Independent* and the *Sheffield Daily Telegraph* led the extensive local coverage, while the *Manchester Guardian*, *The Times* and the *Daily Telegraph* also carried the story of Dr Blakely's controversial acquittal. And it *was* astonishing that the full story was not brought out in court: after all, he had admitted the charge of supplying pituitrin, knowing that his lover was four months pregnant; a timetable for inducing labour had been found in his handwriting; there was persuasive circumstantial evidence that he had injected Phyllis with the drug, knowing that it would be undetectable in post-mortem; and he had been seen taking a parcel away from the house after the miscarriage. But the judge had seen fit to dismiss the case.

The trial had no bearing on Dr Blakely's career. The good standing in which he was held enabled him to continue his work as if the death of Phyllis Staton and her unborn child had never occurred. But the effect on his family was profound. Although David was only five at the time, he was sensitive to the tension at home and years later discussed the case with Ruth, telling her that it had destroyed his parents' marriage.

There was a second element of unhappiness to David's early years: Hillstone Prep in Malvern, the exclusive school that his parents had chosen for him, was recently revealed by writer A.N. Wilson as a deeply disturbing environment in that period. Wilson maintains that the headmaster, Alexander Rudolf Barbour-Simpson, 'was a paedophile who was extremely skilful at hiding his proclivities from other grown-ups' and that his 'beautiful, rather Spanish-looking' wife Barbara was 'a sadist, whose waking hours were devoted to torturing the little boys on whom her sad husband had formed his attachments'.[19] Wilson explains that at the school where David Blakely was a boarder,

> more or less anything was a beating offence: walking on the wrong garden path; not walking on the path; talking after lights out; or being milliseconds late for a lesson or for games . . . There was a cage, shown to prospective parents as the place where we kept our rabbits and guinea pigs. In fact, it was used by Barbara to imprison Rudolf's victims. Sometimes they were left in there all day, until they wet themselves . . . If she spotted there was a particular food you disliked, you were for it. Leaving food, or choosing not to eat it, was never an option.[20]

Wilson recalls that nothing seemed likely to bring down the regime: 'Rudolf continued his fondlings, his canings, his nauseating sex talks. In fact, the sexual abuse got worse. Barbara continued to pick on his crushes.'[21] But in time parents were alerted to the situation and Barbour-Simpson retired at once, albeit as 'a much-respected local magistrate and head teacher praised in the local newspapers for his unforgettable teaching style'.[22]

David's parents' marriage broke down irretrievably while he was at Hillstone. Annie Blakely filed for divorce and was granted a decree nisi on 24 May 1940 on the grounds of her husband's adultery. The divorce became absolute on 2 December 1940. David was then 11 years old and adored both parents; years later when he recalled that time he did so with great sadness. Annie was granted custody and they left Sheffield for Buckinghamshire. Two months later, in February 1941, she married Humphrey Wyndham Cook (who was also divorced with one young son) at the Register Office at Caxton Hall in London. She gave her address as the Hyde Park Hotel and when asked for her father's profession by the Registrar, replied that he was of independent means. After the wedding, the family settled at Humphrey's prestigious address, 38 Upper Brook Street off Park Lane.

David's stepfather was extremely wealthy. Humphrey's father, Wyndham Francis Cook, ran one of the largest English wholesale draperies, Messrs Cook, Son & Co., of St Paul's Churchyard. He died when Humphrey was 12, leaving an estate whose gross value was then almost £1.5 million, plus a thriving family business. Educated at Harrow and Christ Church College, Oxford, Humphrey was a kind-hearted and intensely private man, burly in stature, with a passion for motor racing which he later passed on to his stepson David. He went on to become one of Britain's most well-known racing drivers before the Second World War. In 1925, following his mother's death, Humphrey sold his father's collection of antique gems and medieval jewellery for £75,000 at Christie's. He then immersed himself in motor sports and invested in the production of a team of single-seater racing cars; ERA (English Racing Automobiles) was born. Fired by patriotism and love of the sport, Humphrey ploughed a substantial amount of money into ERA until he withdrew funding in 1939, a year before his marriage to Annie Blakely.

David had never known poverty, but his stepfather was richer than his own father could ever have hoped to be. Humphrey liked tradition and treasured an almost Edwardian style of comfort; a watchmaker visited the Cook household every week to wind the clocks and a cobbler came to inspect shoes and spirit away those that required repair. He was touchingly eager to bond with his stepchildren and made a special effort with David, who became genuinely very fond of him. David's siblings had already flown the nest: his brother Derek was married and had a distinguished career in the RAF; his brother Brian was also in the RAF, and his sister Maureen had joined the Wrens. Humphrey, meanwhile, became a King's Messenger during the war, a courier employed by the British Foreign and Commonwealth Office.

Two years after his mother's wedding, David was enrolled at Shrewsbury School, then a boarding school for boys from the age of thirteen. Founded by Royal Charter in 1552 and identified as one of the 'great' public schools by the Clarendon Commission in 1868, old boys include Charles Darwin, writer Samuel Butler and Astronomer Royal Martin Rees. David was placed in Churchill's Hall during the summer term of 1943, shortly before a new headmaster took charge: John Wolfenden, later Baron Wolfenden, the British educationalist whose 1957 report recommended the decriminalisation of homosexuality.

David's summarised school reports (which did not go out to parents) make for interesting reading when bearing in mind his character during his relationship with Ruth. Comments from his first year include:

> Too spasmodic, lacks resolve . . . Pleasant but not down to it . . . He must do more than this if he is to make a success of his time here. V. backward, badly spoilt. *No* will power . . . Scatterbrained. Works adequately. Maths very weak . . . Must try harder. He still remains overlong at the Preparatory School stage of development.[23]

The following year he began to make something of an effort: 'At last *can* do well, occasionally does try. Better. Not the hoped for upward tendency yet and I think he could do a bit more towards it.'[24] But by the end of summer term, his form tutor warned: 'He had better swallow and try to digest his House Report – no sign of making a success of his term and measles put him back admittedly, but that is a dismal account of four terms here.'[25] Matters did not improve the following year, when David reached 15: 'Willing but weak . . . No sign of determination . . . Both in his work and in other ways there is need of much more determination and ambition.'[26] He displayed some talent in sport and his form tutor noted optimistically: 'His excellent PT performance shows that he has energy and determination, and if he will continue to apply himself to his school work he will find things coming more easily to him . . . PT: first class.'[27] Encouraged, David persevered in other subjects and his 1945 term report reads: 'This is not at all bad. School work does not come easily to him; but he is working well, and with a bit more ambition and still more determination he will go ahead.'[28]

But it was not to be. For some unknowable reason, he slipped back into lethargy and his disappointed form tutor noted:

Not exerting sufficiently . . . Not so good this term. I am sad to see this for I had hoped that he was out of the woods at last. In general ways he is a vastly improved person: but he will have to work a great deal harder than this.[29]

The downward trend resumed the following term:

There is an urgent need for a much more mature attitude towards work. At his present rate of progress he has not the faintest chance of a SC [School Certificate] next July; and the sooner he begins to do some work the better.[30]

Grammar school pupils around 16 years of age took the SC exams to gain admission to university. Matriculation meant passing 'with credit' in five subjects, including English language, maths and a classical or modern language. It was replaced by the General Certificate of Education in 1951.

The likelihood of David passing his SC was low, as his form tutor's half-term report in 1947 acknowledged: 'Far too careless, can't concentrate . . . Not giving work enough attention.'[31] At the end of term the tutor stated grimly: 'The statistics are pretty depressing, and unless there is a sudden gain in concentration and effort I cannot see him passing July's examination. He never really gives his mind to anything for long enough to take it in.'[32] As predicted, David failed his SC and did not graduate to fifth form. The headmaster wrote a final summary before bidding him farewell:

Nobody could feel optimistic about his Certificate result or statistics and comments like these. This present drift must stop sometime and he alone can stop it. If he does he will have a happy and successful future. He certainly has our good wishes for it.[33]

Thus ended David's school years. He was not academic, despite his parents and stepfather giving him every opportunity that money allowed, as well as much encouragement. But his childhood, despite all the privilege, had not been easy and left him insecure and mistrustful. He was perpetually mollycoddled at home, and although he was an affectionate son, stepson and brother, he was too spoiled and simply could not be bothered to knuckle down to any sort of work. He knew that money was never likely to be a serious problem and saw no reason to rack his brains over subjects that he found tedious.

In David's defence, life was unstable during his years at boarding school. In October 1944, *The Times* announced Maureen's engagement to Lieutenant John Fahey of Concord, New Hampshire. David's beloved sister married in Westminster in 1945 and sailed to a new life in February 1946. The *Lewiston Daily Sun* ran an article on Maureen and the other 2,346 GI brides who travelled on the *Queen Mary*, noting: 'New bride Maureen Blakely Fahey, 20, of London, viewed the journey as "an adventure" though admitted she was anxious to have it end.'[34] David must have felt the loss of this sister, to whom he was very close, particularly keenly. His brothers were pursuing brilliant careers in the RAF and his mother, however much she loved him, had the social life of which she had always dreamed, while his father remained in Sheffield. David had never been particularly popular at school, according to the account of a boy named Fawcett, who recalled in 1955:

> The young David Blakely took a positive delight in hurting others. His mercy did not seem to me to exist. I think that if this person's character went on in a progressively worsening way during the last eight years he may well have turned into the sort of person who could so badly hurt someone mentally as to incite that person to lose control of herself and kill him.[35]

Another contemporary ventured that girls and later women were 'naive in the face of [David's] charm, and responded maternally to his apparent need, since I suspect that beneath the surface he was a rather lonely, insecure individual'.[36]

In 1947, at the age of 18, David left Shrewsbury for the Royal Military Academy at Sandhurst, where he joined the Royal Tank Regiment. His public school background helped him win a commission in the Highland Light Infantry for his National Service. He did nothing to distinguish himself in the military field, however, and upon his release in December 1949 he returned to 28 Culross Street, where he was based with his former nanny and a housekeeper. His mother and stepfather occupied 4 Culross Street, scarcely a minute's walk away. Both were elegant mews houses: the entrance to David's home was next to a smart double garage on a quiet street off Park Lane, with the green space of Hyde Park at one end.

David had no idea what he wanted to do with his life. He was an averagely handsome drifter, 5 ft 9 in. tall, dark-haired and slim, unable to arrive anywhere on time and, according to a friend who knew him well, 'a dead unreliable bastard'.[37] With his dismal school career so recently behind him, he loathed 'intellectuals' and would become gloomy if the conversation turned to subjects he didn't understand. Happiest discussing cars, he could be an animated companion when talking to his stepfather about motor racing. Carole Findlater, who was to enter David's life in the near future, said of him, 'How he needed family, my goodness how that boy needed it.'[38] Yet all his siblings were away, having done well for themselves: Maureen was happily settled in America, Derek was working as a BOAC pilot and married with two children, while Brian was serving in Canada with the Fleet Air Arm, the branch of the British Royal Navy responsible for the operation of naval aircraft.

But that lack of purpose ended when David celebrated his 21st birthday on 17 June 1950. His stepfather presented him with a secondhand HRG sports car, and David's idle interest in motor racing flared into a passion. Humphrey, pleased with his stepson's unabashed joy, was keen to foster his enthusiasm, but advised him to learn a trade to fall back on if motor racing didn't work out. With this in mind, he secured David a position as management trainee at the Hyde Park Hotel in Knightsbridge. Originally built in 1889 as an exclusive gentleman's club, it was substantially rebuilt after a fire and reopened in 1902 as London's grandest hotel, garnering a glittering, loyal clientele that included the royal family. The Hyde Park Hotel loomed majestically over the endless streams of traffic, directly opposite a number of exclusive shops, and from the steps of the lavish main entrance, glancing to the right it was possible to see, only a few yards across the road, the bow-fronted windows of the Little Club.

10

David's first venture into employment was no more successful than his time at school or his National Service. He had little interest in the hotel trade, and the trainee rate of pay – 50 shillings a week – was no incentive to him. He relied on the £20 per month allowance from his mother and handouts from his father, when he visited him in Sheffield, to fund his lifestyle. There was one advantage to working at the hotel: it was useful for meeting women, particularly those slightly older than him, which David preferred. His employers were soon displeased with his lack of application and spoke privately to Humphrey, who persuaded them to give David a little longer to prove himself.

In turn, Humphrey had a quiet word with his stepson, but with no discernible effect. David put whatever energy he could muster into priming the HRG for motor racing. He had enlisted the help of an experienced mechanic, Ant Findlater, who together with his wife Carole was at the heart of David's social circle and certainly the closest friends he had ever known.[1] Indeed, the friendship between David and the Findlaters became the source of a great deal of angst for Ruth, and it was only because she wanted to expose the couple in court that she agreed to plead *not* guilty to killing David.

Anthony Seaton Findlater was born on 28 April 1921 into a prosperous, Presbyterian Dublin family. His father, Seaton McCurdy Findlater, was a self-made man through his grocery business, but had come from money and was educated at Harrow in England and Trinity College, Dublin. He was also a talented designer of automobile engines and a successful racing driver, gifts that he passed on to his only son. Their relationship was fraught otherwise; Ant felt that his father undermined him and he was closer to his mother and sisters. The family lived in Lower Wick, Worcester, and Ant was enrolled at the extremely select Hurstpierpoint public school in West Sussex.

After finishing his education, he studied automobile engineering and joined the Royal Air Force, where he met Carole Sonin.

Born Ruth Sonin in 1923, Carole was the daughter of Russian Jewish émigrés who arrived in Britain at the turn of the twentieth century; she also had a brother, Ray. Her father, Albert Sonin, was a manufacturer's agent. Carole trained as a journalist but joined the WAAF when war broke out. She drove a radio truck and became a Leading Aircraft Woman, relishing the social life in the services and studying Russian in her free time. When she met Ant, then a sergeant in the instruments section of the RAF, she was stationed at Sawbridgeworth in Hertfordshire. They attended a Sergeants' Mess Party together shortly before he was posted to Italy and remained in touch until his return, when Ant asked her to marry him. His father approved of the match, but told Carole that he couldn't understand what she saw in his son.

The wedding took place at Kensington Register Office in March 1946. Carole was 22 years old and Ant 24. He took a government course in business administration that year and worked mainly in sales for various engineering companies. Carole went back to journalism and changed her name, becoming a reporter for regional newspapers in Kent and Nottinghamshire, and then assistant press officer for the Royal Society for the Prevention of Accidents. She was offered the position of sub-editor on *Woman* magazine with an income of £20 a week; Ant earned far less as a sales representative for a neon sign manufacturer. Reporter Harry Ashbrook described Carole as 'a powerhouse of ambition and energy' while Ant was 'happy fiddling with carburetors'.[2] Still eager to enter the world of motor racing, it was only after his father's death in 1949 that Ant gave full rein to his interest. Carole presented him with an old Alfa-Romeo sports car and he spent all his time tinkering with it; in 1951 he managed to find work as a fitter for Aston Martin, which suited him far better than his previous jobs.

The couple moved into a flat at 52 Colet Gardens in Hammersmith, but money was tight and they decided to sell the car, advertising it in the press. When a prospective buyer turned up at their flat, he brought along his friend, David Blakely, to look at the car. The man decided not to buy but within a month or so Ant received a call from David, asking him if he would care to look over the HRG his stepfather had bought him. Ant called at Culross Street, where the HRG was parked in the garage, and immediately agreed to David's suggestion that they should work on the car together, sharing the costs, with the aim of creating a winner. In July 1951 David entered the HRG at Silverstone, winning the handicap races, and coming third in the six-hour relay at the track in August that year.

Despite his friendship with Ant and the hours they spent working on the car, David began an affair with Carole, who was the archetypical woman to whom he was attracted: six years his senior, well-spoken, intelligent and confident. Under the pretence of attending Union meetings, she would arrive at the Trevor Arms in Knightsbridge where David awaited her; the pub had a certain notoriety as the place where serial killer Neville Heath had picked up one of his victims in 1946. By autumn the affair between David and Carole was no longer just a bit of fun. A few years later she recalled:

> I left my husband to live with David Blakely. We were in love . . . at least we felt we were. It was a pretty serious business. We lived in hotels and places up and down the country. But there were a number of difficulties – mainly financial. After a few months I returned to my husband. I told him the truth and there was a reconciliation.[3]

When Carole told David that she was staying with Ant, having admitted the affair, he was said to have exploded, 'You stupid bitch. Now look what you've done. Who the bloody hell will tune my car now?'[4] But all three managed to reconcile, as Carole explained: 'Ant, my husband, and David continued to be friends . . . I came to regard David as a dear and close friend – but not my lover.'[5] When questioned about the affair 25 years later, Ant said simply, 'If he'd had the opportunity, David wasn't the sort of man to pass it up.'[6]

In February 1952 Dr John Blakely died at the age of 67 from coronary thrombosis. A small obituary appeared in the *Sheffield Telegraph*: 'Blakely – Suddenly on Feb 24 1952, at 203 School Road, John Blakely, MB, ChB. Service at City Road Crematorium on Friday, Feb 29 at 12.30 p.m. Cut flowers only please, to Messrs John Heath & Sons, Earsham St.' David immersed himself in the HRG to dull the pain of his father's loss. He took part in many high-profile races, including the Jersey International Road Race in July and the nine-hour Goodwood in August, with Ant as his co-driver. His best position was at Goodwood in March, when he finished third in the handicap race. No longer able to feign interest in the hotel trade, in October he had a furious row with the banqueting manager at the Hyde Park Hotel and was fired. As an employee, David had been prohibited from drinking in the hotel bar, but the day after his dismissal he walked in and ordered a gin and tonic, lounging in a chair until he felt he had made his point. Rather than remonstrate with him, his mother bought him a first-class ticket to join her on a cruise to South America; his occupation is recorded as 'student' in the passenger lists of the *Andes* ocean liner. According to a story he related to friends, he was unable to stay out of trouble even on holiday with his mother. He and another traveller drank their way through the bars of one town only to be forgotten when the ship sailed; the two of them had to hire a launch and climb back onboard via a rope ladder.

The ship docked in Southampton in February 1953, exactly one year after his father's death. Dr Blakely had bequeathed each of his children £7,000, and David intended to use his share to build a racing car from scratch.

In the meantime, his stepfather encouraged him to find work again. For the past few years Humphrey and Annie had divided their time between London and a substantial house called Granneys on Witheridge Lane in Penn.[7] Known as 'the Chelsea of the Chilterns' due to the 'calibre' of its inhabitants, Penn was a perfect out-of-town spot: in Buckinghamshire, an hour's drive from London, about three miles north-west of Beaconsfield and surrounded by woodland.[8] Among the locals were novelist Elizabeth Taylor and her family, who became close friends of the Cooks and the Blakely brothers. Elizabeth described the village in her book *In a Summer Season* as being 'in commuting country' with most residents living in 'six-bedroomed villas, built twenty or thirty years ago . . . They had gardens full of flowering trees, bright gravel drives and tennis courts.'[9] Elizabeth's biographer, Nicola Beauman, speculates that David Blakely was the inspiration for the novel's male protagonist, Dermot: 'half-Irish with a "broguey voice"', attracted to older women, fond of driving fast, keen on pubs and clubs and reacting against his father's 'almost neurotic sense of order'.[10] The house in the book is identified as The Old Vicarage, and in the months to come, a house of the same name in Penn would play a significant role in David's relationship with Ruth.

In Penn, David joined the cricket team and, more importantly, through his stepfather's connections, was offered a partnership with Sylicum Pistons Ltd on Hazelmere Road in the village.

An Italian man named Borti ran the firm, whose adverts promised: '24 hour service: we can now supply replacements for most types of motor cars and motor cycles'.[11] In his police statement, Ant recalled that David 'had discussed the job with me before he took it and I visited the works some time later, when I was shown round by David'.[12] The job at the garage in Penn suited him far more than learning the hotel trade. He was also racing again, at Goodwood in March and at the National Castle Combe (Handicap) race in April, which he won. He went on to race at Goodwood that summer, but a minor road accident and then a problem with steering twice forced him to withdraw from European competitions.

David was now well and truly a fixture not only at race meetings, but also at the set's notorious get-togethers in London. One of his few true friends among the group was Cliff Davis, David's co-driver in the 1953 *Daily Express* Rally. Born in Shepherd's Bush in 1917, Cliff began working in a garage at the age of 16 and bought and sold his first car that year. He was taken prisoner during the Second World War, but his skills as a mechanic and his ability to speak German helped him survive. He used his severance pay after the war to buy a Singer Le Mans, which he restored and sold for a tidy fee, and set up Cliff Davis Motors. By the 1950s he was a respected figure on the motor-racing circuit, with an impressive number of wins. He worked with Lionel Leonard, a market gardener who was also a leading sprint driver and 'something of a guru' in MG circles; Leonard was also friendly with David. Tall and ebullient, with an unmistakable bushy moustache, Cliff was in the same racing class as David, who was drawn to his reputation for being able to start a party anywhere.

At the time, there was no distinction between club racing and professional racing drivers, and the same faces appeared at the track and in the drinking dens of London. The racing fraternity regarded David as agreeable and civil when sober but superior and belligerent when drunk. Cliff described him as a

> typical product of the public school system. Well-educated, sophisticated, very supercilious – but I liked David. In my opinion he didn't have a lot of backbone. I found that out when

I took him on that *Daily Express* rally. It went on for a long, long
time and you need a co-driver to give you relief but David just
flaked out after five or six hours. That was it, he was just a sack
of potatoes in the passenger seat.[13]

It was Cliff who introduced David to Archie Scott-Brown. Born with
severe physical disabilities, after winning his first race in 1954 while
working as a travelling salesman Scott-Brown went on to record
seventy-one major races over the next five years. He became part of
the crowd who frequented the Steering Wheel Club where, his
biographer writes: 'Archie and the raffish if spoilt Blakely got on
well.'[14]

On one of their regular inebriated nights at the club, David grabbed
a handful of ice cubes and pushed them down driver Mike Hawthorn's
shirt collar, then squirted the racing ace with a soda syphon. Hawthorn
was livid and went hunting for David, who had simply ducked down
behind the bar, where Cliff saw him crouching when he arrived at the
club. Cliff had a word with Hawthorn, who was still blistering with
anger and took a swipe at him; Cliff dodged the punch but lost his
glasses and the two men ended up in a brawl. It was swiftly resolved and
within minutes Cliff, Hawthorn and David were laughing about the
incident.

Desmond Cussen remained on the fringes of the racing set. Unusually
for the amiable Cliff, he didn't care for Desmond, who struck him as 'a
cagey character'.[15] In his 1955 police statement, Desmond declared that
he had known David through racing 'just over two years – maybe three'
and that 'up to about the end of 1954 we occasionally went out
together'.[16] He recalled that David had recommended the Little Club to
him and that he met Ruth again there. David also pressed Cliff into
visiting the club, which he said was run by a 'smashing blonde'.[17] The
Little became a regular haunt for the racing set, not so expensive as
other nightclubs, relaxed about the licensing laws and always able to
provide girls to 'look after' them. Cliff had enough self-awareness to
recognise that many of the club's members, including his own crowd,
were painfully immature and paid for sex at the club because they
couldn't satisfy their own wives or girlfriends. He and Ruth spent one
night together after he kept telling her that she would be terrific in bed;
he later declared that his instinct was right and she had 'no equal' in that
respect.[18] But there was no possibility of it developing into anything

more: Ruth was a superlative hostess, didn't take offence at anything that was said, and had her own moral code, but Cliff was aware that she was 'nuts' about David, with whom her relationship went far deeper than a mutual sexual attraction.[19]

For her part, Ruth recalled:

I grew to know all the [racing] stars. I liked Mike Hawthorn best of all. Sometimes he would drop into the club for a drink. He was a friend of David. Once Mike asked me to come and look at a new car. I said to Mike, 'Where is it?' He answered, 'Oh, just round the corner.' I said, 'I'll not walk. It's too far. You'll have to carry me.' And he did. David was furious when 'friends' told him about it.[20]

Alexander Engleman was well placed at the Little Club to observe these first stirrings of discontent, particularly the rivalry between David and Desmond. 'I knew David Blakely who was a member and he was a nice boy,' Engleman said in his police statement:

He was very friendly indeed with Ruth and on many occasions she would tell me to leave the door open after the club closed at 11 p.m. so that he could get in. Ruth used to live in the flat above the club. Another member of the club was Desmond Cussen, who was trying to be friendly with Ruth, but she didn't seem to want much to do with him. During the time I was there I only saw Blakely and Cussen speak to each other once, and my impression was that they were not very friendly, and were jealous of each other.[21]

Morrie had also noticed the antagonism between the two men and was displeased by it. He warned Ruth that she must be seen to treat all customers equally – and that included 'loverboy' and Desmond. Ruth's reassurances were convincing and mollified Morrie into hosting her 27th birthday party on 9 October at Carroll's. David sent her a congratulatory telegram: 'Greetings Mrs Ruth Ellis 37 Brompton Road SW1 – Many happy returns on the day, all success to your party, love David.'[22] He arrived that evening with a bouquet of one red and six white carnations, causing a female guest to shudder and exclaim melodramatically: 'No, no – it's a sign of death.'[23]

David spent most week nights at Ruth's flat, returning to Penn at the weekend – a topsy-turvy arrangement given that he worked in Penn. But he was regularly absent from Sylicum Pistons, preferring to socialise in London instead, and told Cliff, 'I can't stand work, it drives me potty.'[24] He divided his time between Ruth's flat, his bachelor pad on Culross Street and the property his stepfather had bought that year in Penn: a sprawling, ivy-clad house named Old Park on Hammersley Lane, where poet Walter de la Mare spent much of the war.

Humphrey had some renovations carried out to provide David with a self-contained flat in one wing and invited his stepson's former nanny to move in to keep an eye on him. David did not mind the latter proviso since he regarded the nanny as family; she doted on him and often accompanied him on trips to the cinema and afternoon drives about the country lanes.

But there was no question of David inviting Ruth to Penn in order to meet his mother and stepfather. The class divide that he was happy to ignore in bed appeared insurmountable when it came to introducing Ruth to his relations. Nor was he serious enough about her to consider bridging that particular gap. Even in the early stages of his relationship with Ruth he pursued other women, including a married American model and a dainty blonde named Faith Roberts, who worked as an usherette at the Prince of Wales Theatre and accepted that she would never be the only woman in David's life. Elizabeth Taylor's biographer surmises that the relationship between the then 43-year-old novelist and David may have been more than friendship, most likely a very mild flirtation, stating that Elizabeth evidently felt a 'tendresse' for him.[25] In a letter Elizabeth wrote about David, a section had been cut away; writer Hilary Spurling glimpsed the letter beforehand and recalled that Elizabeth had written, 'I wondered what would happen if I suddenly said, "Yes, I was in love with him, although I was nearly twenty years older."'[26] Nonetheless, Elizabeth's family strongly dispute the idea of anything other than friendship.

Ruth had yet to find out about David's affairs, but heard endless tales about his horseplay from her customers: he had once driven a Bentley around the Albert Hall at 60 mph and escaped prosecution, and another time he threw a girl into the lake at Frensham Ponds in Surrey after she teased him about his long eyelashes.

Ruth had only been involved with David for a matter of weeks when, on 11 November 1953, a notice appeared in *The Times*:

Forthcoming Marriages: Mr DMD Blakely and Miss M Dawson: The engagement is announced between David Moffett Drummond, youngest son of the late Dr John Blakely of Sheffield, and Mrs Humphrey Cook, of 4 Culross Street, London W1, and Mary, younger daughter of Mr and Mrs W Newton Dawson of Toothill Hall, Brighouse, Yorkshire.[27]

Ruth's reaction can be imagined, although in her statements to the police she insisted that during the first few months she felt scarcely any jealousy. But Mary Newton Dawson was exactly the type of young woman David's mother hoped he would marry. Her father, William Newton Dawson, was an eminent wool manufacturer who had also written a book, *History on Your Doorstep*. Mary lived with her parents and elder sister Patricia at Toothill Hall in Rastrick, near Huddersfield. The property commanded sweeping views across the lower Calder valley and stood in extensive grounds, which included an outdoor swimming pool and a tennis court, but it was the petrol pumps in the garden and tales of a headless hound that delighted David. His friends regarded 20-year-old Mary as a very sweet girl who was too good for him. A regular visitor with her family to the Hyde Park Hotel, Mary attended the various dinner dances and sporting fixtures of the season with David, but he was careful to keep her apart from his boozy nights in London.

Despite his engagement, David ploughed his inheritance into creating the prototype for a new breed of sports car. He chivvied Ant into giving in his notice at Aston Martin to concentrate on the task, offering him a wage of £10 per week. Carole was uneasy about the arrangement; she had recently resigned from her well-paid job at *Woman* after finding out she was pregnant. She and Ant had long discussions about David's proposal and ultimately she told her husband to do whatever he felt best. Fired by his love of motor sports and David's insistence that the cars could be sold for £1,000 each, he agreed to the idea. During the next six months he arrived early almost every morning at the former china warehouse David had rented in Islington. The two men regularly put in eighteen-hour days on the venture, which began with the purchase of the body of the car for £375 and a twin cam version of the 1500 Singer-HRC, supplied to them at a reasonable fee due to the company's confidence in David, who had driven a HRG for the last three seasons. Ant designed the car with a tubular chrome-steel chassis, VW front suspension, de Dion rear end and a full-width aluminum body. He also came up with a name for the prototype: the Emperor, inspired by the eagle on the Findlater coat of arms, which was adopted by Charlemagne to symbolise his position as Holy Roman Emperor. David liked the analogy, so the Emperor it became, registration number VPX66.

In its own way, the car would play almost as large a part in what happened during the next 18 months as the people involved.

*

On 8 March 1954 Ruth had an abortion; the child was David's. In a statement to her solicitor she declared: 'I certainly did not intend to take advantage of such a position. My pregnancy was in fact terminated.'[28] David was aware of the situation. 'I did not ask him for, and he did not pay or offer, any money for the operation,' she wrote, 'although at that time he certainly had some.'[29] Ruth's Holloway hospital case notes state that it was a tubal pregnancy and the operation left her with a scar.

That same month the Findlaters moved into 29 Tanza Road, Hampstead. Their first-floor apartment was situated in a tall Victorian property at the upper end of a quiet, steeply sloping street of semi-detached houses. Steps led up to the front door of the flat, with the bay window of the sitting-room overlooking the street; the rear windows faced the green expanse of Parliament Hill Fields. Ruth had already met Ant when David brought him to the Little Club one evening, but she had yet to meet Carole, who telephoned to invite her to Ant's 33rd birthday party at the new flat on 28 April. The two women took an instant dislike to each other: Carole, wearing horn-rimmed glasses and her trademark scarlet lipstick, recalled that 'shrimplike' Ruth, wearing a low-cut black dress, spent the evening flirting with the men and ignoring her.[30] Her animosity was reciprocated; Ruth scoffed that Carole behaved like a Mother Superior.

The Findlaters never warmed to Ruth, nor she to them. When David brought Ruth along to race meetings that spring, Cliff admired how she made an effort not only to fit in, but also to ensure everyone had a good time; she prepared fantastic champagne picnics, which she shared generously. But Ant was scathing and not to be swayed: 'Ruth did not fit in. She stuck out like a sore thumb.'[31] In their preface to

The Trial of Ruth Ellis, Jonathan Goodman and Patrick Pringle point out:

> All the friends of Blakely's she had met in drinking clubs had been men. At the race meeting she had her first encounter with their wives and fiancées, who treated her with the studied politeness they normally reserved for their charwomen.[32]

Ruth chose to ignore their disdain, happy just to be there:

> Most weekends we spent at motor race tracks, driving there in David's grey-green shooting-brake. Sometimes David took me on practice laps – 'just to bring me luck,' he said. I loved the speed and the feeling of power as we lapped at 100 mph. With David driving I was never afraid. But as I watched him whine past alone, I felt my stomach turn over in fear.[33]

At the Little, Ruth was proving even more successful than Morrie had hoped. She began giving Sunday afternoon parties, which attracted a wider clientele, including actor Richard Greene, who became famous playing Robin Hood in the late 1950s television series. Another regular was Desmond Cussen, although only Ruth made an effort with him. Flattered by his obvious devotion, she confided in Desmond to some extent, but never told him the truth about Andre's father. He was liberal with gifts of money and she admitted to finding him 'so restful compared to David'.[34]

Unfortunately for Desmond, that restfulness could easily seem deadly dull. David was occasionally jealous of him but didn't take him too seriously, reserving his venom for other customers; he accused Ruth of 'tarting' around the bar. 'David was becoming intolerable,' she recalled. 'He criticised me in front of customers by saying, "Look at her – flinging herself at any man."'[35] When she told him not to be so ridiculous, especially since he was present himself most evenings, he glowered at her: 'It's not what you do at nights that worries me – it's what you do in the afternoons.'[36]

In May 1954, Ruth's estranged husband appeared on her doorstep. Repeating past habits, George Ellis left work in Warrington to squander his money in the bars and nightclubs of London. On at least one occasion Ruth agreed to let him sleep on the bed-settee in her flat after he had drunk too much. Despite his own alcoholism, George insisted that Ruth was an unsuitable mother and the flat was no place for their young daughter. He was adamant that they not only needed to discuss the divorce – he was determined to contest the £4 per week that he paid Ruth – but also arrangements for Georgina. He told Ruth about a colleague of his, a wealthy and compassionate woman who could not have children of her own. She and her husband were eager to care for Georgina while agreeing that George and Ruth could remain part of their daughter's life.

He was so persuasive, and Ruth herself was far from happy with the situation (although Andre was at school most of the time), that she began to dither. Her parents had recently gone into service, leaving Ruth without her regular babysitters. She was aware that making new arrangements meant a babysitter whom she would not know or necessarily trust. George's solution would make life much easier, especially with David spending nights at the flat. But Ruth vetoed formal adoption and only agreed to the proposal if she could be kept informed about her daughter's welfare.[37]

Despite her young age – she was not yet three when her father spirited her away from London – Georgina remembers leaving her mother's flat. George proceeded to drink heavily on the train journey and was inebriated by the time of their arrival in Warrington. A large black car waited at the station, with a man sat at the wheel and a woman looking out at them from the back seat. George told his daughter, 'This is your new mother. Go and sit on her knee.'[38] Unsurprisingly, Georgina was confused and very frightened; her father had not explained to her that they would be living with his colleague, Phyllis Lawton, and her husband, who were keen to adopt her but in the meantime were happy enough to provide a home for Georgina and her father. They drove to a beautiful house, where she was shown her new bedroom without further explanation.

Georgina hardly knew her father and hated sharing a room with him. He drank every day, stumbling about before collapsing in a stupor, and it was his skills at the piano, rather than as a father, that she remembered most in later life:

> He had the deftest of touches and could play anything quite beautifully by ear. I play, but nothing like he could. Whenever he was at our home in Warrington, once he got out of bed, he would

make his way to the piano and play *As Time Goes By*. On top of the piano would be a tumbler of neat gin with two raw eggs – his heart starter, as he called it, followed by Andrew's Liver Salts.[39]

Yet George seems to have drawn closer to his small daughter, for when the Lawtons asked to adopt her, he refused and even kept Ruth's parents at bay. Georgina recalled: 'My grandmother wrote to me on a fairly regular basis and sent numerous letters to George imploring him to let her see "Georgina, my baby." He did not accede to her request.'[40] On 26 May 1954 George filed a petition for divorce from Ruth on the grounds of mental cruelty, allegations which she refuted, blaming his reliance on the bottle for the problems in their marriage.

Mercifully, Georgina grew to love Phyllis Lawton, a dentist with Warrington Health Authority, and her husband Peter, who was a veterinary surgeon. They adored her and gave her the best of everything. But she noticed that they never once mentioned her real mother, Ruth.

*

In May 1954, Carole Findlater gave birth to a daughter, Francesca Joy, and David was made godfather. Ant was at home less and less; the Emperor took up far more time, money and exertion than either he or David had anticipated, putting additional strain on the marriage. Carole hated it when Ant accompanied David to the Little Club rather than returning straight home after work, and Ruth was just as irate that David often visited Tanza Road without her. 'I felt she disliked me,' Carole stated:

> She didn't like [David] coming to the flat so often. Yet she tried
> to ingratiate herself by odd shows of generosity. For instance,
> when my child was born she offered to buy the baby a christening
> gown. The months passed and the present did not arrive.[41]

David closed his eyes to the antipathy between Ruth and Carole, and did not get involved in Ant's marital difficulties. He was engrossed in the Emperor and panicked when he realised how swiftly his inheritance had been depleted by the car. For once, Humphrey withstood his stepson's pleas for assistance, having heard that he had frittered away his money in the city's bars and nightclubs.

Infuriated and gloomy, David sought consolation at the Little, where Ruth allowed him to drink at her expense as well as live in the flat free of charge. Morrie was enraged when he found out what was going on. 'The proprietor of the club started charging me a rental of £10 a week for the flat,' Ruth recalled, 'because he knew David was living there and he had already warned me that he objected to it. He considered that it was bad for business.'[42] Ruth asked David to contribute to the rent and bills, but he reminded her that every penny he had was being ploughed into the Emperor, which he was convinced would make his name.

In June, David left for the 24-hour race in Le Mans, promising Ruth he would return before his birthday. On 11 June he sent her a postcard depicting the distinctly unromantic monument to the Fallen of the Great War in Le Mans. On it he scribbled: 'Arrived OK. Haven't had a drink for 3 days!!! Wish you were here. Will see you Tuesday. Love, David.'[43]

Ruth had planned a surprise 25th birthday party for him at the club on 17 June but the only person she succeeded in surprising that evening was Desmond. She had had no word from David since his postcard the week before. Once it became clear he was not going to put in an appearance, Ruth invited Desmond upstairs to her flat and suggested that they go to bed together. Although he had long been attracted to her, Desmond had been too uncertain of himself to make the approach before, and he was sharply aware of Ruth's ongoing relationship with David. But he didn't turn her down. Afterwards, Ruth claimed that she only slept with Desmond in the hope that he would inform David, thereby bringing an end to their increasingly troubled affair; she told Desmond that David refused to leave despite her insistence that he should vacate the flat.

In truth, David's persistent unfaithfulness and his failure to return in time for the party she had planned left Ruth hurt and humiliated. In all probability, she slept with Desmond Cussen out of spite towards David, a scenario guaranteed to cause nothing but ill feeling.

11

Desmond was cautiously optimistic that he and Ruth might have a future after they spent the night together. He told police:

> One night when Blakely was away from her flat, she asked me to stay with her and pointed out she was not married to him and entitled to lead her own life. Later she told me she had thrown him out twice but he kept coming back. She said he drank a lot and from what I gathered he never gave her any money to support herself.[1]

Her absent lover was the main topic of conversation nonetheless: 'She said that David Blakely was in love with her and that she wasn't in love with him, but she would have liked him to remain good friends towards her.'[2]

While David was in France, Ruth gave Desmond a potted history of her past, carefully pruning certain elements and adding others. She told him that she had been married twice, first to Andre's father, whom she said had been killed in the war. She was more truthful about her relationship with George Ellis and her daughter's whereabouts. But if Desmond allowed himself to believe that the affair would develop fully, he was to be bitterly disappointed. One clue to Ruth's feelings for him was between the sheets; in contrast to her other lovers, Desmond described her as 'sexually very mechanical, but great fun to be at a party with'.[3] He was the only man ever to admit dissatisfaction about a sexual encounter with Ruth.

On 2 July, David sent a second postcard, this time from Rheims, showing the Fontaine Subé in the Place Drouet d'Erlon. Either he had suspected something might happen between Ruth and Desmond or he had been told about it, for he wrote: 'Darling, have arrived safely and am having quite a good time. The cars are going very well. Looking forward to seeing you. David. PS. Love to Desmond!!!'[4] And regardless of her earlier protestations that she wanted him out of her life, when David returned from France early that month, Ruth threw him a belated birthday party at the Little Club, even inviting the Findlaters. Seeing him again made her realise the extent of her feelings for him: 'He was tanned from the hot French sun, and his smile was so inviting. I realised with a shock how much I had missed him.'[5] But the evening was not a success: David arrived late for his party and ill-tempered. Looking to vent her frustration while appearing to be merry, Ruth picked up a soda syphon and squirted Carole with it – a practical joke she had evidently learned from David. Carole was unamused, but stuck it out at the party until she laddered her nylons, at which point she departed, her mood spoiled.

After the club had emptied, David followed Ruth upstairs. They began to bicker, but when Ruth asked him if he had set a date for his wedding to Mary Newton Dawson yet, he surprised her with his reply: 'I've got news for you, you are not going to lose me after all. I've broken my engagement.'[6] This was apparently the reason for his late arrival at the party; he had met Mary at the Hyde Park Hotel to end their relationship and she had thrown his engagement ring back at him. Ruth, who could now afford to be magnanimous towards Mary, felt a stab of pity for David's ex-fiancée, recalling that she told him: 'Well, you might have chosen a better day to break it off than your birthday. I think you are callous and heartless.'[7]

Shortly before her execution, Ruth identified David's broken engagement as the turning point in their relationship. She remembered:

> From then on he paid even more attention to me, he literally adored me, my hands, my eyes, everything except my peroxide hair which he always wanted brunette. Now he was free, I am afraid I allowed myself to become very attached to him. At that time I thought the world of him; I put him on the highest of pedestals. He could do nothing wrong and I trusted him implicitly. I still however did not think seriously of the possibility of marriage. I myself was still married and I believed from what he had told me about his family that his mother would never allow such a match.[8]

She told a visiting cleric in Holloway: 'If he had cut his finger, I would have gone to the ends of the earth to bandage it.'[9]

David's feelings for Ruth had apparently undergone a seismic shift, but he remained primarily obsessed with proving himself as a racing driver. Ruth bought him a good luck charm: a tiny gold model of the vintage car Genevieve, from the 1953 film of the same name. He wore it on his keyring chain, but had little success that season in any of his races, which included meetings at Oulton Park, the British GP and Brands Hatch International; his best position was fifth. He had invited Ruth to join him at the International Sports Car meeting at Zandvoort in Holland but although it pained her to refuse a foreign trip with David, she had to come to some decision about Andre's education. David departed for Holland alone, intending to race an MG owned by Lionel Leonard. It was a disaster; *Autosport* featured a photograph of him at the event on 15 August 1954, captioned: 'WOW! David Blakely hastily straps down the Leonard-MG's bonnet after viewing the horrible mess caused by throwing a con rod.'[10] He headed back to London in dismal mood, ruminating on the cost of repairs and how to cover his expenses. Returning to the flat above the Little, inexplicably he suggested that Ruth might move in with him at Culross Street, but she had more sense than to agree. Piqued, he insisted that she apologise to Carole for upsetting her at the party and reminded her that she still hadn't bought a christening gown for Francesca as promised. Ruth immediately went out and spent a small fortune. Carole recalled: 'She sent round a beautiful gown, which I understand cost her £14. By this time the baby was almost nine months old and the gown was obviously too small. The whole business was ridiculous and embarrassing.'[11] Carole put the gift in its box in a drawer. Later she donated it to some Boy Scouts collecting for a jumble sale, warning them not to give it away.

Desmond had offered to pay for Andre to attend a reputable boarding school and accompanied Ruth when she had an interview with the headmaster. She deliberately kept this from David, who was surprisingly fond of her ten-year-old son and was kind to him, perhaps recalling his own experiences during childhood. In September Andre left London to board at a school in Aylesbury, wearing the uniform Desmond had bought him and with his first year fees paid in advance by him. Ruth struggled to afford her weekly rent and could never have sent her son to the school without Desmond's assistance. She was grateful to him for it, and the other amounts of money he surreptitiously put her way.

David was in financial straits of his own. Having invested the bulk of his father's legacy in the Emperor and squandered much of what was left, he could no longer manage to pay Ant a regular wage. Even his income from the partnership at Sylicum Pistons and the generous allowance from his mother could not cover his ambitions for the Emperor or subsidise his lifestyle. Ant decided to look for a job while working on the car in his spare time, but Carole was concerned enough to return to journalism earlier than planned. She was given an enviable assignment by a women's magazine to travel to Russia in order to write a series about life there, for which she was paid the handsome sum of £500. Ant meanwhile found employment as a secondhand car salesman with a man named Derek Simmons, who owned a garage at 12 Rex Place, five minutes' walk from David's flat on Culross Street. Simmons also employed Clive Gunnell, a fair-haired, debonair-looking 30-something who lived near the Findlaters at 45 South Hill Park; Clive was a close personal friend of both Ant and David. Humphrey was unwilling to bail out his stepson, but he did agree to house the Emperor at his garage at 4 Culross Street to cut rental costs.

The person who offered the most financial support to David was the one who could least afford it: Ruth. In court she recalled:

> All his money was going on racing cars. He was not earning anything. He used to stay at his mother's flat in Penn and he came into the club one night and said he had had a row with his stepfather, who had threatened to cut off his allowance. He said he was going to commit suicide . . . I had given the barmaid instructions that if he came to the bar he was to be allowed to drink without paying. He used to eat at the club, and when we went out I gave him the money. If he made out a cheque, I gave him the money afterwards to meet it . . . I realised that if he did get any money it would be spent on his racing car: but I did not mind this. I estimate that, excluding rent, I was spending between £200–250 a year on David.[12]

Despite Ruth's assistance, David exhibited increasingly aggressive behaviour towards her, with consequences not only for her emotional and physical safety but also her livelihood and home. 'In or about October 1954 he started becoming violent,' Ruth recalled:

> He was constantly trying to belittle me in front of my guests and complaining that it was degrading to be associated with me because I ran a Club and generally trying to make me feel as if I was socially inferior to him . . . my nerves began to suffer . . . instead of being cheerful and contented I was becoming moody and ill-tempered and this also was having an effect on the business. I also then started drinking more than I should have done.[13]

There were a number of witnesses to David's violence. One was Jacqueline Dyer, a close friend of Ruth's since they worked together at Carroll's several years earlier. Born in Lyon, Jacqueline was bubbly, smart and outspoken. She worked at the Little Club for a short while in 1953 before deciding it wasn't for her, but Ruth persuaded her to return after they met again in October 1954. 'We became very friendly,' Jacqueline recalled:

> Out of business hours I spent a lot of time with Ruth in her flat above the club . . . We would talk quite a lot about personal matters . . . I met David Blakely, who was living with Ruth in the flat above the club. He seemed to me to be a fool of a man who shouldn't go out with a girl like Ruth. He was very jealous of Ruth and was even jealous of me because she thought a lot of me. They quarrelled frequently and he beat and kicked her. I saw them fighting in the flat one day and he pushed her out of the flat and she fell down six stairs. She was frequently bruised about the body.[14]

Others were witness to the aftermath of David's beatings, if not the attacks themselves. Cliff Davis blamed the couple's mutual mistrust; both were unfaithful and therefore had reason to be jealous. He admitted that David 'knocked her about, no question of it. I met Ruth many times in the Little before David arrived and it would be quiet and she'd been knocked around and have marks on her face.'[15] Those who were sexually intimate with Ruth knew more. In July 1955, a man named Maxwell wrote to the Home Office with evidence he wanted put forward in Ruth's defence. Maxwell explained that in 1954, while his wife was away, he had met Ruth at a club. Although she was 'pretty moody all evening and refused to tell me what the trouble was', he invited her to his flat in Earl's Court Square.[16] There 'she suddenly started talking very excitedly and said, "Do you know David Blakely the racing car driver?" I said I didn't and she then took off her clothes.'[17] Instead of the sexual encounter he had hoped for, Maxwell saw something that would 'live in my memory for ever. Her body was covered with big ugly bruises and in some places the skin had broken.'[18] When he asked her to explain, she replied that the injuries were 'David's work'.[19] He immediately told her to dress and drove her to the Princess Beatrice Hospital in South Kensington. 'She went into the Casualty Department,' he wrote, 'but after I had waited for a long time and she hadn't reappeared, I went in and they told me that she had refused to see anyone and had left by the front door.'[20] He and Ruth never met again, but he had no doubt she was 'undergoing a terrific mental strain'.[21]

The other constant woman in David's life, Faith Roberts, insisted that her lover was as much a victim of domestic violence as Ruth. David told Faith that the scars on his body were due not to Ruth defending herself, but proof of her unprovoked assaults. Faith recalled David arriving very late and agitated at her flat on Gower Street one night:

> We talked for a while and I can't remember what we talked about. Eventually we went to bed and when he got undressed there were some marks on his back. I said, 'What's happened to your back?' He said, 'They're knife marks.' I said, 'Whatever do you mean?' He'd been talking about Ruth and he said, 'Ruth did it.' I said, 'It's not possible, David.' He said, 'I'm terrified of her.' I said, 'Well, leave her if you're that terrified of her. All you've got to do is up and leave.' He said, 'I can't, you don't know her.' And I said, 'That's impossible, David. How can you be frightened of a woman?'[22]

Ironically, it was livid marks on his skin that alerted Ruth to David's affair with Faith. One night when he turned to switch out the bedside light, she saw that his neck and shoulders were replete with love bites. 'I went quite cold with shock,' Ruth recalled:

I told him to get out and leave the flat. He said he could explain everything and started to tell me that someone had bitten him in the neck while he was playing darts at Penn. I said, 'Please get out of my bed and out of my flat and don't come near me again' . . . He did not like it but he went . . . He phoned about an hour after he had left the premises, and he phoned early in the morning and told me he had spent the night at Islington [where the Emperor was originally garaged] and he was very cold and miserable and asked if he could come back, and I said, 'No.' He returned as soon as the bar opened up at three o'clock and asked my barmaid if he could see me. I had already instructed the barmaid that I was not at home to him. He phoned then from the box just in the entrance to the club to my place upstairs, and asked if he could please come up and I said, 'No.' After half an hour he came upstairs and I was fooling around in the flat, doing one thing and another. He was very emotionally upset and he went on his knees, crying and saying, 'I'm sorry, darling. I do love you. I'll prove it,' and he asked me to marry him and I said, 'I don't think your mother or family will agree to this.' . . . He said that if there was any trouble with his family, we could get married secretly.[23]

Ruth gave a slightly modified version of events to Holloway's prison doctor, stating that after the incident in bed David had remained away for a week before appearing in tears, at which point she took him back into her home. In the *Woman's Sunday Mirror*, she tells yet a different story again, stating that David arrived to apologise with a bouquet of red carnations at the club; she made him leave but became concerned, fearing he would do himself harm:

I hurried after him into the Brompton Road. It was raining and cold. He was standing on the kerb. He didn't look round as I went up to him. But he knew I was there. Still staring at the wheels of passing buses and lorries, he said, 'I'll kill myself, Ruth, if you don't forgive me.' I knew he was drunk enough and angry enough to mean it. I pulled him back as he was stepping off the kerb, right into the stream of traffic.[24]

Ruth cited this reconciliation as the deciding factor in making up her mind to agree to George's wishes regarding their divorce and Georgina's future:

> I said I was willing to let it go through undefended, claim no maintenance and allow my husband custody of my little girl. It was a measure of my love for David that I was prepared to give up my child of whom I was very fond.[25]

The phrase 'very fond' in regard to her daughter strikes a discordant note when juxtaposed with Ruth's declaration of love for David, but she spoke the truth; her love for David overrode all other emotional attachments.

An explosive cocktail of mutual jealousy, unfaithfulness and heavy drinking sparked further rows which escalated into physical abuse. David's attitude to Ruth's position at the club worsened by the day. When he tried to provoke her by asking how she expected him to introduce her to 'country' friends, she had the wit to reply: 'Well, if I have to pay their drink bills as well as yours, I'd rather not meet them.'[26] She admitted:

> He was always complaining of my job at the club. Customers who used to be my friends were staying away because of the unpleasant scenes with David. I was tired, nervy and ill with strain and too much drinking . . . David was always urging me to give up my job.[27]

He not only fought Ruth, but frequently clashed with customers – even on one occasion brawling with Ant, whom he then guiltily drove to hospital, where his friend was treated for an injured hand. 'David often attacked me when he was drunk – usually because he objected to my talking with customers,' Ruth stated. 'Even when other women were there he would smack my face and punch me. When we were alone, it was worse. I took it all because I loved him so much.'[28] Cliff confirmed that Ruth was essentially an easy-going character, but David was unwilling to control either his temper or his roving eye. Ruth's response was to mirror his behaviour, leading to further eruptions.

On 12 October 1954, three days after her birthday, Ruth hosted her own party at the Little Club. David sent her a congratulatory telegram from Penn and a birthday card depicting two hands holding champagne glasses; inside he had underlined the printed words 'True Friends' three times and made adjustments to the verse, which read:

> Here's to your health –
> May it always be good (*!!!!*)
> Here's to your plans ('*PARIS*')
> May they go as they should
> Here's to good fortune ('*M. Cononley*')
> True friends and good cheer ('*Desmond and Gregg*')
> And to joy that increases
> Each day in the year.[29]

Underneath he had scrawled: 'Sorry I couldn't find a better card, but in this part of the world they are unheard of. Happy Birthday, Darling. BE GOOD.'[30]

'Paris' referred to David's promise of a long weekend in the city. Ruth recalled: 'We planned to leave on Friday evening and return early on Monday morning. The airport bus was due to leave at 6 p.m. At 5.30 David phoned and said, "Sorry, darling, we can't go. Bad weather. All planes are grounded."'[31] Ruth, waiting at the flat in a new red jacket and with a small suitcase at her side, was disappointed but believed him. However:

> Next morning I read in the paper that a film star had arrived in Paris by air that night from London. I rang the airline. They told me that all services had been normal. Until now David had been everything to me. He could do no wrong. I believed in him implicitly. Now he had lied to me for the first time. Paris was the city of my dreams. I had never been abroad. That lie of David's took the heaven out of my happiness.[32]

She also learned of David's affair with Carole from one of the Little Club regulars. 'I was really upset about it,' Ruth remembered. 'I asked him, "Why on earth didn't you tell me before? It makes me feel such a fool in front of her."'[33] She insisted after her arrest that the knowledge had no bearing on her hatred of the Findlaters nonetheless: 'I was not keen on [David] staying at Hampstead without me and I asked him not to . . . I did not like Carole very much because she was always running people down behind their backs.'[34] David was equally resentful of Ruth's work at the club and began prying her away. He preferred the more upmarket bars of the West End anyway, and Ruth would usually accompany him to his favourite spot, Esmeralda's Barn on Wilton Place, later run by the Kray twins. She attempted to match David drink for drink when they were together in public, downing liberal amounts of Pernod, which she first heard about from Jacqueline, ignoring her advice that it should be mixed with iced water. The potent French aperitif was one of the more expensive spirits at the Little, costing 4/6 a measure; if a customer offered to buy her a drink, Ruth requested Pernod to increase her commission. Her clothes began to smell less of Miss Dior and more of the aniseed reek of her preferred tipple. Occasionally she switched to gin and ginger or champagne. Trying to steady her, Jacqueline would serve Ruth a shot of Pernod followed by water, knowing she was too inebriated to notice:

> I estimate that she would regularly drink half to a bottle of gin a day besides Pernod. She was not the kind to appear drunk, but I could tell when she was having too much because she used to get careless over the running of the business.[35]

Ruth had also begun chain-smoking and easily got through 50 cigarettes a day.

The rows with David were relentless. 'Blakely often arrived intoxicated at seven o'clock in the evening and would go on drinking,' Jacqueline recalled.

> In this condition he was quarrelsome and aggressive towards everyone. Ruth Ellis was not aggressive. There were, however, constant rows between them. I remember on one occasion about a month before Christmas Blakely came into the Little Club about 8 p.m. in a bad temper. Ruth came back with Desmond, having had some dinner with him. Blakely asked her where she'd been and she said she had just had dinner with Desmond. He said, 'You're a liar, you have been sleeping with him.' She said, 'I am not a liar and I do not like being called a liar – please go away.' He went up to her and smacked her hard twice across the face. She was sitting down. I went round the bar to get hold of Blakely and she took hold of my hand and said, 'No, let him alone' and took him upstairs. I heard several thumps. She came

back at 11 o'clock and said she was fed up and wanted to leave him. She had been crying and was crying when she came back. I do not remember whether I saw bruises on that occasion but I have often seen them.[36]

When Ruth's mother stayed at the flat to look after Andre during school holidays, she too witnessed the drinking and the violence; it's fair to assume that Andre himself must have done the same. In a statement to her daughter's solicitor in 1955, Bertha explained that David lived on Ruth's earnings and would 'knock her about terrible'.[37] She heard raised voices one evening while she was in the flat and ran downstairs to find David holding Ruth by the neck, leaving her with 'marks on both sides'.[38] On separate occasions she found the left side of Ruth's face swollen, one eye bruised around the socket and her left leg in bandages. Unsurprisingly, Bertha regarded David as 'a brute . . . the second George Ellis'.[39]

Something had to give at the Little Club, and when Morrie saw that takings had fallen from £200 per week to an average of £80, he exploded. Ruth turned to Desmond for help. He confirmed in his police statement:

Towards the end of 1954 she said she was very broke and thought of leaving the Club and trying to seek a better paid job in another Club. She was still living with Blakely at that time . . . By this time Blakely knew I was fond of her and was taking her out.[40]

In December 1954 Ruth's position at the Little Club came to an end, either of her own volition or because Morrie fired her. In one sense it was a relief:

I felt that if I did not have a rest, I would have a break down. I thought that by leaving my flat David would not be able to come and sleep with me and I thus might find the strength to end the affair.[41]

She continued to work at the Little Club until a new manageress could be found, but vacated the flat.

Again, it was Desmond to whom Ruth turned. She had nowhere else to go. He recalled:

Just before Christmas 1954 she phoned me up and said she could not carry on at the Club and asked if she could come and stay at my flat until she got another job. She asked if she could bring her son along too. I agreed to this and they both came along, just before Christmas. She told me that she had finished with Blakely. He was supposed to be very upset about it, that is, when he heard she was moving into my flat.[42]

Ruth's relationship with David was ongoing, despite her words to Desmond. He was livid when she told him her plans. To placate him, she insisted that it was a temporary arrangement while she looked for work elsewhere – just as he had always wanted her to do. And after all, she said, Desmond could afford to look after her while he could not. Over the past couple of months David had supplemented his income by working on a commission basis for car salesman Derek Simmons, but given his lifestyle and the demands of the Emperor, it was not enough to provide a home for himself, Ruth and Andre.

On 7 December 1954, Ruth left the Little Club. Jacqueline helped to pack her few belongings. Only 18 months earlier, Ruth had climbed the stairs from Brompton Road full of excitement and ambition; now she was leaving it in the knowledge that Morrie would never employ her again. Homeless and unemployed, moving into Desmond's flat at 20 Goodwood Court was not without complications, as Ruth was only too aware. He wanted her for himself, however much he protested afterwards that his motives were purely altruistic: 'To say that we were lovers, that we were living together, gives the wrong impression. I was simply trying to provide a home for Ruth and the kiddie.'[43] He admitted to police that he and Ruth slept together, albeit rarely. His cautious optimism about their future was understandable, especially given his recollection that Ruth told him she hoped 'to get rid of Blakely and not have him bothering her but she still wanted to be friendly'.[44]

But on 18 December 1954, Ruth met David at the Rodney Hotel in South Kensington, about a mile from the Little Club, where they spent the night together. Over the next two months, the couple booked into the hotel on fifteen occasions as Mr and Mrs Blakely of Sheffield. Paying £3 per night for room No.71, they usually arrived around midnight and the following morning had breakfast in bed and a drink in the bar at 11 a.m. before going their separate ways. Ruth told Desmond she was visiting friends or travelling to see Georgina in Warrington. In truth, she felt compelled to be with David: 'Although we quarrelled and he beat me, I just could not part from him.'[45]

Shortly before Christmas, David echoed her words to Cliff: 'I'd give anything to get away from her but as soon as we meet it all starts again.'[46] Caught between the two of them, Cliff listened to Ruth's fears that now they no longer lived together, David would use his freedom to sleep with other women. He witnessed her desperation one night in Esmeralda's Barn, when she confided that she had given David some money and hadn't seen him since, but assumed he was 'poking the arse off some tart'.[47]

As Ruth worked her notice, there were at least two major arguments at the Little Club in the run-up to the festive season. She recalled the first:

Just before Christmas, a customer broke a gramophone record that David had bought for me. It was called *I Still Believe*. The customer may have broken it on purpose for I nearly drove the club members mad playing it. I seemed to find consolation in the words: 'I still believe we were meant for each other.' When David heard that the record was broken, he was furious. 'That's right!' he stormed. 'Let anyone play *our* record and break it!'[48]

Jacqueline recalled the second row, which culminated in a beating for Ruth:

Blakely arrived about 6.30 p.m., dirty, unshaven and slightly under the influence of drink. He said, 'I want to speak to you Ruth, straight away.' She said, 'Just a minute, I am busy, I am speaking to Brian.' He grabbed her by the shoulder and pushed her out of the room and I heard the sound of a blow. She took him up to the [empty] flat and a few seconds afterwards I heard the sound of a blow and she fell down the stairs, bruising herself severely. She told me that she never wanted to see him again but he kept ringing and ringing on the telephone and in the end she answered.[49]

A regular witness to David's abuse, Jacqueline feared that he would kill Ruth one day. She told police that he had come close to it when, during an argument, he had squeezed her neck and lifted her up: 'I always would have thought it would be more him, than her.'[50]

*

Ruth gave David and Desmond identical presents that Christmas: silver cigarette cases. David had arranged to spend Christmas Day in Penn with his family, leaving Ruth free to throw a small party that evening at Goodwood Court. Desmond was duty-bound to attend his work's cocktail party but would be back before 9 p.m., when the guests were told to arrive. Jacqueline turned up early with a businessman friend, Bob Dykehouse, and asked Ruth to join them at a club. They left shortly after 7 p.m., Ruth giggling as she told them about the cigarette cases. She pinned a note with the telephone number of the club to the door for the benefit of any other early revellers and left ten-year-old Andre sleeping in bed, alone in the flat.

David was already on his way to London. He hadn't enjoyed his day in Penn, where his mother and stepfather had gone to a neighbour's house for drinks that morning. He visited The Crown instead, which was largely empty apart from a colleague at Sylicum Pistons. The two men called in at their workplace, where the colleague produced a bottle of rye and they continued drinking. At some point David telephoned Ruth at Desmond's flat, but she made it clear she had nothing to say to him. He invited his colleague to Old Park and they shared a bottle of Pernod before the man had to leave. After a late lunch with his mother, stepfather, brothers Brian and Derek, and Derek's wife Helen and their three children, David left for a second visit to The Crown with Brian. Despite the amount of alcohol in his bloodstream, David then drove his sister-in-law and young nieces and nephew home before heading on to London. In his jacket was a Christmas present for Andre: a toy gun.

It was Andre who let David into the flat. Fuming after reading the note on the door, he gave the boy his present before telephoning the club. When Ruth came on the line, he shouted that she was an unfit mother for leaving Andre alone in the flat, despite knowing perfectly well that she had done the same thing when they had gone drinking together. Desmond was at the club with Ruth and recalled:

> [David] said he was waiting to see us. We arrived back about
> 9 p.m. and found him in the flat, very much the worse for

drink. He had brought Ruth's little boy a Christmas present. A row started between Blakely and Ruth. Apparently they had spoken on the phone earlier that day. She said she had not expected to see him. He said he had been getting into a bad state since he knew she had moved into my flat. Ruth seemed to be worried that he might do something stupid, owing to his condition.[51]

Ruth's anger matched David's own:

He was drunk and unpleasant in front of my friends, calling me a liar . . . he said in front of all our friends 'I am a poor twisted boy and she's the one that's made me twisted. The girl I love sleeping with another man. It's her fault' . . . It was most unpleasant and completely spoiled the party.[52]

As with most drunken rows, this one ended up being about something else entirely: David's affair with Carole. Ruth accused him of continuing to sleep with her, which David dismissed as rubbish before suggesting they drive to Tanza Road to ask Carole herself. To the astonishment of the assembled guests, the couple then drove off in David's car, still arguing heatedly. Desmond immediately climbed into his Ford Zodiac and pursued them to Hampstead, where he glimpsed David letting himself and Ruth into the Findlaters' flat with the key Ant and Carole had given him; they were spending Christmas in Bournemouth. Desmond waited, but it was soon plain that the couple had no intention of leaving the flat before morning. He drove home slowly, knowing he would have to explain Ruth's absence to her son and their guests.

Ruth arrived at Goodwood Court the following morning – Boxing Day – with a story already prepared. Desmond recalled:

She told me that Blakely had been in such a state and wanted her to return to him so, in order to humour him, she had agreed to do so for one evening. He had threatened to do some harm to himself if she did not go back to him.[53]

Whether Desmond believed the tale or not, Ruth excused herself again later that day to watch David debut the Emperor in the Kent Cup at Brands Hatch. He finished a very respectable second to John

Coombs's Lotus MKVIII, then regarded as probably the fastest 1500 cc sports car in Britain. A photograph shows Ruth smiling gamely in the cold, a picnic rug about her shoulders, David tinkering with the Emperor to her left. The subsequent press coverage was glowing: *Autosport* called it 'a splendid debut for the promising new Emperor', while *The Motor* described the car as 'an impressive challenger'.[54] David and Ant threw themselves into preparing the car for the season ahead and even discussed putting it into limited production.

Boxing Day provided a mere lull in the vicious fights between Ruth and David. She captured one argument for posterity, presumably just as a curiosity, using the tape recorder Desmond had given her that Christmas. It opens with the laughter and chatter of a party. What follows is a hopelessly inebriated conversation between Ruth and David, who attempts to explain his activities on Christmas Day but stumbles over his words and loses his train of thought. An extract from the transcript (filed at the National Archives) illustrates the rambling bickering so typical of the two of them after excessive drinking:

> David: 'I bath and have a shave and I go down to the local pub, I go down to the local pub and what happens: I get stinking flipping drunk there on gin. I then go home – no, I don't actually. After that I go up to the factory and I phone to Mrs Ellis. Mrs Ellis says, "No, Desmond's out. I'm in bed."' *Pause.* 'No, that was last night. Desmond's not in yet.' *Pause.* 'No, no, no, it wasn't. I'm sorry. I'm wrong.'
>
> Ruth (*sarcastically*): 'You're wrong. You're wrong. I thank you very much indeed.'
>
> David: 'That was the night before I phoned up and you said you were in bed.'
>
> Ruth: 'Thank you. I thought –'
>
> David: 'I beg your pardon.' *Pause.* 'Anyway, that is my movements for yesterday. No movements today.'
>
> Ruth: 'Thank you, Mr Blakely, very much indeed.' *She addresses a friend:* 'Come along, Bob Dyke. What were you doing yesterday?'
>
> David (*interrupting*): 'If you like to put it on record, just as you've been known to outside, my movements.' *There is a break in the tape, then David speaks again:* ' . . . Flipping playpen, as my

eldest brother had to go wherever it was – Nairobi or something – at 5.30 this morning.' *Pause.* 'I then come back. I have dinner with my brother, my mother and my stepfather, my sister-in-law, my two nieces and nephew. And after that . . . they've got a licence 'til 4 o'clock. So Brian and I walked in there and what happened? They said, "Ah, jolly good, will you help us?" So we said, "Yes" and we got loaded . . . I went back to Old Park and we had tea, then—'

Ruth: 'You had tea? You went to the factory, you mean.'

David: 'No, to home.'

Ruth: 'Oh, I see.'

David: 'And Brian. And then I ran—'

Ruth: 'You ran whoever you were with, home.'

David: 'Yes. My sister-in-law, her three flipping children and her flipping playpen.' *Pause.* 'All right, if you think it's . . . I'm wasting my time telling you the truth. Don't you . . . because you won't ever believe it. Because I never believe the truth you say.'

Ruth: 'Right, have you finished the story now?'

David: 'No, I haven't finished the story. If you want to know, put it all down, go ahead.'

Ruth: 'What did you do Christmas Day – and tell the truth?'

David: 'You don't want to know because you know bloody well I'm telling the truth and it upsets you.'

Ruth: 'Right, well, come on.'

David: 'I think you're one of the biggest bloody liars I've ever met in my life. You can put *that* on record, too.'

Ruth: 'Right, thanks very much. Well, that's all we need from you.'[55]

They squabble back and forth before David, increasingly angry, tells Ruth:

Come on, continue your showing off, Mrs Ellis, and changing your subject. I hope you're finding it interesting . . . And this, ladies and gentlemen, Jackie and Bob, is typical Ruth. She will always change the subject when she's in a tight corner, and that's a flipping lot. Bless you, Ruth, and good luck to you . . . This is what's commonly known as true confessions . . . I'm really drunk.[56]

At the end of the tape, either ignoring David or speaking after he has left, Ruth declares in a voice bubbling with laughter:

> This is Ruth Ellis wishing you a Merry Christmas and a Happy New Year. May Jackie make all the tips she can at the bar and may Ruth have a new coat in the New Year! And may Desmond have all he wants in the New Year![57]

There is a second transcript, of a recording between Ruth and Desmond in which they discuss events over the holidays. On New Year's Eve, David had invited Ruth for a drink at The Crown in Penn, but if she thought it was a precursor to meeting his family, she was mistaken. They set off in high spirits: Ruth playfully dabbed Miss Dior behind David's ears as they left for Penn. But as they drew up outside the large, ivy-clad pub opposite the war memorial, David spied his mother and put his foot down, driving on to the Red Lion in the centre of the village. They had a few drinks with his colleagues from Sylicum Pistons before heading back to The Crown. Ruth waited in the car as instructed while David went inside the pub and spoke to his mother. Unwilling to introduce the two women, he hovered anxiously until his mother was distracted and then returned to the car with two drinks. Ruth knew perfectly well why David didn't want her in the pub, although he tried to joke about it at first, telling her that when he kissed his mother and wished her Happy New Year, she remarked on how nice he smelled. But inevitably a quarrel followed, as Ruth recounted to Desmond on tape: 'David gave me a black eye, sitting in a car park on New Year's night in Penn, Buckinghamshire, at the Crown Hotel.'[58] The row caused them to split up again.

Ruth's complex emotions are manifest in the tape recording with Desmond. Plainly very drunk, she attempts to apologise for not having been honest about her meetings with David:

> Ruth: 'You know something?'
> Desmond: 'What, darling?'
> Ruth: 'When he said he left me, I really believed it. I should have known better, you know.'
> Desmond: 'Don't worry about it, darling.'
> Ruth: 'I feel awful guilty about it all . . . everything, actually.' *She starts to sing 'Answer Me, My Love', recorded by Frankie Laine in*

1953 and a major hit in the US for Nat King Cole in 1954: 'Answer me, oh my love/Just what sin have I been guilty of/Tell me how I came to lose my love/Please answer me, oh Lord.' *Pause.* 'I think that's nice.' *She sings again:* 'He was mine yesterday/I believed that love was here to stay/Tell me, tell me, where I've gone astray/Please answer me, oh Lord/If he's happier without me.' *Pause.* 'I wonder if he still cares . . . ? Do you feel that too? Oh, I'm sorry, oh dear, what a nuisance. I still think my new record's better – *I Believe*. Wonder how [Faith] Roberts is getting on . . . I know what her number is. That Roberts girl, lives in that stinking little dump at the back of Euston Station, in case Mama [David's mother] doesn't know.' *Suddenly she exclaims:* 'No, seriously, Desmond, all joking aside, I think I've been a fool. I was living with that drip eighteen months. Can you imagine it?'

Desmond: 'God, was it as long as all that?'

Ruth: 'Mmm. Bit much, wasn't it?'

Desmond: 'No wonder you're looking haggard, dear.'

Ruth: 'Do I really look haggard? Do I really? Seriously?'

Desmond: 'Mmm.'

Ruth: 'Oh, shut up or I'll give you a black eye . . . I'm still glad it's all over and done with anyway. No, seriously. He's a cheapskate. I think he'd fuck anything, don't you . . . ?'

Desmond: 'Darling, I don't know. I'm not worried in the least about it.'

Ruth: 'Neither am I. I'm rather annoyed, because he's so bloody conceited. But apart from that . . . I'm not worrying about it really. I shall spit at him across the room one day. Or throw a soda syphon all over him. I'd love to do it in a crowded room one day, walk in and say, "Ha, ha, there's my friend Blakely," and squirt the soda syphon of water all over him and make him look silly.'

Desmond: 'Mm. Bit unladylike, would it have been? I'll excuse you for being unladylike.'

Ruth: 'Can you? Do you mind? Do you know what I thought of doing? I thought of taking my flat back again and throwing a party. Building up the Little Club again . . . Isn't it amazing how you can find out somebody? How low, how rotten they really are, basically. You don't really find out, you don't really know . . .

He's the lowest of the low. Just a little skunk. Rotten to the core . . . Anybody can have him as far as I'm concerned. He's just a drip. How he has the nerve to call himself the social life of Buckinghamshire I wouldn't know. If that's social life, God help the man. God help the working class . . . As Miss [Vicki] Martin would say, "Gosh dear, you've done it now." Oh dear.' *She breaks into 'I Still Believe', changing the lyrics:* 'I still believe we were meant for each other/I still believe he'll poke some other.' *She bursts into giggles.*

Desmond: 'Go to sleep, darling.'

Ruth (*snapping*): 'Oh, shut up.'

Desmond: 'Do you want me here?'

Ruth (*placating*): 'Yes, darling.'[59]

Before the tape spools to its end, she begins talking about David again. There was clearly no respite from her thoughts about him. The recording ends with Ruth's high, drunken laughter.[60]

Ruth had referred to her best friend Vicki Martin, who was still enjoying the high life but remained in constant touch. Cooch Behar had commissioned society artist Vasco Lazzolo to paint her portrait; he expected to collect it when he returned from India the following summer, but Vicki decided to sit for it immediately. She attended several parties over Christmas and made an unforgettable entrance at one thrown by her friend Freda Ferrier, who recalled:

> The last time we all saw Vickie was when she came walking down the staircase at our New Year's Eve party. She was dressed in a top hat, white tie and tails. She had these wonderful long legs in black tights. She looked absolutely stunning. As she swept down the stairs everyone held their breath for a moment and just stared.[61]

Nineteen fifty-five was the last New Year that Vicki and Ruth – and David – would ever celebrate. Within four months, all three were dead.

12

Ruth and David were reconciled in early January, spending more nights together at the Rodney. Ruth said nothing to Desmond, but he was not so obtuse as his silence led her to suppose. 'She continued to live at my flat until about the middle of February,' he told police. 'While she was still with me, she went out with Blakely. I had seen it. Blakely would phone to say he had come to take her out. She did not always tell me where she was going.'[1] He knew that she hoped to convince him she felt only pity for David:

> She said after all she had lived with him for two years and that he was still very much in love with her. I did not object to their association, as I felt rather sorry for the fellow. I spoke to her on one or two occasions about going out with him and leaving her child alone in the flat, especially as she stayed away with him for one or two weekends.[2]

Ruth's world revolved around David, and more so when she finished working her notice at the Little Club.

Despite swearing to friends that whenever he tried to leave Ruth she 'creates a scene and forces me back', David continued to pursue her.[3] He often telephoned from Penn in the evening, first at 10 p.m. and again in the early hours of the morning. He rang from a telephone box near the post office, telling Ruth he was on his way home from a Penn nightclub, but she knew that there was no such place in the village. Eventually he let slip that after closing time at The Crown he called in on a friend who lived at the Old Vicarage; he once telephoned Ruth during the day to say he was having an early night and wouldn't be visiting this 'friend'. Ruth instantly smelled a rat: 'I told Desmond that I wanted to catch David out once and for all and that I wanted him to drive me to Penn. I went straight to David's garage and his car was not there.'[4] They drove on to the Old Vicarage, where David emerged in the early hours, just as she had expected. When she asked him the next day how he felt after his early night, he grumbled, 'Awful.'[5] She said nothing about having driven to Penn the night before.

Ruth made a few enquiries and discovered that David was having an affair with Pam Abbott, a 30-year-old ex-actress whose husband often worked away from home; she lived in the Old Vicarage. Months later, Mrs Abbott was questioned by police, who noted that she and David often met for lunch and a game of darts in The Crown: 'This lady says she has known David Blakely and his family for many years, and that he occasionally visited her house, sometimes to talk business with Mr Borti, his employer [who also lived at the Old Vicarage], or to see her family.'[6] But when Ruth and David met at the Rodney on 8 January 1954, she told him she knew about the affair and wanted to meet Mrs Abbott. Panicked, David managed to convince her there was nothing in it, and they spent the night peaceably together. He left the next morning, having told Ruth that he had an important meeting at Sylicum Pistons but would ring her that afternoon. When he failed to call then or the following day, Ruth telephoned Old Park continually, her index finger with its manicured nail repeatedly turning the numbers on the dial: Penn 3157. Finally, David answered. Ruth told him that she intended to visit, not only to see Mrs Abbott, but also to speak to his mother. He replaced the receiver and ignored her calls. She then telegrammed him at Sylicum Pistons to demand: 'Haven't you got the guts to say goodbye to my face – Ruth.'[7]

David retreated to The Crown. Landlord George Beesley had known the Blakelys for years and listened sympathetically to him. In the subsequent police report, Beesley spoke highly of his friend:

> He is convinced that [David] was trying to shake off this woman, who was pestering him and of whom he was frightened. He knows Blakely had a high regard for Mrs Abbott and her family, and he would be prepared to sacrifice himself by remaining friendly with this woman rather than anything unpleasant should happen to Mrs Abbott.[8]

After moping at the bar in Penn, David drove to Hampstead, where

Ant and Carole were more perplexed than sympathetic about the situation with Ruth, asking: 'Could you, with your background, really be happy with this common tart?'[9]

In turn, Ruth sought out Vicki, then living in style at Cadogan Place, to discuss David. The two friends spent an evening together and the shock was all the greater when within days Ruth heard the news that Vicki had been killed in a car crash just outside Maidenhead on 9 January. Initially, both *The Times* and the *News Chronicle* claimed that Vicki was at the wheel, with journalist Terence Robertson a passenger. The *Maidenhead Advertiser* reported otherwise: 'The police have established that Miss Valerie Mewes, 23 year-old model better known as Vickie Martin, was not driving the car in which she was killed.' It transpired that in the early hours of the morning she and Robertson left a restaurant near Henley-on-Thames and were driving home when their car collided with another on the Henley Road. The 41-year-old driver of the other vehicle died instantly; his wife suffered multiple facial fractures. Vicki and Robertson were transferred to Maidenhead Hospital: he had a broken leg and amnesia but Vicki's injuries were horrific and she died soon after being admitted. The press reported that it was her 13th car crash.

The inquest into Vicki's death opened on 11 January and was adjourned until 2 March; the results were not made public. A funeral service was held at the West Chapel, Golders Green Crematorium, on 14 January, with press photographers snapping the many rich and titled people in attendance, including Prince Philip's cousin, the Marquess of Milford Haven. Cooch Behar remained in India. He sent a vast wreath of red roses with a card: 'Goodbye to Méchante. My love always, Tigre.' A year after Vicki's death he married her friend Gina Egan and kept his royal allowance. Stephen Ward recalled that one famous figure was so overcome by Vicki's death that he collapsed. Following the service at Golders Green, Vicki's ashes were interred in a private ceremony at Englefield Green, where the cemetery was covered in thick snow. Film producer Kenneth Harper was there, together with Stephen Ward, who comforted Vicki's grandmother and visited her for years afterwards.

In *An Affair of State: The Profumo Case and the Framing of Stephen Ward* (1987), writers Kennedy and Knightley observe: 'Ward's search for someone as enchanting and unusual as Vickie Martin, his first "Fair Lady", was to contribute to his downfall.'[10] Ward's biographers agree:

In the oddest way, Vicki Martin was a marker for the quicksand of Ward's future. Three years after her death, when Martin's name came up in conversation, another young protégée would exclaim, 'I was at school with her sister!' The girl's name was Christine Keeler.[11]

Losing Vicki distressed Ruth so much that she became ill; later she asked Muriel and Bertha if they had read about the crash. Moreover, on the day of Vicki's funeral, George Ellis was granted a decree nisi and Ruth was told to expect her divorce to be made absolute within six weeks. She no longer loved George – if she ever did – but it was still a blatant reminder of her marriage having failed dismally. She clung to the hope that her relationship with David would end happily, despite her parents asking her to leave him. Months later, Bertha and Arthur Neilson spoke briefly to the prison doctor about this period. He recorded:

> Prisoner allowed [George] to get a divorce on grounds of deceased. [David] was a playboy – spoilt. He used to knock prisoner about. Parents have seen her with black eye and leg in plaster . . . Mother says her daughter expected to marry deceased that is why she had the divorce. They had advised her to keep on with Desmond instead. She said no – she knew her own mind.[12]

But on the evening of Vicki's funeral and the granting of the decree nisi, Ruth and David had a bitter row at the Rodney, during which David taunted her about Vicki: 'That's how you'll end up.'[13]

Tenaciously, Ruth fought for their relationship to work. On Monday, 17 January 1955, she began a course of lessons with the French Institute in Kensington. Jacqueline Dyer recalls that Ruth was motivated by a belief that it would make her more socially acceptable to David's inner circle:

> She thought that they were going to get married . . . when she left the Little Club she was going to learn French to come up to his standard socially and they were going to get married and then they'd be all right.[14]

Cliff Davis confirmed: 'I think that David put her in promised land. I knew his [step]father. He wouldn't have sanctioned a marriage between them. I think he would have cut off the bread.'[15]

The social gulf between the couple grew more pronounced. David told everyone he was broke, but the safety net of familial wealth, few bills to pay and a choice of luxurious homes was ever present; it was a rich boy's version of what it meant to be poor – a world away from the destitution Ruth had known and feared again. Her hard-won security evaporated when she left the Little Club, and she was dependent upon Desmond for a roof over her and ten-year-old Andre's heads. Britain was then mired in 'class consciousness'.[16] When *The People* ran a questionnaire in 1951 asking readers to identify their place in society, 90 per cent of the 11,000 respondents did so unflinchingly. Labour MP Anthony Crosland wrote: 'Class feeling, and general social *malaise*, still persist in England to a deplorable extent. Britain still is, and feels itself to be, a class society.'[17] A person's 'class' was demonstrated in numerous, telling ways: where they lived, where they shopped, where they went to work and where they had gone to school, the newspapers they bought, their choice of entertainment and the sporting events they followed, etc. Social acceptance relied on people behaving in a certain manner and everyone knowing their place despite the vibrations of approaching change. Sex was another factor, inextricably linked to class in the films, books and plays of the 1950s, where it was often the currency that enabled a character to climb another rung of the social ladder. In London's clubs and bars, the facile blurring of class boundaries only lasted for the length of time it took one of the Mayfair set to bed a hostess. Otherwise it proved mostly insurmountable, largely because of the 'distinctly sniffy attitude of the middle class'.[18] The year when the impact of both the Profumo affair and the rapid ascent of the Beatles undermined the Establishment and began breaking down traditional class structures, 1963, was a long way off.

At 3 p.m. on 17 January, Mrs Marie Therese Harris arrived at Goodwood Court to give Ruth her first lesson in French. She recalled Ruth asking if she might pay by cheque since 'her husband' did not have enough cash on him to cover the course fees; Ruth then left the room and returned 'followed by a man whom she introduced as her husband. We shook hands and then he handed me a cheque.'[19] It was signed D.E. Cussen.

The two women worked for an hour, with Ruth unable to refrain from discussing David even then. 'She mentioned that she and her husband were interested in a new racing car which he was building with another man and to be driven by a man named David Blakely,' Mrs Harris remembered:

> She showed me some photographs of a racing car in a motor magazine with David Blakely driving this car. I did not see Blakely. In my idea Ruth Ellis was either living with or married to Desmond Cussen and I thought she might have been a professional woman keeping her single name for business purposes. When I began to teach Ellis, she told me that she had taken a month's holiday from her work as she felt that she would become a nervous wreck due to overwork. I thought that she looked like a person on the verge of a breakdown and had stopped working just in time.[20]

Mrs Harris visited Goodwood Court a second time on 20 January. Ruth was absent and it was Andre – presumably off school due to some illness since it was term time – who let her into the flat. Ruth failed to appear and there was no sign of her 'husband', but Mrs Harris had reason to recall the visit nonetheless. She asked Andre for his mother's exercise book, which she marked and dated for the next lesson. While chatting to Andre, she mentioned how irritated she and her husband were by the noise of pigeons where they lived.

His response shocked her. Mrs Harris informed police several weeks later:

> He said, 'What you want is a gun,' and with that he opened the drawer of the table on which I was writing. In the drawer I noticed, among other things, two guns, which at first I thought were toys. He handed one, the larger one, then said, 'It's all right, it's not loaded.' Then he put it back and closed the drawer and I left the flat.[21]

*

Modernity was finally catching up with Britain by 1955. Meat and bacon rationing had ended in July the previous year and in Trafalgar Square there had been a celebratory ripping up of ration books. Plans were in place to build 12 nuclear power stations, and railways were earmarked for electrification, with steam trains to be gradually phased out. Cars were becoming more prevalent and Britain was coming round to the American idea of hire purchase. 'Another Boom Year Is Here!' declared the *News Chronicle* in early 1955, and announced that 80 per cent of people could expect to earn as much if not more than they had in 1954: 'In booming, buoyant Britain, people are getting ready for a spending spree in which millions will be poured out on TVs, cars, houses, washing machines and refrigerators.'[22] Life was difficult for the 46,850 immigrants arriving between 1955 and 1956 from the Commonwealth who faced an uphill struggle to secure work; a television documentary in January asked: 'Has Britain A Colour Bar?' Typically, the weather brought misery to millions: snow returned in February, with 60 mph blizzards in parts of the country, blocking roads and halting rail travel.

On 26 January, Ruth had her second lesson at last with Mrs Harris at Goodwood Court. The following day, she and David embarked on a lengthy drinking spree. She called briefly at Desmond's flat on 31 January but had gone by the time Mrs Harris arrived for their third French lesson. She spent two more nights with David at the Rodney that week, having told Desmond she was visiting an ill friend. He called in at the Steering Wheel Club and saw her there, drinking with David, but said nothing to either of them. Back at Goodwood Court, he found a crumpled hotel bill for 'Mr and Mrs Blakely' in his wastepaper basket.

Ruth returned to the flat the following day. There were two consecutive French lessons that week, on Wednesday, 2 February, and Thursday, 3 February. In her statement, Mrs Harris told police:

> I remember quite clearly that Ruth Ellis was suffering from extensive bruising, including a left eye, and a bad bruise on the left arm and leg, some time prior to 7th February. This could only have been on 2nd or 3rd February. She had then told me that she had been involved in a car accident.[23]

The following day Desmond drove past the Rodney Hotel and spotted David's car parked outside; he had no illusions that Ruth would stay away from the place. When he went by again some time later, the car was still there.

On the evening of Sunday, 6 February 1955, violence spiralled again. Ruth recalled:

> David drove me back to Desmond's flat. We had been out all day and David had been drinking without eating for about twelve hours. He insisted on coming in for a final drink. Then he wanted me to go off with him but I was too tired. In fact, we'd both had too much to drink. We had a row. Suddenly he lost all control. His fist struck me between the eyes and I fell to the floor. Savagely he beat me as I lay there. I tried to get to the door. David threw me to the floor again. Then he had the nerve to pretend that I would not let him go and he phoned his friends.[24]

David left the flat (in which a telephone was installed) to call Ant, who was out with Clive. He spoke to Carole and gave her Desmond's number, imploring her to make sure Ant called him as soon as he arrived home. He then returned to the flat. When Ant rang a short while later, David answered and said urgently, 'She's taken the keys to my car, will you come and get me?'[25] It was a ridiculous situation; Ruth could hardly be said to be refusing to let him leave when he had managed to slip out to a public call box and then returned to the flat under his own volition.

But Ant and Clive hastened to Goodwood Court, where they found Ruth with a severe black eye, hobbling about on a badly sprained ankle. David's face was scratched and he too had a black eye. They were both extremely drunk. 'She's an absolute bitch, she tried to knife me,' David said loudly.[26] Then he showed Ant and Clive a long scratch on his arm, adding, 'I want to break off with her but she won't let me go.'[27] Ruth made several scornful remarks about David's courage and then everything became confused; what happened outside the flat is unclear. In one version of events, the three men got into Ant's car and Ruth leaned through the window to prevent them leaving. They then got out again and Clive kept Ruth talking while Ant nodded for David to drive off in his own car. According to another account, David made it to his car while Ant and Clive were examining Ruth's injuries but she noticed his absence and ran after him, somehow able to oust David from the driver's seat and sit there herself; the three men then climbed into Ant's car and she attempted to stop them driving away, lying down in the road only for David to escape in his own car. Whatever the precise nature of events, ultimately David drove off alone. Clive and Ant took Ruth for a coffee at a cafe in Great Portland Street before seeing her back to Goodwood Court. There she told Desmond (who must have been absent earlier in the evening) her version of what had happened, insisting that David had beaten her because she refused to live with him again. She then limped off to bed.

That night, Ruth asked Desmond to drive her to Tanza Road, where David had shown Ant, Carole and Clive a number of abrasions on his back. Carole remarked that he would be a fool to return to Ruth if that's what she had done and advised him to view it as a warning. Ruth and Desmond arrived just in time to see them leaving by car. Ruth remarked again on David's inability to fight his battles alone, while Desmond followed them at a safe distance. He parked a short way from the Magdala Tavern, a Charrington's public house at the foot of South Hill Park. The group remained there until closing time, when David drove off by himself again. Ruth was certain he intended to spend the night with Faith Roberts. They drove back to Goodwood Court, where she telephoned a friend for Faith's address. She asked Desmond to drive her there, but it was the wrong flat, and she urged him to make the journey on to Penn, where she hobbled down the driveway of Old Park and rang the bell to David's flat. Desmond recalled: 'She went alone to his house and I waited outside. Apparently he was in bed but he dressed and spoke to her. He then drove off in his car.'[28] Ruth waited with Desmond for David to return, but she was too slow on her injured ankle to catch up with him when he made a dash for the house. She rang the doorbell again, but there was no answer and Desmond persuaded her to get back into the car, telling her firmly that they were going home.

Ruth was exhausted and distraught by the time they reached Goodwood Court. Desmond helped her into bed and noticed the injuries she had sustained the night before. He was appalled, but suggested Ruth should try to sleep for a while at least. She was unable to close her eyes for more than a few minutes and got up, refusing breakfast. Desmond wanted to take her to hospital, but she was only interested in driving back to Penn to get an apology from David. She telephoned Sylicum Pistons but was told he wasn't available and handed the receiver to Desmond. He advised the person who had answered that it would be better for Mr Blakely if he spoke to Ruth, but David declined to take the call. Replacing the receiver, Desmond agreed to drive Ruth back to Penn.

Motoring through the village of Gerrard's Cross, Ruth spotted David's car parked outside The Bull inn; she had visited the pub with David shortly before Christmas, when he had introduced her as his girlfriend to the barman. Desmond pulled the Ford Zodiac into the car park, his temper spoiled. Ruth remained in the car while he strode into the pub to confront David, who was sat at the bar. Dennis Tovell, the cocktail bar attendant, recalled: '[Cussen] went straight up to David, grabbed hold of his lapels and said, "Come on, you bastard, outside." David said nothing but went outside with the little man.'[29] Desmond demanded that he apologise to Ruth for his behaviour, but disingenuously David responded, 'What am I supposed to say?'[30]

'Do you normally go around knocking women about?' Desmond asked. 'As far as I am concerned she has every right to take police action against you.'[31]

At this, David walked across to the car and told Ruth that he was sorry. Desmond was sufficiently het up to challenge his rival: 'Well, here's your opportunity. What about hitting a man instead of a woman?' But David was in no mood to brawl and replied, 'You're stronger than I am. I wouldn't fight you. You're bigger than I am anyway.' Although this last remark was plainly untrue, Desmond allowed it to pass, murmuring, 'You're a gutless little bastard.'[32]

Ruth spoke up then, shaking her head: 'This is no good.' She looked at David and said decisively, 'I am going to see your mother.'[33]

Her threat was effective: David immediately apologised again, more heartfelt than before. Ruth then asked what he had done with all the money she had given him. They argued for a while until she cut him off with the words, 'You've broken my ankle and I'm going to see your mother about it.' Exasperated now, David walked away in disgust, shouting over his shoulder: 'I've got an appointment in London and you've made me late already.'[34]

Incensed and determined to carry out her threat, Ruth asked Desmond to drive her to Penn. On the way he was able to point out that she had won her apology and that a confrontation with David's mother was not in Ruth's best interests if she still harboured a desire to marry him. She saw the logic in this and did not demur when he suggested they should have her injuries properly examined instead.

Ruth's ankle was X-rayed at Middlesex Hospital on Mortimer

Street. A police report later recorded that she had been seen by Dr Robert Hunter Hill on 7 February 1955 at the Casualty Department:

> When the doctor first saw her she was in a wheelchair and gave her name as Ruth Ellis. The doctor says she was suffering from multiple bruises on her right arm, left arm, left hip, both legs and she had a black left eye. The only bruise of any severity was over the left ankle, which caused her some difficulty in walking. Her chest and abdomen were examined but this examination revealed no trace of internal injury. Her left ankle was X-rayed but no injury to the bone could be found. The doctor continued that these bruises could have been caused by any sort of blunt instrument, and when the doctor asked her how she had received these injuries, she told him she had been beaten up by her friend who was a racing car driver. After treatment for these bruises she was told to return to the hospital in three days but the doctor says, according to his notes, she was not seen again.[35]

According to Desmond, Ruth 'thought of taking Court proceedings against [David] but decided not to do so because there might have been a lot of mud-slinging'.[36] When they arrived at the flat, her parents were there. She told them she had been in an accident, but they were not fooled. Later that day a vast spray of red carnations was delivered to Goodwood Court with a card: 'Sorry, darling. I love you, David.'[37] Ruth agreed to meet him that evening and he managed to persuade her that his behaviour was down to frustration at her living arrangements; if only they could find somewhere together, he told her, then all would be well. Ruth wanted to believe him. She knew that he was 'morbidly jealous' of Desmond and decided to look for alternative accommodation.[38]

Mrs Harris telephoned while Ruth was out; she had called at the flat earlier to give Ruth her lesson but found no one home. She spoke to Desmond, who apologised for not having been able to contact her beforehand and explained that her pupil was suffering from a broken ankle. When Ruth arrived home that night, she and Desmond discussed her decision to leave, which she couched in less contentious terms. He recalled: 'She considered that it was not fair to me to be involved in such matters and so decided to look for a room elsewhere.'[39] He agreed to lend her the deposit for a flat, and told her to retain her keys, since she would always be welcome. Ruth promised to return regularly to cook for him and omitted to mention that she was moving in with David until some time later. He described his reaction then: 'I asked her why she allowed it but she did not give any real answer . . . I advised her to see a solicitor about him pestering her. She said she did not want to do that.'[40]

On Tuesday, 8 February 1955, Ruth took a taxi to Egerton Gardens in Kensington, a quiet street of tall red buildings just around the corner from Harrods (and a short walk from the Little Club). Ruth knocked on the door of No.44, which consisted of 14 decently furnished service rooms, owned by a Mrs Kerr and run by Mrs Joan Winstanley and Miss Elizabeth Riley. Ruth spoke to Mrs Winstanley and was surprised when the middle-aged housekeeper explained that she had once owned a club in South Kensington. Ruth introduced herself as Mrs Ellis and requested Room 5 for herself and her 'husband' in the motor world.[41] The rent was approximately £7 per week, with extras including breakfast in bed. Mrs Winstanley recalled:

> The accused paid the rent, in advance . . . When the accused took the room in February, it was for an indefinite period . . . During the ten days before her arrest, that is from 1st April onwards, I think the man I knew as David Ellis was staying there at night. So far as I know, there was no difference in their habits of occupation in the week before Easter.[42]

Yet even while Ruth was making arrangements at Egerton Gardens, David was disparaging her at The Bull at Gerrard's Cross, where Dennis Tovell remembered his arrival early that evening. When Tovell asked how things went the day before, David replied airily, 'Oh that, I've finished with that.'[43] Occasionally David called at the pub again, but Tovell never saw him with Ruth, or at all in the week before the shooting. Quite apart from his words at The Bull, if proof were needed that David had little intention of settling down with Ruth, then his affairs with other women attest to his lack of commitment. His relationship with Faith Roberts was certainly ongoing, and then there was the affair in Penn. In addition, he began dating another girl only six weeks before his death. The Findlaters introduced him to the girl, who later corresponded with Marks and Van den Bergh, telling them she, too, had witnessed marks on David's body: 'When he undressed, there were livid gashes in his arms and back. I asked him where he'd got them. He said, "It was that bitch. She tried to knife me. And that wasn't the first time."[44] The girl claimed that Ruth was 'very violent' when 'on drugs and drink' but admitted she had never actually met her.[45]

The relationship was irretrievably broken, but neither Ruth nor David was quite ready to give up on it completely. They had both come to rely on medication. Ruth is said to have visited Dr Rees in Warlingham, where she was prescribed another course of the tranquilisers she had taken for several years. David used amyl nitrate, which his doctor later testified on oath had not been issued by his surgery, nor did his patient require them for respiratory difficulties. Cliff Davis confirmed in interviews after the shooting that David depended upon the drug to heighten his performance during sexual intercourse. It is certainly true that he was a bundle of neuroses at this time; Carole Findlater afterwards stated that she noticed a marked change in him. He alternated between wanting Ruth and loathing her; often his instinct was to avoid her at all costs, but on other occasions he pursued her ceaselessly, even when she tried to push him away. He wore a permanent expression of anxiety and told Carole that Ruth was behind a beating inflicted on him at Culross Street by gangsters, which may or may not have been true. He also began telling anyone willing to listen: 'Ruth is madly in love with me, but I hate her guts.'[46]

In this maelstrom of emotion, Ruth moved into Egerton Gardens, intending to build a future there with David Blakely. Mrs Winstanley recalled:

> After taking the room she wanted the furniture moved round and borrowed a flower vase. She remarked that her husband Mr Ellis was very particular about having flowers in the room. She took up residence on 9 February 1955 with a slightly-built, dark-haired man about 5 ft 8 ins tall, aged about 27. I accepted this man as Mr Ellis and throughout her tenancy she referred to him as such. I later discovered that his Christian name was David and that he was a racing car driver. They appeared to be an average married couple. On most mornings they used to have a breakfast tray of tea and toast which I used to take up to their room twice a week. I always found them in bed together. Later

in the morning Mr Ellis would leave in his grey and green car to go to work. Mrs Ellis also told me that they wanted only a room in London for use during the week as they were in the habit of spending weekends in the country . . . I didn't know much about their private lives and thought that they really were husband and wife. The room was rented until Monday 11 April 1955. The rent was always paid in advance by Mrs Ellis.[47]

Mrs Winstanley liked Ruth and found David 'pleasant', but was less keen on Desmond, who struck her as surly when he called for Ruth each morning to spend time with her after 'Mr Ellis had gone to work'.[48]

A fortnight after the move, Ruth and David had another violent row about his relationship with Pam Abbott. Ruth sustained severe bruising on one side of her face and about her shoulders, presumably where David had gripped her. When Desmond tackled him about it, David protested that he had been defending himself from Ruth, who had tried to hit him with a bottle of gin. The following day, Mrs Harris called at Goodwood Court, where Ruth was waiting. She recalled:

I gave her a normal lesson. After this she told me that she would be busy for a few days and would contact me in the near future to fix another lesson. Throughout my visits to her flat I found that Ruth Ellis was utterly unable to concentrate. I thought she was a good businesswoman but in my dealings with her she was nervy and unsettled. She used to talk at great length but on the occasion of my last visit I realised that she would not have progressed in her studies and on 5 March 1955 I wrote to her and told her that I felt that it would be a waste of time to go on with the lessons and sent a cheque to refund the unearned fee which I had been paid.[49]

David failed to arrive at Egerton Gardens as expected the day after Ruth's final French lesson. Ruth telephoned Desmond to ask him to drive her to Penn. 'We went down together in the evening,' he remembered, 'and found him in The Crown public house. I went in, as she asked me to see whom he was with. I found him drinking with a few men and a woman.'[50] David was playing darts with a group of friends that included Mr Borti from Sylicum Pistons, and Pam Abbott. In her statement to the police, Mrs Abbott recalled that shortly before the darts game began, David pointed to Desmond and said: 'This man is following me about.'[51] When Desmond left the pub, David slipped out to his car and drove away, then doubled back for The Crown when he was certain Desmond was no longer in the neighbourhood. At 10.30 p.m. he returned to the Old Vicarage with Borti and Pam Abbott, who invited him to stay the night because he seemed 'upset'.[52]

Ruth meanwhile spent a lonely, troubled night at Egerton Gardens. Before dawn, she telephoned Desmond and told him David had not come home. They returned to Penn shortly after 8 a.m. Desmond recalled:

> She wanted to go to his home to see whether his car was in the garage. She found that it was not. She asked me to park the car outside another house . . . About 9 a.m. he came out . . . When he saw us, he walked back into the house . . . She appeared to be jealous of the woman.[53]

According to the police report, based on Mrs Abbott's testimony, David was disturbed by the car outside the house. He told her he hadn't expected 'them' to take matters so far. When she asked him what he meant, David replied, 'She has followed me down here.'[54] Mrs Abbott offered to give David and Mr Borti a lift to the factory, but while she was collecting her car from the garage she noticed the other vehicle and its passenger, a blonde woman with whom David was in conversation. After a while, David returned and Mrs Abbott drove on to Sylicum Pistons but stopped midway so that David might call at the post office. Mrs Abbott noticed 'a car drawn up a little distance behind' and watched the blonde woman climb out and walk towards a nearby telephone box.[55] When David came back, they continued to the factory, after which Mrs Abbott returned home alone. Half an hour later, her housekeeper called to say that there was a woman to see her. She recognised Ruth immediately from that morning.

'I think I'd better apologise,' Ruth said. 'You are the lady who was in the car with David?'[56] Mrs Abbott said she was and invited her into the house.

Ruth gave her own account of the meeting. 'I explained the

situation and she said, "I'm very sorry, it is all my fault. I did not know David had anything so important in London,"' Ruth recalled.

> I said I could not understand why he spent the night there when his home was only just up the road. She said, 'He is not very happy at home.' Knowing David like I do, I know for a fact he would not have spent the night there for nothing. An attractive woman on her own whose husband was always away. Later on, I discovered that they both contradicted one another's stories.[57]

She was referring to David's sleeping arrangements: Mrs Abbott told her he had slept in the spare room but David said he had used the sofa in the lounge. According to the police report:

> Mrs Abbott goes on to say that the woman left her in no doubt that there had been an association between her [Ruth] and David Blakely, but after talking to her and giving her coffee, the woman, who by this time had told Mrs Abbott her name was Ruth, said in a peculiar way, 'So young David is not having an affair at Penn.' She replied, 'As far as I know he is not.'[58]

Ruth left the Old Vicarage in turmoil; she was convinced David *was* having an affair with Pam Abbott and asked Desmond to drive to The Crown for lunch, sensing that David would probably call in during his work break. Before then, she telephoned David and handed the receiver to Desmond, who wanted him to apologise for Ruth's recent injuries. 'Do you want to make a court case out of it?' David asked.[59] With Ruth at his elbow, Desmond replied, 'Don't be ridiculous – come down here and have a drink. I won't hit you.'[60]

David joined them at the pub in his lunch hour, ill-advisedly with Mr Borti and Mrs Abbott in tow. He kept insisting to Ruth that there was nothing going on in Penn, but she refused to believe him. The conversation then turned to the upcoming British Racing Drivers' Club dance at the Hyde Park Hotel. Ruth had wanted David to accompany her but he told her he wasn't interested, leaving her to make alternative arrangements with Desmond. But as he left The Crown to return to work, he suddenly remarked, 'I'll see you at the dance.'[61]

Ruth stared at him for a moment before bursting out: 'You *knew* you were going all the time, you're just trying to annoy me.'[62]

David departed swiftly, leaving Ruth and Desmond to their drinks. But that afternoon they drove on to Sylicum Pistons, where Desmond apologised out of Ruth's earshot for their odd behaviour in following him.

'Would it embarrass you further if Ruth and I went to the dance tonight?' Desmond asked.[63]

David assured him it wouldn't and the two men shook hands.

Ruth was distressed on the journey back to London. At one point she asked Desmond to stop at a telephone box so that she might call David, but afterwards she said nothing of what had passed between them. Desmond drove to Ruth's hairdresser's, Shack's of Shaftesbury Avenue, where she had an appointment that afternoon. He waited until she was ready to return to Egerton Gardens. When he discovered there was no food at the flat, he drove home to make sandwiches for them both, leaving Ruth to change for the dance. He returned and helped mask the bruises on her shoulders with make-up before they sat down to eat.

Suddenly Ruth said, 'I don't know whether I love him, or I am going mad.'[64]

Desmond looked at her, then said softly, 'You're all right, Ruth, you're a bit overwrought.'[65]

They called for drinks at the Steering Wheel Club before heading to the Hyde Park Hotel, where David was waiting for them. He had arrived much earlier with his mother and stepfather, and spent the entire evening telephoning various clubs to ask if anyone had seen Ruth. He was desperate to avoid a row in front of his family, but drank so heavily as the night wore on that by the time he spied Ruth and Desmond in the foyer, his first response was to snap: 'You arrived very late, where have you been all this time?'[66]

Desmond was handing their coats in at the cloakroom but answered lightly, 'Her ladyship was kept a long time at the hairdresser's.'[67] The three of them then walked through to the ballroom, where Ruth divided her time between dancing with Desmond and then David, whom she found 'extremely funny and very rude to people all the evening'.[68] Desmond was puzzled by their sudden closeness, given the farcical nature of the day. As midnight approached, he bought a bottle of champagne and Ruth asked if they might toast her divorce, which she announced had been made absolute that day. David instantly made his excuses, disappearing back to his party.

It was Desmond who drove Ruth home to Egerton Gardens that night. When he had gone, she climbed tiredly into bed and was astonished the following morning to find David next to her. When she said she didn't know how he had the nerve to face her after what had happened in Penn, he responded, 'You know I will always come back to you.'[69]

Later that day Ruth called Desmond to explain, rather embarrassedly, that David had turned up after the dance and they were together again.

But the reconciliation was painfully brief. They separated for a week after the dance and Ruth spent most evenings out drinking with Desmond, whom she pressed into retrieving David's keys for Egerton Gardens. He recalled:

> At her request, I went with her to the Steering Wheel Club, Brick Street . . . to get the keys of her room from Blakely. When I asked him for them, we had an argument and I knocked him down outside the club. He then gave Ruth two keys.[70]

During the fracas, Desmond said in disgust: 'David, you are nothing but a ponce.'[71] His rival replied in fury: 'If I had known that you paid the rent at Number 44, I would have killed her.'[72] He straightened his jacket and returned to the bar.

Ruth recalled that the row about the keys did not end there:

> At a later date I was drinking at the Stirrup Club, talking to some people. I had left my bag at the end of the bar. David walked in, he opened my bag without asking me and said he was looking for his key. I said, 'Leave my bag alone.' I cannot remember whether I smacked him round the mouth or not, I seem to think I did. He left the bar. When I got back to Egerton Gardens, I found him outside. I said, 'What are you doing here?' He said, 'You said if I stopped the affair at Penn everything would be all right.' I said, 'Have you?' He said, 'Yes.' I believed him. He seemed so genuine and sincere. Later on he said, 'I have been wanting to come home to you all the week, it's been hell. I have missed you so much. I have slept with you so long I cannot sleep without you.' I said, 'That is no excuse for sleeping with somebody else.'[73]

David left early the next morning for work in Penn. It was a fine day, which Ruth used as an excuse for asking Desmond to lunch at The Crown. She admitted:

> I also wanted to see if David was telling the truth. I walked in and David was there with her [Mrs Abbott]. When I walked in, he looked very guilty, walked over and bought me a drink. He said, 'I must go.' As he got to the door, she said, 'David, you will drop that chair off for me, won't you?' He just did not know where to look. He said, 'Yes.' I told him once again what I thought of him, on the telephone, but he arrived back full of excuses. He said, 'I cannot help it if she goes into The Crown.' I said, 'It seems one cannot walk in there without finding you with her there. What do you do when your mother comes through?' He said, '[Pam] and I go into the darts room.' I said, 'A very well organised setup, making your mother a fool to the rest of Penn.' He said, 'They all know what my mother is like.' I said, 'I don't believe your mother is as bad as that.' He said, 'That's because you have never met her.'[74]

According to the report compiled by the police, Pamela Abbott told them that on Wednesday, 2 March, David took her to High Wycombe to collect a wheelchair:

> During this journey, Mrs Abbott jokingly said to Blakely, 'How's the girlfriend?' He replied, also jokingly, 'She thinks you are my girlfriend.' She at once pointed out how absurd that was, that she had known his family for so long and asked why he had not told the girl this. On the return to Penn, Blakely and she visited The Crown, where she left him to join some other friends. While with these friends she saw Ruth and the same man – Cussen – enter the lounge and David joined them. Soon afterwards she heard David say he was going for lunch and he left. The couple stayed behind, but she did not speak to them.[75]

The report concluded:

> Mrs Abbott does say that at some time, she cannot say when, David told her that the woman [Ruth] was violently in love with

him but he 'hated her guts'. She was able to gather from all this that David was trying to shake off this woman, but she would not be shaken off.[76]

Ruth told a very different story:

> I asked David if he was in love with [Mrs Abbott]. He said, 'No. I am in love with you.' I asked him what the attraction was. He said, 'She's got something you haven't got, money.' I said, 'Yes, that is so important to you, isn't it?' I also said, 'You get all I ever do get.' He said, 'I know, I'm a rotter and I deserve all I get . . . I shall have to marry you. I shall never be happy if I don't.'[77]

In the midst of all this recurrent upheaval, Ruth met crime reporter Duncan Webb, who was then on Morris Conley's tail, having spent months investigating his various business concerns with a view to exposing the truth. In his 1955 book, *Line Up for Crime*, Webb recalled:

> I had been told that one person who knew a lot about Mr Conley was Ruth Ellis . . . I met her in the bar of a public house not far from the Little Club. If you liked glittering ash blondes, you might have cared for Ruth Ellis. There could be no denying that she was attractive, in a nightclub sort of way, but behind the tinsel-like beauty that led so much to the doom of David Blakely I could not help discerning a certain hardness, a brittle sense of calculation. As we spoke together for more than an hour I detected a note of sadness, almost a far-away wistfulness, in her voice.
>
> Little did I know however, as she sipped the large brandy I bought her, that within a few days the same hand which held the glass a few inches from my nose would be pulling the trigger of the gun that killed David Blakely.[78]

13

On Monday, 7 March 1955, Ruth began a three-week modelling course at the Margery Molyneux Agency on Woodstock Street, just off Oxford Street. Desmond loaned Ruth the 20 guinea fee for the course, which she believed would ease her transition into more conventional modelling, particularly advertising work. Margery Molyneux was one of the leading model agents of her day, but the company had been taken over by ex-model Cherry Marshall, who used to book the girls for shows and photography work. The school Ruth attended was in a huge, rather rundown basement of a Chelsea apartment block, decorated to resemble a 1920s cinema foyer, with a catwalk in the centre and men's lavatories serving as a dressing-room. It was unprepossessing, but at night 'when the place was dimly lit apart from spotlights on the girls as they modelled, it had an air of shabby glamour'.[1]

Marshall remembered Ruth well:

> [She] was never a model in the professional sense, although she was always described as one. She'd done a few pictures for a provincial magazine . . . when I interviewed her I told her she was too short and that she almost certainly wouldn't get any work . . . She was quite pretty and heavily made up in a theatrical way, but when we got rid of her pancake make up she had a rather refined little face, and she looked very good in swimsuits too. Maybe, I said, if a manufacturer wants a petite size model she would be given a chance.[2]

Desmond hoped that the possibility of a modelling career would encourage Ruth to leave David, telling her that to be successful she couldn't afford to be knocked about and bruised. Ruth replied that

David's violence was a thing of the past; he had 'promised to be good now'.[3] But Marshall's recollections show that this was not the case:

> Right from the beginning [Ruth's] appearance in class was erratic. Maggie Wood [who was in charge of the school] complained that she was often late and sometimes didn't turn up at all . . . During the rehearsal of the beachwear scene I noticed Ruth Ellis wasn't taking part, which surprised me. 'What's happened to her?' I asked. 'If she's got any chance at all it's in the sports clothes. Why didn't you tell her she had to wear them?' . . . Maggie bent her head towards me and spoke in a whisper as the girls continued modelling on the platform. 'She's in an awful state, I'm afraid,' she said, 'and she can't possibly wear a swimsuit. God knows what kind of fellow she's tied up with, but she's covered in bruises from head to foot, and she doesn't want anyone to see. Her eyes were red with crying when she came in this morning, but I couldn't get anything out of her' . . . [Maggie] asked if I would have a word privately with Ruth afterwards, but when I did she was no more forthcoming. Well, it was none of my business, and I suggested she made up the lost classes in the next course, taking her passing-out show with them. She seemed relieved, but that was the last we ever saw of her.[4]

Ruth's non-appearance may have been due to the discovery that she was pregnant. She recalled how David reacted to the news: 'He was at first very considerate about it and later changed and started saying nasty things such as, "Well, all I can afford is about seven shillings per week."'[5] For some reason, Ruth took it into her head to speak to Carole Findlater. She was out when Ruth called at Tanza Road, and it was Ant who answered the door. He later told police:

> The gist of Ellis's remarks was that she and David had been quarrelling and I replied to the effect that it was about time she and David either started living together amicably or not living together at all. Her reply was on the lines that it was up to David whether they lived together amicably or not, and that David could end the association any time he liked.[6]

Carole recalled that she was at home when Ruth called again:

She came to see me alone. She said she was going to have a baby and that David was responsible. She described her symptoms and I came to the conclusion she was not telling the truth. I felt she was telling a lie in order to establish a further hold on poor David. He was terrified of her and I don't believe he loved her. I think he hated her – and hated himself for having been involved with her.[7]

David was undoubtedly more interested in his career than thoughts of parenthood. The Bristol Motor Company had selected him to race for them at Le Mans in July and on the afternoon of Tuesday, 25 March, he visited the Studio at Old Rectory Barn in Beaconsfield to have his official team photograph taken. According to a letter written by a member of staff some time after the murder, David talked enthusiastically about motor racing and publicity; he didn't mention Ruth, although that is hardly surprising. But the photograph would feature prominently at the trial in three months' time.

Within a few days, Ruth and David were fighting bitterly again and the fact that she was pregnant did not deter him from using his fists. Ruth recalled:

I said . . . 'You never mention [Pam Abbott's] husband, don't you ever see him?' He said, 'He comes home nights and at weekends.' I said, 'It seems funny you spend the day with her and then at night you come to London when he arrives in Penn, weekends you spend with me when her husband is home. It is no good, David. In my condition at the moment I cannot stand all this. I am feeling ill, you will have to go out of my life.' He then smacked me on the cheek with his fist clenched. I saw stars, my ear was tingling and I seemed to have gone deaf. He then put his two fingers around my throat, with the other hand he punched me in the stomach. I was crying, his fingers pressed tightly around my throat and everything went black. He was like a mad man, the expression on his face was frightening. He said, 'Oh God, don't let me do it.' He repeated it. My throat felt swollen and I was having difficulty in swallowing. I was coughing. In between these bouts I said, 'You are mad, you are stark raving mad.' He said, 'One of these days I will kill you.' I said, 'You have done that already.'[8]

The notes compiled by Ruth's doctor in Holloway confirm that she discussed the beating in prison: '2 weeks ago [David] struck her on the left ear so that she was deaf for some time.'[9]

Ruth lost the baby, but whether David's violence caused her to miscarry or if she had an abortion has never been adequately resolved, although it may have influenced her state of mind prior to the shooting. At the trial, Ruth declared that she had suffered a miscarriage after David had become 'very, very violent . . . I do not know whether that caused the miscarriage or not, but he did thump me in the tummy.'[10] She gave a very different written account:

> On 28th March, I had an abortion, and I was not at all well. On that occasion David took no interest in my welfare and did not even bother to inquire if I was all right. I was very hurt indeed about this and I began to feel a growing contempt for him. The results of my abortion continued until Tuesday 5 April.[11]

Her Holloway hospital case notes state that she had been pregnant three times to David and the prison doctor records: 'One month ago she had an abortion at two months' pregnancy duration and now has a vaginal discharge.'[12] Ruth spoke about the matter on a second occasion to the prison doctor and on 3 May he reported: 'David knew she was pregnant, that she had aborted, but as far as the Findlaters knew she was still pregnant, unless David told them.'[13]

What is certain is that, by the end of March, Ruth's pregnancy had ended and she was very ill throughout the following week. If she had an abortion, as she told the medical staff at Holloway, it was not a straightforward medical procedure and there was an infection of some sort, as was common with backstreet abortions. Dangerous and often excruciating, the operation was usually performed by untrained men and women without anaesthetic or proper surgical instruments. Most abortionists were motivated entirely by money, aware that any number of complications and even fatalities could occur. Ruth spent the first few days in bed after her pregnancy ended, her mind turning on the Findlaters, whom she held responsible for David's unwillingness to commit fully to her.

She did not see much of him that week, but had not expected to since he and Ant were working all hours on the Emperor ahead of the race for the British Empire Trophy at Oulton Park near Chester.

Despite largely blaming the Findlaters for David's fluctuating moods towards her, she realised that alcohol was again a crucial element in ruining a relationship that she hoped to make permanent. Ruth spoke to David about it:

> I said, 'I think you drink too much David, you must stop drinking so much. In fact, we'll both stop drinking.' He said, 'All right, just the occasional one.' I said, 'Anyway, you must get fit for the race.' All that week he worked late on the car. He arrived home about 12.30–1 o'clock, very dirty, smothered in grease and oil. Anthony and David, Dennis [another friend] and Clive worked hard to get the car ready for the race. I was in bed early all that week. He used to phone from Rex Place and check to see if I was in bed like I promised.[14]

On Wednesday, 30 March, David arrived at Egerton Gardens earlier than usual; the conversation supports the likelihood that Ruth had had an abortion. 'He said they had put the racing car in the garage of his mother's flat in Culross Street,' Ruth remembered:

> He said, 'What do you think, darling?' I said, 'Now what's happened?' He said, 'Well, Ant and I and Clive and Dennis were putting the car in the garage when my mother came down and invited us all up for a drink. She was in a very good mood.' I said, 'I am very pleased, that makes us all very happy.' Then he said, 'I wish we had enough money, we could have kept our little David. I didn't want you to get rid of it.' He was then very concerned and said, 'Everything will turn out all right. No one is ever going to part us. I do love you so much, Ruth.'[15]

David's sudden belief in their future continued apace. Jacqueline Dyer recalled that when Ruth called her ten days before the shooting 'she told me that she was very happy and that she and David were going to get married'.[16] Jacqueline hadn't seen Ruth for a couple of months but spoke to her regularly on the telephone. She tried to sound pleased at her friend's news, but experience told her that it was unlikely to last, given the 'sustained terrible strain of her life with Blakely'.[17] In her police statement, Jacqueline declared: '[David] had said to me, and to her in my presence, "If you leave me, Ruth darling,

I will kill you." I heard him say it so often. Their life together alternated between love and beating and he did the beating.'[18]

Ruth and David were due to leave for Chester the following day, Thursday, 31 March. She busied herself producing one of her famous repasts:

> I had prepared a picnic basket, smoked salmon sandwiches and a whole chicken, box of biscuits, sweets and chocolates for David because he liked chocolates while he was driving, also a flask of tea. That day previously I had bought him his new gloves for wearing while driving his racing car.[19]

David had specifically asked for a pair of string-backed gloves but she recalled that he 'forgot to say thank you' for them, which upset her.[20] Far more worrying was the blood loss following the end of Ruth's pregnancy, which depleted her considerably. Determined to ignore it, she set off from London with David in the Emperor while Ant drove David's Vanguard with Dennis as a passenger. Desmond was away in Wales and Ruth had failed to tell him that she was going to the race, although she left an explanatory note in her flat and mentioned it to housekeeper Mrs Winstanley. That night, under the names Mr and Mrs Blakely, Ruth and David booked into the Red Lion, an eighteenth-century inn in the village of Little Budworth, near the racing circuit.

On Friday, 1 April, a persistent rain fell all day. Ruth was still unwell but accompanied David to the track to watch him put the Emperor through its paces on the practice run. *Lilliput* magazine featured a special illustrated article on the car in its April 1955 issue, under the title: 'Building a 130 mph Special'. Written before the race at Oulton Park, the author writes prophetically: 'In the final count the Emperor may crash before it can prove itself (there is no second string to the stable, it may flop or it may become a sensation). Motor racing is too chancy to predict the outcome.'[21] And indeed, the Emperor broke down on its practice run, leaving David and Ant with no option but to withdraw it from the race.

Carole was then women's editor at the *Daily Mail,* where she wrote a piece on women's fashions at the racetrack; she arrived at Oulton Park later that day with a colleague and found everyone in a dark mood. They decided to stay for the race, but that evening David rounded on Ruth, telling her: 'It's your fault, you jinxed me.'[22] He reminded her that she had once said he would never have any luck because of the way he treated her. Ruth replied that she had been right, given that he was unpleasant to everyone one way or another. He responded with the blasé attitude that infuriated her: 'Go on. Say I'm a cad. I'm a rotter. But you're like the rest of them. You like me that way. You'll always come crawling back.'

'You can't walk on me forever,' she warned him quietly. 'I'm only human: I can't stand it.'

'You'll stand it because you love me,' he replied.[23]

The fight may have become physical; Ruth's prison hospital notes record that she had a bruise on her outer thigh, which was 'due to David "knocking me about" last week'.[24]

The British Empire Trophy was won by David's friend Archie Scott-Brown the following day. It was a big win financially and one that David could well have done with at the time. A celebratory party was thrown for Archie that night at the Blossom Hotel in Chester, but at the Red Lion, David, Ruth, Dennis and the Findlaters gathered gloomily in the bar. Carole recalled that Ruth was truculent and sat 'like the Snow Queen', complaining when her champagne didn't arrive.[25] David griped about the cost of repairs for the Emperor and declared the trip an unmitigated disaster.

In London, further misfortune was unfolding. Desmond had returned from Wales to find a telegram from Andre's school; Ruth had not only failed to give them her new address but she had also forgotten term ended before she was due home from Chester. No one had arrived to collect Andre, who was left at school. Desmond immediately telephoned Egerton Gardens, where Mrs Winstanley told him that 'Mr and Mrs Ellis' were not due back until Sunday. She checked the room and found the note from Ruth, asking her to let Desmond know she would ring him on Monday. Andre remained at the school throughout the weekend.

On Sunday, 3 April, David asked Ruth to pay their hotel bill since he didn't have enough cash with him. Ruth gave him £5 but then spotted him at reception, signing a cheque. Asked at the trial what effect this had on her, she replied, 'I just thought it was a mean way of getting money from me when he had sufficient to pay the bill himself, or appeared to have.'[26] She said nothing to David about it and he was too preoccupied with the Emperor – which had to be towed back – to bother with her. When they arrived in London, David ferried the car round to his stepfather's garage before he and Ruth went out drinking. She felt distinctly unwell again and was severely depressed; she drank so heavily that David had to put her to bed.

Desmond called at Egerton Gardens the following morning after David had left for work and found Ruth in bed with a high fever. He told her to stay where she was while he collected Andre. Ruth lay in bed, agitatedly mulling over the situation. She knew that she had changed beyond recognition:

> I used to be good company and fun to be with. [David] had turned me into a surly, miserable woman. I was growing to loathe him, he was so conceited and said that all women loved him. He was so much in love with himself.[27]

She hated the flat and so did Andre, whose feelings upon returning there with Desmond after being forgotten at school can only be imagined. Georgina later recalled how at Egerton Gardens Andre had felt 'like a caged animal. He wanted to run away but there was nowhere to go. He did not even know the area.'[28] No doubt David disliked it too, given the opulence of his other homes: the beautiful old house in Penn and his smart flat on Culross Street were a world away from a furnished service room, no matter how decent. That night and the following evening, he telephoned to say that he would be late back because he was working on the car. Ruth recalled: 'It was either on the Monday or the Tuesday night that I discovered David was at the Steering Wheel spending my money on a party of friends without me.'[29] Asked in court how that made her feel, she replied, 'I felt nothing but contempt for him.'[30]

Ruth and Andre spent almost every day that week at Goodwood Court. Desmond had to work but drove home to have lunch with them before they returned to Egerton Gardens. On Wednesday, 6 April, Ruth began to feel a little better; her fever had gone but she was left with a dry, hacking cough. She and Andre walked to the chemist for some medicine and David arrived at the flat soon after they returned. 'He was quite happy,' Ruth recalled at the trial. 'He was saying everything would be all right, we would soon have some money, and talking about marriage again and all kinds of other little things.'[31] David presented her with a copy of the photograph he had had taken and wrote upon it: 'To Ruth, with all my love, David.' The two of them spent a quiet, happy evening in the flat with Andre. David discussed selling the Emperor to raise money. Ruth told the court: 'I did not want him to . . . he was so fond of motor racing. It seemed such a shame. He had built a car and then wanted to sell it.'[32] His good intentions were dented by his suggestion: 'If you can find me £400, I won't need to sell it.'[33]

The next day Ruth telephoned Desmond. Despite the calm of the previous evening, she wanted to find out whether David had given a copy of the team photograph to another woman and asked if he would drive her to Beaconsfield, having noticed the photographer's stamp. Desmond agreed. Presumably Andre accompanied them on the journey to Beaconsfield, where Ruth asked to be dropped at a pub to check the address of the photographer. She suggested that Desmond drive on to The Crown, just in case David was there with Pamela Abbott. He did so, but found David alone in the pub and left without speaking to him; the two men were no longer feigning cordiality. He then returned to Beaconsfield and collected Ruth. They drove to Egerton Gardens at some speed, since she wanted to be back before David arrived to take her to the theatre that night. A short while later, David called from a telephone box on Western Avenue to say that he was caught in traffic and wouldn't make it home in time for the play. He suggested a visit to the cinema instead.

That evening, Ruth and David left Andre asleep in bed while they went to see *Above Us, the Waves*, a war film starring John Mills. Ruth told the court: 'All through the cinema, which was rather annoying, he was telling me he loved me and all kinds of things – and it was a very good film. He seemed very attentive to me.'[34] Afterwards, they discussed their plans for Easter; it was Good Friday the following day. David said that he had to work on the Emperor again (he was due to race the car at Goodwood on Easter Monday), but asked Ruth to join him for drinks at the Findlaters later. On Saturday, they would take Andre out somewhere. Ruth mentioned her appointment with solicitor Leon Simmons on the Tuesday after Easter to discuss Georgina's future. Most sources claim that the couple then returned to Egerton Gardens for the night, but Marks and Van den Bergh assert that the couple had a blazing row that evening at the Steering Wheel Club, which ended with David punching Ruth full in the face, sickening everyone present. Manageress Gwen Nockolds told Marks and Van den Bergh that she had thrown the couple out, and was surprised not to be subpoenaed for Ruth's trial since the incident occurred so close to the shooting. Ruth said nothing of this, instead telling the court that she and David parted on the very best of terms. It was the last evening they ever spent together.

At 10 a.m. on Good Friday, David left Egerton Gardens, promising to return before 8 p.m. Ruth then telephoned Desmond, explaining that she and Andre were free for the day. He collected them both and they returned to his flat, where they ate lunch before visiting the Plaza cinema in Piccadilly Circus to see *The Conquest of Space*, a science fiction film about a voyage to Mars. Afterwards, he drove them home and left to meet friends while Ruth put Andre to bed, hoping to get him settled for the evening before David arrived.

But David had already decided not to return to Egerton Gardens. According to Ant's statement:

> In the evening [Good Friday] we went to the Magdala Public House for a drink. Whilst we were there David said he had to get away about 8 to 8.30 to meet Ruth Ellis. My wife was with us. I suggested to him that this was foolish, continuing to see this woman, as he wanted to break with her. He said, if I don't she will go to Penn again. I suggested he should stay with my wife and I for the weekend, that if she came along I would cope with her . . . one thing that was obvious to me was that he was afraid to break with Ruth Ellis, this was chiefly because he was frightened of the trouble she would cause at Penn.[35]

Carole was more forthright, telling David, 'Don't be so bloody spineless and silly. Any man can leave any woman. What can she do about it?'[36] He answered, 'It's not as easy as that. You don't know her, you don't know what she's capable of.'[37]

Oddly, Ruth told the Holloway prison doctor that she had been drinking with David that night; she claimed to have had a gin and ginger ale with him at the Hyde Park Hotel, but this seems extremely unlikely, given all the other statements – including Ruth's own – to the contrary. Yet David did not stay with the Findlaters all evening. When Ant was questioned about the events of Good Friday, he replied:

> I do not know where he went when he left me. He did not tell

me. I do not know whether he was going to Egerton Gardens. If
I had been asked at that stage where he probably was after he left
me, I should have said Egerton Gardens, with the accused.[38]

When asked the same question, Clive Gunnell stated that if David
wasn't with the Findlaters, 'I would have been left wondering what
on earth had happened to him and would have had no clue how to
resolve my anxiety about him.'[39] It is a curiosity of the case that both
men professed not to have known where to find David if he were
absent from Egerton Gardens, yet they were perfectly aware that he
might have been at any number of places known to the three of
them.

Wherever he had briefly gone, David eventually turned up at Tanza
Road. He and the Findlaters then called in at a pub in Highgate;
David refused to go to the Magdala in case Ruth turned up. She
telephoned the Findlaters at 9.30 p.m. Lesley, the 19-year-old au pair
who had a room in the basement of No. 29, answered the call. She
told Ruth that her employers were out and, as far as she knew, David
wasn't with them. An hour later, Ruth telephoned again and this time
Ant took the call. In court, Ruth recounted:

> I said to him, 'Anthony, is David with you?' . . . He said, 'No.'
> So I said, 'I am very worried because he should have been back
> to meet me.' I said, 'Do you think he is all right?' Mr Findlater
> replied and said, 'Oh, he is all right.' . . . Just before that he said
> that he had seen him earlier but that he had left . . . He said it
> rather cocky . . . I was furious because I was expecting David to
> come back, and I was not feeling very well.[40]

Ruth's sense of injustice began to burn: 'I knew at once that David
was there and that they were laughing at me behind my back.'[41] She
telephoned Desmond, probably intending to ask him to drive her to
Tanza Road, but he was still out with friends. She tried the Findlaters
again but no one answered the phone.

At Tanza Road, Carole swallowed a sleeping pill before going to bed
and went into the sitting-room where David was preparing to settle
down for the night on the sofa. She was taken aback by how worried
he looked – scared, in fact – and she kissed him on the cheek, reassuring
him, 'Don't worry, David, it will be all right. We still love you.'[42]

The telephone in Desmond's flat rang soon after he arrived back from his night out. He told police:

> About 11.45 p.m. [Ruth] phoned and said that she had stayed in her room all the evening. She had phoned the Findlaters to find out why she had not been picked up and was told that Blakely had called for her at Egerton Gardens at about 7 p.m., but as she was not there, he did not wait. She had asked the Findlaters if David was there but had been told 'no', but she thought he was there. She asked me to drive her there. I picked her up and drove her to Hampstead and dropped her off at the corner of Tanza Road and she asked me to wait for her.[43]

In the dim and leafy street, Ruth saw David's Vanguard parked outside No.29; it had a grey roof and green bodywork. Ruth ran up the steps to the front door of the flat, which was in darkness. She rang the bell: no answer. She rang it again, but still no one came, so she ran back down the steps and to the nearest public telephone box. Her call to the Findlaters' number – 4978 – was answered, but before she could speak, the receiver was replaced. Her anger and humiliation flared. 'I was absolutely furious with David,' Ruth recalled at her trial:

> I just wanted to see him and ask for the keys back . . . All kinds of things were going on. I just wanted him to jump in the lake or go and lose himself – something silly . . . I was feeling just a little – in a peculiar mood then: a rather nasty mood to make them open the door, that was all.[44]

She returned to No. 29 and rang the doorbell again. Desmond was parked nearby on the steep slope; she ran back to his car and reached into the glove compartment, where he kept a rubber-coated torch. She took it out and walked grimly across to the Vanguard, whose commercial metal side panels David had replaced with windows. While Desmond remained in his car, in the darkened street Ruth banged the torch against one of the windows. It fell inwards but did not break.

David watched her from the bay window of No. 29. When he saw her lift the torch again, he went through to the bedroom and woke Ant. Pulling a dressing-gown over his pyjamas, Ant padded over to the telephone. He rang the police and explained quickly about the disturbance outside his flat, then went along the hall to the front door, unlocking it.

Ruth spun on her heel and looked up at him. 'Where is David?' she asked, her voice loud in the silent street. 'I want to speak to him—'

'I don't know where he is,' Ant interrupted.

'*I* know where he is,' Ruth said. 'Ask him to come down.'[45]

At that moment, a police car turned into Tanza Road, its lights picking out the slim figure of Ruth standing in the road with the torch in her hand, and Ant in his pyjamas and dressing-gown, inside the porchway. It was just after 2 a.m.

Inspector Harry Makin climbed out of the car. He approached the steps to No.29, where Ant was the first to speak. Makin recounted:

> Mr Findlater said, 'I want this woman away from here. She is disturbing us. I want to be left in peace.' He alleged that Mrs Ellis had interfered with a motorcar standing outside the house. He stated that the car belonged to Mr David Blakely, who was staying with him. I examined the car . . . and saw that a window on the near side had been forced in. I said to Mrs Ellis, 'Did you cause this damage?' and she said, 'Yes. This car is just as much mine as his. I have been living with him for two years. I shall stay here till I see him. I will pay for the damage.' Mr Findlater said, 'Mr Blakely won't see her, so it's no use her waiting.' Mrs Ellis was behaving in a perfectly normal and quiet manner and as there was no cause for police action I advised Mrs Ellis to leave the vicinity and return home. I then left the scene.[46]

The police car disappeared and the street fell into darkness again, save for the light from the hallway of the Findlaters' flat. Ruth circled the Vanguard slowly. Then she lifted the torch and banged it against two more windows of the vehicle, knocking them inwards without breaking them. Ant left his position at the top of the steps to telephone the police again. It was 2.40 a.m. when Makin returned, and Ruth had already gone. Desmond, who intimated to the police in his statement that he wasn't there when Ruth pushed in the windows of the Vanguard ('When she came back about an hour later – she told me there had been a disturbance in which police were called'), admitted: 'I drove her home. We discussed this incident on the way home. She was upset and said it was just another example of how [David] tried to annoy and upset her.'[47]

Desmond then drove to his own flat, but Ruth did not sleep. She sat up, gazing about the room in the dark, listening to Andre's breathing from the camp-bed: 'I just smoked. I was still in a temper. I was very upset about the whole thing, to think that David was behaving so disgustingly now. I was not well.'[48] In her story as recounted in the *Woman's Sunday Mirror*, she recalled: 'I just sat and howled. I no longer thought of David as the man I loved, but as someone who was trying to make a fool of me. I felt humiliated and frustrated.'[49]

The night passed painfully slowly. At 8 a.m. Ruth dialled 4978 again, but someone cut off the call. She decided against ringing Desmond and instead left Andre still sleeping while she went out to flag down a taxi to take her to Tanza Road. The Hampstead street was slowly coming to life, and she edged herself into a doorway to keep watch on No. 29. After a while, the Findlaters' front door opened. Ant appeared first, glancing up and down the street before inclining his head for David to follow. The two men went down the steps and inspected the Vanguard before climbing into it and driving away. Ruth correctly surmised that they had gone to Rex Place to have it repaired, and walked to a telephone box to call the garage. When Clive answered, Ruth pretended to be one of David's girlfriends and asked to speak to Ant, who came on the line.

'Thank you for calling the Black Maria,' Ruth said, in a voice dripping sarcasm. 'If I had known, I would have waited for it.'[50]

The phone went dead.

Ruth thought for a moment, then telephoned Desmond and asked him to call Rex Place. He did so, pretending to be David's friend Lionel Leonard, but Ant recognised his voice and banged down the receiver. Desmond then called the number of the telephone box where Ruth was waiting and explained to her that he had had no success. Deflated, she returned to Egerton Gardens.

It was almost midday. Ruth made lunch for Andre then gave him some money with the instruction to take himself to London Zoo; she couldn't think with him there. The ten-year-old boy was used to being left to his own devices and often travelled aimlessly on London's underground and bus network until he was expected home.

With Andre out of the flat, Ruth telephoned Desmond again. It was about 2 p.m. when he arrived to drive her to Hampstead, where David and Ant had just returned from a dispiriting morning working on the Emperor. They spent their last £7 on connecting rods only to discover that the HRG had a broken crankshaft and needed further spares, beyond their finances, before it was safe to race again. The two men drove in reflective silence back to Tanza Road. Ant was sympathetic to David's crushed ambitions and understood that his friend was even less inclined to speak to Ruth in his present mood. They decided to drown their sorrows with Carole in the Magdala, which was where Desmond and Ruth saw the Vanguard parked against the kerb as they turned in at South Hill Park. Ruth told Desmond to continue on to Tanza Road, where she intended to wait for David.

A group of workmen were busy outside a house opposite the Findlaters' flat. While Desmond parked the car, Ruth suddenly had an idea and hopped out to approach the labourers, who confirmed that a flat was for sale. Within minutes, she was ensconced in the front room, drinking tea with the owner – by a window with a perfect view of No.29. Her ingenuity was rewarded: she saw the Vanguard pull up outside the Findlaters' flat and watched David, Carole and Ant go up the steps and indoors. An hour later, at 4 p.m., the three emerged again, with Lesley the nanny carrying one-year-old Francesca. They climbed into David's car and drove off towards the Vale of Health, a private road off the Heath. Ruth quickly made her excuses to the owner of the flat and returned to Desmond's car.

Several hours later, after giving Andre his supper and putting him to bed, Ruth and Desmond left Egerton Gardens and drove back to Tanza Road. As they pulled into the street, they saw David's Vanguard outside the Findlaters' flat, where a party was in full swing; a Rolls-Royce belonging to one of the guests was parked nearby. Fuming, Ruth positioned herself close to the steps of No.29, hoping she could not be seen. It was already dark. Cigarette smoke curled from the open bay window, and above the chink of glasses and chattering voices, she could hear David talking loudly, and a woman's laughter. She waited. At about half past nine, the front door opened. Ruth stepped back a little as Ant and David appeared with a young, dark-haired woman. Ruth felt herself grow cold when David said to the girl, 'Let me put my arm around you for support.'[51] She was certain he was with the Findlaters' nanny, Lesley; perhaps it was her laughter she had heard earlier.[52]

She watched from the shadows as the two men and the young woman climbed into the Vanguard and drove off. Ruth returned to Desmond and they left Tanza Road for a while, either for Ruth to answer a call of nature or to tail David's car but without success. Ruth stated that the Vanguard was there again when they returned. At about 12.30 a.m., she later told the court: 'The blind in the nanny's room went down, and the light in the hall went out . . . that was at 12.30.'[53] Now unassailably sure that the Findlaters were driving a wedge between herself and David, Ruth suspected the party had been a ruse to throw Lesley in his path. 'I knew then for certain that the Findlaters were trying to part us,' Ruth recalled, 'and I guessed that David would not have stayed unless there was some female attraction there. I knew him too well and I realised that it was probably the 19-year-old nursemaid.'[54] She stood silent in the street, utterly bereft and humiliated, imagining David with her rival, who was almost ten years younger than she was, a free spirit with no children or ex-husbands to complicate matters. For a while she went on standing there, listening to the sounds of the party still drifting through the open window, a cool April breeze fluttering through the black trees.

Eventually, she retraced her steps to Desmond's car.

*

In Ruth's absence at Egerton Gardens, the housekeeper had let herself quietly into Room 5 to check on Andre. He lay sleeping soundly, a small hunched shape on the rickety camp-bed. Mrs Winstanley was about to shut the door when she sensed that something was different. She paused, frowning as her eyes took in the familiar furniture and Ruth's cast-off belongings. Then it struck her: all the photographs of David had been removed and in their place were snapshots of Ruth, posed stiffly from her time as a model. And there, lying in the flat where she had left it, was one of the last paperbacks Ruth ever read: *Dead Reckoning*, an illustrated book of the 1947 film starring Humphrey Bogart with Lizabeth Scott as a blonde femme fatale. In the denouement of the book, the anti-heroine shoots the wicked nightclub boss, Martinelli, and is seen 'standing by the car in her cape, still clutching her gun with both hands'.[55]

14

When Desmond left Ruth at Egerton Gardens, she let herself quietly into the room she had rented in the hope of building a life with David. She looked down on her sleeping son, whom she was failing to care for in her desperation over a man who no longer loved her – if he ever had. She sat on her bed and lit one cigarette after another in the darkness, the long hours of the night passing in tumultuous thought. 'I was shivering and sick,' she recalled:

> I sat and thought over the last two years. When I first fell in love with David, I was a successful manageress of a prosperous club. I had admirers, money in the bank and a lovely flat. Now all I had was a bedsitting room, no money, no job and a man who swore he loved me one day and couldn't be bothered to collect me on time the next. A man who beat me in private and abused me in public. A man who was relieved when I lost the child he had fathered. A man who, I was convinced, was being unfaithful to me.[1]

The Little Club seemed far distant, a memory as faint as the gramophone records that used to play in the background at the bar. Most terrifying of all, she was virtually destitute, staring straight into the black funnel of poverty that she had always feared.

As the light behind the curtains grew paler with the sounds of the city wakening to the new day, she found she could not move, her emotions passing from grief to fury and encompassing so many painful memories: 'I thought and thought. All kinds of things went through my head – all the things he had said to me and all he had done to me . . . I was raging inside.'[2] Her resentment converged on one person:

> I remember thinking that it must have taken Carole a long time
> to think that one up [using the nanny to tempt David]. She
> wanted to get David away from me and she couldn't get him
> back herself so she did the next best thing. The Findlaters, who
> at that time had very little money, relied on David for their
> social life and I had been taking him away from them.[3]

In Ruth's mind, her bitter enemies had won. It was at that point she
felt the first stirrings of a murderous impulse: 'I had an overwhelming
and peculiar desire to kill David.'[4]

Years later, Ant Findlater dismissed the idea that Lesley had been
used as some sort of 'bait' for David, telling interviewers that the
young nanny had been the size of a horse and stood no nonsense; she
would probably have told David not to be so silly had he tried to
seduce her. He fully refuted the notion that he and Carole had actively
worked to separate the couple, although he did not attempt to deny
that they disliked Ruth. Bluntly, he stated that a woman of Ruth's
background and character would never have proved acceptable to
David's mother and stepfather but – as far as he could see – Ruth
clung to her lover in the hope of a better life. And when she finally
grasped that marriage was out of the question 'she killed him. It was
an open and shut case.'[5]

*

Ruth telephoned the Findlaters' flat at 9 a.m. on Easter Sunday. In
court she confirmed: 'I thought if David was sleeping in the lounge,
and the divan is next to the phone, he would be the first to pick it
up.'[6]

But it was Ant who answered. Hearing his voice, Ruth began to
say, 'I hope you are having an enjoyable holiday—'

He banged the receiver down.

'—because you have ruined mine,' she finished to empty air.[7]

What Ruth did between making the telephone call to the Findlaters
and arriving at their flat that evening remains the subject of speculation.
Asked at the trial about her movements, Ruth replied:

> Mr Cussen picked me up with my son, and we went over and I
> took something to eat at Mr Cussen's flat, and we spent some
> time at the flat . . . I have completely forgotten what I did now.

My son was with us, and we amused him in some way. I do not
know what I did.[8]

In his statement, Desmond Cussen admitted he had spent part of the
day with Ruth and Andre but was firm that he had driven them home
at 7.30 p.m. and had not seen Ruth since then.[9] There are further
theories, based on what emerged in the weeks, months and even years
after the shooting. But for now, the relevant facts are that by early
evening Ruth and Andre had returned to Egerton Gardens, where
housekeeper Betty Riley heard Ruth calling as she closed the front
door, 'We are back.'[10] It was earlier than Desmond remembered; Betty
Riley was certain they arrived at about six o'clock. Ruth and Andre
went straight to their room. The ten-year-old later told journalist
Peter Grisewood that he undressed, washed, got into bed and read a
comic, nibbling an Easter egg his mother had bought him. He
watched her repair her make-up, change her shoes and skirt, and put
on a black coat. She leant over his camp-bed, smelling of perfume and
powder, to kiss him goodnight. 'I won't be long,' she said softly and
then she went out.[11]

He never saw her again.

Betty Riley met Ruth as she came downstairs; an hour had passed
since she heard her call. She, too, recalled that Ruth wore black. The
issue of clothing is important: Ruth was said to be wearing a black
two-piece suit when she left Egerton Gardens, yet at her arrest later
that night, she was dressed in a *grey* two-piece suit with a green polo
neck. If so, then clearly before arriving at Tanza Road Ruth had
changed her clothes somewhere.

She left the flat, closing the door with a slight click, and stepped
out into the dark street wearing her horn-rimmed spectacles. There
was only one thought in her mind: what to do about David. Asked
in court about her mood that night, she replied, 'I was very upset.'
Then she paused and said, 'I had a peculiar feeling I wanted to kill
him.'[12]

With that in her heart, she emerged from the brick porch of
Egerton Gardens and walked away with a quick, light step.

*

David's movements throughout Easter Sunday were more
straightforward. Together with Ant and Carole, he met Clive and

another friend named Michael Webb in the Magdala for lunch. Someone suggested a get-together that evening again at 29 Tanza Road. Clive offered to bring his record player along; David told him he would call for him in the car later. He then approached the bar and asked landlord John Colson to cash him a cheque for £5, which Colson was happy to do, having known David since the Findlaters moved into the neighbourhood and made the Magdala their local. After lunch, David and the Findlaters said goodbye to Clive and Michael and returned to the flat. Lesley was ready to leave for home. She usually caught a bus or tube to Victoria Station, but David obligingly drove her there instead. It was a while before he returned; he told Ant that he had visited the cinema for an hour, which may have been true, since he was a devoted picture-goer.

During the early part of the evening, David and the Findlaters took advantage of the good weather by visiting the Easter fairground on Hampstead Heath. David strolled about with his goddaughter Francesca perched on his shoulders; the sun glittered on the water and there was a haze across the city rooftops. They spent a pleasant few hours wandering about the busy stalls and rides before walking back to Tanza Road, where they spruced themselves up for the evening ahead.

Cutting a sharp figure in a dark grey worsted suit, blue shirt, waistcoat, Old Salopian tie and black shoes, David climbed into the Vanguard to collect Clive and the gramophone. Carole accompanied him, leaving Francesca at home with Ant. They drove down to the junction of South Hill Park then took a sharp right up the slope to No.45, where Clive was waiting for them. They stopped at the Magdala for one drink before driving back to Tanza Road, where a small party had already begun.

At 9 p.m., Carole found she had run out of cigarettes. David offered to drive to the Magdala again to fetch cigarettes and more beer, and Clive volunteered to go with him. The streetlamps were just flickering into life as they left the flat. The muted glow failed to pick out a woman watching a short distance away.

David swerved the Vanguard across the road to park directly next to the entrance to the pub, facing downhill. Although he had fitted the vehicle with 'banger caps' that would explode like fireworks if anyone tried to steal it, he locked the Vanguard before heading for the bar with Clive. A sticker on the rear window of the car advertised the forthcoming *Daily Express* trophy meeting at Silverstone on 7 May 1955.

There were two doors to the Magdala: one into the airy main room with a serving area on the right, the other into the saloon bar with its panelled walls, plush seats and ornate fireplace. It was busy throughout, with people enjoying a drink in the knowledge that they didn't have to work the next day. David and Clive pitched up rowdily at the saloon bar, where John Colson served them after changing another £5 cheque for David, who asked for a gin and tonic. Clive had a beer, and he and David spent the better part of £1 on drinks and provisions for the party.

While they melted into the crowd inside the Magdala, Ruth walked purposefully down past the houses and flats of Parliament Hill, her high heels clicking sharply on the pavement. 'I felt somehow outside of myself,' she recalled afterwards. 'Although I seemed to be registering impressions quite clearly, it did not seem to be me. I was in a sort of daze.'[13]

She passed the flats of Parliament Court to her left, just before the railings where the ground dropped steeply away to Hampstead Heath Rail Station, bombed during the war. The lights of the Magdala burned at the foot of the hill, and faint sounds from the bar drifted towards her. David's Vanguard was a humped shape against the kerb. She crossed the road at the junction with South Hill Park and remembered standing 'for a few minutes a little way up the hill from the back of the car, on the pavement'.[14]

Inside the Magdala, sitting with a group in the corner seat near the windows, was off-duty Metropolitan police officer Alan Stewart Thompson:

> I'd been out with friends over Hampstead Heath, having a stroll, and we looked at Hampstead Heath fair, and we just came in for a drink before going home. I noticed Blakely and Gunnell come into the saloon bar – I think everyone else in the pub did because they were in a fairly boisterous mood.[15]

Thompson was dimly aware of someone pacing the pavement outside the bar. At about 9.15 p.m. he saw a woman's face pressed against the glass of the left-hand window, below the word 'WINES'. The rippled effect on the window distorted her face only slightly; he noticed she wore spectacles and was fair-haired before she drew back into the darkness.

After peering in at the window, Ruth walked down towards the main road and back up again, past the Vanguard. Her fingers tightened on her handbag as she stopped outside the tall, curved bulk of the Magdala.

Next door to the pub was Hanshaw's newsagent's. George McLaughlin Stephen, a 17-year-old student at Epsom College, had been visiting a friend's flat in South Hill Park Gardens, where he met David James Lusty, an 18-year-old apprentice engineer who lived just yards away on Parliament Hill. Lusty had decided to walk with Stephen and they stood chatting together by the news-stands and overhead signs advertising Will's Capstan cigarettes and Gold Flake tobacco.

Across the road, almost at the junction of South Hill Park and Parliament Hill, were a middle-aged couple, Donald Maclean Yule – a bank official – and his wife of almost 15 years, Gladys Kensington Yule. The Easter holiday had been a nightmare for them; Mrs Yule's 22-year-old son from her first marriage had committed suicide on Good Friday. Not knowing what to do with themselves, they decided to call at the Magdala for a drink. Mrs Yule recalled in her statement:

> Just before we reached the junction ... I noticed a blonde, hatless woman wearing a light grey suit and horn-rimmed glasses, walking slowly up and down on the pavement outside the Magdala public house. I also noticed a large motorcar outside the pub. The woman seemed to be waiting for somebody.[16]

Inside the pub at the bar, David and Clive drained their glasses in good humour, then collected their cigarettes and the three quarts of light ale to carry out. Clive was ahead of David as they threaded their way through the crowd and called goodbye to the landlord. Colson put up a hand briefly before returning to serve customers. It was 9.20 p.m.

The two men emerged in high spirits from the pub. Mrs Yule spotted them: 'As we got to the corner, two young men ran out of the pub with port bottles in their hands ... I said to my husband, "I say, this is a party," seeing the boys run out with the bottles.'[17]

Clive went round the front of the Vanguard to the passenger door, waiting for David to unlock it. He didn't notice the small figure standing with her back to the wall of the Magdala, near the windows of the saloon bar.

David reached the driver's door, balancing the bottles as he fumbled for his keys. There was a movement behind him and he turned.

Ruth stepped forward. 'I have a vague impression that he saw me but went to the door of the car without taking any notice of me,' she recalled. 'I know I was in a frightful temper and I think I started forward and took the pistol out of my handbag as I was walking towards him. I believe I stopped a few paces away from him.'[18]

David saw the revolver Ruth held out. In terror, he began to run towards the back of the Vanguard, still clutching the bottles and car keys to his chest.

Ruth's small fingers closed around the trigger.

'Clive!' David screamed.

Ruth fired twice, the mouth of the gun emitting small white flashes in the darkness:

> I didn't know what David was doing or whether he was facing me or had his back to me – I cannot say – I just do not know. I did not hear him call out but he started running round the back of the Vanguard. I had no experience in firing a gun before and I did not think he had been hit because he was running. I think I followed and when I was beside Clive I said, 'Stand still, Clive,' or something like that.[19]

'Get out of the way, Clive!' Ruth shouted as David scrambled around the Vanguard. But Clive stood rooted to the ground in bewildered panic. He heard 'two bangs' which were not like revolver shots because 'they sounded more muffled'.[20] He thought the noise came from the anti-theft devices attached to the Vanguard.

Almost directly opposite at the road junction, the Yules watched in horror. 'I saw a flash and heard a shot fired,' Gladys Kensington Yule recalled:

> I did not see where the flash came from. I saw a young man trying to get in the car through the door nearest the public house. He didn't get in and he ran round the car. The lady chased

him. There was another shot. The man was then round the back of the car. He staggered round.[21]

Her husband echoed in his statement:

I saw the dark-haired man running along the nearside of the car, chased by the woman. His back was toward me and I heard the sound of another shot. The man was chased in a clockwise direction round the car and when they both reached the pavement again, almost opposite the Saloon bar of the public house, he seemed to face her.[22]

Ruth was dimly aware that Clive looked 'petrified':

When I got to the front of the bonnet of the car I think I fired again – David was still running and I must have followed because when I got back to the other side of the Vanguard on the pavement near the rear he was running along the pavement up the hill towards Tanza Road – he looked round as I shot again and he fell forward flat on his face.[23]

David collapsed on the pavement almost at the feet of George McLaughlin Stephen and David James Lusty. The two boys could not believe what they were seeing and hearing. Stephen had thought it

some sort of prank and that she was firing a 'cap' pistol. By the time I heard the fourth or fifth shots, I realised that the bangs were too loud for a cap pistol. The man stumbled as he ran round the car and when he had completed a circuit of the car, he fell face downwards on the pavement between the public house door and the car. All the time he was running, the woman was pursuing at a distance of about two yards and firing continuously. After the man had fallen onto his face, the woman stood over him and I saw her fire the gun once; the gun was pointed at the man's body.[24]

Beside him, Lusty watched as the man crumpled to the ground while 'the woman stood over him and fired two or three shots at him'.[25]

Directly across the road, Mrs Yule saw the figure lying on the pavement 'raise himself up on one elbow'. More than twenty years later, standing in that same spot, she stated emphatically: 'I shall *never* forget the look of appeal in his eyes. She put two more bullets into him, deliberately. I was petrified – I couldn't move on my corner.'[26]

David lay twitching on the ground, his head level with the billboards outside Hanshaw's, and Ruth fired again, point-blank into him.

Clive recalled helplessly:

> I couldn't see through the windows of the Vanguard what was happening on the other side of it . . . When I had got round the back of the car he was already on the ground . . . he was lying with his head near the beginning of the newsagent's shop and his feet between the two windows. He was lying . . . in the middle of the pavement. He never moved after I first saw him. The accused was at his feet between him and the public house. I saw her firing. From the time I first saw that to the end of it appeared to me to be a second or two. Then it was all over.[27]

Inside the Magdala, landlord John Colson heard the reverberations:

> We were very busy, it being Easter Sunday, and suddenly I heard this noise going on outside – shots. Nobody seemed to think it was shots, we all thought it was a car backfiring and nobody took a lot of notice of it.[28]

Outside, on the pavement, David's life was ebbing away.

'I ran over,' Clive remembered, 'and picked his head up and blood was spurting out of his mouth. David said nothing and I stood up.'[29]

Ruth said afterwards that David lay on the ground 'covered with blood. He was gurgling and slowly dropping. Clive stayed as if he was petrified.'[30]

For a brief moment, nothing happened. Then, standing against the wall of the Magdala, Ruth very deliberately brought the gun up to her temple, pressing it under a lock of blonde hair. Her fingers closed again around the trigger.

'She couldn't do it,' Mrs Yule said heavily during a televised interview years later. 'She went like that [she put down her hand] and the bullet hit the road and ricocheted clean through this hand of mine and into the wall behind me.'[31]

Ruth recalled:

> During the whole of this time I felt that I was in a kind of cold frenzy. But I am certain in my own mind that I did not fire at him when he was lying on the ground. At one time I seem to remember someone saying, 'Stop it, Ruth' – it may have been David – it may have been Clive, but I cannot see how it could have been David. In fact, I do not remember firing any more shots although the pistol must have been empty because I vaguely remember it clicking. I am sure there were no more shots because I meant to shoot myself.[32]

David James Lusty stated: 'She emptied the gun. I heard two or three clicks from the gun after the last shot . . . I just stood and looked, I was so surprised that I didn't realise what had happened.'[33] His friend confirmed: 'She fired again, but this time all I heard was a click, as though the gun was empty. I heard a man, who was standing beside the Public House entrance, shout, "Look what you've done, Ruth."'[34]

The bullet that hit Gladys Kensington Yule ricocheted off the paving slab and passed through the base of her thumb, fracturing a bone. 'I felt a searing pain in my right hand,' she recalled, 'and I knew I had been shot . . . When I saw these things happen and I was hit, my husband and I were in the gutter at the junction of South Hill Park and Parliament Hill.'[35] The pain in her thumb caused Mrs Yule to drop her handbag to the ground.

Ruth had fired six shots. Four found their target, one disappeared and the other hit Mrs Yule, whose thumb bled profusely. 'At that moment a taxi cab came down Parliament Hill and passed us,' Donald Maclean Yule recalled in his statement:

> I shouted at the driver and he stopped almost immediately opposite the Magdala. We ran up to it and after a little argument, I persuaded him to take my wife and I to the Hampstead General Hospital. Just as I was helping my wife into the taxi, I recollect that I saw the blonde woman standing rigid on the pavement at the foot of the man lying there. I do not remember seeing a gun.[36]

In her evidence, Gladys felt certain she had been the one to flag down the vehicle: 'A taxi cab came along the road from Parliament Hill and I shouted and ran after it.'[37] The driver baulked when he noticed Mrs Yule's bloody thumb and it took some persuasion for him to agree to allow the injured woman and her husband into the cab. His main concern was not the welfare of his wounded passenger but that his seats should not be stained. He insisted that Mrs Yule travel with her hand out of the window.

Ruth stood at David's feet, between his body and the wall of the pub. She turned slowly to look at Clive through her horn-rimmed spectacles, the spent revolver in her hand. She was trembling. 'Go and call the police,' she said quietly.[38]

Inside the Magdala, Colson jerked his head up as the door was thrown open.

> Clive rushed back in . . . and said, 'She's got him.' Almost at once I realised that the woman who had been troubling Blakely [Colson had heard about Ruth pushing in the windows of the Vanguard] must have shot him. I immediately phoned for police and an ambulance . . . I did not leave the bar until much later, after the arrival of the local police. I did not see the woman concerned.[39]

PC Alan Thompson rose from the corner seat of the saloon bar and made his way outside:

> The first thing I saw was a man lying on the pavement . . . He was bleeding. Blood was coming from his mouth. And a woman, who I now know was Ruth Ellis, was standing over him with a gun, kind of at a right angle. Pointing at his body.[40]

Ruth turned to peer at Thompson. 'Phone the police,' she repeated.

Gently, he removed the gun from her right hand. 'I am a police officer,' he told her. Then he knelt down next to David. 'I could see that I could do nothing for him,' he recalled later. 'It was obvious to me that he was dying.'[41]

Ruth's black handbag dangled from its strap in her left hand. She gazed down at David. Blood oozed from his mouth onto the pavement under his head. She watched him in a completely detached sort of way – I did not feel anything, except I seemed to be fascinated by the blood – I have never seen so much blood. He seemed to gasp two or three times, heaved and then relaxed. I think that must have been when he died. I saw his outstretched arm – his watch, and signet ring. I was rooted to the spot – I neither moved nor spoke. I seemed to be looking at things in a sort of haze rather as if I were drunk – I remember Clive coming round . . . Someone felt David's pulse and said, 'He's gone.' Clive was hysterical and screaming, 'Why did you kill him? Why didn't you kill me? What good is he to you dead? You'll both die now.' Someone said, 'Pull yourself together, you're a man, aren't you?'[42]

PC Thompson cautioned Ruth outside the Magdala. She made no reply but seemed to remember afterwards asking him to fetch an ambulance. He told her to wait where she was and offered her a cigarette. 'No, thank you,' she said. Thompson looked at her, puzzled. 'She showed no emotion whatsoever,' he recalled afterwards.[43]

George McLaughlin Stephen handed his coat to his friend. 'Realising the gun was empty, I went towards the woman with the intention of taking the gun away from her,' he stated:

When I reached the woman, the gun had already been taken from her. The man was laying on the ground; he was quite still and a lot of blood was coming out of his mouth . . . All the time we were waiting for the ambulance and the police, I never lost sight of the woman, although I did not actually see her being taken away. After the shooting finished, she stood near the man and seemed quite composed. I never heard her say anything.[44]

The lights of the Magdala glinted on David's expensive watch and ring. His head was turned to the right on his arm and the pavement beneath him was thick with congealed blood. Eventually the sirens of an ambulance sounded, racing down the road from New End Hospital. It had taken only five minutes to reach the Magdala, but Ruth thought it was far longer, as her prison doctor recalled:

The ambulance did not come for 10 or 15 minutes and the prisoner stood beside David on the pavement. There was a great deal of blood. She thinks David was dead before he got in the ambulance as he stayed down.[45]

Paramedic Ernest Pett examined David, watched silently by the crowd now gathered outside the Magdala. Ruth stood nearby with PC Thompson and Clive. 'When the ambulance arrived, they were slow putting him in,' she remembered. 'They asked lots of silly questions like "What's happened?" They put him in face down as he was. Clive said to the ambulance man – "I will go with you" and he went in the ambulance.'[46]

The doors of the vehicle slammed shut. It pulled away slowly and made the turn at the junction, then headed down to the main road. Ruth stared after the ambulance as it paused for a moment, sirens wailing, and then disappeared into the night, taking David out of her life forever. She recalled: 'I heard someone say, "Who did it?" And someone answered, "She did." It all seemed rather far away, but I had a curious feeling of relief.'[47]

Not long after the ambulance had gone, a police car appeared. There was a delay outside the pub while a policewoman could be found to accompany Ruth to Hampstead Police Station. Eventually, WPC Frances Garrad arrived. In her 40s, the former parlour maid and bus conductress had joined the force 12 years earlier. She recalled:

A police constable who had been off duty and drinking in the pub brought Ruth Ellis out. He was there when the shooting started . . . I had to arrange for two PC's [*sic*] to look after her. Ruth was very quiet. People said she was drunk, but she wasn't.[48]

It was only a short distance to the station. Sitting next to WPC Garrad in the back seat, Ruth said nothing during the journey. She felt no regret for what she had done, but her memory of it was already confused. She kept trying to think how many times she had shot David and what part of his body the bullets had torn into; she felt sure she had not shot him in the head. Of that she was certain, and that her actions had been justified, as she told surprised prison staff a few days later: 'He deserved what he got.'[49]

At Hampstead General Hospital, resident surgeon Dr John Nicholas Rae examined Mrs Yule's injured thumb. He diagnosed 'a penetrating wound at the base of the right thumb' and 'a fracture of the first metacarpel bone'. The injuries were 'compatible with a bullet wound, a bullet having passed right through the hand'. He told her that she would probably find her thumb was 'permanently stiff'.[50]

In the ambulance, travelling through the dark streets, Clive sat numbly alongside his friend. Paramedic Ernest Pett observed the still figure of David, now having been turned onto his back on the stretcher, from whom 'there was no apparent sign of life'.[51] In the small compartment, Pett leaned forward, moving David's shirt aside to examine him, and noticed something in the light, 'protruding slightly through the skin on the right hand side below the lower rib'.[52] It was a bullet.

The ambulance pulled into the yard at New End Hospital. Pett opened the doors and the cold night air swept in like a breath as Dr Elizabeth Beattie climbed into the vehicle and bent over David. 'He was dead,' she said simply in her statement. 'The body was still warm.'[53] She told Clive gently that there was no more he could do. In a daze he watched as his friend's body was covered and wheeled on its stretcher to the tunnel connecting the hospital to the mortuary, a small, white church-like building on the opposite side of the narrow street.

At Tanza Road, the Findlaters were puzzled by David and Clive's long absence from their party. Only a few hundred yards away, in the lights outside the Magdala, those who knew the reason for it began to disperse, talking in hushed tones about the death of the young man whose blood lay in a dark, viscous pool on the pavement. The beer from the broken bottles he had clutched to his chest mingled with the blood, and the deep red froth seeped into the drain at the foot of the hill.

IV

Table of Drops

Holloway Gaol, Easter Monday 1955 – Holloway Gaol, Execution
Day, 13 July 1955

15

Hampstead Police Station, on the corner of Rosslyn Hill and Downshire Hill, remains almost unchanged since the Easter Sunday evening in 1955 when Ruth Ellis was brought there. An imposing, salmon-coloured building dating from 1913, it retains the old-fashioned blue lamps on either side of the entrance steps. Ruth was driven into the courtyard at the rear of the station and led up a closed iron stairwell into the building.

Detective Constable George Claiden recalled:

> If I remember rightly, Ruth Ellis was brought into the station by the wireless car and that's where I first took charge of her and that sort of thing . . . I sat her down in the CID office. She had a cigarette and she was absolutely and completely calm. Chatting away. I formed the impression then, and very much confirmed later, that she really couldn't care less what was going to happen to her . . . She was quite calm, more calm than we were, I suppose.[1]

Ruth's property was confiscated upon arrival. She struggled to remove the signet ring from her finger; it had been 'bent all shapes due to the fights I had had with David'.[2] The arresting officer made a list of her possessions on a charge sheet:

List of Property of Mrs Ruth Ellis taken by Police:
One .38 revolver containing six empty cartridge cases.
One handbag.
Sixpence copper.
Two keys for 44 Egerton Gardens.
One nail file.

One paint brush.

One lip brush.

One cigarette lighter.

One packet of cigarettes.

One powder compact.

One book of matches.

One lip stick.

One note book in plastic case.

Two combs.

One mirror.

One bottle of make-up.

Seven visiting cards.

One pair of earclips.

One yellow metal wrist watch.

One cigarette holder.

One yellow metal ring.

One pair of spectacles.

One pair of gloves.[3]

She was taken to a cell, housed in a small area behind another heavy door that had to be held open. The cell was narrow and high-ceilinged, with a hard bench on which to lie or sit and a toilet in one corner. A barred window set almost in the roof showed a patch of night sky. She was offered a cup of tea and left alone behind the locked metal door. 'I seemed to be waiting a long time,' she recalled.[4]

At 11 p.m., mortuary attendant Sidney King showed Detective Chief Inspector Leslie Davies and Detective Superintendent Leonard William Crawford the body of David Blakely at New End Hospital. The Vanguard had been towed from the Magdala to the courtyard of the police station for further analysis. Police photographs appear to show the rear doors splashed with blood, and further flecks on the chrome bumper, the bodywork and windows of the driver's side. Witness statements were taken and two officers dispatched to speak to the Findlaters. Another had the task of informing Ruth's parents, then living only a few streets away at Ferncroft Avenue in Hampstead. There is no record of when or by whom David's family was informed of his death, but the police compiled a list of his possessions taken from his person and the Vanguard:

Metropolitan Police Hampstead Station, 'S' Division

Property of the late David Moffat [*sic*] Drummond Blakely now in possession of the police:

One 'Standard Vanguard' motor van, index no. OPH615

Four £1 Bank of England notes.

Eight shillings and sixpence silver.

Threepence bronze.

One cheque book of the National Provincial Bank, Beaconsfield, containing three cheques, nos. 924210 to 924212.

Twenty-three keys.

Three key rings.

One biro pen.

One petrol lighter.

One metal toy whistle.

One box containing capsules of amyl nitrate.

One pair of sunglasses.

One leather case containing a comb and a metal nail file.

One plastic clothes peg with safety pin attached.

Six packets of 'whizz bangs.'

One log book relative to Standard motor van, index no. OPH615.

One certificate of insurance No CV 5455997 relative to Standard motor van, index no. OPH615.

One log book relative to motor car, index no. HLO168

One certificate of insurance No P.M. (1) 5444704 relative to motor car

[The next line is indecipherable, partly due to the paper having been torn; the list then continues:]

Two pairs of driving gloves.

One pair of sunglasses.

One dynamo type torch.

One pair of soft leather black lace-up boots.

One pair of grey socks.

One green jersey.

One pale green jersey with badge on breast pocket.

One pair of black tracksuit trousers.

One cream coloured sleeveless pullover.

One cloth helmet.

One red scarf.

One bottle containing a colourless fluid.

One tin containing car polish.

One tie.

One woolen car rug.

One pen knife.

One pair of leather mittens.

Two pairs of gloves.[5]

Upon his return from the mortuary, Detective Chief Inspector Leslie Davies joined two other CID officers to begin questioning Ruth. Davies was in his late 40s and had joined the Metropolitan Police in 1929; Detective Superintendent Leonard William Crawford was in his early 50s and had joined the force two years earlier than Davies, while Detective Inspector Peter Smith Gill was the youngest at forty-six and, like Davies, had become a member of the Met in 1929.

Ruth was brought into the interview room at 11.30 p.m. to face the three men. Crawford opened the exchange: 'I've seen the dead body of David Blakely at Hampstead Mortuary. I understand you know something about it.'[6] Nine months earlier in the same spot, he had interviewed fifty-one-year-old Styllou Christofi about the death of her daughter-in-law; Christofi was found guilty of her murder and executed at Holloway in December 1954. He cautioned Ruth: 'You are not obliged to say anything at all about this unless you wish to do so, but whatever you say will be taken down in writing and may be given in evidence.'

'I am guilty,' Ruth said decisively. Then she hesitated: 'I am rather confused.' She took a breath and began, 'It all started about two years ago. When I met David. At the Little Club. In Knightsbridge.'

Crawford raised his hand slightly. 'Would you like this to be written down?'

Ruth nodded. 'Yes.'[7]

After signing another caution, she answered the questions put to her, which then became her statement. She had not yet been charged and there was no solicitor present, which today could render a statement inadmissible, but as the law then stood, there was nothing untoward in the absence of legal representation. The detectives were taken aback by Ruth's excessive calm, but her statement was made within three hours of killing the man she loved, with all the implications that entailed. The cool facade may have been just that: a barrier, enabling her to disengage from what she had done – and what had been done to her. She was undoubtedly in shock, smoking one cigarette after another, and gulping down the tea placed before her. She heard the voices of the detectives but could see nothing but David's blood, 'a lot of blood', she recalled later:

> I was talking more or less mechanically as though I were in a dream. I know they asked me all sorts of questions like, 'When did you decide to do this? Did you plan to kill him tonight? Did you intend to kill him when you put the gun in your bag? Where did you get the gun from?' A man with glasses [DCI Davies] was asking all the questions.[8]

Her statement was taken down by Detective Inspector Gill:

> I understand what has been said. I am guilty. I am rather confused.
>
> About two years ago I met David Blakely when I was manageress of the Little Club, Knightsbridge. My flat was above that. I had known him for about a fortnight when he started to live with me and has done so continuously until last year, when he went away to Le Mans for about three weeks, motor racing. He came back to me and remained living with me until Good Friday morning.
>
> He left me about ten o'clock a.m. and promised to be back by 8 p.m. to take me out. I waited until half past nine and he had not phoned, although he always had done in the past. I was rather worried at that stage as he had had trouble with his racing car and had been drinking.
>
> I rang some friends of his named Findlater at Hampstead, but they told me he was not there, although David had told me he was visiting them. I was speaking to Findlater, and I asked if David was all right. He laughed and said: 'Oh yes, he's all right.' I did not believe he was not there, and I took a taxi to Hampstead, where I saw David's car outside Findlater's flat at 28 [she was mistaken; it was No.29] Tanza Road. I then telephoned from nearby, and when my voice was recognised they hung up on me.
>
> I went to the flat and continually rang the doorbell, but they would not answer. I became very furious and went to David's car, which was still standing there, and pushed in three of the side windows. The noise I made must have aroused the Findlaters,

as the police came along and spoke to me. Mr Findlater came out of his flat and the police also spoke to him.

David did not come home on Saturday, and at nine o'clock this morning (Sunday) I phoned the Findlaters again, and Mr Findlater answered. I said to him: 'I hope you are having an enjoyable holiday' and was about to say: 'because you have ruined mine', and he banged the receiver down.

I waited all day for David to phone, but he did not do so. About eight o'clock this evening (Sunday) I put my son Andria to bed. I then took a gun which I had hidden and put it in my handbag. This gun was given to me about three years ago in a club by a man whose name I do not remember. It was security for money, but I accepted it as a curiosity. I did not know it was loaded when it was given to me, but I knew next morning when I looked at it. When I put the gun in my bag, I intended to find David and shoot him.

I took a taxi to Tanza Road, and as I arrived, David's car drove away from the Findlaters' address. I dismissed the taxi and walked back down the road to the nearest pub, where I saw David's car outside. I waited outside until he came out with a friend I know as Clive. David went to his car door to open it. I was a little way away from him. He turned and saw me and then turned away from me, and I took the gun from my bag and I shot him. He turned around and ran a few steps around the car. I thought I had missed him, so I fired again. He was still running, and I fired the third shot. I don't remember firing any more but I must have done. I remember he was lying on the footway and I was standing beside him. He was bleeding badly and it seemed ages before an ambulance came.

I remember a man came up, and I said: 'Will you call the police and an ambulance?' He said: 'I am a policeman.' I said: 'Please take this gun and arrest me.'

This statement has been read over to me and it is true.

Ruth Ellis.[9]

'When I put the gun in my bag I intended to find David and shoot him . . . ' There could be no more telling phrase. When her case came to trial and the jurors took their transcript of the interview with them into the jury room to consider their verdict, that line would leap out

at them. A defendant's statement is generally closely scrutinised, particularly since it is often made within hours of the arrest. Yet, as barrister Helena Kennedy points out in her book *Eve Was Framed: Women and British Justice* (2005):

> Rarely is this going to be their best and most complete account, because of the state they are likely to be in ... Inevitably interviews are interrogator-led, and one frequently finds that the defendant's story is told inadequately because the answers reflect the limitations of the questions. If, for example, a woman is never asked whether her husband beat her, she may not mention it at that stage, especially if she is finding the atmosphere unsympathetic.[10]

Ruth made no mention of the physical or emotional abuse she had suffered at David's hands. Nor did she refer to the part Desmond Cussen had played in events over the Easter weekend, telling the police she had taken a taxi to Hampstead on the evening of Good Friday, omitting that she had seen him on Saturday and Sunday, and claiming to have arrived at Tanza Road by taxi that evening, which may or may not have been true. But it was the first time she had spoken about her son, and Detective Chief Inspector Davies was alarmed, fearing that her 'apparent indifference' might imply she had killed the child before she set out for Hampstead with the revolver in her handbag.[11] He immediately dispatched an officer to 44 Egerton Gardens, where housekeeper Joan Winstanley was amazed to be 'woken up in the early hours by the police and told [Mrs Ellis] had shot her young man'.[12] Wordlessly she opened the door to Room 5, where Andre slept soundly on his camp-bed.

Ruth was led back to her cell, where WPC Eleanor Hogg kept watch on her. The night passed in a blur: 'Policemen, cars, statements, cold rooms in Hampstead Police Station, cups of sweet tea, a feeling that my mind was somehow detached from my body.'[13] There was a crackle of interest inside the building as everyone discussed the unlikeliness of the crime. Ruth struck them all as quiet and fragile; she was only 5 ft 2 in. in her stockinged heels and weighed less than 7 st. There was nothing in her behaviour that suggested the raging emotions that might cause a person to kill and, despite their combined years of experience, detectives were puzzled by the case.

PC Thompson, who cautioned Ruth outside the Magdala, had brought in the revolver. It was examined by each of the officers in turn, who took no more care to preserve fingerprints than he had done, having already assumed that it was a straightforward murder. But they all agreed on one thing: the gun was too well-oiled to have been left in a drawer for three years.

*

At 9.30 a.m. on Easter Monday, a post-mortem examination was carried out on David by Dr Albert Hunt, lecturer in the Department of Forensic Medicine at the London Hospital Medical College, in the presence of DCI Davies and DC Claiden.

Hunt's post-mortem report and sketches of David's clothing show the bullet entry and exit wounds together with details of how they occurred. There were 'small, circular tears' in those articles covering the right side of David's lower back (his jacket, waistcoat, singlet and the upper material of his trousers), and similar holes on the left side of the upper back through the jacket, waistcoat, shirt and singlet.[14] Further holes had been torn in the jacket, trousers and pants over the left hip and there were two holes on the inner side of the left sleeve of the jacket where David's arm was grazed by a bullet.

Hunt describes the four wounds, numbering them in turn. Entry wound one was 'just above the outer part of the left hip bone, penetrating skin and underlying fat only, with an exit wound quite close by'.[15] Entry wound two was 'below the angle of the left shoulder blade' and the resultant track passed

> between the ninth and tenth rib upwards piercing the lung and passing out of the chest cavity in front of the spine, through the aorta and across the trachea and up the right side of the neck. The bullet is lying in the deep muscle of the right side of the tongue.[16]

This wound caused 'a large amount of blood in the chest cavity'.[17] Entry wound three was in the lower part of the back on the right-hand side and had passed 'through the muscle and abdominal cavity, through the second part of the duodenum, through the lower part of the liver and out through an oval wound just below the rib'.[18] The exit wound left a large black hole in David's chest. The fourth wound was a deep graze below his left elbow. Hunt believed that it may have been caused by the trajectory of the same bullet that formed wound one – the shallow wound above David's hip bone – 'but it might equally have been caused by a separate bullet'.[19] He observed:

> Each of the bullet wounds have entered through the back. There are no entry wounds in the front. Looking at the track of wound numbered two, it suggests that the deceased was either bending down or lying prostrate. Number three passes through the body almost horizontal with the ground when the man is in a standing position. Number one goes slightly upwards and forwards. This suggests he might have been bending forward . . . These have caused death from *Shock* and *Haemorrhage* due to gun shot wounds.[20]

For further clarification, Hunt added: 'The wound which entered the chest [entry wound two] . . . was in my opinion the wound which played the greater part in causing death. I cannot express any opinion as to the order in which the wounds were caused.'[21] He also noted the presence of 'partly digested food and a blackish fluid which had an alcoholic smell' in David's stomach.[22] From his jacket pocket, a Boots tin with a blue and white label was removed; inside were 12 unused capsules of amyl nitrate. Hunt also found eight ampoules in silk wrappings secured with red cotton, a plastic tray containing cotton wool and one spansule packed with white, yellow and orange particles.

Two bullets were removed from David's body: one from his ribs, which Ernest Pett had carefully extracted during the journey to hospital, and the other from his tongue at post-mortem. The police already had the first and Hunt passed the second to DC Claiden after the examination. DC Claiden also took possession of a blood sample from David, two samples of his stomach contents, the tablets from David's pocket and four garments in which there were bullet holes. All these he eventually deposited, together with the gun, at the Metropolitan Police Laboratory at Scotland Yard.

Detective Constable Thomas Macmacken, who had already taken shots of the crime scene and the Vanguard, arrived to photograph David's body. Laying him on a white sheet on the ground, with a wooden block propped beneath to allow for the necessary angles, DC Macmacken filed four photographs as exhibits: '1. Shews fully clothed body. 2. Shews head and shoulders. 3. Shews bullet wounds on back. 4. Shews bullet wound on front of body.'[23]

DCI Davies returned to Hampstead Police Station. Ruth was brought from her cell into his office, where he gave her a piercing look from behind his spectacles. Then he addressed her: 'Ruth Ellis, as a result of a post-mortem examination conducted on the body of David Blakely, you will be charged with murdering him.'[24] She was cautioned, charged and cautioned again.

'Thanks,' she replied.[25]

It was 12.30 p.m. She was told she would be appearing at Hampstead Magistrates' Court 15 minutes later; it was within the same building. WPC Garrad explained that she would accompany her into court and sit with her while the charge was read out. Ruth nodded, then remarked, 'An eye for an eye, a tooth for a tooth. I will hang.'[26]

WPC Garrad shook her head, 'Don't say that.'[27]

Ruth still seemed preternaturally calm despite her words. WPC Garrad tried to engage her in small talk. Ruth responded normally but without interest until she spoke of her son. Then it was time to leave for the court; Ruth was escorted to the heavy door and out into the cold air to the covered stairwell that ran the length of the station yard. As she descended, she could see David's squat Vanguard parked among the police cars. WPC Garrad remained at her elbow as they entered a separate area of small offices, interview rooms and then the waiting room of the Magistrates' Court, which had been specially reconvened for an Easter Monday.

Prompted, Ruth entered the court through the Prisoners' Door on the right. Inside was a surprisingly small room with wood panelling and a glass ceiling that did nothing to dispel a sense of claustrophobia. To the left of the door was a cubicle, walled in wood and glass and entered through a separate door, where the public would normally sit. The odd little dock was directly in front: a narrow platform with a correspondingly narrow bench bordered by rails, it resembled a seat on a Victorian fairground ride. To the right of the room were the witness boxes. The magistrates' chair was in the centre of the room with the seats for legal representatives in front.

Ruth stepped up into the dock and sat next to WPC Garrad, who recalled holding Mrs Christofi's hand throughout her hearings. Afterwards, Ruth described her state of mind:

I remember thinking, as I sat in Hampstead Magistrates' Court, 'How many women would be in this position if they had a gun in their dressing table?' I remember that tune humming in my head: '*I still believe we were meant for each other*'.[28]

Proceedings were brief: DCI Davies gave evidence of Ruth's arrest and she was granted legal aid, with a solicitor in Whetstone assigned to represent her. The magistrate then gave the instruction for her to be remanded in custody; she would appear in the same court on 20 April 1955.

There were fewer reporters than might have been expected in court, due to the strike that had affected most national daily and Sunday newspapers since 25 March. Those who were present concentrated on investigating the main characters involved and soon 'the first pornographic pictures of Ruth, taken in the back seat of a motorcar, were trawled up'.[29] The *Manchester Guardian*, which wasn't taking part in the industrial action, featured the case in a small column on the front page:

Man Shot Outside Public House: A man was shot outside a public house in South Hill Park, Hampstead, London, last night. He was dead on arrival at hospital. Later a woman went to Hampstead Police Station to help the CID with enquiries.[30]

Otherwise the story received little coverage, apart from a brief reference on the BBC's *Six O'Clock News* to Ruth's appearance in court. But two newspapermen were keen to explore the background to the case: crime reporter Duncan Webb, working at the *Sunday People*, and his rival Dougie Howell at the *Daily Mirror*. Both were eager to buy Ruth's story and probe further. Although Webb had already met Ruth, Howell caught a taxi to Ruth's address at Egerton Gardens and managed to persuade Mrs Winstanley to join him for a drink in the Bunch of Grapes on Brompton Road.

Howell asked the housekeeper if Ruth could afford a good lawyer, explaining that the Mirror Group were willing to buy her life story for a sum that would cover all legal costs. He then pulled out a letter, which he said he had taken the liberty of drawing up earlier; Mrs Winstanley's signature would ensure that his friend, a solicitor with a formidable record, was willing to handle Ruth's case. It was a far better option than legal aid, Howell added. Mrs Winstanley hesitated, then took the pen and signed.[31]

At Goodwood Court, Desmond had received a call from Hampstead Police Station informing him that Ruth had been charged with David's murder. Muriel claims that Desmond appeared at her door later that day, with her parents and Andre. When Andre ran upstairs to play with his cousins, Bertha told Muriel of the previous night's events. Muriel, who knew nothing of her sister's life during recent months, recalls that her mother told her not to speak to anyone about it. Andre remained with Muriel while her parents departed with Desmond; Bertha and Arthur travelled to Hemel Hempstead to impart the news to Granville and Desmond drove to Hampstead Police Station.[32]

Giving his occupation as a director of Cussen & Co., Desmond made a statement about his relationship with Ruth and described the past two years in some detail, admitting to a certain competitiveness for Ruth with David. He discussed the beatings Ruth had received, mentioning the visit to Middlesex Hospital, and also his part as an unofficial chauffeur for Ruth when she and David fought. He was candid about the financial assistance he had given her, and her stay at Goodwood Court. But regarding the Easter weekend, he was oddly vague. He provided a few particulars about Good Friday but told police: 'I cannot remember what happened on Saturday, certainly nothing of any importance.'[33] His account of the previous day, Easter Sunday, was banally brief:

> I met her by arrangement during the morning. She and the boy
> – Andria – came to my flat where she cooked a meal and they
> stopped with me until about 7.30 p.m. During the day there was
> some slight reference to David, but Ruth certainly did not
> mention any intention of harming him. I drove them back to
> her room about 7.30 p.m. and that is the last I saw of her. I next
> heard from Hampstead Police that she was in custody.[34]

His recall of events from just an hour or so earlier – that is, immediately before his arrival at the station – are noticeably different from Muriel's account: 'I later drove Ruth's parents and the boy to London Bridge Station today.'[35] There is no mention of a visit to Ruth's sister's flat and, according to Desmond's statement, Andre accompanied his grandparents to Hemel Hempstead. He concludes: 'Although she lived with me, at no time have I seen a gun in Ruth's possession nor have I heard her talk about one.'[36]

Other statements were taken that day, and CID officers visited Clive at South Hill Park before collecting Ant from Tanza Road for the journey to New End Mortuary, where he had the unbearable task of identifying the body of his best friend. In his statement to police he described Ruth's appearances at Tanza Road and the damage to the Vanguard on Good Friday. Regarding Easter Sunday, he explained that David had left the party that evening with Clive at about 8.30 p.m., adding wretchedly: 'That was the last I saw of Blakely, until I went to Hampstead Mortuary at 2.35 p.m. on 11th April, where I saw his dead body.'[37] An inevitable cold fury towards Ruth pervades his statement and, as the case unfolded, that feeling would only deepen. He was aware even as he spoke to police that afternoon that David should have been taking part in the BARC International race meeting at Goodwood; the 2000cc sports car race was won by David's friend Archie Scott-Brown.

There was no possibility of a chance encounter with Ruth at Hampstead Police Station as Ant departed for home. Immediately after leaving the Magistrates' Court, Ruth was driven to the place where she would spend the few remaining weeks of her life: Holloway Gaol.

16

Joan Henry's 1952 book *Who Lie in Gaol* documents life as a prisoner in HMP Holloway shortly before Ruth's incarceration there. Henry, a debutante turned romance writer, was convicted in 1951 of passing a fraudulent cheque and sentenced to twelve months' imprisonment, of which she served eight months, in Holloway and Askham Grange respectively. *Who Lie in Gaol* became a best-seller, creating a wave of controversy in its depiction of the prison service. She followed it with a novel about a young woman's experiences in the condemned cell; published in 1954, the book was called *Yield to the Night*.

Holloway Gaol as Joan Henry and Ruth Ellis knew it no longer exists; it was razed to the ground and rebuilt in the early 1970s. The original building where they were imprisoned was described as 'Victorian Gothic in its most overpowering form'.[1] The castellated Gothic front, ornate battlements, towers and innumerable buildings spread over 10 acres, with an 18 ft wall surrounding the entire complex. Initially housing both male and female prisoners, in 1902 it became the city's first women-only prison and underwent significant renovation in the 1930s, remaining virtually unchanged until its demolition 40 years later.

Ruth's first glimpse of the formidable gates of Holloway was from the back of a police car, with an officer either side of her, at 2.50 p.m. on Easter Monday 1955. She was led upstairs to reception, where the process of depersonalisation began. In a small office she gave details of her occupation, religion, date of birth and next of kin before the contents of her handbag were listed one by one. A female doctor weighed, searched and superficially examined her, looking for signs of venereal disease and foreign bodies in her hair. Remand prisoners were subject to almost the same regime as convicted criminals, except that they were permitted to wear their own clothing. By late afternoon Ruth Ellis was simply Prisoner No.9656.

The prison hospital, to which she was assigned, was on the ground floor and reached through the centre of the main building. Floors of cells and connecting iron staircases were visible all the way up to the roof, with wire nets hung across the landings to catch suicidal prisoners. Yellow fog suffused the place. On the ground floor a wide stone passage led to the hospital complex containing padded cells, punishment cells and the block for mothers and infants. A lavatory marked with a large red cross was set aside for those with venereal disease. Upstairs were three wards: one for those suffering mental health problems, another mainly for expectant mothers and a third general ward. Ruth was shown to a bed with a hard mattress and stiff pillow. Beside it was a chair and small wooden cupboard on the brown linoleum floor. Light filtered through the thickly barred windows. In the centre of the room was a large table where prisoners ate and, at the far end, a gas fire. All inmates had to make their beds before breakfast and help clean the ward, bathroom and toilet before the head sister appeared with the doctor and matron on their daily rounds.

Remand prisoners were afforded certain privileges, including daily visits and access to reading materials from friends and family on the outside, although court cases were cut from newspapers before being handed over. Smoking was not permitted except during exercise in the yard, where there were two narrow circular stone pathways: remand prisoners walked on the inner path, convicted prisoners on the outer one. Babies in Moses baskets were laid out on a patch of grass and left in the care of a trusted prisoner during exercise. When infants reached the age of nine months, they were removed from their mothers.[2]

Ruth's hospital case notes – unlike her actual prison records, which are thought to have been stolen from Holloway in 1964 – have been preserved. They show that she was examined that day between 5.10 p.m. and 5.43 p.m., then interviewed until 6.10 p.m. She had suffered a nosebleed earlier, which the doctor thought was due to stress but Ruth told him it was because she had banged her nose somehow the previous evening, although there was no obvious bruising.

The person who conducted Ruth's interview describes her as 'a heavily made-up woman' with 'bleached platinum hair', 'composed but rather hard-faced and abrupt in manner' although 'very cooperative'.[3] Ruth referred to David as 'my boyfriend' and explained that she was divorced with two children, 'a boy aged 10 years in a boarding school at Aylesbury and a daughter aged 4 years who has been given into the husband's custody'.[4] Ruth then described the past week, having been warned not to discuss anything she had not already admitted to police. The interviewer made extensive notes, including:

> States she has been living with David Blakely for two years. On Friday he left her after a quarrel. She determined to shoot him. On Sunday she went from her flat to the flat of a friend. Afterwards when she had been refused admission she saw him drive away in his car. She assumed he had gone to the local public house. She followed him there and shot him six times with a service revolver she had. There were eyewitnesses of what happened. It would be about 9.30 p.m. that night. It was in the street in Hampstead. She states all the above she has stated in a written statement to the police. She thinks that although he had left her that he would return again. He had gone racing at Le Mans before and returned to her. She states that she has not given a full account of the quarrel to the police as it would have entailed dragging in the names of other people whom she did not want to mention.[5]

There are a number of interesting lines in this part of the report. 'She determined to shoot him' and 'she followed him there and shot him six times with a service revolver she had' make it plain, if it were not already so, that Ruth intended to take full responsibility for David's death.[6] Equally significant is her intimation that another person was involved in some capacity: 'She states that she has not given a full account of the quarrel to the police as it would have entailed dragging in the names of other people whom she did not want to mention.'[7] Ruth was not protecting the Findlaters, whom she loathed; it is far more likely that she was referring to Desmond Cussen.

The interview continued. Prompted by the medical examination, Ruth admitted David had been violent towards her:

> States bruise on thigh is due to David 'knocking me about' last week. States 2 weeks ago he struck her on the left ear so that she was deaf for some time. Test of hearing . . . shows no obvious impairment of hearing now.[8]

When asked about any previous convictions, Ruth stated that she had none, replying 'sharply' and appearing 'shocked by the suggestion'.[9] The notes reveal more about her frame of mind:

> She is well orientated and appears to show no confusion over dates and times. She gives a lucid coherent account of herself spontaneously and with no prompting. There is an almost complete absence of display of emotion, but she is obviously very tense and keyed up, and trying hard to be matter of fact.[10]

The opinion of the interviewer is summed up in a single line: Ruth was 'a jealous woman who felt herself scorned'.[11] Afterwards Ruth asked for a Bible and a photograph of David; she was then sedated and slept throughout the night.

A visitor called to see her that evening but was turned away. Fifty-three-year-old solicitor John George Arscot Bickford had been urged to present himself at Holloway by reporter Dougie Howell. Bickford worked for the firm of Cardew-Smith & Ross; part of the defence team in the sensational Rattenbury and Stoner murder trial in 1935, he also served as Public Prosecutor in the British Zone in Austria after the war. Bickford claimed that he initially refused to visit Ruth because it was Easter Monday, but when Howell turned up at the office with Mrs Winstanley's written instructions, he 'went down to the prison in the evening. When I arrived, I was told Mrs Ellis was under sedation, so I left a note for her and arranged to call the following morning.'[12]

Ruth's first meetings that day were with the Governor, chaplain and welfare officer. The former, Woking-born Dr Charity Taylor, was a firm but compassionate woman, an avid proponent for prison reform, introducing practical and academic classes for inmates, permitting them to wear make-up and allowing those who gave birth in prison to keep their babies as long as the law allowed. She gave occasional interviews in the press to highlight areas where the system could be improved and said that being a wife and mother made her better able to govern Holloway. She and Ruth would meet often during the next few weeks.

Bickford called later that morning and was astonished by Ruth's vehemence that she did not want him to plead for her life to be spared. After giving him the gist of her statement – which was not yet available to Bickford – she told him that she would declare at her trial how she had fully intended to shoot David. Bickford asked her to consider a plea of insanity but Ruth dismissed the idea, using the same words she had spoken to WPC Garrad the day before: 'An eye for an eye. A life for a life. I took David's life and I don't ask you to save mine. I don't want to live.'[13] She repeated too that she felt justified in her action and hoped that he would bring this out in court. Flabbergasted, Bickford urged her to live for her children and said he would find out as much as he could about the background to her case. He asked if there was anything else he could do. Ruth asked him to visit her mother and to keep her belongings safe.

He was about to depart when she suddenly seized upon something; she asked him to give a message to Desmond Cussen. 'I realised it must be terribly significant,' Bickford recalled, 'because she was so insistent that I should give it to him. She said that she had forgotten to tell him that she had got the gun from a fellow at the Little Club who handed it over for security for £5 or something like that. And she said that she had told the police this and she wanted me to tell Cussen.'[14]

Ruth reeled off Desmond's address and telephone number.

After leaving Holloway, Bickford called on Ruth's mother at her place of work. He told Bertha that he had spoken to her daughter, who appeared quite well. He then 'collected certain domestic articles' belonging to Ruth and telephoned Desmond to arrange a meeting for the following day.[15] He made another call, this time to Victor Mishcon & Co., where Leon Simmons was astonished to hear why Ruth had not arrived for her 2.15 p.m. appointment. He agreed that Bickford should handle her trial for murder, since his firm were not criminal defence solicitors.

In Holloway's hospital wing, Ruth asked for pen and paper. She then steeled herself to write a letter to David's mother (the spelling errors are Ruth's own):

Dear Mrs Cook

No dought these last few days have been a shock to you.

Please try to believe me, when I say, how deeply sorry I am to have caused you this unpleasantness. No dought you will hear all kinds of stories regarding David and I. Please do forgive him for deceiving you, has regarding myself. David and I have spent many happy times together.

Thursday, 7ᵗʰ April, David arrived home at 7.15 p.m., he gave me the latest photograph he had had, a few days hence had taken, he told me he had given you one.

Friday morning at 10 o'clock he left and promised to return at 8 o'clock, but never did. The two people I blame for David's death, and my own, are the Findlayters. No dought you will not understand this but perhaps before I hang you will know what I mean. Please excuse my writing, but the pen is shocking. I implore you to try to forgive David for living with me, but we were very much in love with one and other unfortunately David was not satisfied with one woman in his life.

I have forgiven David, I only wish I could have found it in my heart to have forgiven when he was alive.

Once again, I say I am very sorry to have caused you this misery and heartache. I shall die loving your son. And you should feel content that his death has been repaid.

Goodbye

Ruth Ellis.[16]

The peculiarly stiff tone of the letter may be explained by Ruth's desire to write a formal apology to the woman whose son she had killed – a woman regarded as having some social standing – and her own repressed emotions. In the short letter, there are three references to Ruth's own incipient death; there can be no doubt that she expected to be hanged.

Ruth's state of mind during her time on remand in Holloway can only be imagined. In *Who Lie in Gaol*, Joan Henry writes:

> When you hit bottom everything is levelled. It does not matter whether you are standing next to the most wicked woman in the world or whether you yourself have not been meted out half the punishment you deserve. You are still human beings, sad, and far from home. If somebody smiles at you in prison – you may have never seen them before – you will remember it all day.[17]

Many inmates suffered 'nerve storms', destroying everything in their cells, which either released the pent-up emotion or led to a complete breakdown. Henry refers to the 'terrible dreams' no prisoner was able to escape; Ruth found it impossible to sleep without medication, mirroring Henry's experience: 'There is no escape from the long night which in time would make even the most energetic listless and lethargic.'[18] Daytime brought the harsh reality of the situation more firmly to bear, as Henry writes:

> It is impossible to walk along the landings and endless passages to work, to exercise, to church, without being aware of the misery, the tears, the despair, which those drab stone walls have witnessed. This atmosphere of suffering was to me almost like a living thing.[19]

As Ruth's first full day in prison drew to a close, her name appeared again in a small column in the *Manchester Guardian*:

> Remanded on Murder Charge: Ruth Ellis, 28, a model, of Egerton Gardens, Kensington, was at Hampstead yesterday charged with the murder on Sunday night of David Blakely. She was remanded in custody until a week tomorrow. Blakely was found shot outside a public house in South Hill Park, London.[20]

*

On Wednesday, 13 April, Bickford called at Goodwood Court.[21] During the coming weeks, Desmond would inundate Ruth with letters, books, make-up, perfume and flowers, and visited her in Holloway as often as possible. His first meeting with Bickford was contentious because the two men could not agree afterwards on what was said – but the solicitor was resolute that what Desmond told him that day amounted to a confession of being an accessory to the shooting in Hampstead.

In a televised interview for the 1977 *Story of Ruth Ellis* documentary, Bickford declares that after passing on Ruth's message, Desmond replied, 'Well, the truth is that I gave Ruth the gun, but the police don't know that.'[22] In a written account five years before, Bickford gives more detail:

> [Desmond] was intimately concerned with both Ruth Ellis and David Blakely and knew as much as anybody of the association and was quite clearly on the side of Ruth Ellis. So much that,

having been assured by me that I only had Ruth Ellis's interests at heart, he told me of the part which he had played in the affair. Amongst other things, he told me that he had supplied her with the revolver. He said that he had cleaned and oiled it. He wiped the bullets and loaded it. He showed her how it worked, his explanation being that she knew that he had a collection of three or four guns, she was so beside herself and so persistent and he was so much in love with her that he, eventually, gave way.

Throughout Good Friday and Saturday, she had been in constant touch with him and he had driven her wherever she wished to go, in search of Blakely.

She was quite beside herself with grief, jealousy, frustration and, consequently, anger. From recollection and without reference to papers, I feel sure he told me that it was on Easter Sunday morning at his flat that he prepared and gave her the gun.

Probably about midday or in the early afternoon, Mrs Ellis and Cussens [*sic*], together with her young son Andrew or 'Andy' as she called him, aged then between 10 and 13, drove to Penn, Buckinghamshire, in search of Blakely. They did not find him and started off on the return journey. On the way back, I think near Gerrards Cross, they stopped by a wood and Ruth Ellis got out of the car and fired at a tree. It is just possible that the son may recollect this. They continued on their way and when going over one of the bridges over the Thames, I am not at the moment certain which one he said it was, Cussens stopped the car and having previously reloaded the gun with another bullet to replace the one which had been fired, he threw the remaining spare bullets and the cleaning materials, which he had used, into the Thames.

They drove back to Mrs Ellis' flat in Egerton Gardens and I seem to recollect that he said he left her there with the boy. Whether he waited or not, I cannot now say, but she put Andy to bed, took the gun in her handbag and was driven to Tanza Road by Desmond Cussens, where he left her and drove back home.[23]

It was startling information and, armed with what Desmond had told him, Bickford dashed back to Holloway, where Ruth's response left him nonplussed. He recalled: 'She immediately said, "Yes, but I don't want Cussen involved in any circumstances whatsoever."'[24] According to Bickford, she admitted that Desmond had spoken the truth but she was to blame for putting him in such an untenable position. 'She said that she had over-persuaded him,' Bickford recalled,

> because she knew he loved her . . . She told me she thought she was guilty and just wanted to get the whole thing over with, so that she could die and join David Blakely. I talked about her responsibility to her children and so on and urged her to make an effort. She made it quite plain that she was quite prepared to die; but wanted her story told so that her friends and relatives would know why she had done what she did . . . She was most anxious that nobody else should be involved, she did not then want to defend herself but she wanted to tell her story.[25]

Bickford succeeded in convincing Ruth that if she wanted to condemn the Findlaters publicly then she had no choice but to plead *not* guilty so that it might all come out in court. Ruth wrote to a friend shortly before the trial that this was indeed her aim: 'What I want is that the jury should hear my full story.'[26]

Bickford departed from Holloway that afternoon 'in a quandary'.[27] He felt the value of Desmond's information was negligible in that it did little to help Ruth's case,

> because if evidence had been available that she had been acting in concert with someone else . . . her chances of an alternative verdict of manslaughter on the possible grounds of lack of premeditation were virtually nil, and likewise, her then very feasible chance of a reprieve, would virtually have vanished.[28]

He seems to have dismissed the idea of Desmond as instigator of a murder plot, perhaps because Ruth had already insisted that she had had to plead with him to let her have the gun, rather than him putting her up to it.

Nonetheless, Bickford was deeply uncomfortable at the idea of deliberately withholding information and agonised for some time about which path he should take. After much soul-searching, he resolved to remain silent:

> My first duty was to my Client . . . I therefore decided, in the interests of my client and, having regard to the professionally confidential relationship, which then existed, that it was my duty to withhold this information and to recommend Cussen to go to another solicitor, which he did.[29]

In an unpublished letter he added that he advised Desmond to consult a different solicitor 'before I knew he would be called as a witness for the prosecution, as indeed at that time it seemed to me to be unlikely'.[30] Having reached a decision, Bickford did not waver from it, but the moral and legal dilemma caused him endless torment, which worsened in the years to come.

For the time being, he had obtained 'a picture of sorts and various names and addresses' from Ruth to investigate further. And despite having advised Desmond to speak to another solicitor, the two men met again: 'He helped me to collect her things and was most co-operative.'[31] Bickford gave no further hint of anything Desmond may have said to him while he was deliberating how best to present Ruth's case.

Ultimately, Bickford settled on aiming for a verdict of manslaughter and if that failed, a recommendation of mercy that would give him room to press for a reprieve. There was a significantly weak spot in obtaining a manslaughter verdict: the absence of contact between Ruth and David from Good Friday to Easter Sunday. It was difficult to argue that the shooting was an impulsive act caused by provocation when the last time Ruth saw David was more than 48 hours before. Her refusal to account for her activities on the afternoon and early evening of the shooting further depleted her chances of being convicted of manslaughter rather than murder.

The defence of diminished responsibility, which would almost certainly have saved Ruth from the gallows, was not recognised in English law in 1955.

Following her meeting with Bickford, Ruth had an appointment with the prison doctor. She discussed her background with him in detail and was frank about her past, although less so when giving her occupation ('I am a professional model and mannequin since December 1954'), and spoke at length about David, including his death.[32] The doctor noted:

On day of offence she went home and got a revolver which she
had hidden . . . She shot at David . . . 'He deserved what he got'
. . . Cause of actions appears jealousy . . . States she did not
mind what happened to her, at the time she was in such a rage at
the way David and his friends were dealing with her.[33]

The police continued to obtain statements from witnesses and various
people involved in Ruth and David's lives. On Thursday, 14 April,
Bickford's firm of Cardew-Smith & Ross wrote to ask the Director of
Public Prosecutions for a copy of any statement that Ruth had given
to police, adding: 'We also understand that a Mr Desmond Cussen
also made a statement to the Police and we have his authority to ask
you if we may have a copy of this statement as well.'[34] The office of the
Director of Public Prosecutions replied the following day, explaining
that they had not yet received any papers on the matter. Ruth's parents
arrived at Holloway that afternoon for an interview with the prison
doctor, who recorded their names as Mr and Mrs George Neilson;
Ruth's father was then working as an animal technician at the British
Medical Research Laboratory in Colindale. There was no mention of
physical or sexual abuse within the family, nor of any mental or
nervous illness, although they discussed both George Ellis's and David
Blakely's assaults on their daughter. The doctor eccentrically noted
that Ruth had 'chocolates, cigarettes and many flowers in cell. Also
has ornamental pair of spectacles. Reading weekly, by Ethel M Dell.'[35]
Ruth's parents attempted to persuade their daughter to enter a plea
of insanity but she refused, telling them defiantly: 'It's no use. I was
sane when I did it and I meant to do it. I won't go to prison for ten
years or more and come out old and finished.'[36]
Death, unsurprisingly, occupied much of Ruth's thoughts. When
Jacqueline Dyer visited for the first time, Ruth asked her immediately:
'Are they going to hang me?' While Jacqueline drew in her breath,
Ruth said quickly, 'I don't mind, but go and see him [David] and tell
me what he looks like.'[37] Reluctantly, Jacqueline did as she was asked.
In readiness for the funeral, David's body lay in a white, satin-lined
coffin at an undertaker's in Sloane Street, a chapel of ease only a few
minutes from Egerton Gardens. When Jacqueline reported back,
Ruth responded that she was very pleased David was 'being properly
cared for'.[38]
Among those giving statements was Ruth's former French teacher,

Marie Therese Harris. Having heard about her pupil's arrest, she telephoned Commander Jones of Special Branch, who was a neighbour. That same evening, 16 April, DC Claiden called at her flat just before supper. Mrs Harris remembered him afterwards as a pleasant man who talked until she and her husband were faint with hunger. Eventually, she suggested they all eat together and they sat down to a dinner of eggs and bacon. DC Claiden departed with a full stomach and a statement about the guns Mrs Harris had seen in the drawer at Goodwood Court.[39]

Detectives were also investigating the matter of the amyl nitrate found in David's possession, hoping to pin down whether it had been for medical reasons or recreational use; it was very much the Viagra of its day. Since March 1954, David had been registered with a Dr McGregor, who assured detectives: 'I have never at any time given him capsules of amyl nitrate.'[40] However, he had given David 'two capsules or ampoules of Dexedrine', a type of amphetamine developed in the 1920s and originally used to combat depression and excessive weight gain. Potentially very addictive, among its side effects are fluctuations in mood. In the 1950s it was fairly widely used both as a diet pill and an amphetamine. Dr McGregor explained:

> Some weeks ago [David] informed me he was entering a motor car race [Oulton Park] and after a discussion I gave him two capsules or ampoules of Dexedrine, which were so compiled as to give a prolonged effect of alertness and concentration. As his racing car broke down during the practice run I presume he did not use the capsules but I made no further enquiries in the matter. During the period I have known him his health has been excellent and he always seemed in first class physical condition.[41]

Ruth's hospital case notes began recording her well-being at regular intervals from 17 April; she had put on four pounds during her first week in prison, probably as a result of eating properly. The notes from 17 April read:

> Day report: Has been quietly reading most of the day. Makes no complaint. Evening report: Reading at intervals during the evening. Stated eyes ached at times. Conversation seems quite rational, but patient shows no emotion whatsoever. Took her

supper. Medication at 8 p.m. Night report: Slept well. Very little to say. Had breakfast.[42]

The following day she was 'quiet. Has been reading most of the day. Makes no complaints. Taken fair amount of diet.'[43]

Police attention had now turned firmly to the murder weapon. On 18 April, DCI Davies and DC Claiden called on Cussen to ask whether he had ever given a revolver to Ruth or indeed owned one. He replied that he had not, on both counts. When confronted with Mrs Harris's statement, he told them that he couldn't understand it, and obligingly searched the drawers in his flat. He showed them a Webley air pistol and an Em-ge starter pistol, which produced a moment of farce when one of the detectives accidently pulled the trigger. The guns were taken away for examination. DCI Davies and DC Claiden then visited Mrs Harris to ask if she recognised the guns but she was unable to be specific. Absurdly, the .38 Smith & Wesson that killed David Blakely was not among those shown to Mrs Harris, since it was in the Metropolitan Police Laboratory. Neither she nor Desmond were asked to make further statements.

Ruth's hospital case notes for the following day record:

> Reading quietly in bed. (something) of indifference. Day report:
> Quiet and composed. Resting this afternoon. No complaints.
> Taken diet. Evening report: Sitting reading. Calm and pleasant
> in manner. Taken cocoa. Night report: (medication) 9.30 p.m.
> Slept well. Very composed. Had breakfast. To court this am.[44]

DC Claiden and WPC Garrad arrived at Holloway early that morning to collect Ruth for her appearance at Hampstead Magistrates' Court at 9.30 a.m. DC Claiden recalled: '[Ruth] used to sit in the back of the car and a WPC was with her, and just chat away about things in general. She wondered if I was married, had children, that sort of thing. Just as if she were being taken to a tea party.'[45]

In Hampstead, Ruth was driven into the courtyard of the police station and led up the familiar closed stairwell. DCI Davies questioned her about the gun, but all she would say was that she had kept it concealed in a towel, which forensic tests proved untrue. The detective told her bluntly that they didn't believe her story about how she had been given the gun. Then he added that they had found the name of a notorious East End gangster in her diary; Ruth replied that he certainly was not responsible. DCI Davies persevered, telling her that they knew the gun had been cleaned and recently oiled, rather than hidden away for three years.

Ruth looked at him for a moment. Then she lifted her shoulders and said: 'Was it? I know nothing about it, I am sorry.' [46]

In court, Bickford represented Ruth for the first time as she sat in the dock next to WPC Garrad, listening to DCI Davies as he conferred with the magistrates' clerk about a date for committal proceedings; it was decided they would begin on Thursday, 28 April. Bickford asked for copies of any relevant statements and DCI Davies duly informed the court that he would bring the request to the attention of the Department for Public Prosecutions. By eleven o'clock Ruth was already back on the hospital ward in Holloway, where a prison officer noted she remained 'very calm and composed', spent much of the day reading, and appeared 'very indifferent in attitude'. [47]

The question of the gun and what he knew about its origins continued to plague Bickford. Many years later, he responded to the suggestion that Ruth's case had seemed incontrovertibly 'open and shut' by nodding: 'It looked like it, and that's why the police didn't bother to trace the story of the gun originally. I think they thought they had it in the bag and that was it.' [48] But the police report, compiled by DCI Davies and dated 20 April 1955 (the date of Ruth's second appearance at Hampstead Magistrates' Court), reveals that there were other issues involved: the twin prejudices of class and gender.

17

DCI Davies's report on the case opened with a brief summary of Ruth's early life without mentioning any form of abuse during her childhood and teens. He then skimmed the surface of her marriage to George Ellis, stating that Ruth's husband had filed for a divorce,

> on the grounds of mental cruelty by his wife. In the petition he alleged that they frequently quarrelled, that she shouted, abused and nagged him, and accused him of having improper relations with other women. These allegations were denied by Mrs Ellis, who blamed her husband's excessive drinking for the break-up of the marriage.[1]

Again, there was no reference to the violence Ruth had suffered at the hands of her husband, a considerable oversight since her parents had told police in some detail about the injuries caused to their daughter.

DCI Davies then turned his attention to David, summarising his background and noting: 'This family are of some standing and are highly respected in the neighbourhood . . . Blakely was very popular and well respected among his circle of friends, who are all, generally, of the motor racing fraternity.'[2] Unfortunately the police failed to interview Cliff Davies, who was the most honest of David's friends regarding his shortcomings and Ruth's strengths; they spoke only to the Findlaters, who disliked Ruth – particularly after the shooting – and Clive Gunnell, who never had a bad word to say about anyone. Other than that, the police relied on the respective landlords of the Magdala and The Crown, and the cocktail bar attendant at The Bull for additional insight, each of whom had listened to David's often inebriated complaints about Ruth, and none of whom were familiar with her.

Regarding the relationship between the couple, DCI Davies observed:

> There is some conflicting evidence as to who was at fault here because, on Ellis' side, it is said she was trying to leave Blakely, while on his side, it is said he was trying to leave her. We do know that she 'chased' him and even called upon friends of his at Penn in Buckinghamshire. This caused Blakely some concern.[3]

He then referred to Easter Sunday:

> At about 8 p.m. that evening she put her son, Andria, to bed, took a gun she had hidden and put it into her handbag. She says the gun was given to her about three years ago in a club by a man whose name she does not remember. It was as a security for some money but she accepted it as a curiosity. She did not know it was loaded when it was given to her, although she knew the following morning. She says that when she put the gun in her handbag she intended to find David and shoot him.[4]

There is further reference to the gun: 'Efforts have been made to trace from whom Mrs Ellis obtained the revolver used by her in this offence, but so far without success. Enquiries are being continued with this end in view.'[5] He stated that the taxi driver whom Ruth alleged had driven her to Hampstead on the evening of the shooting had not yet been traced. If this struck DCI Davies as puzzling (one would imagine that a cabbie would recall this particular fare, given that it involved a blonde who asked to be dropped off close to where a killing occurred that same evening), he said nothing about it in his report.

He then described Ruth's pursuit of David after he spent the night at Pamela Abbott's house in Penn, largely basing his information on Mrs Abbott's testimony. This section of the report ends:

> Mrs Abbott does say that at some time, she cannot say when, David told her that the woman Ruth was violently in love with him but he 'hated her guts'. She was able to gather from all this that David was trying to shake off this woman but she would not be shaken off.[6]

DCI Davies briefly turned to the matter of David's violent temper: 'There is confirmation of the fact that Ruth Ellis did suffer some injuries as referred to by Cussen in his statement.'[7] He quoted Dr Robert Hunter Hill on the occasion when he examined Ruth at Middlesex Hospital and found her to have 'multiple bruises on her right arm, left arm, left hip, both legs and she had a black left eye. The only bruise of any severity was over the left ankle.'[8] In view of the repeated beatings Ruth suffered, this section of the report is wholly inadequate, although it must be remembered that Ruth herself was unforthcoming on the subject.

Regarding the last few weeks at Egerton Gardens, according to the report, David only returned to live with Ruth

in order to prevent her creating any further disturbances as far as his friends were concerned . . . However, it seems that in spite of going back with her, Blakely did not intend that this arrangement should last very long, and it was when she decided that he had left her following Good Friday that she made up her mind to take this drastic step.[9]

DCI Davies's conclusions are damning against Ruth:

This is clearly a case of jealousy on the part of Ellis, coupled with the fear that Blakely was leaving her. In spite of what Cussen says that Ellis wanted to be rid of Blakely and he would not leave, the weight of evidence points quite clearly to the position being completely reversed. The two people concerned, Blakely and Ellis, are of completely different stations in life. Her parents Mr and Mrs George Nelson [sic], have for some months been residing in two rooms at 3 Ferncroft Avenue, Hampstead, where Mrs Neilson is the Cook and General Domestic. For this she receives 30/-d per week and the two rooms free of rent. Her husband has never fully recovered from the effects of his injuries received during the bombing of London and is now an animal attendant at a laboratory in Colindale at a wage of four pounds 6.0d for a 7-day week. It will thus be seen that this girl has tried to rise above her humble beginnings and is considered by her parents to have done very well for herself. However, they both agree their daughter has always had a violent temper. On meeting Blakely and realising that his class was much above her own, and finding him sufficiently interested in her to live with her and, if we are to believe Cussen, to promise her marriage, it seems she was prepared to go to any lengths to keep him. Finding this impossible, she appears to have decided to wreak her vengeance upon him.[10]

Thus DCI Davies relegated David's attacks on Ruth to a matter of little or no importance, condemning Ruth as a working-class floozy who saw an opportunity to better herself and took revenge when thwarted in her social-climbing, pecuniary ambitions. David's own excessive jealousy, violence and infidelity, together with his reliance on her which led to the loss of her position, income, home and self-respect was disregarded. Any mitigating circumstances for Ruth's actions on Easter Sunday were lost in the detective's deeply subjective and discriminatory assessment of her character.

In a footnote to his findings, DCI Davies referred to Ruth's letter to David's mother, which Mrs Cook had handed to her solicitors, Bliss, Sons & Covell of High Wycombe, who then forwarded it to Hampstead Police Station, where it arrived that very day. Enclosed with it was the telegram Ruth had sent to David on 10 January, asking if he had the guts to say goodbye to her face.

DCI Davies's report, together with 26 witness statements, was submitted to the Director of Public Prosecutions. Mrs Harris's statement about the guns she claimed to have seen in Desmond's flat was not included, and there was no mention of her evidence in the report. However, a copy of her statement was given to Bickford, who spoke to her with a view to calling her as a witness. She was not subpoenaed, despite the fact that she could have told the court not only about the guns but also about Ruth's disposition in the weeks before the murder, and the injuries she had seen inflicted on her.

DCI Davies's conclusions were transparent:

> It is certain that [Ruth's] action was coldly premeditated because, without thought to her son to whom she is said to be very attached, she left him alone to come to Hampstead with her mind made up to commit this murder.[11]

His report is among hundreds of papers from this period in a thick file in the National Archives, including a yellowing sheet dated 22 April.

The signature is illegible but the comment is clear: 'Straightforward case of shooting – with eyewitnesses and admissions and REAMS of "background".'[12]

*

In Holloway, the subject of the report informed Bickford that she 'did not intend to go through with sentence if found guilty' and planned to obtain 'a drug' from her old boss, Morrie Conley, to end her life.[13] There would be other indications that, despite her determination not to be reprieved, Ruth intended to commit suicide rather than face the hangman.

Her hospital case notes record that the day after this revelation there was no discernable change in her manner: 'Remains composed and pleasant. Reading for long periods . . . Made no complaint.'[14] Although Ruth relied on sedatives at night, the following day she told the wardress that she had found it very difficult to sleep. She was 'very talkative and bright when visited' and 'appeared rather strained'.[15]

Bickford was among Ruth's visitors that day, 22 April; he also spoke to Holloway's Principal Medical Officer, Dr Mervyn Ralph Penry Williams, about Ruth's mental health. After Bickford left, Ruth seemed keen to talk to someone; her hospital case notes record that she began reminiscing about her past and how she had expected David to marry her after her divorce, adding that she had 'several love notes from him and a signed photograph' from the Thursday before the crime.[16] Ruth then stated that she had 'not drunk heavily for at least two weeks' before the shooting and 'expressed regret' for having wounded a bystander.[17]

That same day the *Daily Mail* ran an article on the shooting, stressing David's background as the apparently well-educated son of a doctor with a promising career in motor racing. Ruth was portrayed as 'a 28yr old model . . . Her hair was short, stylish, her dress exclusive, but she failed to rid herself of a Manchester accent . . . She felt it a barrier to Mayfair.'[18] Ruth had never had a Manchester accent but the article continued with a description of how she had striven to overcome her humble beginnings, although 'every turn failed, for Blakely was still ashamed of her'.[19] The *Daily Mail* also referred to David's funeral, 'attended by many leading motorists'.[20] He had been laid to rest at the Holy Trinity churchyard in Penn, his grave in a small cemetery dominated by the 900-year-old church. Locals were appalled by the tragedy of his death, remembering a very different David to the man described by the press. Novelist Elizabeth Taylor recalled how, when her son fell seriously ill with pneumonia earlier that year, David had sat with him for hours, and that her 14-year old daughter 'adored' him, as did his 'little niece' and countless others.[21] To them he was 'a dear young man . . . so kind and gay . . . whom we all loved very much'.[22] The revelations about David's 'double life' in London had rocked the village; Elizabeth wrote that he had been 'caught up in a strange net of ugliness and fear' with 'a very frightening sort of woman'.[23] She was so distressed by his death that when she heard Ruth's trial was set for 14 June, she left to stay in Ireland with her friend Elizabeth Bowen. A change in circumstance saw the trial date altered, resulting in Elizabeth being in Penn after all; Bowen comforted her, 'I was glad for you that it was over so quickly. Also, nothing horrible about David. I wish I had known him.'[24]

Ruth had asked someone – probably her mother – to send 'spring flowers' to David's funeral on her behalf. News of the service did not disturb her apparent equilibrium, however.[25] On 23 April, Ruth's hospital case notes record: 'Day report: Composed, pleasant, co-operative, taken diet well. Evening report: Quiet evening. Resting in bed, smoking cigarettes and reading books. Does not complain. Taken cocoa. Night report: Slept well during the night. Had breakfast.'[26] The following day her mood was much the same, apart from a complaint about a pain in the left side of her chest. Visitors found her 'rather talkative' and she mused that it had been 'a very long day'.[27] She spent much of the following day reading and writing letters, relieved that the pain in her chest had gone. One of her correspondents was Clive Gunnell, who had put aside his feelings about David's death to support her. She replied:

Dear Clive

Thanks for your letter. No dought you have been shocked rather badly.

Thanks for all the racing news, it is nice hearing all about Peter and the rest. How is the girlfriend, you know who I mean.

Give my best regards to all the people I know, who are still my friends.

Well at least Clive, you can say, I told you so. You have been right all the time.

Holloway is a jolly nice place better than Butlins holiday camp you are always talking about peace and quiet.

Everyone is jolly nice here it has surprised me.

Thanks for your advice regarding Rose H, the lawyer has already fixed everything.

I am rather surprised that you are continuing to race your car, I seem to remember you telling me, that you were giving it up.

Sorry about the writing, the pen is definitely not my type at all. Has you know Mr Bickford is my lawyer, I feel sure he will do his best, but I have no (faulse (I have forgotten how to spell) idears about my position, so do not worry (friend) I shall be able to take it.

I have a visitor everyday which breaks the monetary [monotony], I have seen Morry C and Mrs C [Conley and his wife Hannah], he is as faulse has ever.

Please excuse the writing paper, heading, but the printers could not get my own crest printed in time.

Well, Clive, I am in court Hampstead police station? on the 28th Thursday, so you will be reading more about things, so don't forget to order your copy right away.

Bye for Now. Clive.

Thanks Once Again.

R. Ellis.[28]

Clive's statement was among those passed to the Director of Public Prosecutions and now under discussion. Although he gave a fair and detailed account of the shooting, he made no attempt to analyse the relationship between Ruth and David or disclose anything that David had said to him previously about her. Ant had given a second statement in which he discussed Ruth's visit to Carole a few weeks prior to the murder. He had already given a full account of his view of the relationship and the rows he had witnessed. He had little to add, apart from: 'I heard all about the ups and downs of this affair [with Ruth] from David, and although I saw Ellis fairly regularly, the matter was not discussed by us.'[29] Several other witnesses had also given further statements.

Bickford was keen to obtain as much information as possible from the Director of Public Prosecutions and on 23 April the papers he had requested were sent to him. To Bickford's surprise, he learned that 'Mr Desmond Cussen will be called as a witness for the prosecution', resulting in his statement being withheld.[30] In what appeared to be a complete reversal of interests, Desmond was no longer part of Ruth's inner circle but instead had joined those whose testimony would be used to convict her of murder. Bickford had fully intended to call him as a witness for the defence; in his pre-trial notes, 'Brief to Counsel to Appear on Behalf of the Accused', he writes that Desmond

> has frequently visited her in prison and is likely to be of assistance to the defence if he is not attacked. He was frequently at the club during the material times and can confirm much of what she says. She told him a great deal of her association with Blakely but sometimes misrepresented the position . . . It is believed that the Police may suspect him of having originally possessed the gun. But the Accused is quite definite that this was not so and she certainly does not want anything to be said or done, which might involve him in any way.[31]

There were further surprises in store. Bickford had contacted DCI Davies to ask if he would approach the Director of Public Prosecutions for a list of prosecution witnesses and those persons interviewed but not expecting to be called, with a copy of any relevant statements. The office of the Director of Public Prosecutions subsequently telephoned Bickford to explain that they 'couldn't let him have a copy of the statements' and would 'explain the position to him at court in Thursday week'.[32] Among those not being called were the two youths who had witnessed the shooting, David James Lusty and George McLaughlin Stephen, and Dr Robert Hunter Hill, who had examined Ruth's injuries at Middlesex Hospital.

Bickford had also requested 'a list of the articles in the possession of the Police, which were either removed from our client or her flat at 44 Egerton Gardens and an opportunity for inspection'.[33] Ruth had complained on several occasions that the police confiscated her spectacles shortly after her arrest, but according to the Director of Public Prosecutions, these had since been returned to her along with her keys, cigarette lighter, cigarettes, lipstick, two combs and a bottle of make-up. The letter from the Public Prosecutions office declared: 'I understood nothing was removed from the flat', a comment repeated at the foot of the list of Ruth's personal effects: 'No property was taken by police from Mrs Ellis's flat at 44 Egerton Gardens.'[34]

On 27 April 1955, Lewis Charles Nickolls of the Metropolitan Police Laboratory filed his report on the revolver, the air pistol recovered from Desmond's flat and the oils in both guns. In his book *Forty Years of Murder*, forensic pathologist Keith Simpson discloses:

> Because of our national dearth of gunmen, until the 1960s there was no ballistics expert on the staff at Scotland Yard. The police relied on the help of private gunsmiths, of whom the most famous was Robert Churchill. For the police surgeon and the pathologist the crucial question in a fatal shooting is whether the wound indicates murder, accident or suicide; each has its distinct features.[35]

Nickolls was thorough in his examination of the guns and oils; he had worked on several high-profile cases before, including the Craig and Bentley case. In his report he explained that although 'on receipt the Smith and Wesson revolver was in working order', during the course of firing in the laboratory, 'the cylinder catch broke as the result of a long standing crack in the shank'.[36] In effect, had this fault shown up on the night of the shooting, the barrel would not have revolved as it should, making it impossible to fire. Nickolls outlined the defect in his statement at Hampstead Magistrates' Court the following day but said nothing about it during Ruth's trial at the Old Bailey, perhaps judging it of lesser significance since the gun had fired normally that night in Hampstead. In his report he explained:

> The trigger pull is 9 and a half – 10 lbs uncocked, and 3 lbs cocked . . . the cylinder contained, on receipt, 6 spent cartridges. In order to fire these 6 cartridges it is necessary to cock the trigger 6 times, as in the case of a revolver pulling the trigger only fires one shot. To pull a trigger of 10 lbs requires a definite and deliberate muscular effort . . . The revolver could only have been discharged by cocking the hammer and releasing it.[37]

He stated that the oil on the revolver 'is a mineral oil. It is similar to the oil on the Webley air pistol but it is not possible to say whether they are the same oils.'[38]

The point Nickolls was making when referring to a 'definite and deliberate muscular effort' was that it wasn't particularly easy to fire the gun – especially with little or no tuition – and in order to do so, Ruth must have been determined to shoot David that night, for all

Ruth at primary school
(© Rex Features)

Ruth before she became a platinum
blonde (photo credit unknown)

Bertha, Arthur, Ruth and Betty Neilson,
c. Christmas 1953 (photo credit unknown)

George Johnston Ellis, whom
Ruth married in 1950. They
divorced in 1955
(© Getty Images)

The Little Club at 37 Brompton
Road, Knightsbridge. The club was
on the first floor, above the shop;
Ruth's flat was on the second floor
(author photo)

Ruth with Morris Conley, c.1953/4 (© Mirrorpix)

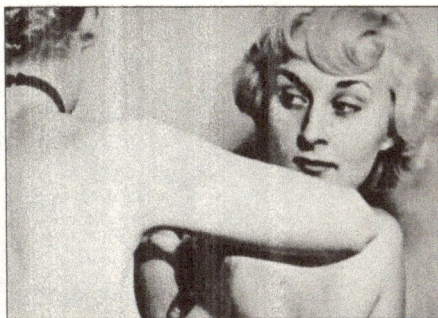

Ruth in a risqué photograph thought to
date from 1953 (copyright unknown)

Carole Findlater, Ant Findlater, Ruth and
David Blakely at the Little Club
(© Mirrorpix)

Ruth, in her flat above the Little Club,
*c.*1954. (© Getty Images)

Tanza Road, Hampstead. The Findlaters' flat is the first building on the left (author photo)

Ruth (third from right) and Desmond Cussen (third from left) (© Mirrorpix)

Goodwood Court, where Desmond Cussen lived at flat 20. Ruth and Andre moved in with him for a while in December 1954 (author photo)

The flat where Ruth and David lived at the time of the shooting, 44 Egerton Gardens, Knightsbridge (author photo)

The Magdala Tavern, South Hill Park, Hampstead. On the night of the murder, David's car was parked directly outside the entrance of the pub; Ruth waited against the wall, near the windows on the right, for him to emerge (© Getty Images)

The Magdala Tavern, Easter 2012 (author photo)

Hampstead Police Station on Rosslyn Hill, where Ruth was taken immediately after her arrest and kept overnight. The following day she appeared at Hampstead Magistrates' Court; the entrance door (second from right) can be seen at the side of the building (author photo)

Young boys standing on a wall to get a better view outside Holloway Gaol on the morning of Ruth's execution, 13 July 1955
(© Getty Images)

Ruth's son, Andre. He sits on the second row from the front, third boy from the right (used by kind permission of Mr C. de la Salle)

Ruth's daughter, Georgina (© Rex Features)

At Ruth's request, her mother laid carnations at David's grave in Penn
(photo credit unknown)

Executioner Albert Pierrepoint at Ruth's grave, 1977
(© *The Sun*/NI Syndication)

her nerves and poor eyesight. Muriel claims that she was physically incapable of doing so, an issue that is discussed in the appendix; Marks and Van den Burgh point out that without someone having tutored Ruth beforehand it is unlikely that she would have shot David at all, let alone four times. This is not necessarily the case, since Ruth was directly behind David when she first fired, and close on his heels as he ran from her; the final shot came as he lay incapacitated on the ground and was aimed into his back from mere inches away. However, had the gun been handled more carefully after Ruth's arrest, other fingerprints might have been detected. Equally, there is no record of Ruth's clothes or person being inspected for oil residue or bloodstains. WPC Eleanor Hogg could not recall any telltale marks on Ruth's clothing when she arrived at Hampstead Police Station.

While Nickolls filed his report, Ruth prepared herself for her third and final appearance at Hampstead Magistrates' Court the next day. Her brittle manner didn't go unnoticed by the prison staff, who noted that evening: 'Appears composed but shows signs of mental strain.'[39] The following morning she dressed in a grey and black tweed suit with velvet piping and black suede shoes, and applied heavy eye make-up and a pale lipstick.

The police car that collected Ruth from Holloway drove swiftly into the station yard to avoid the large crowd of reporters and photographers gathered outside the courtroom doors on Downshire Hill. Among them was Tim Leuty from the Manchester office of the *Sunday Pictorial*; he had brought a guest, who stumbled into the foyer of the court completely inebriated, the tails of his camel overcoat flapping.

'Stop the trial, stop the trial! I want to see my wife's lawyers!' shouted George Ellis, insisting that he had evidence to help Ruth.[40]

One of the Cardew-Smith & Ross staff took him aside, but he had nothing useful to add and was quickly returned to Tim Leuty, who bundled him away to a nearby pub. Leuty's newspaper bought George's life story but when the piece was sent to his solicitors for approval, the ghostwriter's memo was accidently left attached to it; he had flagged up George's alcoholism and position as a dental officer, advocating: 'I suggest we expose this bastard.'[41] George's solicitors immediately contacted the *Sunday Pictorial* editor to ask him to retract the series, which would spell professional disaster for their client. He agreed, but kept the story on file and ran it a few years later after George's death.

Someone else was clearly agitated before the hearing began. In the small waiting room Mrs Winstanley watched as Desmond Cussen paced up and down either side of the seats in the middle of the room. Sweat poured from his receding hairline and gathered on his clipped moustache. Eventually, Ruth's former housekeeper stood up and asked if he was quite well, but he made no reply and turned away.

When they were called in, Ruth walked straight to the iron-railed dock with WPC Garrad, keeping her eyes averted from the people squeezing onto the benches of the public booth. Morris Conley slid his bulk along the seats, having let it be known that he could not understand why Ruth had expressed a wish for no more visits from him; Mrs Winstanley was of the opinion that he was piqued his former employee had not asked him for financial assistance either. When the benches were filled, Ruth glanced round just long enough to notice that the Findlaters' nanny was there. The realisation inflamed her.

Mr Sebag Shaw represented Ruth against the charge that 'on the 10th April 1955, at South Hill Park, Hampstead, in the County of London, she did murder David Moffett Drummond Blakely, Against the Peace of our Sovereign Lady the Queen, Her Crown and Dignity'.[42]

He entered Ruth's plea of not guilty. The case was then put forward for the Crown, with prosecutor Mr Claxon stating that before the shooting, whenever David left the flat, 'Mr Cussen would come round and more often than not Mrs Ellis went out with him.'[43]

Ruth clicked in irritation but composed herself while her statement was read out by DCI Davies. She betrayed no emotion as the revolver was produced, or when the lead witnesses gave their evidence. PC Thompson demonstrated how he had encountered Ruth outside the Magdala, pointing the gun at David's prone body. Gladys Kensington Yule, wearing an elaborate hat and fur coat, gave her account with her thumb bandaged and in a sling. The *Daily Sketch* reported: 'Ellis, in a grey and black tweed costume, toyed ceaselessly with an embroidered handkerchief . . . she propped her black suede shoes against the railings of the cage-like dock of the tiny panelled court.'[44] Her 'eyes narrowed' when the photograph of David taken for the Bristol Motor Team was produced.[45]

It was not until the court reconvened after lunch, when she returned with a folded coat to make sitting on the dock bench more comfortable, that Ruth showed any sign of emotion. As Desmond stepped up into the witness box a few feet to her right, Ruth put on her horn-rimmed spectacles and peered at him. Then she dropped her gaze again. But as he spoke about his affair with her and how she had shared his flat, borrowed money from him and asked him to drive her to Tanza Road on several occasions, she began slowly tapping first one black high-heeled suede shoe against the iron rails and then the other. The sharp tapping was plainly audible in the small courtroom. Desmond perspired profusely but focused his attention on the questions put to him. He was the last witness for the Crown.

The magistrates then committed Ruth for trial at the Old Bailey and the court emptied. Before returning to Holloway, Ruth was shown into one of the small cubicles that passed for an interview room. Mr Sebag Shaw asked her how she felt it had gone. 'Why do you say I'm not guilty when I am?' she demanded, even though she had agreed to it in order to expose the Findlaters. 'I killed him, and I've got to die for it.'[46] As she left the building via the enclosed stairwell, a representative from the Blakely family's solicitors asked to speak to one of the detectives in charge of the case; he asked for David's possessions to be deposited with his firm 'to proceed with the winding up of Blakely's estate'.[47] He was told to put the request in writing.

It was 5.45 p.m. when Ruth arrived back at Holloway. She was exhausted and only remained awake long enough to be given the news that the *Woman's Sunday Mirror* had bought her life story. She hoped it would generate enough income to leave a small nest egg to Andre and had either forgotten or not been told that the fee would cover the costs of her defence. Her hospital case notes record: 'Very tired on return from court at 5.45 p.m. To bed at 6 p.m. Quiet and polite in manner.'[48] The following morning she appeared 'refreshed and cheerful' after a sedated sleep.[49] Throughout the day she was 'rather talkative' and inclined to 'fidget'.[50]

For the next two days, the newspapers were a blaze of sensational headlines and gossip generated by the court hearing. The *Daily Mail* led with: 'Six revolver shots shattered the Easter Sunday calm of Hampstead and a beautiful platinum blonde stood with her back to the wall. In her hand was a revolver.'[51] The *Daily Herald* headline was punchier: 'Hostess with Two Lovers Shot One'. There were many more, including the *Daily Express*'s 'Court Hears of Loves of the Little Club Girl'; the *Daily Telegraph*'s 'Model Shot Car Ace in the Back, Say Police'; and another from the *Daily Mail*, 'Four Bullets As He Lay Dying'.[52] The public devoured them eagerly. Cherry Marshall, who ran the Margery Molyneux Agency, was exasperated by the description of Ruth as a model, but admitted that she and her pupils at the agency were 'curious to read all about it':

> The fact that she had two lovers shocked a lot of people more than the actual killing, while we were more curious to know which one did the beating up. But we didn't read anything about that, which we thought a pity as it would have gained her some sympathy. Or so we imagined, although a few people I mentioned it to said they weren't surprised she'd got a bashing if she was playing around with two men ... [but] Maggie Wood kept saying to me that if she'd been in the same state as Ruth when she was in the school she'd have gone berserk herself. We all felt tremendously involved.[53]

Ruth's composure crumbled a little in the days following committal proceedings. Her hospital case notes record on 1 May: 'Appears calm and detached superficially but deep down worried, restrained' and the next day: 'Quiet evening. Arranging flowers and reading until 11.30 p.m. Appeared to have slept, but says had terrible night, not slept at all. Tea only given for breakfast.'[54] The following day Ruth was sent for a mental health assessment at Kelvin House, where Dr Dennis Williams performed an electro-encephalic examination. He found 'nothing to suggest either the presence of organic brain disorder or epilepsy'.[55] She returned to Holloway at midday and spoke to the doctor about the examination, then began talking about her past behaviour ('prisoner states she never used drugs but would often drink 12 gins'), before mentioning that the Findlaters' nanny had been in court.[56] The doctor noted that Ruth still believed Lesley was 'the inducement' to keep David at Tanza Road.[57] Ruth was keen to talk. She told him that David's mother hadn't even known she existed as her son's girlfriend until after he died and that 'Anthony Findlater had covered up by saying David was with him.'[58] She referred to David's affair with Carole and said she was looking forward to being able to 'tell the truth' about the Findlaters at her trial 'although of course it does not excuse what I did'.[59] When Ruth returned to the ward, sleeping through the afternoon, the doctor wrote his report:

> Prisoner appears a very jealous woman based on her own almost amoral behaviour. States David knew she was pregnant, that she had aborted but as far as Findlaters knew she was still pregnant, unless David told them. She had forbidden David to visit the Findlaters because of his previous affair with Carole Findlater. He had obeyed until the weekend when his mother rang up the Findlaters.[60]

On the same date, the prison's Principal Medical Officer, Dr Penry Williams, drafted a letter to the offices of the Central Criminal Court:

> Sir,
>
> I have the honour to report, as follows, regarding the mental condition of the above prisoner:-
>
> She was admitted to this prison on 11.4.55 and has since been under observation by day and night in the prison hospital. I have twice interviewed her and have some knowledge of the circumstances of her alleged offence, but I have not read the depositions. I have interviewed her parents and seen her almost every day.
>
> I have no knowledge of any personal or family history of mental disease or epilepsy.
>
> She states that she attended a primary school to the age of 14 years. She has followed the occupations of housewife, mannequin, model, hostess and manageress of night clubs. She has been married and has two living children.
>
> When she was fifteen years old she states she developed rheumatic fever and spent a considerable period in Dulwich Hospital. Three years ago she had a tubal pregnancy for which an operation was required. In March of this year she had two abortions. On Wednesday April 6th she says she had a severe chill as a result of being soaked by rain. Generally her health has been satisfactory.
>
> Upon admission to prison she was found to be in good health except for a genital infection of non-venereal type for which she has had treatment whilst in custody. She had a bruise upon the left thigh and a more recent bruise on the right forearm.

The only defect of her central nervous system was a minor defect of vision corrected by spectacles. I could find no evidence of mental disease, she realised her position and shewed no gross abnormality of mood.

Since she has been in custody her behaviour has remained rational and restrained. She has been co-operative to examination and maintained a keen interest in her surroundings and legal position and shews no evidence of mental disease.

Examination of her blood revealed no evidence of venereal disease. She appears to be of about average intelligence.

Today, 3rd May 1955, she has with her consent gone to have an electro-encephalograph examination performed and the result will be forwarded as soon as this is available.

With regard to her alleged offence there appears to be little or no impairment of memory. There is no suggestion that she was under the influence of drugs or alcohol.

The deceased was a person with whom she had been on terms of intimate affection, but there appears to have been some breach in this affection during the two days preceding the happening in question.

I have found no medical condition which would be likely to cause the prisoner to be unaware of what she was doing or whether it was wrong at the time of the alleged offence.

She is fit to plead.

I am, Sir,

Your obedient Servant,

M R Penry Williams,

Principal Medical Officer.[61]

For much of the following week, according to her hospital case notes, Ruth was 'inclined to be rather talkative' but 'calm exteriorly'. She spent hours in bed, 'surrounded with books' and although she was sedated at night she 'seemed restless during sleep, position altered frequently'.[62] On 8 May she was allowed to have her hair washed and retinted and as a result, was 'quite cheerful all day'.[63] The next afternoon she returned 'fairly cheerful' from a meeting with Bickford and was overwhelmed by a visit from a group of women she had worked with years ago in the Court Club. In turn, they were relieved to find Ruth in a brighter mood than they had expected, but she stunned them by announcing: 'I want to die because David was the love of my life.'[64]

Afterwards, Ruth wrote to thank them, addressing her letter to ex-hostess Joan Green:

> Dear Joan,
> Just a line, thanking you for the lovely flowers, I would like you to thank Betty, Ronnie, and Lisa.
> I must say, it was rather a surprise, seeing you all here. I really did think, you all where [were] fairly wonderful.
> Well Joan, I hope that club live [life] is still going strong, my best regards, to the few I know.
> Bye for now.
> Yours,
> Ruth Ellis.[65]

Despite her apparent equanimity, Ruth told the warders that she 'would be grateful' if she might continue to have a nightly sedative; she found it almost impossible to sleep otherwise.[66] On 11 May she made a brief appearance at the Central Criminal Court of the Old Bailey before Mr Justice Barrie. Her counsel, Mr Melford Stevenson, applied for a postponement of the trial until after 14 June, 'owing to the large number of enquiries still to be made by the defence'.[67] The application was granted. The list of witnesses who would give evidence at the trial had been finalised the day before, together with a list of exhibits, which included the clothes David was wearing when shot, two bullets, the revolver and six spent cartridge cases. The press had already begun applying for seats, with Dougie Howell and Duncan Webb at the forefront.

Among the defence enquiries was the search for a precedent. In 1955, under English law there were four defences to a murder charge: insanity (Ruth's doctors had stated that she was 'fit to plead'), self-defence (inarguable given the length of time that had elapsed since David's last assault on her), proof that the defendant had not committed the act (all the evidence showed that she had) and, finally, provocation, which was defined as an act that might reasonably cause a person of sound mind to suffer 'a sudden and temporary loss of self-control, rendering the accused so subject to passion as to make him or her not master of his mind'.[68] Bickford remained convinced that their best hope was for the murder charge to be reduced to manslaughter on grounds of provocation, despite the legal difficulty. He directed his team to scour records in England and America for similar cases, despite neither country recognising 'slow burn' provocation as a defence. With diminished responsibility not yet a legal term, it may be that this was why David's violence over the past 18 months, together with his persistent infidelity and emotional abuse, were deemed irrelevant in court.

Yet the possibility of the charge against Ruth being downgraded from murder to manslaughter was not beyond reason. Bickford would have been aware of the case of Elvira Barney, although it was not quite the precedent he and his team were aiming to find. On 30 May 1932, Elvira Barney, a rich socialite who was separated from her violent husband, dined with her lover Michael Stephen at the Café de Paris in Piccadilly after hosting a party at their Knightsbridge home. Following drinks at the Blue Angel they returned home, where neighbours were awoken in the early hours by screaming. Elvira was reputed to have shouted, 'Get out, I will shoot you!' before a pistol shot cracked the night air. Elvira's doctor arrived at the property soon afterwards, summoned by Elvira herself, who told him there had been 'a terrible accident'.[69] He found Michael lying dead on the staircase, shot in the chest. Near his body was a five-chambered Smith & Wesson revolver which when examined by police was discovered to have two empty chambers. Elvira admitted she had rowed with her lover after he threatened to leave her; she had threatened to shoot herself with the gun, which she kept at her bedside. They had tussled, she told police, and the gun went off, accidentally causing the wound to Michael's chest. There was a bullet hole in the bedroom wall, which she was unable to adequately explain. The discussion with the police became heated; at one point Elvira smacked the face of the inspector in charge, yet incredibly she was allowed to return home to her parents after making a statement.

Almost certainly, the careful way in which Elvira's case was handled was due to the fact that her parents were Sir John and Lady Mullens, and the family home was in Belgrave Square. When Elvira was charged with murder on 3 June, Sir John asked former Attorney General Sir Patrick Hastings to defend his daughter. He did so brilliantly, convincing the jury that it was perfectly possible that the revolver had fired inadvertently, since it had no safety catch and an easy trigger pull. The matter of witnesses having heard the couple quarrelling often and violently, and an earlier incident when Elvira was said to have shot at her lover, was said to be without merit; the jury found her not guilty. Outside the court, she was met by a cheering crowd and within days, according to a reporter, she was dancing up a storm in the Café de Paris, shouting: 'I am the one who shot her lover – so take a good look at me!'[70] But four years later Elvira was dead, after a night spent drinking and snorting cocaine in the bedroom of a Paris hotel.

*

Several notable figures had been assigned duties in Ruth's upcoming trial at the Old Bailey in June. Mr Melford Stevenson QC would lead her defence. Born in 1902, he became a barrister at the age of 23 and served as a Deputy Judge Advocate during the Second World War. After being appointed a King's Counsel in 1943, Stevenson served at the Nuremberg Trials and was an outspoken proponent of capital punishment. Barrister Helena Kennedy describes him in *Eve Was Framed*, her 2005 study of women and the legal system, as: 'The scourge of the Old Bailey . . . He was held in very low esteem by many of my generation as a judge of the old school, dogmatic and misogynistic.'[71] She recalled her disgust when, early in her own career, she heard him extending leniency to a rape defendant because, Stevenson said, 'the girl was asking for it', having been hitchhiking at the time of the attack.[72] He dismissed the offence as 'an anaemic affair as rapes go'.[73] In 1955, he was still largely a divorce practitioner and had little experience of criminal court.

Better suited to the task of representing Ruth were either of Stevenson's junior counsel, Mr Peter Rawlinson and Mr Sebag Shaw, the latter of whom had represented her at Hampstead Magistrates' Court. Thirty-five-year-old Rawlinson was then libel reader for the *Daily Mirror* group, who funded Ruth's defence. He published a book of poetry in 1943 and continued writing throughout his legal career, during which he actively opposed the abolition of capital punishment. Very tall and possessed of a fair amount of charm, Rawlinson was called to the bar in 1946 and joined Walter Monckton's chambers, where his first major case was the Towpath Murder in 1953. In his autobiography he recalled Bickford as 'a conscientious and kindly man who did all that could be done' for Ruth.[74] Even before her trial, however, Rawlinson doubted they could win and, if they lost, then he felt the legal system would be to blame, rather than her team: 'As the law stood in 1955 there could be no real defence on her behalf to the charge of murder.'[75]

Presiding over the prosecution was Travers Christmas Humphreys, son of a respected barrister and judge after whom he was named. An ardent admirer of Shakespeare, ballet and Chinese art, he had written several books concerning his religious beliefs and in 1924 founded what became the London Buddhist Society. Humphreys was called to the bar that year. Appointed Junior Treasury Counsel at the Old Bailey in 1934, he had been Senior Prosecuting Counsel for five years at the time of Ruth's trial. After the Second World War he participated in the Tokyo war crimes trials and prosecuted in several high-profile and controversial cases during the 1940s and 1950s, including the trials of Timothy Evans and Derek Bentley, although he did not support capital punishment. Both men were posthumously pardoned after their executions. In his autobiography, Humphreys refers to Ruth in a few lines, recalling that, in his cross-examination of her, one 'deadly' question was sufficient to convince the court of her guilt.[76] He then reflected:

> If it was my karma to prosecute, it was the karma of the prisoner not only to be prosecuted by me but also to have committed that crime or at least to be on trial for it . . . and his death, if he were hanged, it would be the result of his causing, and might, as it were, wipe out the causing in the infinitely complex, infinitely subtle weaving of this cosmic web.[77]

These, then, were the men who would prove pivotal to Ruth's fate.

18

'The photographs of Ruth Ellis in the newspapers showed a young woman with bright blonde hair. That was not how she looked when I saw her in a cell in the Old Bailey,' Peter Rawlinson, then junior counsel, recalled.[1] They met briefly on 11 May, when Ruth made her first, three-minute appearance at the Old Bailey, after Justice Barrie remanded her for trial at the next session. Bickford had asked Rawlinson to see his client before she was returned to Holloway Gaol, and Rawlinson made his way down the steps inside the dock – as robed barristers were permitted – to the corridors beneath the court.

'The surroundings were grim,' he remembered. 'The air reflected the tensions and anxieties which were daily experienced in that place, although mostly by persons without merit who had given no mercy and deserved little in return.'[2] Bickford had to take the longer route and thus Rawlinson arrived a while before him. Ruth was sitting at a small table with a wardress, who left as soon as he entered the cell.

> We shook hands, hers a small, limp hand matching the listless face and the hair from which the dye had faded. I explained to her what had been decided by the Court. She had of course been present, but John Bickford had wanted to ensure that she understood what had happened and also give her the opportunity to tell me anything further that she might wish to say.[3]

Rawlinson sat opposite her at the table and she listened while he explained that the trial would begin on 20 June.

'She looked at me steadily, quite composed but with dull eyes,' he recalled.

I asked if she wanted anything. Was there anything that I could do? She flicked her faded hair back with a toss of her head. 'You will make certain, won't you,' she said quietly, 'that I shall be hanged? That is the only way that I can join him.' I caught my breath and said that she must not talk like that. But she shook her head and repeated, 'I want to join him. I want to join him.' Again I said that she must not speak or think like that, but she made a gesture as though to brush me and my words aside. Clearly, she implied, I did not understand. John Bickford arrived in the room. She stood up. She said she wanted nothing. She made it clear that she wanted to say no more. She wanted to return to Holloway. A little while later I shook her hand and left her with Bickford. I climbed up the steep stairs into the large dock of No.1 Court where a trial was being heard. As I appeared as though from the floor and moved to the door of the dock and was let out by the warder, the judge glanced up and then back to his notes. The traffic of counsel between court and the cells was quite usual. But I felt greatly disturbed.[4]

It was dark when Ruth arrived back in Holloway, ostensibly less upset than her defence, for the wardress noted: 'Returned. Comfortable, composed.'[5] She spent much of the following day reading and her hospital case notes record her manner: 'Self-possessed as usual.'[6] She remained outwardly stoical; the wardress described her on 14 May:

> Still putting on a brave face. Says she knows what will happen to her, her conscience will not allow her to want to live. Stated: 'an eye for an eye. I am prepared to give my life for having taken one.' Read and smoked during the evening. Took supper.[7]

The ledger has a similar entry two days later:

> Composed. Pleasant. Talks freely of the prospect of a short life. States that she gets very depressed at times. Had supper. Night report: Slept until 3 a.m., could not get to sleep again, alarmed at being awake in night.[8]

Ruth was relieved by the news that permission had been granted for her hair to be bleached, which she desperately wanted before her trial.

In Bickford's 'Supplementary Brief to Counsel for the Accused', under 'Accused Personal Appearance' he had written:

> Efforts have been made to enable the Accused to have her hair attended to because it is now changing colour patchily as a result of continued neglect . . . but the Governor has stated that she has no authority to grant such a request. An interview is being sought with the Governor in order to see what can be done: it is submitted that it is of considerable importance to the Accused that she should be able to look her best at the trial . . . Counsel's views are sought as to what steps ought to be taken for the purpose.[9]

Having learned that her request had been granted, Ruth was asked to put her signature to a printed note: 'I, Ruth Ellis, hold no one responsible for the bleaching of my hair which is being done at my own request.'[10] Principal Officer Cherry, who was often on duty with her, witnessed her signature.

That evening Bickford called at Holloway to speak to Ruth. There is no record of what transpired between them, but when she returned to the ward she appeared 'rather tense'.[11] Being woken in the night by a banging window upset her, but she managed to fall asleep again eventually.

On 19 May, Ruth was set several aptitude tests in the prison hospital and scored 98 in an IQ test. She protested that staff had tried to hurry her in completing the tests. The doctor noted: 'Followed test by speaking about club she ran. Proud that she was the youngest manager of a club in London.'[12] Ruth spent the following morning 'arranging flowers, writing letters and reading' and was 'relaxed and chatty' with everyone, including the chaplain when he visited her.[13] Her good mood continued the next day, and she was eager to discuss the books she had been reading. At four o'clock her parents and brother visited. Granville recalled his sister telling them:

> Don't worry about me. There's nothing to be done. It's hopeless. I'm not worried and I've no regrets as to what lies ahead for me. The children are provided for and you are all right at home. I won't let them plead insanity for me. I'm not crazy. I know exactly what will happen. They are going to hang me.[14]

Two days later her spirits deteriorated. She slept during the day but still complained of feeling tired and told the warders: 'Reading doesn't help any more, I'm beginning to find it difficult to concentrate.'[15] She played patience over and over again and a visit from her mother and a friend one morning failed to lift her mood. Her hospital case notes for 25 May read:

> Looked poorly this a.m. and said she did not feel too well. Lying in bed doing nothing most of the morning . . . Tries hard to keep cheerful but states she thinks her 'nerves are going'. Has been restless and talkative all day. Visited this afternoon by lawyer and friends. Evening report: Appears to be on edge and nervy though trying to remain outwardly calm. Night report: States unable to concentrate, finds reading difficult . . . slept after 10.30 p.m., position altered frequently during sleep.[16]

The prison doctor encouraged her to talk and recorded her 'interest in motoring events, [she] likes magazines covering this. Speaks of her acquaintanceship with various people – in motor racing.'[17] Ruth briefly rallied after a visit from Bickford. But during the night of 26 May she told warders she felt 'weak and listless'.[18] A heavy period contributed to her 'very pale' complexion and lack of energy. She slept intermittently throughout the day and was pleasant but clearly tense. On 29 May, she told the wardress: 'I don't like Sundays here. It's so quiet and we don't have visitors.'[19] The following day, after playing patience all evening, she 'talked in a detached manner about arrangements for her children "afterwards".'[20]

As May turned to June, Ruth rallied again and was once more 'fairly cheerful, very self-controlled and composed'.[21] She remarked often how cold it was for the time of year and had taken to reading most of the day in bed. Principal Medical Officer Penry Williams spoke to her at length on 3 June and wrote a detailed account that day:

> During the continued period of observation her only complaint has been of occasional difficulty in sleeping for which she has when necessary been given drugs. She has been pleasant and co-operative in manner, and has maintained her interest in her friends and acquaintances in the outside world. Her behaviour

has been rational and she has fully appreciated the gravity of her position. She has spent much of the time reading.

The further period of observation has revealed no evidence of mental disease. She has maintained her physical health and her normal menstrual periods.

On May 11th she appeared at the Central Criminal Court, and in her hearing her trial was postponed to the next sessions, commencing June 14th 1955.

With regard to her alleged offence, she states her divorce had recently been completed, and she thought she was being unfairly treated by the deceased to whom she had shewn much kindness in the past, and whom she had been living with for a considerable time.

I have not found evidence of any condition which would lead me to think that at the time of the alleged offence she would be incapable of realising the nature and quality of her actions or whether they were wrong.

She is fit to plead.[22]

Attached to his letter was a report of the electro-encephalogram, which found no abnormality.

A few days before, Bickford had approached Dr Duncan Whittaker, a Member of the Royal College of Surgeons and a Licentiate of the Royal College of Physicians, for his opinion on Ruth's mental health. A traditionalist and ardent churchman, with a thick moustache, black-rimmed spectacles and 'curtained' hair, he visited Ruth as a psychiatrist for the defence on Saturday, 4 June. Penry Williams noted his visit and suggested obtaining a second opinion 'as insanity may well be the only defence considered open for her' although her behaviour was 'essentially normal and rational'.[23] Whittaker's report, addressed to Bickford, makes for exasperating reading. He began by stating:

I think it is quite fair to say that provocation-inflaming jealousy has a far more powerful effect upon a woman than upon a man . . . Women are far more interested in inter-personal relationships than men. Women cannot so easily as men separate their sexual experiences with men from their total personal relationship. There are, of course, exceptions, but most people would agree that this is so … Women cannot help being more totally involved in the sexual relationships because they run the risk of having the whole of their life changed by childbirth. From all this it follows that a woman is more upset in the depth of her being by unfaithfulness on the part of her lover. Above all, women are more prone to hysterical reactions than men. The word hysteria comes from the Greek hysteros, the womb, because they thought that the symptoms of hysteria were due to movements of the womb … The occurrence of hysterial symptoms is a sign of emotional immaturity, not necessarily of low intellectual ability.[24]

After quoting Swiss psychiatrist Bleuler on the methods by which hysterical women betrayed themselves with 'erotic smiles', etc. Whittaker turned to his two-hour interview with Ruth:

The feature which impressed me most was her equanimity. She had drifted into a situation which was for her intolerable, she could find no way out, she had not a sufficiently hysterical personality to solve her problem by a complete loss of memory, she knew that, although Blakely was, in her view, being unfaithful to her, and she would not be able to refuse him, and that this thing would go on and on. She had been a successful manageress of her club, and was now living in one room because of his possessiveness and jealousy had made her position at the Club impossible. Her jealousy made her hate him, although she knew she loved him. Finally, when he was dead, she experienced a feeling of relief. An emotionally mature woman would have been prevented from this action by thoughts of her children. I asked her about this point, and she told me that she never once thought of them.

She indignantly denies that her behaviour over the weekend was hysterical, and said that she is on the whole a calm person. Nevertheless, her whole history is that of an emotionally immature person, and her present equanimity is 'la belle indifference de l'hysterique', whose intolerable problem has been solved at an immature level of behaviour and who is prepared to pay the price for this solution. Jealousy, of course, played a very large part, but it was her incapacity to get out of an intolerable situation which finally precipitated her action.

When she had her second child at Dulwich Hospital, her husband became a voluntary patient at Warlingham Park Hospital, and she appears to have had a nervous breakdown of an hysterical type, although I have not seen a report of it but only have her statement.

To sum up, the provocation of jealousy has a more marked effect upon a woman than a man; women are more prone to solve their problems at an hysterical, or at least, immature emotional level. Mrs Ellis is emotionally immature, although intelligent, and did solve her problem at an immature level, although of course, only after great and prolonged provocation.

Although she was not in an hysterical fugue when the action took place, she had during the weekend, experienced mounting emotional tension, frustration, rage and humiliation and, if Blakely had not, in her view, been hiding behind his friends, but had spoken to her even on the telephone and given her the chance of blowing off her tension by upbraiding him, the emotional safety valve, so to speak, would have let down the tension, and this act would, in my view, not have occurred. To this we have to add the fact that he had already let her down on a number of occasions before, but it is not for me to give details of the provocation. In my view the basic cause was the intolerableness of the situation for her, and the actual precipitating cause, the fact that over the weekend he gave her no chance of 'letting off steam'. The final and ultimate provocation was thus not what he did, but what he did not do, i.e., give her the chance to lower her emotional tension.[25]

The Prison Commission wrote to the Director of Public Prosecutions about Whittaker's examination of Ruth. The irony is that all those involved in weighing up her mental and emotional state did not contact Dr Rees at Warlingham; equally, the case was by then on everyone's lips and it seems strange that he did not come forward, although he may simply have assumed that Ruth had informed her solicitor about her past medical history. But Ruth did not want to reveal any more than she was forced to do; over the weekend she told a wardress that there would be a great deal of 'mud slinging' at her trial. The wardress noted: 'Remains only outwardly calm.'[26]

On 9 June, Dr Alexander Charles Dalzell, medical superintendent at Friern Hospital and formerly of the Royal Army Medical Corps, arrived at Holloway to examine Ruth on behalf of the prosecution. He found her to be cooperative and fairly open, although she did not expand on any of her answers to his questions. She said plainly that she had intended to kill David that Easter Sunday and did not regret it. Dalzell judged her to be of sound mind and believed that she had been intent upon killing David when she set out from Egerton Gardens that evening and understood the consequences of her actions. At the end of their meeting, Ruth said she had no objections to a second visit. But her hospital case notes for the following day read:

> Is very distressed at times today. Quietly reading most of the time. Still has a heavy cold. Is very upset about childrens' future, says she regrets that she won't be able to see them grow up. Spent evening sitting by her bed playing patience. Has a heavy cold and looks poorly.[27]

On Saturday, 11 June, Ruth was shocked by news from France: the 24-hour race at Le Mans, in which David had been due to drive for the Bristol Motor Company, hit the headlines when more than 80 spectators were killed by burning debris flying into the crowd after an accident on the track. Mike Hawthorn, the blond, gregarious driver who used to visit the Little Club, was involved; driver Pierre Levegh was killed and over 1,000 spectators badly injured. Ruth's mother recalled: 'When that terrible accident happened at Le Mans, she talked to me a lot about that. It's as though [racing] were in her blood like he was.'[28]

A warder noted the following day that Ruth seemed a little improved: 'Fairly cheerful and still outwardly calm. Cold is subsiding but patient looks rather poorly still. Is very talkative when visited, quietly reading in bed most of the time. Weight 102 lbs.'[29] In the afternoon Dalzell called again; Bickford was turned away because she was with the prosecution psychiatrist. When Bickford saw Ruth afterwards, she said that 'a gentleman with a beard had just been to see her and he said he was a doctor and wanted to ask her some questions. She asked whether he had been sent by her lawyer and he said he did not know who had sent him.'[30] Her hospital case notes for the evening record that she was calm but very 'anxious to talk of the past' and 'worried about her next visit to the Old Bailey'.[31]

Bickford was displeased by Dalzell's visit, deeming it underhand. A representative from his firm Cardew-Smith & Ross wrote to Governor Charity Taylor, describing the visit as a 'somewhat extraordinary situation'.[32] They asked for Dalzell's name and stated that they were 'most perturbed that this interview should have taken place without our knowledge and approval and without our being able to see the doctor or our client beforehand'.[33] In the interim, Dalzell had already dispatched his report on Ruth to the Director of Public Prosecutions, which was not substantially different in its conclusions from Whittaker's findings:

> I found her to be fully co-operative and she expressed herself in a clear and intelligent manner, neither evading any particular points nor going into elaborate and unnecessary details. Her mood was not disturbed; she showed no depression, and though somewhat more obviously cheerful on the second interview, was not elated or excited.
>
> She gave no history of any previous mental illness or nervous trouble, and no history of violent behaviour, uncontrolled outbursts of temper, or undue aggression. She summarised the events of the last two years, and the events leading up to the weekend of April 9th and 10th.
>
> There were no points in her story as discussed at either of the interviews, which appeared inconsistent or contradictory. She stated that she became extremely angry with David Blakely on Friday the 8th of April as he had left her after having made arrangements to spend the weekend with her. She became increasingly angry with him on the Saturday and Sunday owing to his failure to return or to telephone, and her inability to get in touch with him, although she knew where he was. She stated that when she left her home on Sunday evening, she took with her a loaded gun with the intention of shooting David Blakely. She stated that at the time she felt 'tired and run down'; that she had a cold, and had a two months miscarriage some ten days previously, though this did not necessitate any medical attention.
>
> She stated that after having shot David Blakely she felt no regret, and considered that she was justified in having done what she did because of the way in which he had treated her, and that she still felt so justified.

There was nothing to suggest at either interview that Mrs Ellis was suffering from, or had been suffering from delusions, hallucinations or any other symptom of mental disorder. In my opinion she knew the nature of the act which she performed and knew that it was wrong; that she formed the intention of carrying out this act some time beforehand, and that she was aware of the possible consequences to herself.

I do not consider that she is of unsound mind, and I consider that she is fit to plead.[34]

Bickford later claimed in a letter to the Under Secretary of State that Ruth 'was most indignant and flatly denied' ever having said that she felt justified in shooting David, although the defence's psychiatrist had reported her declaring the same thing.[35]

Ruth had an interview with the prison doctor later that day. During their discussion, Ruth produced photographs of Andre and Georgina, explaining the situation with Georgina but adding that she had retained legal custody of her daughter. The doctor noted:

She is thinking of letting her husband's partner, a dental surgeon – a woman – adopt Georgina as the woman is very fond of children and anxious to adopt. States Andria is with relatives and is shortly to return to school but not to the school in which he was previously.[36]

This last remark is curious, perhaps suggesting that Desmond had withdrawn his offer to pay Andre's school fees. It isn't made explicit in the doctor's report, which continues:

States her divorce was made absolute in the third week of February [Ruth was mistaken; it was March]. Discusses a recent serious accident at Le Mans racing track in France and explains that the car driver who was involved [Hawthorn] and not killed was well known to her and used to visit her club . . . Takes great care with her personal appearance. Writes letters poorly spelt but business like.[37]

Another meeting, this time with Bickford, upset Ruth greatly and finally penetrated the shell she had so carefully constructed; at her request he brought with him the police photographs of David's corpse, taken in New End Mortuary soon after the shooting. The hospital case notes record: 'Upset on return from solicitor's visit, had been crying. Said she had insisted on seeing the photographs of "David". They were worse than she imagined. States it is the first time she has cried since she has been here.'[38] Ruth was unable to sleep that night, despite taking a sedative. The next morning she seemed superficially cheerful, talking nineteen-to-the-dozen, and a wardress reported that she appeared 'more excitable, not so composed as usual'.[39] After a little quiet time spent playing patience and reading, she suddenly told the warders: 'I wish I didn't have so much time to think.'[40] They made a note that she seemed 'rather worried'.[41] But the following day, 15 June, she showed a grim humour in a letter to a former friend named Alex (possibly Alexander Engleman, the doorman of the Little Club):

> Dear Alex,
>
> I am writing to you, again, because I hate the thought of you, being without money. Perhaps you can get another £5 for this letter, like you got for the last one.
>
> Yes, Alex, I still have a sense of humour.
>
> Goodbye,
>
> R Ellis.
>
> It's always nice to know, Alex, at times like this, who's one's friends are.[42]

Ruth's trial at the Old Bailey was just five days away. In conversations with the prison staff she spoke about it often, 'and the photographs of "David"'.[43] Her lingering cold was beginning to go at last, but on 17 June, the hospital case notes record that she was very poorly, with pains again on the left side of her chest and looked 'worrying frail'.[44] She kept up a constant chatter nonetheless and was 'cheerful on return from solicitor's visit at 6.25 p.m.'.[45] The meeting with Bickford was to discuss her amended proof of evidence, which ran to 23 pages and is dated 17 June 1955. It ends with her conviction:

> I feel I ought to die – 'An eye for an eye and a tooth for a tooth.'
> I am sorry for what I did insofar as it affects other people: but not so far as it affects myself and David. I am sure he really did

love me; but it was the interference of other people that caused all the trouble.

My great mistake was when I went to live at Desmond's flat – that gave the Findlaters a weapon with which to work on David and I am sure they were urging him to break with me. It accounts for all that business with the nanny – David had become so weak where women were concerned. He used not to be when I first met him, I think the fact that he was hard to get in the first place, was part of his attraction to me when he originally started coming to the Little Club.

I have given in detail the whole history of my association with David and, as I feel now, after full consideration, all I want is that my Counsel should see to it that I can tell my story.

I know the penalty for what I have done and I am willing to pay it. As I am now I would not have done it; but as I was then, with circumstances as they were, I cannot help feeling that it was inevitable.[46]

That day, 17 June 1955, would have been David's 26th birthday. When Ruth's parents visited her, they brought a gift from an apparent well-wisher. Ruth recoiled when she saw the bouquet of one red and six white carnations: David had presented her with an identical bouquet on her own birthday two years earlier. Ruth refused the flowers, shaking her head: 'Someone is trying to frighten me.'[47]

*

The following morning, Ruth was determinedly cheerful and chatty again. She wanted to discuss the clothes she would wear to court; always sharply aware of how she presented herself after years of working in the clubs, she wondered aloud whether her hair would 'look nice'.[48] Bickford and her defence team, who met with her that weekend, were very uncomfortable with the idea, sensing that Ruth's brightly bleached hair would only encourage the press and public – and, more importantly, the jury – to view her with disdain. But the day before the trial was a Sunday, and the Governor had been granted permission from the Home Office to allow her charge to have a full peroxide rinse. Ruth's regular hairdresser, Shack's of Shaftsbury Avenue, sent in everything needed for her usual treatment, together with detailed instructions for a nervous wardress. Ruth was not completely satisfied with the results, but was relieved not to have to appear in court with dark roots. The hospital case notes record: 'She used to get her hair bleached twice a week in a hairdressers as it grew so fast ... Bleaching of her hair appears satisfactory. Prisoner says quite good but cold rinsing has made hair a little too blue.'[49]

While Ruth was having her hair coloured and set, Carole Findlater was in a Hampstead pub giving an interview about her old adversary. She knew *Sunday Pictorial* journalist Harry Ashbrook well and confided in him: 'I'm dreadfully afraid I'll be dragged into the case. Perhaps her solicitors know about David and me.'[50] For two hours, she went over all that she could remember of the past eighteen months, even divulging her earlier affair with David, and shortly before leaving the pub told Ashbrook: 'Poor David. He was terrified of her and I don't believe he loved her. I think he hated her – and hated himself for having been involved with her. I disliked the woman.'[51]

Ruth's trial began at the Old Bailey the very next day.

19

At daybreak on Monday, 20 June 1955, a long queue of people hoping to gain access to the public gallery of Court No.1 at the Old Bailey started to form under warm and cloudy skies. Ticket touts were able to ask £30 a seat, such was the level of interest. Reporters crowded onto the benches behind the dock; Duncan Webb took his place with a studied appraisal of the scene:

> It had been some time since the Old Bailey had witnessed such a 'fashionable' murder trial. By that I mean a trial in which so much public interest was aroused. The public seats were filled with the smart set from Mayfair, the sophisticates of Chelsea and Knightsbridge, the vulgarly inquisitive from the highways and byways.[1]

Ruth's parents and brother Granville were there, but other family stayed away.

Built in 1907, the Old Bailey suffered bomb damage during the war and had only recently been restored. Court No.1 was not a large room, but it was imposing, with light oak panelling on the walls below a ceiling of white arches, under a circular skylight. The judge's bench, with its six tall green chairs and four desks, dominated the space. Below was the clerk of court's table and, in the well of the court, the space where counsel sat. The witness box was to the right of the judge's bench and beyond that, the jury seats. Members of the bar and eminent guests occupied the green leather benches of the City Lands Committee. The octagonal dock was large enough to accommodate a group of people and surrounded by glass panels.

Below court were the various rooms for the legal fraternity, prisoner cells and witness rooms. When Ruth arrived that morning, the police escort party led her through myriad stone passages to a room where she had a brief meeting with her counsel. Bickford stated afterwards: 'Each counsel in turn had an opportunity of meeting the Accused and each was remarkably impressed by her outwardly entirely calm demeanour and her obvious candour.'[2] From there Ruth was taken into the cells. Nearby was a lavatory in a 'narrow, rather dirty cold room where there was no fastening of the door'.[3]

Overhead, the prosecution took their seats. Christmas Humphreys would be assisted during the trial by Hampstead-born John Mervyn Guthrie Griffith-Jones, educated at Eton and Cambridge. Griffith-Jones was 'the incarnation of upper class morality' who earned a place in history five years later with his infamously pompous question at the *Lady Chatterley's Lover* obscenity trial: 'Is this a book you would wish your wife and servants to read?'[4] Also assisting Humphreys was Miss Jean Southworth, a graduate of St Anne's College, Oxford, who was called to the bar in 1954. Ruth's defence team – Melford Stevenson QC, Mr Sebag Shaw and Mr Peter Rawlinson – filed into their seats after the meeting with their client. Presiding over them all was 65-year-old Mr Justice Havers, a High Court judge since 1951 and head of a legal dynasty.[5]

There was a stir and a few low coughs in the hushed courtroom as Ruth was brought up from the cells below. Wearing a black suit with astrakhan-fur collar and cuffs and a white silk blouse, her make-up perfect, it was the immaculately coiffed platinum hair that caught everyone's eye. 'Blonde tart,' said a voice from the public gallery. Ruth did not flinch. She stood next to the wardress who had accompanied her from Holloway and gave a small smile.

Mr Justice Havers recalled afterwards:

> She was extremely calm and cool from when she came into the dock until the end of the trial. I must admit it rather surprised me. I came to the conclusion that she was certain that she was going to be convicted and had made up her mind that she'd got to face it.[6]

The clerk of court stood to address her: 'Ruth Ellis, you are charged that on 10 April last you murdered David Moffett Drummond Blakely. How say you, are you guilty or not guilty?'[7]

'Not guilty,' Ruth replied in a clear, high voice.[8]

The twelve members of the jury – ten men and two women – were sworn in. Their task, of determining whether the woman in the dock was guilty or not, had to be made entirely on the evidence before them. This was not completely subjective, as former family law barrister Leonora Klein explains:

> The evidence is like a script and it has been carefully drafted and re-drafted by the police and the lawyers over the preceding weeks and months. The initial creative force behind this production are the police – how they conduct the investigation, which lines of inquiry they pursue and which they leave out, will determine the essential quality of the final performance ... When the prosecution see the police statements there is another rewrite. The prosecution lawyers may want more evidence to strengthen their case or they may not like all the evidence that the police have gathered – there may be material that they do not want the jury or even the defence lawyers to see. Once the defence have some idea of the evidence they will also want to make changes, and if the lawyers cannot reach agreement on exactly what evidence should go before the jury, the judge will decide ... The jury are only allowed to see the finished version of the script and they are required to accept it as the only version ... These are the rules of evidence and they create a necessary fiction which underpins the whole jury system.[9]

The clerk of the court addressed them:

> Members of the jury, the prisoner at the bar, Ruth Ellis, is charged with the murder of David Blakely on the tenth of April last. To this indictment she has pleaded not guilty, and it is your charge to say, having heard the evidence, whether she be guilty or not.[10]

Humphreys then stood to open the case on behalf of the Crown:

> Mrs Ellis is a woman of twenty-eight, divorced, and the story which you are going to hear outlined is this, that in 1954 and 1955 she was having simultaneous love affairs with two men, one of whom was the deceased and the other a man called

Cussen, whom I shall call before you. It would seem that lately, Blakely, the deceased man, was trying to break off the connection and that the accused woman was angry at the thought that he should leave her, even though she had another lover at the time. She therefore took a gun, which she knew to be loaded, which she put in her bag. She says in a statement, which she signed: 'When I put the gun in my bag I intended to find David and shoot him.' She found David and she shot him by emptying that revolver at him, four bullets going into his body, one hitting a bystander in the hand, and the sixth going we know not where.[11]

Humphreys paused to read extracts from Ruth's statement and gave a number of details about her relationships. He then urged the jury not to let this information influence them:

You are not here in the least concerned with adultery or any sexual misconduct. You are not trying for immorality but for murder, and the only importance of these movements between her and these various men is that it will help you to see the frame of mind she was in when she did what it cannot be denied in fact she did.[12]

Curiously, he referred specifically to prosecution witness Desmond Cussen, almost as if to deflect the question of whether he played a more crucial role in the events of Easter Sunday: 'The only comment I would make upon her statement is that she never mentions Mr Cussen from start to end.'[13]

After reading further extracts from Ruth's statement, Humphreys completed his speech:

Members of the jury, there in its stark simplicity is the case for the Crown, and whatever be the background and whatever may have been in her mind when she took that gun, if you have no doubt that she took that gun with the sole purpose of finding and shooting David Blakely and that she then shot him dead, in my submission to you, subject to his Lordship's ruling in law, the only verdict is willful murder. If, during the trial, any matters arise which enable you, under his Lordship's direction, to find some lesser verdict, then you will do so.[14]

He gave a slight bow. 'Now, with the assistance of my learned friends, I will call the evidence before you.'[15]

The first three witnesses were examined by Miss Southworth: PC Philip Banyard, who drew up the plan of the scene around the Magdala; DC Thomas Macmacken, who photographed David's corpse; and Mrs Winstanley, who confirmed that Ruth and David had lived together at Egerton Gardens. She was soon out of the witness box, where her place was taken by Desmond Cussen. Rawlinson glanced over at Ruth. She sat very still and straight-backed in the dock and he felt himself very 'impressed by her detachment from all that was going on'.[16]

Desmond, in contrast, was visibly nervous. His complexion was unusually pale. Tiny beads of sweat gathered on his temples and about his neat moustache. Prompted, he confirmed that he had known Ruth 'about two years' and had been her lover 'for a short time'.[17] Humphreys led him very briefly through the events of Easter Sunday. Desmond stated that he had last seen Ruth at 7.30 p.m. that evening. Melford Stevenson then rose to cross-examine him:

'You have told the jury that you and this young woman were lovers for a short time in June 1954. Is that right?'

'Yes.'

'And that was a time when Blakely was away, was it not – at the Le Mans race in France?'

'Yes.'

'Were you very much in love with this young woman?'

'I was terribly fond of her at the time, yes.'

'Did she tell you from time to time that she would like to get away from Blakely but could not, or words to that effect?' Stevenson asked.

'Yes.'

'And at that time did she repeatedly go back to him?'

'Yes.'

'At a time when you were begging her to marry you if she could?'

'Yes.'

'Have you ever seen any marks or bruises on her?'

'Yes.'

'How often?'

'On several occasions.'

'How recently before Easter had you seen marks of that kind?'

'On one occasion when I was taking her to a dance.'

'When was that?'

'The twenty-fifth of February.'

Mr Justice Havers leaned forward in his chair. 'Of this year?' he asked.

Desmond looked at him, 'Yes, my Lord.'

'"When I was taking her to a dance"?' the judge repeated.

'Yes.'

Stevenson resumed his questioning: 'Did you help to disguise bruises on her shoulders?'

'Yes.'

'Were they bad bruises?'

Desmond gave a nod: 'Yes, and they required quite heavy make-up too.'

'I do not want to press you for details,' Stevenson said, most peculiarly, 'but how often have you seen that sort of mark on her?'

'It must be on half a dozen occasions.'

'Did you on one occasion take her to the Middlesex Hospital?'

'Yes, I did.'

'Why was that?'

'She came back when she was staying at my flat, and when I arrived back I found her in a very bad condition.'

'In what respect?'

'She had definitely been very badly bruised all over the body,' Desmond replied.

'Did she receive treatment for that condition at Middlesex Hospital?'

'Yes,' he said.[18]

Incredibly, that was the end of the cross-examination. Desmond left the witness box having given what can scarcely be described as the bare minimum of information about Ruth's life over the past two years. There was no attempt to gain insight into his or David's relationship with her, nor to explore his story about the day of the shooting, or to ask him about the revolver. Stevenson had raised the matter of David's violence, with its physical and emotional scars, only to drop it like the proverbial hot cake. Desmond knew more than anyone how increasingly angry, hurt and humiliated Ruth had been during the Easter weekend when David refused to speak to her, yet none of that was brought out either. Reflecting on his cross-examination, it is hard to resist the temptation to view it as a whitewash. Stevenson would explain his approach afterwards, but not necessarily convincingly.

Desmond left the witness box without even glancing at Ruth. The man who had been so devoted to her during the long months of her troubled relationship with David and during the aftermath of her arrest was finished with her; Ruth never heard from him again. He could not escape the Old Bailey quickly enough.

The next witness was Ant Findlater. Ruth immediately sat forward, reeling from Desmond's lack of description about the Findlaters' role, as she saw it, in the breakdown of her relationship with David. Desmond had disappointed her appallingly, but she felt certain that Stevenson's cross-examination of David's mechanic and best friend would reveal the truth to those gathered in court.

It was not to be. Humphreys' questioning of Ant Findlater was brief and merely gave him the chance to tell the court of her 'sarcasm' on the night when he and Clive had called at Goodwood Court to collect David following the row at Desmond's flat, and about her pushing in the windows of David's Vanguard. When Humphreys sat down, Stevenson began the cross-examination, establishing that Ant's sole source of income 'for some time' had been the £10 David paid him to work on the Emperor. He then moved on to Ruth's state of mind during the call that preceded her superficially damaging the Vanguard:

'Was it quite plain when you spoke to her on the telephone that she was in a desperate state of emotion?'

Ant looked at him. 'No.'

Stevenson seemed slightly nonplussed. 'What?' he asked.

'I said no.'

'Do you mean she was quite calm?' Stevenson pressed, incredulously. 'Do you really mean that?'

Ant gave a verbal shrug: 'It was *just* a telephone conversation. She rang me up, as she had done hundreds of times, and asked if I knew where David was. It was just a telephone conversation.'

Somewhat impatiently, Stevenson retorted: 'I *know* it was just a telephone conversation. Just bear in mind what she said and the way she said it and the fact that she afterwards pushed out those windows. Did you observe *no* indication of her being a very desperate woman at that time?'

'No,' Ant replied, almost mutinously.

'Never mind the word "desperate",' Stevenson said, sounding desperate himself. 'Was it obvious to you that she was in a state of considerable emotional disturbance?'

Ant moved his head slowly from side to side. 'Well, I did not get that impression over the phone. She might have been.'

Stevenson frowned and narrowed his eyes. 'Perhaps you are not very good at judging that sort of thing on the telephone . . . Are you?'

Another verbal shrug: 'I think so.'[19]

All of Ant's replies were couched in this air of thinly veiled belligerence. Asked whether on the evening of Easter Saturday there was a Rolls-Royce outside his house, he replied yes, but asked if he and David went 'with this young woman' (Lesley, the nanny) to get into the car he replied, 'I can't remember.'[20] It seems unlikely that he could not recall a drive in such a luxurious car, especially since – as Marks and Van den Burgh point out – he was able to remember with clarity Ruth's tone of voice in a telephone call three months earlier.

If Ruth hoped the question about the nanny would lead to Ant being pinned down on the issue of whether he and Carole had deliberately foisted Lesley on David to lure him away, she was bitterly disappointed by her defence's failure to pursue the subject. It fell instead to Humphreys, the prosecution, to query him about it:

'You will appreciate what is being suggested: that there is some reason for Ruth Ellis being jealous of some new woman being on the stage?'

'I did not even know that Mrs Ellis knew we had a nanny,' Ant replied. 'She knew we had one, but this was quite a new one.'

Humphreys tried again: 'What my friend is putting is that Ruth Ellis, in hanging about, might have seen Blakely in the presence of an entirely new young woman. I am sure you will help us if you can, if you were fooling about or anything of that sort. Was there any incident with a young woman outside the house that you can remember?'

'No.'[21]

Ant's time in the witness box was over. Ruth's ambition to expose the Findlaters as 'malicious snobs' who had destroyed her relationship with David and were responsible for his death – and her own – was in ruins.[22] She had been fiercely opposed to pleading not guilty, and had been persuaded to do so only in the hope of seeing Ant and Carole squirm. But it was finished; although Carole had been subpoenaed, it was decided not to call her, and there was no one else who might 'unmask' the Findlaters as Ruth had so keenly wished.

The trial was moving spectacularly quickly. Clive gave evidence next, describing the incident outside Goodwood Court in a single breath. He spoke almost equally swiftly about Easter Sunday, when he had witnessed his friend's violent death:

> Blakely and I left to go to the Magdala public house to fetch more [beer]. We stayed there ten or fifteen minutes, leaving Blakely's Vanguard parked outside. I came out first, carrying a bottle. I went round to the passenger seat, but the door was locked, so I had to wait for David Blakely. While I was waiting, I heard two bangs and a shout of 'Clive'. I went round the back of the car and saw David lying on the ground. Mrs Ellis was firing a gun into his back. I ran to Blakely and heard Mrs Ellis say, 'Now call the police.'[23]

There was no cross-examination.

Lewis Charles Nickolls followed Clive into the witness box. When Humphreys called him, he did so with the astonishing comment: 'My Lord, I will now call Mr Nickolls because he is anxious to get away.'[24] The director of the Metropolitan Police Laboratory then testified as to the items he had received from Chief Inspector Davies and Detective Constable Claiden on the day after the shooting. He spent a minute explaining the properties and purposes of amyl nitrate, and the single spansule of amphetamine sulphate found on David's body, before stating that the revolver was 'in working order' when he took possession of it; he did not mention the fault that showed up in the laboratory during his examination. 'The barrel was foul and consistent with having been recently fired,' he confirmed, 'otherwise the revolver was in clean condition and was oily.'[25] He added that the recovered bullets had been fired from the same gun.

'Can you help us at all as to the distance from the body at which any of the bullets had been fired in respect of the wounds found in the body?' Humphreys asked.

'Yes,' Nickolls responded. 'I examined the clothing of the deceased man, and I found that on the left shoulder at the back of the jacket there was a bullet hole. This had been fired at a distance of less than three inches.'[26]

There were several gasps and low whistles from the public gallery. Humphreys, not distracted, asked him to identify David's dark grey jacket, which was then passed from Nickolls to the jury, with the bullet hole in plain view.

Mr Justice Havers enquired, 'Why do you say that?'

'That is because of the circle of powder fouling round the hole,' Nickolls told him. 'The others are all fired from a distance.'

'A powder fouling?'

'Yes. There is a circular powder residue. All the other shots had been fired at a distance.'[27] Humphreys did not ask him to estimate the actual distance and Nickolls did not volunteer a guess.

PC Thompson was next in the witness box. He told the court how he had seen Ruth peering through the mottled glass of the Magdala's saloon bar before David was shot outside the pub where he, Thompson, arrested her. Gladys Kensington Yule gave her evidence afterwards, questioned by Miss Southworth. Asked if Ruth had chased David around the car after shooting him, Yule replied, 'Yes.'

'After the shots were fired at the man did you hear another one?'[28]

'I heard two,' Yule confirmed in a loud, precise voice, 'and when he fell, two more.'[29] She then described how she had been shot in the thumb and was taken by taxi to Hampstead General Hospital for treatment.

Dr Albert Charles Hunt gave evidence of his post-mortem examination of David and the discovery of a bullet lodged in the dead man's tongue; he confirmed that cause of death was shock and haemorrhage due to gunshot wounds. DC Claiden then told the court that he had taken possession of two bullets removed from David's corpse.

Detective Chief Inspector Leslie Davies was the final witness for the prosecution. He described Ruth's arrival at Hampstead Police Station and her subsequent interview, adding that he was 'most impressed by the fact that she seemed "very composed"'.[30] He then read Ruth's statement in full to the court.

With that, the case for the Crown was complete. It had taken less than the time allocated for the morning session to hear all the evidence, largely because Ruth's defence, led by Stevenson, chose not to cross-examine all but two of the witnesses. Bickford claimed afterwards that the decision to follow this course was taken prior to the court sitting and without Ruth's knowledge. In a letter to the

Home Office eight days later he wrote: 'Mr Melford Stevenson decided on Monday morning just before the trial that he would subject the witnesses of the prosecution to the minimum of cross-examination.'[31]

Twenty years later he stated with the same conviction on camera:

> I had explained to counsel, absolutely clearly, that in my view to save Ruth Ellis it was essential to have the witnesses for the prosecution cross-examined in the way in which the case had been prepared. Please forgive me, I had a magnificent team and I am not blaming any single one of them – they did their best, God bless them . . . [but] I was completely stunned because my leader [Stevenson], whom I met in the hall of the Old Bailey, with the court all sitting waiting for him, said, 'I'm not cross-examining the witnesses for the prosecution.' We were late, the trial was overdue, I also turned to counsel and said, 'So sorry, I can't accept that.'[32]

Stevenson refuted Bickford's claims, insisting that Ruth's solicitor had never challenged any of his decisions. He explained that he chose not to cross-examine more thoroughly because he felt the witnesses would not add anything to Ruth's case that might prove useful for the defence. Ex-barrister Leonora Klein believes that his approach may have been driven by other considerations:

> Stevenson could have given the jury another version of Ellis's story by exposing the full extent of Blakely's violence and infidelity, but he chose not to dwell on any unpleasantness because Blakely was a man and a member of his own class.[33]

Bickford was adamant that the lack of cross-examination destroyed Ruth's spirit and undermined how she had intended to present herself when the time came for her to step into the witness box. He described Stevenson's failure to question Ant Findlater properly as 'absolutely horrifying' and said he himself 'just wanted to crawl under the table. Because I'd built my whole case on it.'[34] He added that Stevenson's approach resulted in the trial moving 'at such speed that Mrs Ellis was in the witness box before I could explain to her the decision [not to cross-examine] had been made' and thus she gave evidence on her own behalf feeling 'disheartened and somewhat bewildered'.[35] Asked during the 1977 documentary whether he had tried to give Ruth some encouragement and prevent her further depleting her chances of a not guilty verdict, Bickford replied: 'Couldn't. Well, I don't know . . . if I'd been a stronger man or a more determined fellow, or didn't mind making a spectacle of myself perhaps.' His eyes welled with tears: 'Sorry.'[36] Interviewed for the same documentary, Mr Justice Havers described Ruth's defence as 'so weak I think you could say it was non-existent'.[37]

For all his protestations, according to his own testimony, Bickford himself withheld information from the jury. In a letter already quoted from 1972 he gave his reasons, writing that he had felt it 'unwise' to call the first-hand evidence he apparently had from Desmond Cussen, regarding how he had 'driven her to Hampstead, provided the gun, and had goaded her into shooting Blakely to remove a love-rival from the scene'.[38] His feeling that Ruth's chance of a manslaughter verdict and the possibility then of a reprieve would have been reduced by evidence 'that she had been acting in concert with someone else' convinced him to remain silent.[39] Yet if Bickford had pursued the line of Desmond 'goading' Ruth, and if the true nature of her violent relationship with David had been revealed in court, there was at least the sliver of a chance that the jury would have been more sympathetic towards her. Bickford's concern that it might have appeared to be a conspiracy to murder was worth risking, surely. In his defence, it is obvious that Ruth was no help in this regard; she was determined that nothing should implicate Desmond in David's death.

All those involved in the legal process suspected Ruth of prevaricating when it came to the question of who gave her the gun and taught her to shoot. Mr Justice Havers stated more than 20 years after the trial:

> She did give some explanation as to how she came into the possession of that revolver but it was never very convincing. And nobody ever really knew how she did get it. I didn't believe her explanation on that. I suspected somebody had given it to her.[40]

But it was hopeless, for as the judge explained: 'The defence counsel never mentioned it and I can only act on the evidence put before me.'[41]

*

Melford Stevenson rose to make his opening speech on behalf of the defence. He began by stating unequivocally that Ruth was guilty of the crime:

> It cannot happen often in this court that in a case of this importance, fraught with such deep significance for the accused, the whole of the prosecution's story passes without any challenge from those concerned to advance the defence. Let me make this abundantly plain: there is no question here but this woman shot this man. No one is going to raise any sort of doubt in your mind about that. You will not hear one word from me – or from the lady herself – questioning that. She is charged with murder and one of the ingredients in that offence is what lawyers call malice; and the law of England, in its mercy, provides that if a person finding themselves in the position in which this unhappy young woman now is, has been the subject of such emotional disturbance operating upon her mind so as for the time being to unseat her judgement, to inhibit and cut off those censors which ordinarily control our conduct, then it is open to you, the jury who are charged with the dreadful duty of trying her, to say that the offence of which she is guilty is not the offence of murder, but the offence of manslaughter, and that, members of the jury, is what we, on her behalf, ask you to do in this case.[42]

He felt it necessary to remind them, as the prosecution had done, that it was not their task to make a moral judgement. He then went on to outline something of what Ruth had endured in the months before the shooting, beginning:

> It is always an unpleasant thing to say anything disagreeable about someone who is dead, but I venture to think the story she will unfold to you can leave no doubt in your minds that he [Blakely] was a most unpleasant person.[43]

His next words were unfortunate in echoing the belief that Ruth had shot David simply because she could not bear to lose him to anyone else:

> The fact stands out like a beacon that this young man became an absolute necessity to this young woman. However brutally he behaved, and however much he consorted with other people, he ultimately came back to her, and always she forgave him.[44]

His speech thus embedded the idea deeper in the minds of those in court that Ruth had murdered David because she could not live without him, a misapprehension that was both more straightforward to explain and easier to understand than the more complex truth. Stevenson went on:

> She found herself in something like an emotional prison guarded by this young man, from which there seemed to be no escape . . . You make take the view that there really is no doubt that this young woman was driven by the suffering she endured at the hands of this man to do what she did, and it so operated on her mind that her judgement for the time being was unseated, her understanding was gone, and that malice, which is an essential ingredient in the offence of murder, was absent from this case, so that you can perfectly properly return a verdict of manslaughter rather than a verdict of willful murder. Members of the jury, that will depend upon the view you take of this girl when you see her here in the witness box. You will observe that she is now a calm and undisturbed person. You have got to try to put yourselves in the situation in which she found herself during that Easter weekend, when this man, whom she needed as one of the fundamental requirements of her existence, having as you will hear, promised to spend that weekend with her, having as you will hear, shortly before amended his conduct and behaved towards her in a way that gave her every hope for the future and bestowed on her all the marks of attention as before, went away and chose to consort with these rather odd people in Hampstead.[45]

He ended his speech with particular reference to women's rationale, or rather lack of it:

You will hear – and I am going to call a very eminent psychologist who will tell you – that the effect of jealousy upon that feminine mind can so work as to unseat the reason and can operate to a degree in which a male mind is quite incapable of operating. Now, members of the jury, there are dozens and dozens of cases in which the courts have considered this matter which is called provocation. It always has to be considered on the facts which arise in the individual case; but never before, as far as I know, and as far as all the industry of those associated with me can reveal, has any court had to consider a case in which the defence rely upon jealousy, and the state of mind in which a woman gets when a man to whom she is devoted behaves as this one did, as constituting this defence of provocation.[46]

He then called Ruth to the witness box.

She stood. All eyes in court were upon her as she walked from the dock, her high heels clicking on the parquet floor.

Here at last was Stevenson's opportunity to show the reality of what had led up to that night in Hampstead two months earlier. Barrister Helena Kennedy describes how a defence lawyer works in court:

> Taking a defendant through the evidence may seem like a straightforward process to the onlooker, but there is a special skill involved in choreographing a witness's account so that, while coherent, it also gives the jury a sense of the misery and turmoil that can lead to behaviour that would normally never even be contemplated. The counsel's task is to enable the client to communicate their sense of desperation, or whatever other aspects of their emotional state figured in the offence. It should be like watching a *pas de deux* and the parties must be in step.[47]

But there was none of the crucial trust and understanding between Ruth and Stevenson, and his lack of experience in criminal court was a further hindrance. This deeply unhappy state of affairs was exacerbated by Ruth's own utter indifference to the outcome now that she knew the Findlaters had 'got off'. Bickford admitted: 'She grossly understated her case . . . she gave her evidence almost wilfully badly . . . she tended to exculpate Blakely as regards the various assaults.'[48] From the very beginning, Ruth's replies to Stevenson's questions were abrupt and careless of the impression she made on those in court. His starting point was her securing the position of manageress of the Little Club, where David would visit:

'Did he come and live with you in a flat which you occupied above the club?'

'Yes.'

'At that time, how did he behave towards you?'

'He was very concerned about me. He seemed very devoted.'

'At that time, were you still married?'

'Yes.'

'Did he come to sleep at your flat nearly every night, and did he spend the weekends at Penn?'

'He stayed there from Monday to Friday, and spent the weekends in Penn.'

'And at that time were you very much in love with him?'

Ruth gave a slight shrug: 'Not really.'[49]

Mr Justice Havers watched her reactions carefully. 'I didn't look at her hardly at all, I must say, during the case for the prosecution,' he recalled:

> but then she came into the witness box and of course I have to look at a witness in the witness box because one of the things we have to try and do is make out if the witness is telling the truth, and you have to observe their demeanour. Of course I was bound to look at her then. As a matter of fact she was telling the truth for most of it I am sure. Unfortunately, the truth for her was fatal.[50]

The offhand manner in which she discussed her abortion of David's child in December 1954 did little to endear her to the jury:

> Although he was engaged to another girl, he offered to marry me, and he said it seemed unnecessary for me to get rid of the child, but I did not want to take advantage of him . . . I was not really in love with him at the time and it was quite unnecessary to marry me. I thought I could get out of the mess quite easily.[51]

Stevenson was taken aback: 'What "mess"?'

'I decided I could get out of the mess quite easily,' she repeated.

Mr Justice Havers leaned forward with a frown. 'You mean the *child*?' he enquired.

'Yes,' Ruth replied.

'Without him *marrying* you?' he asked.

'Yes.'[52]

Ruth then explained that she hadn't taken her affair with David seriously until he broke off his engagement: 'I tried to tell him that our association was not good for the club business, and we should stop living together. Mr Blakely didn't like the idea of ending our affair at all.'[53] Her next seemingly heedless remark – that she had instigated an affair with Desmond because she thought it might finish David's interest in her – likewise did nothing to gain the sympathy of those listening.

The idea planted by her defence – that she had been so obsessed with David that she was eventually driven to kill him when he abandoned her – took a severe knock when she said she couldn't remember when David first proposed to her. She followed this with an excessively bland description of her feelings for him: 'He was a very likeable person and I got very attached to him.'[54]

Briefly, she described how she had supported David by stating that she had 'given him money, bought him clothes and paid for his cigarettes and drink bill', and was painfully muted on the subject of his violence: 'It was always because of jealousy in the bar. At the end of the evening when we got upstairs it was always about the things he had been seeing me do, and so on and so forth.'[55] Asked how this violence manifested itself, she replied: 'He only used to hit me with his fists and hands, but I bruise very easily, and I was full of bruises on many occasions.'[56] Her seeming apathy may be attributed not only to her sense of hopelessness at the progress of the trial, but was perhaps also a 'coping mechanism', learned early in life. The matter-of-fact, listless responses she gave to Stevenson's attempts to draw her out made her appear callously rational, instead of revealing the very real inner deadness and despair behind the facade. Leslie Boyd, clerk of court at Ruth's trial, described her afterwards as 'cold and calculating, an example of evil womanhood'.[57]

Stevenson asked, 'When he complained about your working in the club, and exhibiting his jealousy, how did you take it?'

'I often told him to go and not come back sort of thing, but whether I meant it or not . . . I said it anyway.'

'When you said that, did he ever go?'

'No,' said Ruth.[58]

At this point, the court adjourned for lunch. During the break Ruth was given something to eat, watched over by the escort party who had accompanied her from Holloway, but she did not speak to Bickford or any of her defence team. When the court reconvened, Ruth returned to the witness box and described leaving the Little Club and moving in with Desmond. Stevenson then led onto the farcical chasing of David in Penn. When asked how she had felt upon seeing David emerge from Mrs Abbott's house, Ruth replied:

> I was obviously jealous of him now. I mean, the tables had been turned. I was jealous of him, whereas he before had been jealous of me. I had now given up my business – what he had wanted me to do – left all my friends behind and connected with clubs and things, and it was my turn to be jealous of him.[59]

She said she had taken him back 'because I was in love with him'.[60] Stevenson asked about her recent pregnancy, which in court she claimed ended in a miscarriage rather than an abortion, adding that David had 'got very, very violent. I do not know whether that caused the miscarriage or not, but he did thump me in the tummy.'[61]

Stevenson made no further attempt to discover exactly how this particular episode of violence had begun and precisely what it entailed, despite an obvious opportunity to enlighten the court with a solid example of the injuries Ruth had sustained at David's hands. Equally puzzling is Bickford's apparent failure to locate the doctor who examined Ruth following her 'miscarriage', with a view to providing medical evidence about the abuse. But Dr Robert Hunter Hill's statement had not led to his being called as a witness either. It is possible that Ruth herself vetoed any efforts Bickford may have made in this respect; a note in her files dictates: 'A supplementary proof dealing with the Accused's past history is attached. Unless material, she does not want too much detail – particularly relating to previous pregnancies referred to below – to come out.'[62]

Stevenson then came to the matter of the race meeting at Oulton Park and the reconciliation afterwards. Ruth recalled that, on the Wednesday before Easter, David 'was quite happy, and he was saying everything would be all right, we would soon have some money, and talking about marriage again and all kinds of other little things'.

'Did he bring you anything on that occasion?' Stevenson asked.

'Yes, he brought me the latest photograph he had had taken.'

'Was that a recent photograph?'

'It was a photograph he had had taken. He was going to race a car, a Bristol, at Le Mans this year, and he had to have a photograph taken you see, and he had an enlargement which I had.'

'He brought it to you, did he?'

'Yes.'

'Did he write on it in your presence?'

'Yes, "To Ruth, with all my love, from David."'

'Is that the photograph?' Stevenson indicated the exhibit brought before her.[63]

To the astonishment of the court, Ruth began to cry. It was the one moment in her entire testimony where the real emotion she felt made itself apparent.

Stevenson, somewhat surprised himself, asked if she might be permitted to sit down. Mr Justice Havers agreed at once, but Ruth shook her head and said through stifled sobs, 'No, it is quite all right.'

'Do, by all means,' the judge told her.

She shook her head again and said in a firmer voice, 'I do not want to sit down.'[64] Wiping her eyes, she waited for her counsel to continue.

Stevenson then led her to the day of the shooting, having touched upon the chaotic events of Good Friday evening and Easter Saturday, when Ruth admitted she had behaved 'like a typically jealous woman'. Asked how she had spent the afternoon of Easter Sunday, she gave the response: 'I have completely forgotten what I did now. My son was with us, and we amused him in some way. I do not know what I did.'[65] Stevenson did not seem to notice the switch from 'I' to 'we'.

He asked what time she had put her son to bed.

'Seven thirty,' she replied.

'You had gone back to your flat by this time, had you?' Mr Justice Havers enquired, understandably confused by all the expeditions between Tanza Road, Egerton Gardens, Goodwood Court and Penn.

'Yes,' Ruth replied.

'And what did you do next?' asked Stevenson.

'I put my son to bed,' Ruth repeated.

'Yes, go on.'

'I was very upset, and I had a peculiar idea I wanted to kill him.'

There were intakes of breath and a very startled Stevenson blurted, 'You had *what*?'

'I had an idea I wanted to kill him.'[66]

After a moment's hesitation, Stevenson plunged on: 'And we have had the evidence about your taking a revolver up to Hampstead and shooting him. Is that right?'

'Quite correct,' Ruth replied.

'Why did you do it?'

She looked at him. After a pause, she said, 'I do not really know, quite seriously. I was just very upset.'[67]

The judge repeated: '"I do not really know why I shot him." Is that right?'

'Yes,' she said.

Stevenson then asked pointlessly: 'When you say you had a peculiar idea that you wanted to kill him, were you able to control it?'

'No.'

'And then you went up, in fact, and shot him. Is that right?'

'Yes,' she said.[68]

Thus ended Ruth's counsel's attempt to save her from an appointment with Albert Pierrepoint. She had been in the witness box for almost two hours and despite everything, as authors Goodman and Pringle point out, she had not said

> a mean or vindictive word against anyone. She had not mentioned the Findlaters; she said nothing spiteful about their new nanny; she co-operated when her counsel asked her not to name the married woman Blakely had slept with at Penn. And she could not quite bring herself to castigate Blakely.[69]

Most significantly of all, she said nothing about where she had obtained the gun.

From his vantage point in the press seats, Webb observed Ruth's distinctly eerie calm and the

> complete silence in the court as she stood there, a lone figure in that witness box, within touching distance of the jury. She seemed diminutive beneath the overpowering awe of the large plaque of the City Arms fixed in the wall above the judge. Then the tall, angular figure of Mr Christmas Humphreys, leading the prosecution, stood up to face her.[70]

As Humphreys unbent from his seat, he had only one question to ask, prepared in advance. The man who wrote in his autobiography that he far preferred the 'dispassion' of prosecuting to the 'persuasion' of defence, recalled that when it came to cross-examining Ruth:

> For the first and only time in my life I wrote down the question.
> I wanted to be perfectly cold and clear and I wanted a cold and
> clear answer. I wanted the effect of a plea of guilty to the offence
> by an admission of the ingredients which made up the offence.[71]

The court was silent and still as Humphreys turned his cool, grey gaze on Ruth. In a voice as clear and piercing as a Shakespearean actor, he demanded: 'Mrs Ellis, when you fired that revolver at close range into the body of David Blakely, what did you intend to do?'[72]

Ruth returned his unclouded stare. 'It is obvious,' she said calmly, 'that when I shot him I intended to kill him.'[73]

The court drew in a loud, collective breath.

Humphreys, with a slight bow, said, 'Thank you,' and sat down.[74]

Mr Justice Havers indicated that Ruth should return to the dock. She did so, her heels clicking again on the parquet floor, a little more slowly than before, as the dust motes revolved in the stupefied silence, in the shafts of sunlight filtering down from the ceiling.

20

The defence called one other witness: Dr Duncan Whittaker. After stating his credentials at length, the psychiatrist announced: 'I agree with the view of Professor Jung that women cannot so easily as men separate their sexual experiences with men from their total personal relationships.'[1]

Stevenson prompted: 'You mean that a man's love is a man's boast, a woman's is her existence?'

'They are more prone to hysterical reactions than men.'

'And under the influence of these hysterical reactions, what becomes of their standards of conduct and control?'

'They are inclined to lose some of their inhibitory capacity and solve their problems on a more primitive level. This is not applying to women in general, but if they *do* have hysterical reactions, they are more prone to hysterical reactions than men.'[2] Dr Whittaker paused before launching into a discourse: 'A man in the firing line in a war sometimes gets a paralysis that ensures his removal from the front . . .'[3]

'I thought we were talking about women,' Mr Justice Havers interrupted, visibly irritated. 'What has the firing line got to do with a woman? If you want to talk about men, very well, but I thought we were talking about this woman.'[4]

Stevenson hastily brought his witness back to Ruth, and their interview in Holloway. Dr Whittaker told the court that he had been most impressed by her 'equanimity', then lost the interest of much of the public gallery as he clarified his observations in language better suited to the lecture theatre: 'She had drifted into a situation, which was for her intolerable, but she could find no way out, and she was not a sufficiently hysterical personality to solve her problems by a complete loss of memory.'[5] He explained that although Ruth was 'very disturbed' at the time of the murder, 'she was not disturbed when I saw her . . . The situation was absolutely intolerable for her. She considered that he was being unfaithful at that moment, but she was convinced that he would return . . . she both hated him and loved him.'[6] He allowed that Ruth possessed 'some degree of emotional immaturity – not intellectual but emotional'.[7] Dr Whittaker then made a statement guaranteed to alienate Ruth further from the jury: 'I asked her if she thought about her children. She said she did not think about them at all.'[8]

Humphreys' cross-examination of his expert witness was opportunely brief:

'Dr Whittaker, do you regard her as being somewhat emotionally immature?'

'Yes.'

'From the psychological point of view, something of an hysteric?'

'Yes, but not a gross hysteric.'

'In your view, there was such emotional tension over the weekend, without relief, that she felt impelled to resort to violent action to release that suppressed emotion?'

'Yes.'

'In your view, at the time of the killing she was mentally capable of forming the intent to kill?'

'Yes.'

'In your view, was she at the time within the meaning of the English law, sane or insane?'

'Sane.'[9]

Stevenson rose: 'That is my case, my Lord.'[10]

Years later, when asked why Dr Whittaker was called as an expert after having only spoken to Ruth for two hours, Bickford responded:

> I was endeavouring to get all the sympathy I could, and there was just a possibility of a verdict of manslaughter on the grounds of lack of premeditation. This was an extremely weak case . . . Ruth Ellis had gone through all the transports of rage and jealousy until I am quite convinced she had got into a very calm state of mind where she was in a sort of stratosphere of emotion . . . Of course we consulted the psychiatrist.[11]

It would have been more effective, perhaps, to call Ruth's friend Jacqueline Dyer, who had witnessed Ruth's psychological and physical battering at David's hands. But as barrister Helena Kennedy explains, seeking psychiatric explanations for women's crime,

> is a way of trying to make it invisible, a profound expression of our worst fears about the social fabric falling apart. Women are still the glue that cements the family unit, providing cohesion and continuity, and we do not like to admit to the possibility that there is a potential for crime in us all.[12]

It is interesting to note that Ruth's anger and despair were often referred to as 'hysterical', when the often unhinged behaviour of the two most prominent men in her life – David Blakely and George Ellis – was never described in such terms. 'Hysterical', along with 'nagging' and 'promiscuous', are words only ever applied to female defendants, and, in the case of the latter term, gay men. Dr Whittaker's testimony did nothing to help the jury understand the defence of provocation following cumulative bouts of physical and emotional abuse.

Mr Justice Havers then released the jury in order to discuss a matter of law that he said need not trouble them: to consider whether Ruth's balance of mind had been disturbed sufficiently through provocation to justify a manslaughter verdict. Stevenson submitted that this was in fact the case, causing Mr Justice Havers to exclaim: 'But this is new law!'[13] After Stevenson was forced to admit that none of his team had been able to find such a precedent in England or America, the judge enquired:

> Does your proposition come to this, putting it in its simplest form: if a man associates with a woman, and he then leaves her suddenly, and does not communicate with her, and she is a jealous woman, emotionally disturbed, and goes out and shoots him, that is sufficient ground for the jury to reduce the crime of murder to manslaughter?[14]

Pared and simplified to that extent, with no reference to David's violence, infidelity and emotional abuse, it did indeed sound preposterous. Stevenson struggled to give a straightforward reply. Humphreys interjected thoughtfully:

> I accept my learned friend's proposition that this woman was disgracefully treated by the man who died, and I accept my

learned friend's proposition that it would tend to lead her into an intensely emotional condition, even as that hypothetical person, 'the ordinary, reasonable human being'. These conditions may well apply elsewhere. But was she brought more than into a state where it would be reasonable for her to hit and hurt him? One must take into account that the actual crime was planned and prepared. There was some pursuit of that purpose through the streets of London, and during the time of an hour or two, and finally, the man she killed was an unarmed man and without any semblance of a struggle, she shot him in the back.[15]

Stevenson said nothing. Afterwards he admitted that this was the end, that he had been 'left with virtually no defence'.[16] The court adjourned until the following day, the room emptying slowly of its inhabitants, and Ruth returned to the cells below, preparing herself for the long night ahead in Holloway.

*

Bickford's aim of securing a manslaughter verdict was eradicated by the end of that first day at the Old Bailey. The best he could realistically hope for was that his client was found guilty of murder with a recommendation of mercy. As Mr Justice Havers clarified years later, he and the jury could only act on the evidence put before them, and there had been no real attempt to demonstrate the torment Ruth had suffered in her relationship with David, nor to explore his violence and exploitation of her, no medical evidence about her injuries, nothing said about her state of mind by a doctor who knew her well, no substantial mention of her children or any effort to determine her emotions when she shot David that night in Hampstead, and no probing to discover who had actually given her the gun and why.

The questions put to Ruth by her defence were not sufficiently phrased to demonstrate how that first glimpse of David outside the Magdala on Easter Sunday, after he and his friends had deliberately shunted her from his life, led to that all-important loss of control. He had seen her and turned away; Stevenson omitted to ask whether she thought a response from him might have prevented her from squeezing the trigger. It was a particularly valid question in light of Dr Whittaker's belief that had she been able to speak to David, the 'emotional tension would have been released and the incident would not have occurred'.[17]

The events leading up to that moment were thinly described; Stevenson's inability to connect with Ruth resulted in clipped, methodical responses rather than an exploration of her emotions and intentions over the Easter weekend, and indeed the months before. Ruth had spent many intense hours trailing David between Hampstead and Penn; when he wouldn't see her or even speak to her – abetted by people whom she knew regarded her as socially inferior – she was reduced to a 'long vigil' outside the flat where he partied with those same people. Her reaction was dismissed in court as that of a typically scorned female, rather than 'as the response of someone who had been systematically abused, exploited and humiliated'.[18]

The element of snobbery was present not only in the breakdown of Ruth's relationship with David but also in court itself:

> In 1955 the barristers and judges . . . were almost all men with a public school education and a private income. This doesn't necessarily mean that Ellis's trial was less fair than it would be today, but it *does* mean that it was conducted in a very rarefied atmosphere. When Ellis was charged with murder she entered a world inhabited by people who spoke a different language and operated according to a different set of rules. They were acting according to the rules of the law and the rules of their own class.[19]

It is a peculiarity of the case that those who viewed Ruth's primary interest in David as motivated by a wish to escape her working-class background failed to realise that if she had simply wanted a man who could provide her with a more comfortable lifestyle then Desmond Cussen was the ideal candidate, particularly since he not only wanted to provide a home for Ruth and her son, but was willing to marry her.

The deciding of Ruth's fate also had much to do with the fact that she did not conform to the stereotype of a wronged woman – or even a hysterical one who had killed her lover through jealousy. She appeared in court with the platinum hair that caused such a frenzy in the press, was calm under questioning, frank about her sexual relationships with David and Desmond, did not present herself as a victim and appeared unemotional. Even her own counsel, Peter Rawlinson, recalled: 'After she had given her evidence she returned from the witness box to the dock, looking assured and without

regret.'[20] Her lack of remorse and absence of tears was seen as hard
and unnatural; Ruth's quick recovery when she broke down upon
being handed David's photograph did nothing to challenge that
assumption.

She did not look or act as an abused woman was expected to look
and act, and therefore the court found it almost impossible to
understand how she could have been victimised by her partners.
Bickford was prudent not to draw attention to Ruth's abuse by her
ex-husband, since that could well have been interpreted, as it so often
is, as being her fault, that she was the sort of woman who deliberately
or passively somehow provoked men into violence. Equally, police,
solicitors, judge and jury found it difficult to reconcile the notion of
Ruth as an abused and helpless partner with her work as a nightclub
hostess and her sexually confident past – and more so with her decisive
action against David. The 'slow burn' provocation of the long-term
violence she had suffered, her feelings of being overwhelmed by
David's persistent use of alcohol and his infidelity (and her own), the
spiralling of her life out of control and her gradual loss of rationality
had not been sufficiently demonstrated to warrant that verdict of
manslaughter. Her defence had failed to communicate the 'snapping
in slow motion' that culminated in her pacing the pavement outside
the Magdala with a revolver in her handbag.[21]

The fact that Ruth was a mother, often a mitigating factor, worked
against her; she was seen as undeserving of motherhood. Again
Barrister Helena Kennedy explains:

> I learned very quickly, like every other lawyer worth her salt and
> a brief fee, that the nearer I could get to painting my female
> client as a paragon of traditional womanhood, the more likely
> she was to experience the quality of mercy . . . I have no doubt
> that sexuality and reproduction play a role in the judging of
> women which is not only irrelevant but unequalled by anything
> that happens to men.[22]

Ruth's working background did her no favours either, nor the salacious
revelations about her personal life in the press. The moral was simple:
she was a bad girl, and girls like her came to bad ends.

And yet for all that, Bickford worked hard to win a case which was
never going to be straightforward and which received a great deal of

press attention. Ruth had refused to plead insanity, she would not cooperate with his enquiries about the gun and made it plain she did not want Desmond's name brought into the equation. With all that in place, Bickford set out to do his best with what he had to work with, and spent a great deal of time honing his instructions to her legal team. Ruth's performance in the witness box, quite apart from Stevenson's line of questioning, did nothing to help the case he had worked on so tirelessly. She had told him she wanted to die, and after that first day at the Old Bailey, he knew that she would get her wish.

*

The court reconvened at 10.30 a.m. on 21 June 1955. In Ruth's presence but before the jury returned, Mr Justice Havers addressed the barristers for the prosecution and the defence:

> I feel constrained to rule that there is not sufficient material, even on a view of the evidence most favourable to the accused, for a reasonable jury to form the view that a reasonable person so provoked could be driven, through the transport of passion and loss of self-control, to the degree and method and continuance of violence which produced the death. Consequently it is my duty as a judge and as a matter of law, to direct the jury that the evidence in this case does not support a verdict of manslaughter on the grounds of provocation.[23]

Melford Stevenson responded:

> In view of the ruling which your Lordship has just pronounced, it is desirable that I should say that I cannot now with propriety address the jury at all, because it would be impossible for me to do so without inviting the jury to disregard your Lordship's ruling.[24]

Bluntly stated, Ruth's defence accepted that it was pointless to try and make any further appeal on their client's behalf. It was now for the jury to decide whether or not Ruth Ellis had murdered David Blakely. After they were called in, Stevenson very briefly explained his position, followed by Humphreys' simple remark: 'In the circumstances, I have nothing to say.'[25]

Mr Justice Havers then addressed the jury:

> You will approach this case without any thoughts of sympathy
> either for the man or for the accused, who is a young woman –
> and, you may think, a young woman badly treated by the
> deceased man. Nothing of that sort must enter into your
> consideration.[26]

He then explained the murder charge and the fact that, of six shots
fired from a Smith & Wesson,

> three or four were fired into the body of Blakely, and one was
> fired at extremely close range . . . you will have to ask yourself
> this very serious question: whether you would not be compelled
> to the conclusion that there was, in the circumstances of this
> case, at least an intention to do grievous bodily harm, if not to
> kill. If all the evidence compels you to that conclusion, and you
> are satisfied that Mrs Ellis intentionally fired the shots, then that
> would amount to a verdict of guilty of murder. [27]

He then stated his own views on the case heard in court:

> I am bound to tell you that even if you accept the full evidence
> of this woman, it does not seem to me that it establishes any sort
> of defence to the charge of murder. According to our law,
> members of the jury, it is no defence for a woman who is charged
> with the murder of her lover to prove that she was a jealous
> woman and had been badly treated by her lover and was in ill-
> health.[28]

Again he drew the jury's attention to Ruth's perceived lack of morals
by asking them to ignore it:

> You will not allow your judgement to be swayed or your minds
> prejudiced in the least degree because, on her own admission,
> when Mrs Ellis was a married woman she committed adultery,
> or because she was having two persons at different times as
> lovers. Dismiss those questions from your minds.[29]

Finally, he summarised the limited options open to them regarding the verdict:

> If you are satisfied that the accused deliberately fired those shots at Blakely and as a result he died, it is not open to you to find a verdict of not guilty. If, on a review of the whole evidence, you are left in reasonable doubt whether at the time she fired those shots she intended to kill or do grievous bodily harm, you will find her guilty of manslaughter. If, on the consideration of the whole evidence, you are satisfied that at the time she fired those shots she had the intention of killing or doing grievous bodily harm, then your duty is to find her guilty of willful murder.[30]

The jury retired. It was 11.52 a.m.

Ruth was removed to the holding cells below while court officials then swore in the jury for another case. The clerk read out the charge of buggery, causing murmurs of disgust from the public gallery, who were there solely for the Hampstead murder.

In a nondescript side room, the 12 jurors sitting around a table to decide Ruth's fate felt there was little to discuss. One man alone tried to insist on a manslaughter verdict, arguing that they were all men of the world who knew what went on in those clubs and surely they could understand the jealousy that motivated her to kill. But no one else seemed to agree, including juror Jack Dunkley, who recalled afterwards:

> It was premeditated murder, plain as that. There was no other verdict that we could bring in. The evidence proved that she was a determined woman who knew what she was going to do. It was the old 'Frank and Johnnie – he done her wrong' and that was it.[31]

Ruth's only defender, realising that he had lost the argument, asked whether they oughtn't to be lenient towards her nonetheless. Someone else pointed out that the judge had not directed them towards that. There was no more to say: their spokesman let a clerk know that they had reached a verdict. The other case being heard in Court No.1 was adjourned at 12.15 p.m.

Ruth had scarcely sat down in her cell when the message was relayed that the jury was filing back into court. She was led quickly through the corridors and up the steps into the dock again less than half an hour after she had left it.

The clerk of the court spoke clearly: 'Members of the jury, will your foreman please stand? Mr Foreman of the jury, are you agreed upon your verdict?'

'We are,' the foreman replied.

'Do you find the prisoner at the Bar, Ruth Ellis, guilty or not guilty of the murder of David Blakely?'

'Guilty.'

'You find her guilty, and that is the verdict of you all?' asked the clerk.

'Yes,' said the foreman.[32]

The clerk turned to Ruth. 'Prisoner at the Bar, you stand convicted of murder. Have you anything to say before judgment of death is passed according to law?'

Ruth said nothing, but stood very still and straight, awaiting the inevitable words.

Mr Justice Havers slowly picked up the small black square of silk and placed it on his head. Then he turned to address her: 'Ruth Ellis, the jury have convicted you of murder. In my view, it was the only verdict possible. You will be taken hence to the prison in which you were last confined and from there to a place of execution where you will suffer death by hanging and thereafter your body buried within the precincts of the prison, and may the Lord have mercy upon your soul.'[33]

'Amen,' intoned the chaplain.

Ruth bowed her head and said quietly, 'Thanks.'[34]

The wardress by her side put out a hand, but Ruth gently brushed her off and glanced across at her parents and Granville. She gave them a quick smile before turning for the steps that led down from the dock. In the brief silence all that could be heard was the smart clicking of her heels gradually growing fainter as she descended to the corridors below. And then the court seemed to move as one: chairs were scraped back and papers collected up by the judiciary; the public gathered their bags and coats, and reporters dashed from the court to the pressroom to telephone through their copy.

Underneath the Old Bailey, Ruth's family was allowed a short time with her before Bickford went in to her. She was crying but said it was nothing to do with the death sentence being passed and everything to do with the Findlaters: 'I don't mind hanging. But why should *they* get away with it?'[35] She insisted she did not want to appeal.

When Bickford left, Ruth was driven back to Holloway. She remained on the hospital wing for a while and was visited again that day by her parents and Granville. She repeated that she had no wish to fight the sentence of the court but although she had said, time and again that she did not wish to live, she was terrified by the thought of being hanged. She managed to write a note without being seen by the wardresses, and pushed it into Granville's hand as he was leaving.

Outside, once he and his parents were on the main road with the walls of the prison behind them, Granville unfolded the scrap of paper. His sister had written down the details of a lethal drug she wanted him to procure for her, so that she might take her own life. He showed the note to his father, who said at once they should try to do as she asked. But Granville knew that Bickford intended to push for a reprieve, and he could not risk her life when it might yet be saved.

He tore up the scrap of paper.

21

Hanging as a form of capital punishment in Britain is thought to date back to Saxon times. It was convenient and ostensibly less cruel than many of the other punishments meted out to wrong-doers, including drowning, drawing and quartering, decapitation, burning at the stake and boiling alive. In the Middle Ages, the prisoner usually stood on a ladder or stool and was tied to a sturdy tree with a rope, then 'turned off' their foothold. A little later, this was modified: the prisoner was placed on a horse-drawn cart which was brought beneath a tree while a noose was put about the neck; the horse was then led swiftly away, leaving the prisoner to hang. Eventually, gallows were introduced. These consisted of a single upright post with a crossbeam, or two upright posts and a crossbeam, under which the prisoner would stand on a stool or box that was removed when the noose was in place, leaving the condemned suspended.

Tyburn had become the place of execution for London by 1177. On 1 June 1571, a permanent gallows was erected at a spot close to today's Marble Arch; the notorious 'Triple Tree' served the City of London and County of Middlesex. Often death was painfully slow, resulting in the prisoner writhing for up to three minutes ('dancing the Tyburn jig') while a crowd 100,000 deep watched in thinly veiled delight. Street hawkers sold food and souvenirs, and broadsheet peddlers urged them to read the prisoners' alleged last speeches and confessions. Seats could be bought for a hefty sum in the fashionable galleries of Mother Proctor's Pews. After death, the bodies were cut down and either passed to family and friends for burial or dispatched to Surgeons' Hall for dissection. Over 2,000 prisoners, including some 150 women, met a ghastly end at Tyburn during the eighteenth century. In summer 1759 the Triple Tree was dismantled and a portable gallows, comprising two parallel beams on an elongated raised platform, replaced it. The platform had trapdoors opened by a lever and could accommodate 12 prisoners, but the new drop still wasn't sufficient to dislocate the neck of those condemned to die and hundreds slowly strangled to death. Complaints from residents about traffic congestion during the executions led to highwayman John Austin being the last person to hang at Tyburn in November 1783; thereafter prisoners were dispatched in the grounds of Newgate Gaol. Crowds gathered there to watch the hangings, with wealthy spectators renting rooms and even rooftops opposite the Debtors' Door for a better view.

In the nineteenth century the population boom was matched by an increase in executions: over 4,000 men, women and occasionally even children were executed. Two hundred crimes carried the death penalty. There was a sharp decline in executions following the reclassification of offences and with the introduction of transportation to America and then Australia as alternatives to the death sentence. In 1838 there were only six hangings in England and Wales, but they remained a popular spectacle, with people willing to journey many miles to watch 'a good hanging'. Extra trains were brought in to cope with the demand and executions outside London were usually carried out on market days to ensure a vast crowd, with parties of school children brought along to be taught a lesson about criminality. There were several superstitions regarding capital punishment, including the belief that bits of the gibbet were a useful cure for toothache, and it was not uncommon to see women holding their infants up to the scaffold to touch the hand of the corpse, which was thought to cure a number of ills.

Newspapers became more readily available during the nineteenth century, with criminal trials and hangings providing a steady readership. In February 1864, the *Illustrated Police News* superseded the old execution broadsheets, featuring lurid details of murder cases, trials and executions, with graphic pen-and-ink drawings. The public interest in crime, especially murder, exploded under Queen Victoria's rule, and displays of death masks from infamous felons proved hugely popular, as did Madame Tussaud's Chamber of Horrors, where the wax figures were often dressed in clothes bought from the hangman. There was little support for a campaign to end capital punishment under the circumstances; those in favour of abolition concentrated instead on banning the public from executions. Charles Dickens,

William Thackeray and Sir Robert Peel were among those who supported the Capital Punishment (Amendment) Act, introduced on 29 May 1868, which decreed that all executions should take place within county prisons. Seven years earlier, the Criminal Law Consolidation Act of 1861 narrowed the number of capital crimes to four: murder, high treason, piracy and arson in a Royal Dockyard.

Most executions were carried out in purpose-built sheds within the prison grounds. By the turn of the twentieth century, a scaffold intended for assembly inside the prison adjacent to the condemned cell became common. The scaffold was designed to allow for an accurate adjustment of the drop; the beams were usually 8 ft high and set into the walls at either end of the execution chamber. The hangman chalked a 'T' on the join in the trapdoors to indicate precisely where the prisoner should stand, imparting one source of the phrase 'to toe the line'. By the turn of the twentieth century, rope-maker John Edgington & Co. of Old Kent Road supplied the Home Office with every noose: 13 ft of Italian hemp, bound in leather around the neck (to lessen the likelihood of flesh being torn and lesions on the skin) and with a serrated rubber washer to keep it in place. Tailoring the drop to each prisoner was crucial: too long and the prisoner might be decapitated, too short and they would strangle. It became a scientific process, calculating a prisoner's age, weight, height and general build against the necessary length of rope. Executioners adapted the statutory 'table of drops' to meet the needs of the prisoner for whom they were responsible. To guarantee a precise drop, new ropes were stretched the night before a hanging, using a sandbag that matched the prisoner's weight. The noose had to be put over the prisoner's head so that the eyelet was just beneath the jaw, thereby causing the head to jerk backwards and thrusting the force into the neck vertebrae rather than it being taken on the throat.

Immediately prior to hanging, the prisoner's legs and arms were pinioned and a white cotton hood covered the head. The hood was used during the days of public hangings to spare the audience, rather than the prisoner. Following the Act that limited executions to closed confines within prisons, the hood was retained to save the condemned inmate the sight of the executioner reaching for the lever that would set the apparatus in motion. When the trapdoors opened, the prisoner's body accelerated through the gap and the sudden stop at the end of the rope dislocated the neck and ruptured the spinal cord.

Death was usually – although not always – instantaneous.

Before 1800, most hangmen were drafted from the ranks of condemned criminals who escaped execution by agreeing to hang their fellow prisoners. Subsequently, the post of executioner became a sought-after job, with the successful applicant having undergone a police check, an interview with a local prison governor, a medical examination and then a week's training at Pentonville Gaol before their name was added to the list of official executioners. There are no records of female executioners other than two in eighteenth-century Ireland.

Of the 1,485 prisoners sentenced to death in England and Wales between 1900 and 1965 (when the last executions took place), just over half – 755 – were hanged. No one younger than 16 is thought to have been executed after 1833, although it was not until the Children's Act of 1908 that minors were officially excluded from the death penalty. A pregnant woman could 'plead her belly' in order to exchange the death sentence for life imprisonment.

In Britain between 1735 and 1955 (and Southern Ireland before 1923), more than 600 women were executed. Among those present at the hanging of Elizabeth Martha Brown in Dorset on 9 August 1856 was writer Thomas Hardy. Aged 16, Hardy and a friend climbed a tree near the gallows that had been erected outside the gates of Dorchester Gaol, where a crowd of 3,000 people had gathered to watch the hanging that morning. Brown was an attractive woman who had axed her younger, abusive husband to death following a quarrel about his infidelity. Dressed in a long, close-fitting black silk gown, she would not agree to be driven to the gallows but walked instead in the pattering rain. From his spot in the nearby tree, Hardy watched her die and stayed while she was left hanging on the rope, her face concealed by the rain-drenched hood, noting 'what a fine figure she showed against the sky as she hung in the misty rain, and how the tight black silk gown set off her shape as she wheeled half round and back'.[1] He clearly found the spectacle of the dead woman erotic, writing about it in old age, and drew inspiration from her death for his novel *Tess of the D'Urbevilles*.

Frances Kidder was the last woman to be hanged in public; she was executed in Maidstone on 2 April 1868 after being convicted of drowning her ten-year-old stepdaughter. In London, female executions were initially carried out at Newgate Gaol but, on 3 February 1903, convicted baby farmers Annie Walters and Amelia Sach were the first women to be hanged at Holloway. Between 1908 and 1922 no women were put to death in Britain, but in 1923, the execution of Edie Thompson – with its attendant rumours of a horrific, bloody death on the scaffold – caused substantial outrage.

In his autobiography, Albert Pierrepoint observes:

> The principal differences in the prison atmosphere during the execution of a woman were the appalling effect it often had on the woman prison officers, and the degree of commotion outside the gates. Soon after I began my duties Mrs Van der Elst, the wealthy propagandist against capital punishment, was beginning her emotional campaign and she generally attracted more support when protesting against the hanging of a woman. She would stretch the pathos of the moment of execution to an almost unendurable pitch by playing hymns through amplifiers carried on cars outside the prison gates . . . This affecting music stopped on the stroke of the hour. The crowd strained to hear the crash of the trapdoors. They never could hear it, but some abolitionist would obligingly thump the door panel of a car with a flat hand. Then the tension snapped into savage hysteria as the mob rushed the gates of the prison.[2]

Five more women were executed in the thirty years between Edith Thompson's death and 1953. The last of these was 46-year-old Louisa Merrifield, who, together with her husband, was charged with killing an elderly widow for her money; they mixed her jam with Rodine, a phosphorus-based rat poison. Merrifield's husband was acquitted, but she was hanged by Pierrepoint on 18 September 1953. The following year, on 15 December 1954, 51-year-old Styllou Christofi – a near neighbour of Clive Gunnell in South Hill Park – was executed for the murder of her daughter-in-law; after hitting the young woman with an ash pan and then strangling her, she burned her body in the back garden. Christofi was the first hanging at Holloway since Edith Thompson. Afterwards it was revealed that she had been tried for the murder of her mother-in-law in Cyprus in 1925; on that occasion she had thrust a burning torch down the woman's throat. There were no voices of protest at her death, nor that of Louisa Merrifield; both were middle-aged women of unremarkable appearance.

Nonetheless, opposition to capital punishment was growing, particularly after the Second World War. When Labour came into government in 1945, the Prime Minister, Clement Attlee, chose James Chuter-Ede as his Home Secretary; Chuter-Ede was a supporter of abolition, as were many in the Labour Party, including Sydney Silverman, who founded the National Campaign for the Abolition of Capital Punishment. Silverman introduced a Bill to suspend the death penalty for five years; in April 1948 the House of Commons voted in favour of the Bill and Chuter-Ede pledged to reprieve all condemned prisoners until it was resolved. Thus there were no executions between March and October 1948.

The Bill was rejected by the House of Lords, but in November that year Chuter-Ede announced the setting up of a Royal Commission to look into all aspects of execution. During the next four years the Commission's ten men and two women listened to everyone involved with the process, from prison governors and warders to hangman Albert Pierrepoint. The Commission, less its two female members, observed a simulated execution carried out by Pierrepoint. They concluded that hanging was the most expedient and humane means of capital punishment, even though they doubted its effectiveness as a deterrent to crime. The Commission's published findings led to several minor changes in the system, but capital punishment was to be maintained until the public majority demanded otherwise.

But there *were* reprieves.

In April 1955, the month that Ruth Ellis shot David Blakely outside the Magdala Tavern, twenty-eight-year-old Alfred 'Jake' Wayman was pardoned four days before he was due to be executed for the fatal stabbing of his girlfriend. Wayman had cut his own throat after the murder and it was feared that the wound might open and cause an unholy mess on the scaffold. He served 12 years of a life sentence instead. In a similar case the previous November, the Home Secretary reprieved a man who pleaded guilty to murdering his former fiancée; the man had tried to commit suicide by throwing himself under a train. He survived but lost both legs in the process. Major Lloyd George thought 'humanity and decency demanded that a legless man should not to be carried to the drop'.[3] He refused to permit his execution.

In June, the month when Ruth's trial was held at the Old Bailey, Sergeant Emmett Dunne was reprieved following the murder of his lover's husband, a colleague of his at a British Army base in Germany. The offence happened on British Sovereign territory, but German law did not recognise capital punishment, regardless of the nationality of the murderer. Dunne was imprisoned and released in 1965.

In July, one week before Ruth's execution, Mrs Sarah Lloyd was reprieved after being sentenced to death for the murder of her eighty-six-year-old neighbour, with whom she had had a long-running feud. Mrs Lloyd stove in the elderly woman's head with a spade after pouring boiling carrots and onions over her; she then stood chatting to other neighbours while an ambulance arrived and went to the pictures that evening with her 13-year-old daughter. Following her trial, she was placed in the condemned cell in Strangeways Gaol with an execution date set for 7 July 1955. Her case attracted very little publicity and Mrs Lloyd's husband was the only person to speak up in her defence. But two days before she was due to hang, Mrs Lloyd's solicitor announced that she had been granted a reprieve; the Home Secretary had given no reason 'but the plea of provocation might have had something to do with it'.[4] Sarah Lloyd served seven years of a life sentence.

On 21 June 1955 Ruth left the prison hospital in Holloway and entered the condemned cell where she would remain until death.

*

'There is a strange kind of excitement in the prison when there is a woman in the condemned cell,' wrote Joan Henry. 'The condemned cell itself is really a small flat, with lavatory and bathroom adjoining, and the scaffold through a locked door. The condemned woman is never left alone day or night.'[5]

Situated on CC wing and reached via a flight of stone steps, the cell was to be Ruth's home for the next three weeks until the long green screen at the foot of her bed was removed to reveal the door into the execution chamber. Day and night, the electric bulb on the ceiling burned and she was watched over constantly by wardresses working shifts, a ruling enforced after the suicide of Mary Ann Milner, convicted of poisoning her sister-in-law; Milner 'cheated' the executioner by hanging herself the night before she was due to be executed in July 1847. The condemned prisoner and those who were charged with her care established a strange relationship – not exactly a friendship but a certain mutual respect and dependency.

Wardress Evelyn Galilee worked many shifts in the condemned cell with Ruth. She went against her parents' wishes to become a prison officer in 1951, following the death of her husband in a farming accident three years after they married. A young, childless widow, she found life at Holloway impossible at first. 'It was like a spider web,' she recalled. 'I thought "I don't belong here", and I didn't. I never did. But I had such a stubborn nature.'[6] There were many assaults from inmates in the first few months of her time at Holloway: 'You weren't a fully-fledged officer until you took a beating.'[7] She was approached to work in the condemned cell immediately after Ruth's sentencing: 'I was given a minute's notice [to decide if she would do it]. I took it. I didn't want it . . . I have a guilt. I am disgusted at myself for doing it.'[8]

After her initial surprise at how small, dainty and quiet Ruth was, Officer Galilee rapidly found herself warming to her charge. 'I liked her officer to woman,' she recalled. 'Ruth was helpful. She wasn't a bother and didn't throw a wobbler. Ruth Ellis was first class.'[9] The Home Office rules for life in the condemned cell were followed to the letter: Ruth passed her time mostly reading books (particularly the Bible, in which she now found comfort), playing patience, meticulously sewing dolls from the scraps of material sent in to her by her mother, doing jigsaws, writing letters and carefully tending the goldfish she was allowed to keep in a bowl on the table. She ate the unexciting food when it was brought into her and drank tea but refused the beer that formed part of her 'privileges'. Mostly, she smoked and was glad when the clock turned each day to the hour of her walk in the walled prison yard. It was summer, after all.

Governor Dr Charity Taylor called in daily to ask after her welfare and to see if there was anything she wanted to discuss. Otherwise, Ruth received her visitors in the partitioned cell on the other side of the bathroom. The bouquets brought in for her were removed to the prison chapel, where she could see them every Sunday; no flowers were allowed in the condemned cell. She shocked some of her visitors and correspondents with a faintly macabre twist to her naturally wicked humour; Bickford was lost for words when she told him: 'I gave David a lot of rope – come to think of it, he's giving me quite a bit now.'[10]

Ruth insisted that as far as she was concerned, the verdict of the court had been just and she grew annoyed whenever anyone tried to raise the matter of an appeal. But Bickford, acting mainly on the wishes of Ruth's family, had already begun putting together the argument for a reprieve. Her future was now entirely in the hands of Major Gwilym Lloyd George, Home Secretary since May 1954, when the Conservatives won the general election. Although he had been in favour of the suspension of the death penalty when it was debated in 1948, one of the Tory party's key election pledges was the retention of capital punishment.

On 22 June, the newspapers were emblazoned with reports of the trial. The *Daily Mail* leader read:

> Model *Smiles* At Murder Verdict: Mrs Ruth Ellis turned to a nurse attendant in the dock at the Old Bailey yesterday and smiled as the jury announced their verdict: guilty of murder . . . That smile was the first sign of emotion the 28yr old platinum blonde had given during her trial.[11]

The newspaper also featured two other stories about Ruth: 'Model Weeps: I Was a Jealous Woman' and 'Ruth Ellis: I Shot to Kill Him'. Her mother's story appeared in the *Sunday Dispatch*, Jacqueline Dyer's in the *Empire News* and Granville's in the *Empire News* and *Sunday Graphic*, while Ruth's 'own' story ran in the *Woman's Sunday Mirror* between 26 June and 17 July.

On 23 June 1955 Dr Charity Taylor wrote to the prison service declaring that the date of Ruth's execution had been set:

> 9656 Ruth Ellis
>
> The execution date of the above named woman has been fixed by the Under Sheriff for Wednesday, the 13th July at nine o'clock in the morning.
>
> The Under Sheriff will attend the prison on Tuesday, the 12th July at four thirty in the afternoon for the purpose of testing the apparatus.
>
> Governor.[12]

Jacqueline Dyer was determined to do whatever she could to help spare Ruth's life. She had already written to the Queen, asking her to consider Ruth's children and to intervene 'as a mother', but on 25 June she took more decisive action, sending a letter to the Home Secretary with information he could not ignore: Desmond Cussen had provided Ruth with the revolver. 'Mrs Ellis had told me that she knew there was a gun in Cussen's flat and this gun had been seen by two other women,' Jacqueline wrote:

> She killed the man she loved and was determined to join him by not offering a shred of evidence in her own defence . . . I knew them both so well, and nothing surprised me more than that it was *she* who shot *him* . . . There is much more I would gladly tell police officers of the sustained terrible strain of her life with Blakely, a strain which I am sure on the fateful night turned into a temporary state of insanity when Blakely would not speak to her.[13]

The Home Office forwarded her letter to Scotland Yard for investigation and it landed on the desk of DCI Davies at Hampstead Police Station. He contacted Jacqueline to ask her to make a formal statement.

Despite her friend's pleading during visits, Ruth flatly refused to discuss the gun any further. Jacqueline then approached George Rogers, her local MP, who had recently campaigned to clear Timothy Evans's name. Rogers was in his late 40s and had been elected as Labour MP for Kensington North. He found Jacqueline waiting for him one afternoon in the lobby of the House of Commons. He listened to her story, the gist of which was that, after enduring months of David's abuse, on Easter Sunday Ruth had been plied with drink by someone who gave her a gun, drove her to Hampstead and urged her to shoot David Blakely. Rogers was intrigued. He agreed to speak to the Home Secretary and applied for permission to visit Ruth in Holloway.

On 26 June, an article appeared about the Little Club in *Reynolds News*. Reporter John Knight observed:

> Last night in the Little Club, up the staircase in the Brompton Road, there were anxious looks on the staff's faces. For Ruth Ellis, the ash blonde who slew her lover by shooting him down, was manageress there . . . And the club is bravely turning its music higher, laughing louder to live down that dreadful story . . . Lonely men drifted up the stairs into the let's-be-madly-gay atmosphere and found romance – which never survived . . . It was a club of unhappy people. A well-

known racing driver would go there only when he lost a race. Another
visitor was found later in a gas-filled room. The Unhappy Little Club
... On many nights I have sat there and seen have-been and never-
will-be celebrities trying to be so gay. The girl with the fair hair was
always among them, talking, smoking, drinking ... Ruth Ellis, as
manageress, confided in me two summers ago: 'If only some of the
members here knew what I thought of them ... But I have to be
charming to them all ... ' Ruth Ellis is gone. It is becoming plain
Little Club again: happy if pretentious.[14]

In the meantime Bickford was working industriously on Ruth's behalf;
he sent a seven-page letter to the Home Secretary requesting a reprieve,
stating that his client was 'a woman of quite incredible self control
and courage ... she has done her utmost to tell the whole truth so far
as she is concerned'.[15] Regarding the murder, he cited the 'recent
miscarriage' as a principal factor, adding: 'Cussen saw evidence of this
when he went round to Egerton Gardens to collect the linen.'[16] He
also named Ruth's high temperature and addiction to 'heavy drinking',
together with her 'highly nervous and tense condition' as contributing
factors, asserting: 'As she said to me on more than one occasion, "He
[David] could have chosen any other weekend but that one to play
me up."'[17]

Ruth ignored Bickford's attempts to discuss a reprieve with her.
She was even less forthcoming when George Rogers visited her on
29 June. The MP afterwards declared himself shocked by her
appearance, which was such a contrast to the photographs in the
newspapers and even in court: 'She was rather thin and very pale. A
rather fragile sort of person ... Her eyes were rather shallow, not
much depth to them.'[18] The 'weeks of suffering' had 'much refined'
her; he felt that 'in normal conditions she was probably a hard,
brassy blonde'.[19] He was impressed by her, despite himself: 'She
certainly had much courage and had resigned herself to death. She
was quite sure she would meet her victim in the next world.'[20] He
noticed Ruth's powder compact, which when opened played a
mournful 'La Vie en rose'; the song remained with him after their
meeting, which did not go well. His attempts to draw Ruth out on
the subject of the gun in the 'unpleasant' hour he spent with her
were catastrophic; he left overcome with a headache that lasted three
days, while Ruth was more disturbed by his visit than any other.[21]

The wardresses were equally upset by the pressure Rogers had brought to bear upon their charge, and Principal Officer Griffin put her observations in writing for the purposes of an investigation:

> I was present when Mr Rogers MP visited 9656 Ruth Ellis at 5.40 p.m. this afternoon.
>
> He introduced himself, then said that all her friends and relatives were distressed at her position, in particular, J Dyer had approached him and asked him to do all he could for her. He kept onto her about living for her child's sake, her attitude in wanting to die was all wrong, did she believe in the After World, she needn't think that by her dying she would be with David Blakely. She should live to expedite her crime on earth. Would she give him authority to approach the Home Secretary for clemency. Did she believe in God, because if she did, she should have the will to live.
>
> Ellis, in reply, said she did not want to live and that her child was being taken proper care of. She had no wish or desire to live.
>
> Mr Rogers was so persistent that Ellis very grudgingly said, What if you do ask for clemency and it fails, I shall still be in the same place. Mr Rogers reply was, 'I never fail.' Mr Rodgers [*sic*] said she hadn't told them about when she got the gun. Ellis told him that Mr Bickford had all the information necessary. Mr Rodgers [*sic*] then told her to pray and think about it. Ellis said she would, but for him to fail. Ellis said that if he wanted to he could, but she still did not want to live.[22]

When the Governor called to see Ruth that evening, she found her still deeply affected. In a letter to the prison commissioners, Dr Taylor recalled:

> At approximately 7.10 p.m. on the 29th June I paid a routine visit to Ruth Ellis in the condemned cell. She told me that the MP I had told her of during the morning had been to see her. She said he was a great talker and she was too tired to argue with him. She said that she had agreed with him that there were matters she had not disclosed, but she did not want to as she did not want more scandal. She told me she hoped he would fail in his efforts and she would pray that he did.

I have never seen Ruth Ellis so distressed, and the officers reported that for the first time she cried. She told me she supposed it was too late to change her mind as he was going to the Home Secretary in the morning.

I did not ask her, but I formed the strong impression she did not wish Mr Rogers to pursue the subject of a reprieve.

When I visited the Centre of the Prison, Principal Officer Griffin reported that she had taken the visit with Ellis and Mr Rogers and that he had 'badgered' her.

I spoke to Mr Paice on the telephone and he instructed that my statement and Miss Griffin's should be sent by hand to the Under Secretary of State on the morning of 30th June.[23]

The Governor sent a copy of her letter to the Home Office, enclosing Principal Officer Griffin's report. The following day she confirmed that she had given permission for the MP to visit Ruth 'as he professed some degree of constituency interest' and had understood that he intended to work for a reprieve but had not foreseen that he 'proposed to browbeat her into authorising him to do so. As his visit caused Mrs Ellis so much distress he should not be allowed to visit again.'[24]

Ruth's hospital case notes for the day of their meeting read simply: 'Upset by visit of MP Mr Rogers – wanted permission to organise petition.'[25] Rogers' unsuccessful visit had a correspondingly unsuccessful outcome: his letters to the Home Office were ignored.

Ruth still had no wish to live.

22

Despite Ruth's opposition to anyone fighting for clemency on her behalf, public demand that she should be granted a reprieve was gaining momentum. Several well-known authors were among those adding their voices to those condemning the death sentence. Playwright Guy Bolton wrote from the Hotel Westminster in Paris:

> If Ruth Ellis is hanged a day will certainly come when the act will be condemned as one of subservience to an outworn legal code. The ladder is a long one and man has mounted slowly from the depths of brutality. When we stood but a dozen rungs lower we acquiesced in the hanging of man for stealing a sheep.[1]

The *Evening Standard* published a letter from American thriller writer Raymond Chandler, then visiting London, which ended:

> This thing haunts and, so far as I may say it, disgusts me as something obscene. I am not referring to the trial, of course, but to the medieval savagery of the law . . . I have been tormented for a week at the idea that a highly civilised people should put a rope round the neck of Ruth Ellis and drop her through a trap and break her neck. This was a crime of passion under considerable provocation. No other country in the world would hang this woman.[2]

Many readers wrote in support, including MPs Sir Beverley Baxter, Anthony Greenwood and Emanuel Shinwell, and publisher Victor Gollancz, who stated:

I am reminded of words written by Thackeray after witnessing an execution: 'I came away from Snow Hill that morning with a disgust for murder, but it was for the murder I saw done. I pray to Almighty God to cause this disgraceful sin to pass from among us and to cleanse our land of blood.'[3]

Raymond Chandler spoke again about Ruth's case in an interview with the *Daily Express*:

The death sentence on Ruth Ellis has upset me. How can the British law be so savage? The case of Ruth Ellis was no bestial or sadistic killing. There was nothing slow about it, like a poisoning, nothing like the murder of a child. It was a crime of passion committed, I feel certain, under a kind of shock which may have flared up uncontrollably . . . The phrase 'cold blooded' doesn't come into it. This woman was hot blooded.[4]

One writer who openly declared himself in favour of Ruth's execution was Dennis Wheatley:

I think Ruth Ellis should hang. She was convicted of a cold-blooded murder and we do not recognise *crimes passionelle* in this country. In the same way as Derek Bentley was hanged for his part in the shooting of a policeman in Croydon, justice must be maintained.[5]

Perhaps the most eloquent damning voice belonged to journalist William Connor. Writing under the pseudonym 'Cassandra' in his regular *Daily Mirror* column, he declared that Ruth faced,

a shameful doom in a prison yard . . . Pity comes hard after such dreadful deeds. Compassion weeps but is silent. Yet, had I the power I would save her. This was a murder of love and hate. The one as fierce as the other – the storm of tenderness matching the fury of revenge. In human nature where passion is involved, love and hate walk hand in hand and side by side. The difference between them is a hair's breadth. The one can change to the other in a trice. Infinite sweetness and affection become infinite wickedness and black insensate cruelty . . . There are thirteen more days to go . . . Ruth Ellis does not matter . . .

But what we do to her – you and I – matters very much. And if we do it, and we continue to do it to her successors, then we all bear the guilt of savagery, untinged with mercy.[6]

Other newspapers and abolition campaigners joined the debate, which spread to the far reaches of the globe as members of the public wrote to the British press and the Home Office pleading for Ruth's life to be spared. Petitions of 50,000 signatures were collected and forwarded to the Home Secretary, arriving from Norway, France, Denmark, Germany, Italy, Australia, America, Argentina and so on. Among the papers that form the National Archives file is a thick red exercise book, its pages filled with name after name after name, begging for a reprieve. Dr Mary Kidd wrote to ask the Home Office whether they had considered if premenstrual tension might have been a contributing factor to Ruth's decisive action in Hampstead, while Cherry Marshall and the girls from the Chelsea modelling school were similarly moved:

> It seemed to us that she was hardly given a chance . . . we sent a telegram from the office, signed by dozens of models, telling of the bruises on her body in the vain hope it would make some kind of difference.[7]

Ruth's parents wrote individually to the Home Secretary to ask him to overturn the verdict. Her father implored:

> I respectfully beg of you to use your great influence to spare my poor daughter's life (Ruth Ellis). This terrible tragedy has been a terrible shock to me . . . Sir you will understand my nerves have gone to pieces under the strain. My daughter I would have thought to be the last person to become involved in such a crime as a child she was shy and reserved and never gave me any cause for anxiety and later on she was a devoted mother to her two children. I blame the whole sequence of events to the fact of such an unhappy experience of three bad men [Ellis, Conley and Blakely], the details of which you will know. I ask you as a distraught father to show her mercy.[8]

But for all those who believed Ruth should live, there was an equally vociferous group who urged that she should hang. The letters preserved in the Home Office files include several from married men who feared that a reprieve for Ruth would impel women to run amok. Mr Bitter from Lewisham urged:

> I am married to a woman similar in nature to Ruth Ellis; eaten up with jealousy through and through ... my wife begrudges me everything ... I greatly fear that my future personal safety would be at stake if you granted a reprieve. PLEASE, DEAR SIR, GRANT NO REPRIEVE.[9]

Mr Brindhlaw of Kentish Town warned the same: 'I should judge wisely otherwise wifes [*sic*] will be shooting there [*sic*] husbands if a woman just says good morning to him ... it would be a riot among wives.'[10] One man declared himself appalled at Raymond Chandler's defence of Ruth, condemning him as 'one "ex-Yankee" purveyor of gangster-thrillers full of dash-and-bash', adding that he firmly believed Ruth should hang because 'the professional harlot may have a right to present the meanderings of a man she supports from her filthy gain [but] Ruth Ellis did not claim even that excuse'.[11]

A large proportion of the letters supporting Ruth's execution came from women expressing concern about her 'immorality', adhering to the view that men were at the mercy of their own appetites, and it was up to the female of the species to bring order to society. In their eyes, Ruth was a symbol of all women who broke the accepted rules about feminine behaviour; she was so abhorrent and unnatural that she did not deserve to live. Mrs Spoczynska of London admired the Home Secretary's 'courage and devotion to duty' in upholding the sentence of the court:

> As a mother of two children, British by birth and descent and proud of it, and having dedicated my life to campaigning and writing to further the cause of our British Christian traditions of honourable family life and decent living, I wish to express my personal appreciation ... The fate of this self-confessed openly immoral and shameless woman will, I feel, prove a deterrent to many who might otherwise have been tempted to let lust rule their lives. Such women are a menace to our national standards, and there is now one such less to corrupt others by her example.[12]

Another married woman wrote from Portsmouth in the same vein:

I expect you have had a lot of appeals from sentimental crackpots and also from people themselves living immoral lives asking for the reprieve of that murdering trollop Ruth Ellis . . . I am a married woman and I have a son. I hope it may never happen but either my husband or my son may fall for a foul harpy . . . they'd come to their sense sooner or later. Men do . . . If you let her off hundreds of homes will shake and God knows the marriage tie is weak enough as it is.[13]

Children's author Jacqueline Wilson remembers the reaction of her mother, Biddy, to the newspaper serialisation of Ruth's story: 'I read over Biddy's shoulder. She tutted over Ruth's blonde hair and pencilled eyebrows and dark lips. "She's obviously just a good time girl. Look at that peroxide hair! Talk about common!"'[14]

In their 1961 paean to abolition, *Hanged by the Neck*, Arthur Koestler and C.H. Rolph put forward an interesting argument as to why so many women were adamant that Ruth should die:

When Ruth Ellis had shot her former lover in a frenzy of jealousy and resentment, women were in general less inclined to demand a reprieve than men. Many of them, involved in similarly unhappy circumstances, may have felt some unconscious envy at the thought that if they were denying themselves the luxury of murdering a faithless lover or husband, then those who indulged in it ought to pay the price. What appeared to be moral indignation was a mixture of envy and vindictiveness. Sexually frustrated women will persecute their luckier sisters under the same cloak of moral righteousness.[15]

*

On 1 July 1955, Jacqueline Dyer gave a formal statement at Hampstead Police Station, detailing her friendship with Ruth, the violence she had witnessed ('I feel that Ruth shot David because of the way he treated her and in my opinion he asked for what he got') and explaining why she had written to the Home Secretary: 'I wanted to help my friend and because she must have been driven to it by the way Blakely had treated her.'[16] She then declared:

During one of my visits to Ruth I gathered from her that Cussen had given her the gun, and that he had driven her to Hampstead on the night of the shooting. She later denied that Cussen had given her the gun but I cannot see who else would have given it to her. I still press this question every time I see Ruth, because I think she is telling lies when she says he did not give it to her. It is also my opinion that Ruth did not go to Hampstead by taxi but was taken there in Cussen's car.[17]

Jacqueline ended her statement stubbornly: 'I intend to do everything in my power to save my friend's life because I think it is only justice and I know the life she had to lead with Blakely.'[18]

DCI Davies drafted a long, careful report after interviewing Jacqueline and taking her statement. In it, he admitted: 'Ellis's story that she had had the gun in her possession for three years was not believed from the outset because of the clean, well-oiled condition it was in. As a consequence, inquiries were made to trace its origin but without success.'[19] He described how he and DC Claiden had visited Desmond at Goodwood Court on 18 April, and that Desmond had 'emphatically denied that he had ever given a revolver to Ruth Ellis or in fact that he had ever had one in his possession'.[20] He explained that,

during the remand period I several times questioned Ruth Ellis as to the authenticity of her story ... Throughout she was adamant that this story was true. In view of this we were forced to accept the fact that Cussen did not give the revolver to her.[21]

He referred to Ruth's statement and the issue of how she arrived in Hampstead on the evening of Easter Sunday:

It will be seen that she says that she travelled to Hampstead by taxi cab on the night of the shooting. This taxi cab was never traced, but it is significant that she does not mention her movements on the day of the murder until 8 p.m.[22]

DCI Davies then made clear his position: 'I am of the opinion that Cussen did not supply the gun, neither did he drive Mrs Ellis to Hampstead on that night.'[23] After highlighting Jacqueline's testimony regarding David's violence and the statement of Dr Robert Hunter Hill, he concluded:

> Nothing further calling for inquiry has emerged from the letter of Mrs Dyer, but it is my opinion that, being a Frenchwoman, she finds it difficult to believe that Ellis should pay the supreme penalty for a crime of this nature. I think she is genuine in her efforts to save her friend, but unfortunately she cannot say anything that we do not already know and has not been inquired into.[24]

His report was forwarded to the Home Office, where a note was added to their file on Ruth that very day; it concerned MP George Rogers and his belief that there was a case for a reprieve. The Home Office official was less convinced, writing:

> It seems to me that even if Mrs Dyer's theory about the gun is true, it is not directly relevant to the question of premeditation and it does not affect the fact that Mrs Ellis went out on the evening in question in Hampstead armed with a gun, which she then used against Blakely.[25]

Nor did the Home Office attach any value to the letter sent in by the married man whose one night stand with Ruth was cut short after he glimpsed her appalling injuries; his detailed description was filed and forgotten.

Bickford wrote again to the Home Office on 3 July, imploring them to give due consideration to Ruth's mother's letter, which he felt was a 'convincing but somewhat illiterate statement'.[26] But the following day, Philip Allen, the Assistant Under Secretary, wrote with reference to the voluminous papers in Ruth's file:

> A serious view has always been taken of the deliberate use of firearms in this country to commit crime, and it is difficult to see what extenuating features there are in this case to warrant a merciful view being taken of this premeditated shooting.[27]

Among those writers stirred enough to contact the letter pages of the London press was *Who Lie in Gaol* author Joan Henry:

In a country that claims to lead the world in matters of reform, capital punishment is, indeed, a blot. If one could, truly, believe that the death penalty is a deterrent to the would-be murderer, possibly one should suppress one's revulsion against it – but this has never been proven to be so . . . Surely it is time that we followed the example of the thirty other states who have abolished capital punishment with no evidence of any increase in the murder rate, and did away with the gallows.[28]

Three days later, crime writer F. Tennyson Jesse – author of *A Pin to See the Peepshow*, a novel based on the life of Edie Thompson – wrote expressing another view:

Mrs Ruth Ellis's killing of David Blakely could not possibly have been manslaughter; if she had lied she could not have made it seem so. She loaded all six chambers of her gun and she fired them all. One bullet hit an unfortunate passer-by in the thumb; anyone might have been killed. That Blakely was a lamentable specimen of humanity is neither here nor there . . . It is true to say that untidy morally as the life was that Mrs Ellis led we do not hang people for immorality. She had been unfaithful, even to Blakely, and it is difficult to understand why she should take his wish to leave her so seriously. But unpleasant as he was, he is dead, and the English are much too apt to forget the first corpse . . . If the prerogative of mercy is granted, there is still no reason to minimise the seriousness of the crime, for that crime was murder.[29]

Her words provoked an angry protest from David's brother Derek and his wife, then living in Beaconsfield:

We have read Miss Tennyson Jesse's letter referring to Ruth Ellis and David Blakely. We notice she refers to him as 'a lamentable specimen of humanity'. Those of us, and there are many, who knew and loved David for years, wish to register our protest at these remarks. We should require a great deal more proof than that provided by the defence at the trial that any of the allegations against his character were founded on fact.[30]

In Holloway, Ruth read Derek's letter and was pleased by his loyalty to David but disappointed by his remark about her case in court. On

5 July she wrote to her friend Frank Neale, expressing gratitude to all those fighting on her behalf while making it clear that she did not invite their efforts:

> Dear Frank
> Thank you for your letter, and lovely flowers, yes, I was allowed to see them, they are now in the church, I shall see them again, on Sunday. Sorry to hear of your accident, hope you get well soon.
>
> I am overwhelmed with the thought of so many people, wanting to help me. And am, deeply great ful, to one, and all.
>
> No dought you have heard, I do not want to live. You may find this very hard to believe, but that is what I want.
>
> I am, quite well and happy, under the circumstances, and very well looked after. I have plenty to amuse me.
>
> Well Frank this must be all for now.
> Thanks Once Again
> Yours
> Ruth Ellis.[31]

As the weather grew hotter, increasing numbers of people spoke up on Ruth's behalf, including former Little Club employee Alexander Engleman, who informed the Home Office that Desmond Cussen had owned a taxi, which he suspected was used to drive Ruth to Hampstead on Easter Sunday. The Home Office forwarded the letter to DC Claiden, who interviewed Engleman at his home off Tottenham Court Road. Engleman spoke about the rivalry between David and Desmond, and recalled how one evening in 1954 he had accepted a lift home by Desmond, who drove an old taxi and even doffed a chauffeur's cap for the journey.

After leaving Engleman's flat, Claiden set out for Goodwood Court, but Desmond was not at home. In his 8 July report on the matter, Claiden recalled:

> I made inquiries of a number of friends of both Blakely and Cussen, but none could remember Cussen ever having used an old taxi cab. It may well be that he did so when driving Engleman home but it would appear that it was an isolated incident [according to Engleman, Desmond mentioned he had 'borrowed' the cab while his own car was being serviced]. No information

could be obtained concerning the possible ownership of the machine. Cussen has not been seen, and although intensive inquiries were made to trace him, he could not be found. It is believed that he returned to London during the afternoon of 6 July 1955, but his present whereabouts are unknown. If, within the next few days, Cussen is traced he will be interrogated in respect of the use of the taxicab with Engleman, and of the possibility that he drove Ellis to the scene of the murder.[32]

Then he added:

Even if it is established that Cussen drove her to Hampstead on that evening, it would have little bearing on the culpability of Ellis in this matter, but so far there is not a shred of evidence to show that Cussen did take her to the scene of the crime.[33]

Ruth had five days to live.

*

On Friday, 8 July, the *Daily Mirror* front-page headline read: 'LAST BID TO SAVE RUTH ELLIS'. The article highlighted the letters, petitions, telegrams and even poems flooding into the Home Office from across the globe to plead for Ruth's reprieve. The Women's Social Labour Organisation of British Guiana on the northern coast of South America sent a telegram to the Home Secretary entreating: 'Consider children alone in the world. Act of mercy will be great boon to International Womanhood.'[34]

One person who felt little sympathy for Ruth's fate was David's friend Archie Scott-Brown. The prospect of her execution

gave Archie grim and rather untypical satisfaction. Archie was on record as having been very much in the pro-hanging lobby on this occasion, unlike much of the country, whose friend Blakely was not. Archie was outraged at Ellis's action, which suggests that he did not know much of her complicated and tawdry life, or her relationship with Blakely. Perhaps he felt that Blakely's own death sentence for the minor misdemeanor of having a 'loose zipper' was, to say the least, unjustified.[35]

But the majority of those contacting the Home Office and the press hoped that Ruth would be saved; one anonymous writer had even asked the Home Secretary to look into the death of Phyllis Staton, believing that something could be gained from investigating David's father's own trial for murder. Unsurprisingly, nothing came of it.

Later that Friday, the Home Secretary left London for a weekend with his sister Lady Megan Lloyd George in Wales, taking with him all the papers on Ruth's case. If the police were not overly concerned about the original owner of the gun, the press were beginning to scent a story worth investigating. The *Evening News* hinted very loosely at Desmond's involvement: 'The man who gave it to her has never been named, but it is believed he was an army officer . . . Possibly Mrs Ellis may have forgotten the identity of the man who made that illegal transaction.'[36]

Desmond returned to London that day, unable to avoid the headlines and clamour. On Saturday, 9 July, the *Daily Mirror* offered another banner headline: '"I'M CONTENT TO DIE" SAYS RUTH ELLIS'. There was a feeling of oppressive tension in the air, caused by the uncertain fate of the woman in the condemned cell and the strange, broiling weather. Islington schoolteacher Gladys Langford wrote in her diary: 'How grim the intervening hours must be for her and her parents. Poor unfortunate children too. Thank God I had a good mother. Bad thunderstorm tonight and such clammy weather all day.'[37]

Bickford sensed that he was losing any chance of saving his client but persisted until the end, hoping that further evidence about her mental health in the days before the shooting might help sway the Home Secretary. He contacted Vernon Symonds, a specialist in alcoholism therapy, for his professional opinion. Symonds responded that Ruth was 'almost certainly an alcoholic according to the reports of the proceedings which I have seen'.[38] Bickford did his best to develop the idea that alcoholism was partly to blame for Ruth's actions outside the Magdala, despite evidence (including the testimonies of PC Thompson and WPC Garrard) to the contrary.

'Mrs Ellis confirmed the facts regarding her drinking to me,' Bickford wrote to the Under Secretary of State on 9 July, 'and has told me that she remembers on one occasion drinking as much as a bottle and a half of Pernod within the space of a few hours.'[39] He described her as 'continually drugged by drink . . . ill and weak', yet Ruth had told the prison doctor upon admission to Holloway that she 'had not drunk heavily for at least two weeks'.[40] But Bickford ploughed on, raising virtually every point in his desperation but that of the origins of the gun. He quoted from an interview he had conducted with Dr Hertzel Creditor of Hampstead, adding that the doctor was prepared to support his statements on oath 'although most of them amount to theory or hearsay; but are, in my respectful submission, of value'.[41] In fact, they were no such thing, being no more than libelous tittle-tattle by a man who had apparently 'brought Carole Findlater in the world' and was 'a great personal friend' of her brother.[42] The Home Office quietly ignored Bickford's desperate attempt to persuade them to pursue the matter.

At Goodwood Court, DCI Davies and DC Claiden had succeeded in obtaining a statement from Desmond:

> I have been asked if I ever owned a taxi cab. I did. I bought it early in 1954 . . . I ran it for several months until about June 1954, then loaned it to several of my staff to use on their holidays, then disposed of it to my brother, William David Cussen . . . in about August or September the same year. I have not used it since. On Sunday, 10th April 1955, I dropped Mrs Ellis and son at about 7.30 p.m. at 44 Egerton Gardens and did not see her again that day. I certainly did not drive her to Hampstead that evening, by taxi or otherwise. I have seen Ruth Ellis in prison since she was sentenced and at no time have we discussed the origin of this gun.[43]

After concluding their interview, the detectives sent a message to the Home Office explaining the outcome:

> Re: man named Cussen alleged to have driven Ruth Ellis to Hampstead on the night of the shooting. Cussen has been interviewed this morning and denies having driven Ellis to Hampstead on the evening of 10/4/55 in a taxicab or any other vehicle. He did own a taxicab from Feb to September 1954. He drove it from Feb 54 to June 54, and then lent to members of his staff to go on holiday. He sold it to his brother at Windsor in September 1954 and has not seen or used it since.[44]

The following day, Sunday, 10 July, Ruth attended the prison chapel, as she did every week, except that this visit would be her last. The chapel was large and modern, with garish red, blue and green stripes underneath the windows. It was empty when Ruth entered with two wardresses. She sat where she always did, in a pew at the front, surrounded on three sides by thick green curtains to protect her from the curious eyes of the other inmates. The place was filled with flowers brought in to Ruth by her visitors. She spoke for a while afterwards with the chaplain and was later visited in her cell by the Bishop of Stepney, Joost de Blank; Holloway Gaol was part of his diocese. He recalled that Ruth said during their meeting: 'It is quite clear to me that I was not the person who shot him. When I saw myself with the revolver I knew I was another person.'[45]

More contentiously, the Bishop claimed that during his visit to Ruth in the condemned cell he was,

> horrified and aghast beyond words to find that Holloway prisoners could hear hammering going on as a scaffold was being built. I reject the death penalty because of its absolute nature, its questionable nature and its revolting nature.[46]

The matter was raised in Parliament on 8 December 1955, when Harford Montgomery Hyde, Ulster Unionist MP for Belfast North, asked the Home Secretary,

> if he is aware that the prisoners and staff in Holloway Prison were greatly disturbed shortly before the execution of the late Mrs Ruth Ellis, by the noise caused through hammering in the erection of the scaffold on which she was subsequently hanged; and whether he will take steps to prevent inconveniences of this kind in future in all Her Majesty's Prisons where executions are carried out.[47]

Lloyd George replied: 'My Hon Friend is under a misapprehension. No scaffold was erected in Holloway prison before the execution of Mrs Ellis.'[48] Incredibly careful steps were taken to ensure that neither the condemned prisoner nor any other inmate should be aware of the practicalities of execution, and it was this shrouding of secrecy – with politicians as uninformed as the public – that led to so much extreme and persistent rumour.

Monday, 11 July was another day of soaring temperatures, with thunderstorms breaking over London and other parts of southern England in the afternoon and evening. It was the hottest day of the year until then, but followed within hours of dawn with heavy rain and lightning. The London Fire Brigade were inundated with more than one hundred and forty calls, mostly about flooding; parked cars were suddenly moated in six inches of water and, at Paddington Station, lightning struck, dislodging a piece of brickwork which fell, smashing four panes of glass in the roof above platform one. Miraculously, no one was harmed.

Bickford made his way to Holloway Gaol early that morning, where the prisoners too were feeling the heat. He asked Ruth about Dr Creditor's claims, but she dismissed them as nonsense. Bickford then spoke to Dr Ralph Penry Williams to clear up one or two medical issues and, upon returning to his office at Cardew-Smith & Ross, he drafted a letter to the Home Office, stating that Ruth had refuted beyond doubt any truth in Dr Creditor's claims, but,

> still insists vehemently that it was due to the Findlaters keeping David back in those peculiar circumstances that she acted as she did. On looking back she is convinced nothing of the sort could or would have happened if it had not been (a) for her continual drinking of spirits, which she had taken to during the last six months, owing to the nerve-strain she had been enduring. This robbed her of her normal powers of judgement. (b) To the miscarriage shortly before the event, which she insists was not induced and believes may well have been caused by one particularly violent attack by Blakely shortly before . . . (c) To her generally low state of health including the effects of the severe cold she had had with a high temperature and (d) to the events, which have already been described, which led to the tragedy.[49]

He added:

> When I first saw her within days of the event she still seemed to feel that what she had done was the only thing she could have done; but she could only give vague and inconclusive reasons. Later she became far more lucid about it and obviously realised what a frightful thing she had done.[50]

Bickford enclosed the transcript of Carole Findlater's interview with *Sunday Pictorial* journalist Harry Ashbrook, who hoped that it might somehow prove useful in obtaining a reprieve.

A letter supporting the death sentence on Ruth was received at the Home Office later that day; the writer (a woman) asked:

> Will you forgive my saying that the majority of women do not join in the hysterical clamour to reprieve Ruth Ellis? . . . If she is reprieved it creates a precedent whereby every prostitute who thinks herself slighted by a former lover will think herself entitled to butcher him.[51]

One woman who fervently disagreed was twenty-nine-year-old Frieda Platt. Although she and Ruth had never met, Platt spent upwards of 12 hours every day at London's mainline stations, asking people to sign a petition in favour of a reprieve. Four years earlier, Platt had been accused of the attempted murder of her own husband and was determined that Ruth should not hang.

But the Home Secretary, aided by a secret committee he himself appointed, had reached a decision. One of the committee members – a Catholic priest who had also been a prison chaplain – pleaded for clemency, but the others – a Home Office official and a psychiatrist – recommended no reprieve. The Home Secretary listened to their arguments that morning upon his return from Wales and issued a statement:

> I have given the most careful and anxious consideration to this case.
>
> As I conceive my duty, it is to review all the circumstances of a capital case in order to see if there are such mitigating circumstances as would justify me in recommending interference with the due course of law. It is no part of the duty of a Home Secretary to give any weight to his own approval, or detestation of the penalty prescribed by law; and least of all is it his duty to alter the law merely on the grounds that he thinks that a penalty which is appropriate for a man is inappropriate for a woman.
>
> There may be circumstances in a capital case where special considerations apply to a woman which would not be applicable in the case of a man. A recent example is the case of Mrs Sarah

Lloyd [the Leeds woman who was convicted of beating to death her elderly neighbour; these 'special considerations' in her case were never explained]. I can find no such special circumstances, however, in the present case. The crime was a premeditated one and was carried out with deliberation. The prisoner has expressed no remorse. I can find nothing to justify my taking a less serious view of this case than of other similar cases where the crime was of a callous and calculated nature.

I have been pressed from many quarters to exercise clemency in this case on the grounds of the prisoner's sex and of her yielding to jealousy which is alleged by some people to be stronger in the case of a woman than in the case of a man. But our law takes no special account of the so-called *crime passionel*, and I am not prepared to differentiate between sexes on the grounds that one sex is more susceptible to jealousy than the other.

Cases may arise from time to time where a husband deserts a wife, or a wife deserts a husband, or where one spouse is deceived by the other spouse in the most provocative circumstances, and clemency may be appropriate in such a case. In the present instance there is no such element: and the woman was as unfaithful to her lover as he was to her.

I have consulted the trial judge and discussed all the details of the case with him. He told me that he was unable to suggest any mitigating circumstances, and although he naturally disowned any responsibility for the ultimate decision, he said that he himself could find no sufficient grounds for suggesting that clemency would be appropriate.

If a reprieve were granted in this case, I think that we should have seriously to consider whether capital punishment should be retained as a penalty.

The fact that many people have signed letters and petitions on behalf of the prisoner is a factor to which I have given due weight. I do not think that it is a conclusive factor.

After much anxious thought I have come to the conclusion that this is a case in which the law should be allowed to take its course.[52]

That same sentence is written across the Home Office file containing

Lloyd George's statement in the National Archives: 'THE LAW MUST TAKE ITS COURSE.'[53]

Ten years later, when he was no longer Home Secretary, Lloyd George spoke to barrister-turned-author Fenton Bresler about his decision:

> For a start, I do not think that a press campaign should affect the Home Secretary one way or the other. I'd have reprieved everyone if I could, but as Home Secretary I had to administer the law of England ... This was no inflamed murder in the heat of the moment. She travelled all the way up to Hampstead from her home in Kensington, looked in the window of the public house, waited for him to come out and then shot him six times. It was a deliberate killing![54]

He expanded:

> We cannot have people shooting off firearms in the street. This was a public thoroughfare where Ruth Ellis stalked and shot her quarry. And remember that she did not only kill David Blakely; she also injured a passer-by. As long as I was Home Secretary I was determined to ensure that people could use the streets without fear of a bullet.[55]

The injured bystander expressed her views in the *Evening Standard*'s letter page that day, 11 July:

> Don't let us turn Ruth Ellis into a national heroine. I stood petrified and watched her kill David Blakely in cold blood, even putting two further bullets into him as he lay bleeding to death on the ground.
>
> What right had Ruth Ellis to be jealous of Blakely, jealous to the point of killing, even if there had been 'another woman'? She had another lover during the same period; that has been proved in evidence. What proof have we that the allegations against Blakely are true? He is dead and cannot defend himself. It is therefore distasteful and cruel to start a smear campaign against the boy to try and justify a dastardly murder.
>
> Those hysterical people, getting up petitions for a reprieve,

and those rushing to sign them – do they realise that Ruth Ellis shot Blakely to the danger of the public?

She might easily have killed me, an innocent passer-by, a complete stranger. As it is I have a partly crippled right hand for life, for which there is no compensation.

If Ruth Ellis is reprieved, we may have other vindictive and jealous young women shooting their boyfriends in public and probably innocent blood on their hands.

Crime passionel indeed! What if other countries would let her off from her just punishment? When has Britain followed the lead of others?

Let us remain a law abiding country where citizens can live and walk abroad in peace and safety.[56]

Gladys Kensington Yule did not have to worry: the wheels of officialdom began to turn, moving towards the hour of Ruth's death. Acting Under Sheriff, Harold Gedge, who was to be present at the execution, received a letter informing him: 'the law is to take its course in this case'.[57] Upon receipt of the letter, Gedge immediately contacted the landlord of the Rose and Crown pub, just off the A59 at Much Hoole near Preston, with instructions to present himself at Holloway Gaol the following afternoon.

*

'When I leave school, I should like to be Chief Executioner,' 11-year-old Albert Pierrpoint had written in an essay, much to the disapproval of his mother. She was married to a chief executioner (Henry Pierrepoint) and counted another as her brother-in-law (Tom Pierrepoint). 'You'll have no luck at all as long as you live if you take that job,' she told her son.[58] Albert was employed in a cotton mill near the family home in Huddersfield until the end of the 1920s, when he became deliveryman for a grocer. But then he decided to follow his calling, and began acting as his uncle's assistant at executions, bypassing the usual routes into the profession. In 1941 he was appointed chief executioner at last and his first appointment was to hang gangster Antonio 'Babe' Mancini, who surprised the entire execution party by calling 'cheerio' when Albert placed the hood over his head.

The Guinness Book of Records credits Albert with hanging 530 men and 20 women during his long career; this includes Lord Haw-Haw,

John George Haigh, Neville Heath, Timothy Evans, John Christie, Derek Bentley and a number of Nazi war criminals. The latter group he dispatched in Germany, flown there secretly after a meeting with Field Marshal Montgomery. When the British press discovered the purpose of his sojourn in Germany, he became a celebrity almost overnight. He was not always comfortable with his newfound fame, but it did him no harm when he and his wife Anne decided to manage a pub in Hollinwood, between Oldham and Manchester. The unfortunately appropriate name, 'Help the Poor Struggler', drew the crowds even more, although Albert refused to discuss his work as an executioner and was furious about stories of a sign in the bar that read: 'No Hanging About'. In June 1952, he and Anne left the pub in Hollinwood for the Rose and Crown in Much Hoole, where they remained until retirement.

Albert prided himself on his professionalism and speed (his fastest recorded hanging took just seven seconds) and spoke in hallowed tones about the condemned prisoner:

> Decisions have been made which I cannot alter. He is a man, she is a woman who, the church says, still merits some mercy. The supreme mercy I can extend to them is to give them and sustain in them their dignity in dying and in death. The gentleness must remain.[59]

He would not allow anyone in his party to make jokes about the prisoner and insisted on cutting down the noose himself after an execution, as well as undressing the corpse and covering it in readiness for the post-mortem.

He had no patience with abolitionists, and described the uproar over Ruth's execution as 'the last great sentimental protest against capital punishment in Great Britain'.[60] With some justification, he pointed out the difference between opposition to Ruth's death and the planned execution of Mrs Sarah Lloyd, writing in his autobiography:

> At the same time that I held in my files the written appointment for the execution of Ruth Ellis I had another date in my diary. I was to go to Strangeways Gaol, Manchester, a week earlier and hang a woman of forty [Sarah Lloyd] . . . Two women therefore lay under sentence of death at the same time. For one a powerful

> series of national petitions was launched – someone even sent
> me a cheque for ninety pounds and said it was my fee if I did not
> carry out the execution: I have the cheque still. For the other,
> nobody except her devoted husband lifted a finger.[61]

As Albert made arrangements to catch the train from Preston to
Euston the next morning, at quarter to three on Monday afternoon a
Home Office official travelled by taxi to Holloway to inform Dr
Taylor that a reprieve had been refused. It was she who had the task of
walking through the hot, airless warren of the prison to the isolated
room at the top of the stone steps to tell Ruth that she had less than
two days left to live. As the Governor quietly but firmly explained the
Home Secretary's decision, Ruth's fragile shell disintegrated. She
collapsed on her bed, weeping: '*I don't want to die. I don't want to
die.*'[62] Dr Taylor left the cell silently, and wrote to the Home Office in
the emotionless language that concealed the horror of the news she
had just imparted, confirming receipt of the letter, 'informing me that
the Under Secretary of State has failed to discover any sufficient
ground to justify him in advising Her Majesty to interfere with the
due course of law. The woman has been informed accordingly.'[63]

23

Bickford was the first person to visit Ruth after she had been informed there would be no reprieve. Appalled by the news ('I couldn't believe they would hang her'), he was in for an even greater shock.[1]

In the visitor's cell he took his seat, intending to ask Ruth to finally allow him to reveal the story of the gun. His client entered the room, accompanied by a wardress, and sat down.

'Now, look, this isn't the finish of everything—' Bickford began.

Ruth cut him off with a cold stare: 'I've been wondering what your game was.' She spoke slowly: 'I know now. No wonder you haven't been to see me.' Her next words took the wind out of his sails: 'You've been taking money from Cussen to see that I go down and he goes free.'[2]

Bickford was aghast. 'She accused me of deliberately throwing away her case,' he recalled, 'and of having accepted a bribe from Cussen to ensure that she was hanged and he got away.'[3] Asked years later whether he had in fact ever received any sort of financial remuneration from Desmond, the solicitor reacted angrily: 'Certainly *not*, my friend.'[4]

After leaving Holloway, Bickford telephoned Leon Simmons. He had recently spoken to him to ask if he would assist Ruth in drawing up her will, and again to request that he contact the Home Office to support a reprieve. Bickford now told Simmons in consternation about his meeting with Ruth, admitting that she had more confidence in her old solicitor. Simmons spoke urgently to the head of the firm, Victor Mishcon, and they decided to visit Ruth together, agreeing to speak to Bickford first the following morning.

Following Bickford's departure, Ruth received another visitor: MP George Rogers. A note in her file reveals that Rogers had spoken to 'Mr Allen' (Philip Allen, Assistant Under Secretary at the Home

Office) and was given permission to visit her again despite their disastrous first encounter:

> In consultation with Mr Allen, Mr Rogers was allowed to pay a second visit. Mrs Ellis said at first that she would not see him unless her solicitor agreed, but it is understood that he did agree . . . On the day before her execution, Mr Rogers was allowed to pay a final visit. His request that Mrs Rogers might accompany him was refused.[5]

The MP had a proposal for Ruth: that Andre should stay with him for a while. Inexplicably, given that Rogers had only recently come into her life and then under fractious circumstances, Ruth agreed. Arrangements were made for Andre to be taken to the Rogers' large country home in Sudbury. 'The boy had been kept in the dark as there was still a little hope,' Rogers recalled. 'And we thought it would be better to keep him away from his normal surroundings where he might learn the truth rather brutally.'[6] In her memoir, Muriel claims that Ruth wrote to her after the trial asking her to take care of her children, but she destroyed the letter because she didn't want her own children to read it; the inference is that Rogers and his wife were simply seeking the limelight in taking Andre to live with them, but this still does not explain Ruth's motivations in removing her son from his family to be deposited with a couple whom he did not know. During his visit, Rogers again raised the question of who gave her the gun; whether Ruth told him or not is unclear, but she did insist that she desperately needed to speak to Leon Simmons.

Ruth's other visitor that day was Jacqueline Dyer, who noticed that her friend's eyes were red-rimmed but had no idea why and did not ask.

At some point, when all her visitors were gone, Ruth was weighed again, as she had been at regular intervals in Holloway, and a note was made: '103 lbs'.[7] Observing her weight was part of medical regulations, but this time it had another purpose: the measurement would be handed, with Ruth's other details, to Albert Pierrepoint so that he could make his final calculations for the rope.

*

Tuesday, 12 July 1955 was Ruth's last full day on earth. A newspaper headline announced that Britain was 'hotter than Africa'.[8] The noon temperature on the Air Ministry roof in London was 75 degrees and, unusually, it was hotter still by early evening. There were powerful storms in Dorset and Wales, leaving buildings damaged, families homeless and crops destroyed, but elsewhere there was nothing but brilliant sunshine and intense, inescapable heat.

Ruth's mother called three times at Holloway that day. On the first occasion she was with Muriel, who recalls that she was 'sneaked in', although her name was on the official visitors' list:

> My mother and I went up these concrete steps, which were all worn away in the middle where people had walked before. Ruth was standing in front of a grille, with two prison officers behind her. Her hair and makeup were done. I wasn't allowed to ask any questions but my eyes pleaded with her to tell me the truth, to tell me what had happened.[9]

She remembered Ruth as 'very calm . . . I'd just had a new baby and she said what was he like, and she said she liked the dress I had on. I believe she thought that at the last minute they'd say, "You'll go to prison instead."'[10] As the visit came to an end Muriel was 'so choked I couldn't say goodbye. I just collapsed on the steps and sobbed.'[11]

Victor Mishcon and Leon Simmons called on Bickford in his office before their visit to Ruth. Bickford, apparently still feeling constrained by client confidentiality, made a suggestion to the two men. Mishcon recalled:

> I asked him . . . whether there was anything he could think of which would give me a lead, even at this stage, to save her life. He looked at me and said, 'Try and get her to tell you who gave her the gun.' Nothing more than that.[12]

Questioned afterwards about whether or not he should have been more explicit in his instructions, Bickford responded:

> I don't think so. I'd have very willingly done so if it had been counsel or somebody, yes . . . but a solicitor coming in, in those circumstances, I hadn't been freed from this bond of confidence . . . I thought I've still been told not to involve this fellow, and the only indirect way I could do it was to ask him to ask her that direct question.[13]

Pressed further, Bickford faltered:

> Well, in the events that happened I think that it proves I should
> have done, willy-nilly. But I didn't. Because I was trying to make
> the best decision I could in those circumstances, in the
> atmosphere I was in and the feeling at the time . . . I'd been at it
> 'til I was nearly dead, so perhaps my judgement was at fault, I
> don't know . . . If it was, I apologise to Ruth Ellis. I'm sorry, I
> made a mistake.[14]

Mishcon and Simmons arrived at Holloway at 11.15 a.m. They
climbed the stairs to the condemned cell, where Ruth was waiting for
them. She struck Mishcon as 'quite remarkable'.[15] He remembered:

> I must say I was quite amazed at [her] calm . . . There was a little
> of the actress about her. She wore a dressing-gown over prison
> clothes, yet completely acted the charming hostess. 'How kind
> of you to come,' she greeted us. 'I wanted Mr Simmons to know
> certain facts which I think may have some bearing on my will.'[16]

He had no doubt that she had resigned herself to death and she told
them, in a speech that sounded as if it had been prepared in advance:

> I'm not asking for a reprieve. I am now completely composed. I
> know that I am going to die, and I'm ready to do so. You won't
> hear anything from me that says I didn't kill David. I did kill
> him. And whatever the circumstances you as a lawyer will
> appreciate that it's a life for a life. Isn't that just?[17]

Mishcon looked at her steadily, bearing in mind what Bickford had
intimated. He told her, 'Yes, I understand what you're saying, but
please don't limit facts to those which you think affects the alteration
of the will.'[18] Ruth asked him whether he wanted her to say anything
that might help him obtain a reprieve for her, adding that she wasn't
interested in that at all. 'I thought I'd got a duty to carry on pressing
her to tell me the truth,' Mishcon remembered:

> and the only way I got her to tell me the truth – as it undoubtedly
> was – was when I asked her whether she thought it was right that

her son when he grew up should merely get her version of what had happened from what he read in the newspapers – if that was right for her, if that was right for her family. And that at last got her and she told me, 'Yes, alright. I will tell you facts and I will tell you the truth which hasn't yet been completely known by any manner of means.'[19]

After a pause, Ruth said: 'You're the only person who has been able to persuade me to do this. I suppose the truth would have been found out anyway after I've gone. I'll tell you what happened if you'll promise not to use it to try and save me.'[20]

'Tell us what happened,' Mishcon said, 'and we can discuss afterwards whether or not we have your permission to do anything with it.'[21]

Ruth frowned: 'I don't want to get anyone else into trouble – one life for a life is enough. I didn't say anything about it up to now because it seemed traitorous – absolutely traitorous.'[22]

Principal Officer Griffin was also present. Afterwards, she drafted a report for the Governer:

> Mr Mishcon was very persistent in asking Ellis about the gun, stating that it was only fair that the Home Secretary knew the true facts of the gun, he did not suppose it would help Ellis but the truth could be put on record. Ellis said that she didn't want to say anything that would get anyone else in trouble, the solicitor assured her it would not and if only she would tell him what he wanted to know, they would discuss it after and see if it would help her and after repeated attempts by Mr Mishcon, Ellis, with very, very great reluctance said, alright I will tell you, but, I can't in front of the Officer.
>
> After a little more persuasion Ellis said that she hadn't had the gun for 3 years, but was given it by Desmond Cousins [sic] on the night she shot Blakely (Easter Sunday). He loaded it, and oiled it before giving it to her. She says she was muddled through all the drink she had had and can't remember the conversation that passed when D Cousins [sic] gave her the gun. She knows she was drinking Vurnat [Pernod], a greenish liquid, from 8.30 p.m. til 3 a.m., most days and she was dreadfully muddled, but clearly remembers rushing out of the room when given the gun.

She came back a few moments later, and asked D. Cousins [*sic*] to drive her to Hampstead, which he did without asking any questions. She had never seen the gun before, only an air pistol in the flat, Blakely was more jealous of Cousins [*sic*] than Cousins [*sic*] of Blakely.

She still says she doesn't want to live, if she did, she could have pleaded insanity at her trial. She said that she went to the flat to seek Desmond and it was her suggestion that she had the gun.

The rest of the visit was to add a codicil to the will, making her Parents Executors and transferring the whole business to Mr Simmons.[23]

After listening to Ruth's story, Mishcon asked her to make a formal statement, which she did. It read:

I, Ruth Ellis, have been advised by Mr Victor Mishcon to tell the whole truth in regard to the circumstances leading up to the killing of David Blakely and it is only with the greatest reluctance that I have decided to tell how it was that I got the gun with which I shot Blakely. I did not do so before because I felt that I was needlessly getting someone into possible trouble.

I had been drinking Pernod (I think that is how it is spelt) in Desmond Cussen's flat and Desmond had been drinking it too. This was about 8.30 p.m. We had been drinking for some time. I had been telling Desmond about Blakely's treatment of me. I was in a terribly depressed state. All I remember is that Desmond gave me a loaded gun. Desmond was jealous of Blakely as in fact Blakely was of Desmond. I would say that they hated each other. I was in such a dazed state that I cannot remember what was said. I rushed out as soon as he gave me the gun. He stayed in the flat. I rushed back after a second or two and said 'Will you drive me to Hampstead?' He did so and left me at the top of Tanza Road.

I had never seen that gun before. The only gun I had ever seen there was a small air pistol used as a game with a target.

Signed Ruth Ellis.[24]

Mishcon read the statement aloud in the narrow confines of the visitor cell. After Ruth signed the paper, he added the time and date: 12.30 p.m., 12 July 1955. Both he and Leon Simmons stressed again that it was her duty to let the authorities know the truth. They asked for her permission to put the statement before the Home Secretary.

'Well, if you want to, you can,' Ruth said indifferently.[25]

Then, almost as an afterthought, she mentioned that on Easter Sunday Desmond had driven her to Epping Forest, where he taught her how to fire the revolver; Andre was with them. For some reason, Mishcon did not add this to her statement and nor did he add – according to Principal Officer Griffin's report to the Home Office – her remark that *she* had asked Desmond for the gun.

Twenty minutes after Ruth made her statement, Mishcon and Simmons gathered up their papers and bid her a swift farewell. There was no time to waste: at that very moment, the train from Preston was nearing Euston with Albert Pierrepoint onboard. His assistant, 36-year-old publican Royston Rickard, likewise had already departed his home on Milton Street in Maidstone. Ruth was due to be hanged the next day at 9 a.m. After leaving Holloway, Mishcon telephoned the Home Office to request an urgent meeting, while the Governor waited for Principal Officer Griffin's report before dispatching it, too, to the Home Office.

Mishcon and Simmons raced to Whitehall and asked to speak to Sir Frank Newsam, Permanent Under Secretary of State. Frustratingly, he was at Ascot, but Philip Allen saw them and read Ruth's statement. He assured them that a thorough investigation would be made.

'Is that possible,' Mishcon asked, 'given the time left to us?'

Allen's reply did not instill him with much hope: 'I cannot say that the facts, even if verified, will necessarily justify a reprieve.'[26]

While her solicitors were at the Home Office, in Holloway Ruth received several visitors. Jacqueline Dyer arrived with her husband James and thought Ruth looked different:

Her face was white, her hair silver rather than ash blonde. It had grown quite long and was combed back over her head and behind her ears. She had regained her composure . . . Her dress was blue, the front tied with bows. With the words choked in my throat all I could say was, 'You have bows on your dress,' like a stupid child. Ruth laughed. She said, 'Have you heard the big news?' I nodded. I said, 'I realise you had heard yesterday before I came.' Talking was difficult . . . Ruth sensed my confusion. She said, 'All your efforts to help me have not been in vain. You will know this later.'[27]

During one of Jacqueline's earlier visits, Ruth had referred to her impending death: 'Don't worry, it's like having a tooth out and they'll give me a glass of brandy beforehand.'[28] Now that flippancy had gone; she told Jacqueline that she wanted her to have her beauty box 'afterwards'. When she tried to light a cigarette, a wardress had to help her – a habit Jacqueline remembered of old. Too soon the visit was over, but Jacqueline could not bring herself to say anything other than: 'I will see you later,' when the wardress indicated that it was time for them to leave.[29] Ruth nodded. 'My husband and I had the feeling that she didn't want us to go,' Jacqueline recalled.

> The wardress said we must leave and added, 'You are not allowed to come back. You should not say you will.' Afraid Ruth had heard this, I whispered, 'Ssh. I'm trying to say for me it's not goodbye.' There was a strange and peculiar look on Ruth's face. I cannot put it into words. Suddenly she turned and went through the door to that place where she had lived ever since her trial.[30]

Jacqueline left Holloway that afternoon with a knot of twisted emotion in her stomach. She could not forget how Ruth had looked at them before returning to the condemned cell: 'She always had this facade but I am sure when I left on Tuesday that she broke down.'[31]

Ruth's parents visited with Granville and his wife at 2 p.m. Granville recalled:

> Ruth appeared to be absolutely calm and unafraid of what was going to happen to her. On her cheeks was a fresh bloom, which she said she got as a result of walks in the sunshine in the prison garden. She asked, 'How's everything?' then said she had made a change in her will.[32]

On the other side of the prison gates, the press had got hold of the story that Ruth Ellis had finally broken her silence to make a sensational confession which might overturn the Home Secretary's decision. A cluster of reporters rushed at Mishcon and Simmons as they emerged from Whitehall at 2 p.m. Irritated, Mishcon refused to tell them what was happening: 'It is far better that I say nothing at this stage. A life is at stake.'[33]

Inside the building, Philip Allen told his secretary, Miss Baines, to make two telephone calls: one to Sir Frank Newsam, the Permanent

Under Secretary of State, at Ascot and the other to Hampstead Police Station, asking DCI Davies to make his way immediately to Scotland Yard. Miss Baines' first call resulted in an announcement over the tannoy in the Royal Enclosure, where it was heard by several reporters who quickly made calls of their own to various newsrooms in London (the *Daily Sketch* headline read: 'Drama of Ascot Race Bid to Save Ruth Ellis'). Sir Frank agreed to leave for the Home Office straightaway. The duty officer taking Miss Baines' call at Hampstead Police Station explained that DCI Davies was off sick with influenza; Detective Constable Claiden stepped in and drove straight to Scotland Yard, where he was informed that he was needed at the Home Office. Upon arrival, DC Claiden was interviewed by Philip Allen and then returned to Scotland Yard, where Detective Inspector Peter Gill (who had taken Ruth's original statement on Easter Sunday) noted the main points of what had been said at the Home Office:

> Mr Allen informed the officer that there was a last minute inquiry concerning the death sentence imposed on Ellis, and asked a number of questions respecting the revolver used by Ellis in the commission of the crime. The officer replied to the effect that it had not been believed that Ellis had had the weapon for three years, but the police could not prove otherwise as they had been unable to trace its origin.
>
> Mr Allen seemed particularly interested in the possibility that it had been given to her by Cussen ... DC Claiden observed that it was possible that Cussen had given it to her, but the only evidence of Cussen's possession of guns tended to show that he was not in possession of a revolver a week or two before the tragedy. This information had been culled from Mrs Harris, who had seen two pistols in a drawer in Cussen's flat some time before the shooting occurred. It subsequently transpired that these were an air pistol and a starter's pistol, afterwards taken by police from Cussen's flat and identified by Mrs Harris as those she had seen there – although she had earlier been unable to be specific about the guns. Throughout the inquiry police obtained no evidence to connect Cussen with the revolver in question.
>
> Mr Allen then asked if it was possible that Cussen could have driven Ellis to Hampstead on the night of the shooting, and again he was told that it was possible but nothing had arisen to

confirm that suspicion. DC Claiden was then asked by Mr Allen that if Ellis had made a statement to the effect that Cussen had given her the revolver and had driven her to Hampstead on that night, would it then be possible to charge Cussen with having been an accessory to the crime. Mr Allen was told that, given sufficient evidence, including these two points, it might be possible to charge Cussen, but the most important consideration must be that Cussen knew that the revolver he had given her was to be used for the purpose of shooting Blakely, and this must be substantiated by evidence other than Ellis's, which would then be that of an accomplice.

The discussion terminated at this point as Mr Allen was due to report to the Home Secretary on this matter. DC Claiden returned to New Scotland Yard, where he joined me. With Deputy Commander Rawlings we then went to see the ACC [Assistant Commissioner for Crime], where a further discussion took place.[34]

At Scotland Yard, the discussion between the three policemen was interrupted by a telephone call from Philip Allen at the House of Commons, who asked if they might meet him there. Upon arrival, he handed them a copy of Ruth's new statement to read, which they discussed at length. As a result, DC Claiden and DI Gill were instructed to track Desmond down and 'interrogate him in the light of matters raised therein'.[35] They left the House of Commons at 4.30 p.m. and headed straight to Goodwood Court.

Outside Holloway, crowds had begun to gather in the afternoon sun. Their numbers swelled as schools broke up for the day. A former pupil of nearby Burghley Road Primary recalled that although none of the children in his class read the newspapers, somehow,

> we all knew about Ruth Ellis and her rapidly approaching
> execution. Holloway Prison was only a mile from the school and
> an occasional subject for playground discussion. Some of the
> boys who lived closest to the prison claimed that during her trial
> they had seen Ruth Ellis leaving the prison every morning for
> the Old Bailey. As the date of actual execution approached the
> stories became more detailed. The boys who had claimed to have
> seen Ruth Ellis leaving to go to the Old Bailey were now claiming

that they had seen Albert Pierrepoint, the hangman, arriving to test the scaffold. One boy who lived in a tall block of flats overlooking the prison said that he had heard the crash of the trapdoor being tested and actually seen Ruth Ellis exercising in the prison yard. In the days before the execution a morbid atmosphere descended over the school. Boys spent ages talking about what was going to happen, often referring back to other hangings that had taken place in our short lifetime.[36]

The children hung around the prison gates as long as they dared, mingling with the crowd in the sunlight that slanted through the tall trees. A few people brought along portable wirelesses: the thud of cricket balls and a smatter of applause could be heard from Test Match commentaries, and a light jazz programme played, competing with the rumble of buses, lorries and beeping cars. Somebody called the Fire Brigade for a prank; the noise of the engines added to the jangling nerves of the crowd, who began hammering on the vast double doors of the prison. The police forced them back to the other side of the road.

The boys who claimed to have seen Albert Pierrepoint may not have been fantasising. At 4.30 p.m., a taxi carrying the executioner arrived at the prison. The crowd fell silent as it purred past and disappeared behind the gates. Inside Holloway, Albert reported to the Governor; Royston, his assistant, arrived in Dr Taylor's office at the same time and they shared a pot of tea before being shown to their rooms.

Outside Holloway, the news placards shrieked that a last-minute reprieve was imminent; special editions of the evening papers were filled with the story that the condemned woman had suddenly appointed a new solicitor, who had sprinted to the Home Office that very afternoon. There were so many letters protesting the execution that the newspapers struggled to print only a small section. In the *Evening Standard*, Sir Beverley Baxter MP warned: 'If this woman hangs then the shame of it will be upon us all.'[37] In the *Daily Herald*, Methodist leader Dr Donald Soper urged: 'The killing of a woman would be sordid, shameful and useless . . . Christian punishment must be reformatory.'[38] Frank Owen, a *Daily Express* journalist, fired off a telegram to the Home Office:

Mrs Ellis had a miscarriage three days before she committed murder. If she had given birth to a child and killed it she would have escaped the death penalty under the plea of infanticide. The justification being that her mind had been unhinged by the birth. As it is she shot her lover. Could her mind have been unhinged by reason of the miscarriage? I beg of you to make a last moment decision of mercy.[39]

But in the visitors' cell at the top of the stone steps, Ruth's parents visited their daughter for the last time. Granville was with them again, and later told reporters that his sister 'remained quite calm throughout the last meeting. She appeared to be untroubled. We stayed together for thirty minutes. But much of this time was spent in silence.'[40] Ruth told them about the statement she had given Mishcon and Simmons that morning, but said she had no hope, nor desire, for a reprieve. Granville recalled:

We could not think what to say after her statement about being drunk at the time of the killing and the business of the gun. None of us could understand why she did not release this information earlier. Obviously she was trying to shield someone.[41]

There was no more time for questions: the visit came to an end and Ruth said goodbye to her family, requesting only that they look after Andre: 'When he grows up, see that he understands about me and try to show him that, whatever I did, I loved him all the time.'[42]

*

'In the evening, say at five o'clock or six o'clock, we see the prisoner, probably at exercise or in his cell,' Albert Pierrepoint wrote in his memoirs. 'Then we ask for his age, height and weight and in the evening we make out his drop. Every person has a different drop.'[43]

When Ruth's visitors had gone and she was alone again in the condemned cell with her warders and the pair of goldfish swimming endlessly inside their bowl, Albert and Royston walked quietly up to her door. Albert, chief executioner, swivelled an eye to the Judas hole. 'She was sat down at a table,' he remembered, 'with two wardresses on either side of her.'[44] He moved to one side slightly to allow Royston his turn to look. They stepped back without speaking and Albert was handed the file containing Ruth's weight, height and several other details.[45] The small party of prison officers and hangmen then walked to the execution chamber. Ruth was taken out into the prison yard for an impromptu stroll while they made their preparations. Albert briefed the prison officers who would take over from the wardresses the following morning. He showed them where to stand on the two planks laid across the drop either side of the noose, and how to support Ruth from just slightly behind, keeping a hand flat between her upper arm and ribs, and putting upward pressure in her armpits so that when she fell they could remove themselves quickly. When he was certain they understood, Albert tested the drop using a sandbag that matched Ruth's weight. He made a few final adjustments to the rope and set the drop at 8 ft 4 in. Officer Galilee later described the measurement as 'vicious' and it was – Ruth was only 5 ft 2 in.[46] Under the watchful gaze of Dr Taylor, Albert pulled the lever and the sandbag disappeared into the pit.

The crash of the trapdoors, loud as they were, could not be heard down in the prison yard.

The executioners returned to their rooms for the night, having said a polite goodbye to the Governor and warders; they would meet again the following morning. In her office, Dr Taylor could hear the swell of anger from the crowd and she rang for police assistance to keep order at the gates. Violet Van der Elst, a portly woman of 73 wearing long, rather Victorian clothes, led the chants that hot July evening. '*Evans–Bentley–Ellis . . . Evans–Bentley–Ellis.*' The voices rose above the roar of the traffic, and punters outside the Holloway Castle pub opposite the prison gates joined in. *The Times* reported:

Crowds Demand to See Mrs Ellis: Police reinforcements were sent to Holloway Prison, London, last night to control crowds . . . They had been sent for by the Governor of the prison, who complained of the noise of singing and shouting which had been going on for several hours. Last night a petition urging further consideration of a reprieve, signed by thirty-five members of London County Council, was sent to the House of Commons . . . One section of the crowd chanted, 'Evans – Bentley – Ellis', and the chorus was taken up by all those watching. Before they were moved across the road by the police some people broke through a thin cordon at the entrance to the prison and knocked at the gates demanding to see Mrs Ellis. They apparently sought an opportunity of asking her 'to kneel in prayer with them' but they were told that Mrs Ellis did not wish to see anyone.[47]

Elsewhere in the city, DI Gill and DC Claiden were gloomily reflecting on their efforts to track down Desmond:

> We first telephoned his office, and were told that twenty minutes earlier he had left and was believed to be returning to his flat. We went straight there but found that he was not at home. Telephone inquiries of a number of his associates and also places known to be frequented by him were made, but without success.[48]

The two men reported back to Scotland Yard before deciding to sink a couple of pints in the Red Lion on Parliament Street. They were joined by DCI Davies, who had hauled himself from his sick bed to help.

In the condemned cell far away from everything and everyone, Ruth spent a quiet evening writing letters against a faint backdrop of shouts from the crowd below. The heat of the day had given way to a balmy night, sticky and unpleasant. She wrote to Jacqueline: 'I am quite happy with the verdict, but not the way the story was told. There is so much people don't know about.'[49] She thanked Frank Neale for his last letter 'or should I say epistle, I enjoyed reading it . . . but never mind friend we will all meet again, not to worry'.[50] She expressed her gratitude to MP George Rogers for taking in her young son: 'I am quite well – my family have been wonderful. Once again I thank you and your wife. Goodbye.'[51] And finally she wrote to Leon Simmons, referring less obliquely to the 'untold story' behind David's death and her own:

> Just a line to thank you for coming along, with Mr Mishcon this morning.
>
> I have given, Mr George Rogers authority, to take Clare Andria away for a holiday.
>
> I am now content and satisfied that my affairs will be dealt with satisfactorily.
>
> I also, ask you to make known the true story regarding Mrs Finlater [*sic*] and her plan to break up David & I – she should feel content, now her plan ended so tragically.

Would you please ask my mother to go to David's grave, and put flowers, Pink and White Carnations. (Ask her to do it for me.)

I would also, like to answer David's, brother's, (newspaper remarks).

I admire Derek, for defending, his brother. I would have been cross with him, if he had not. – But he said he would have to have more proof than he heard in court before he would believe my story. –

My reply, to Derek is, I am sorry. I can not, give him any more proof, than I have.

I did not defend myself. I say, a life for a life. What more proof can he want?

I have spoken the truth, and I want you to make the truth known for my family, & son's sake.

Well, Mr Simmons, the time is 9.30. I am quite well & not worrying about anything.

Thanks Once Again.

Ruth Ellis. [52]

A Home Office memorandum states:

> It is common practice for the Governor to visit the prisoner before he retires for the night to talk to him and give him an opportunity to say anything he may wish. Some like to take advantage of this opportunity, others do not, but no one is forced to say anything.[53]

Ruth had only one request to make of the Governor: she asked if all the letters she had received during her time in prison could be sent to Leon Simmons, who was dealing with her personal affairs. Dr Taylor recalled: 'I did not make any definite reply, but said that I would see what could be done.'[54] Ultimately Dr Taylor decided it was better 'to destroy them rather than to revive interest in the case by sending them out'.[55]

The crowd at the prison walls began thinning out at about half past eleven. A solitary figure remained under the lamp close to the gates of Holloway; Ruth's brother Granville recalled: 'I spoke to the matron in charge but Ruth sent back a message saying she did not want to see me or anyone, and that she was quite well but very tired. She said she wanted peace.'[56]

In Whitehall, DCI Davies left the Red Lion to return home, while

DI Gill and DC Claiden retraced their journey to Goodwood Court: 'We kept observation on his flat until late in the evening when, on telephoned instructions from Deputy Commander Rawlings we withdrew, having been unable to see Cussen, who has not yet been again interrogated.'[57] It was just before midnight when they were told to abandon the search.

Journalist Peter Grisewood later made his own enquiries about Desmond's movements that day. In his report, Grisewood wrote that he had spoken to both porters at Goodwood Court, one of whom told him that on 12 July at 9.15 a.m., Desmond emerged on the rear staircase with a suitcase in his hand. He seemed startled to be seen and mentioned that he was going to the country for a few days. After asking the porter to check the street for journalists – which was quite natural, under the circumstances – Desmond climbed into his car and drove away. The porter who worked the following shift at Goodwood Court recalled noticing the two detectives, who were clearly hoping to spot Desmond.

They were not the only ones hunting Desmond that evening; a reporter (thought to be Dougie Howell but never publicly named) approached Granville with the idea of finding Desmond and forcing him to admit his part in David's murder and Ruth's downfall. 'I started by going to Mr Mishcon,' Granville recalled, 'but he didn't want to see me. We then went to the Home Secretary's place but he didn't want to see us either. We then began our search throughout London looking for Cussen. But this resulted in little success.'[58] Several years later, Granville told a very different version of his activities that day. He claimed that he and the reporter had found Desmond in bed with a woman in someone else's flat, whereupon Ruth's former lover told both men to get lost. Muriel has a slightly modified account of this in her memoir, giving the date of the confrontation as 11 July, whereas Granville stated it happened on 12 July. Again the reporter was not named but was thought to be Dougie Howell, who said in a 1970s interview that on the last night of Ruth's life, Desmond *was* at home. All of which begs the question: why didn't the reporter and Granville contact the police with the news that Desmond had been found? Yet another version emerged of his whereabouts that evening in Robert Hancock's book *Ruth Ellis*; he claims that Desmond spent that night with friends in Kensington.

Victor Mishcon had no idea that Desmond could not be found, but doubted very much whether the statement he had extracted from Ruth earlier in the day could be corroborated before the morning:

> I don't know how the most efficient police officers could have done the job in the time. I had hoped that the very least the Home Secretary would have done would be to postpone the execution, so that proper inquiries could be made.[59]

His words were repeated several years later to the former Home Secretary, Lloyd George, who insisted:

> The police were, in fact, able to make considerable inquiries but anyway, it made no difference. If anything, if Mrs Ellis's final story was true it made her offence all the greater. Instead of a woman merely acting suddenly on impulse, here you had an actual plot to commit murder, deliberately thought out and conceived with some little care.[60]

His real motivation in not granting a stay of execution was expressed privately: 'If she isn't hanged tomorrow, she never will be.'[61]

There is a note on Ruth's file initialled 'F.N.' (presumably Sir Frank Newsam), dated 12 July 1955, which reveals the Home Office perspective:

> This uncorroborated statement by the prisoner does not add anything material to the information before the Secretary of State when he decided not to interfere. The discrepancy between the officer's report [Principal Officer Griffin's report] and Mr Mishcon's statement is interesting and illuminating.[62]

This last remark refers to the solicitor's failure to include in the statement Ruth's comment that she had asked Desmond for a gun, rather than one being foisted upon her. Mishcon, for his part, took a dim view of F.N.'s note: 'With great respect, he didn't allow much time for the light to illuminate.'[63]

In 1999, former Assistant Under Secretary at the Home Office, Philip Allen, reflected on Ruth's case:

You may say we came to the wrong conclusion. I don't know.
Perhaps we did . . . I gradually became a convinced abolitionist,
having dealt with a number of these cases. It didn't seem to me
to be right that an individual life should be taken. But we had to
operate on the basis of what the law was and the law said that the
punishment for murder is death by hanging.[64]

Mishcon stayed awake, waiting for the Home Office to call. Some
time after 2 a.m., the telephone rang: the new evidence changed
nothing. Ruth would be executed in seven hours. He replaced the
receiver and went to bed.

In the empty chamber next to Ruth's cell in Holloway, just a few
paces from where she slept, the sandbag turned slowly on its rope in
the darkness.

V

The Loss-ness of Everything

Holloway Gaol, 13 July 1955 and After

24

No one who knew Ruth remained unmoved by her hanging, whatever their relationship to her. Julian Neilson stood at the forefront of the crowds outside Holloway that morning, clutching a spray of white carnations; he had asked to see his half-sister before her execution but it was too late – visits to the condemned cell were not permitted at that stage. Ruth's parents were there too, waiting by the gate. In her flat in St Paul's Cray, Muriel walked into the sitting-room, switched on the wireless and broke down when the chimes of Big Ben were followed by the declaration that Ruth was dead. Granville heard the clock intoning the hour from a newspaper office in Fleet Street: 'I was watching the ticker-tape machine. I was actually waiting in anticipation, hoping that there would be a last minute reprieve. I watched it come over the ticker-tape and tears were rolling down my face.'[1]

Policewoman Frances Garrad remembered that morning as 'dreadful'.[2] It was another scorcher of a day, and she walked over to Hampstead Heath, only a few minutes from the Magdala: 'I went right out across the heath so that I wouldn't meet anyone. The heath-keepers knew not to speak to me about it, but they gave me a cup of tea.'[3] Ruth's ousted solicitor, John Bickford, also took himself off for a long walk, across Blackheath Common, where he too felt 'quite dreadful'.[4] In his imagination he heard the tinkling music of Ruth's powder compact playing endlessly. Peter Rawlinson, the junior defence council at Ruth's trial, recalled: 'I could think only of what she had said to me in that bleak room under the dock of No.1 Court at the Old Bailey.'[5]

'I want to join him,' she had said. 'I want to join him.'

Cherry Marshall, head of the modelling school where Ruth had taken a course only a month before the shooting in Hampstead, declared:

I'll never forget the morning of her death. No one could quite grasp that she was going to die and a deep gloom was felt everywhere . . . I thought I'd be unable to read the reports of her last hours but I felt compelled to. It seemed important to follow her story through to the very end, and never to forget it.[6]

In Warrington, four-year-old Georgina knew nothing of what had happened to her mother that day, and in Surrey, George Rogers and his wife tried to shield Ruth's son from the news; Andre was under the impression that his mother had gone to Italy, modelling swimsuits. Rogers recalled: 'We thought it best that it should be broken to him gently a while afterwards. But I think he knew.'[7]

What the Findlaters and Desmond Cussen did that morning is not known. No one ever asked them and they never said. But in the churchyard of the Holy Trinity in Penn, an anonymous benefactor placed three bowls of freshly cut roses on David Blakely's grave.

The man who pulled the lever that saw Ruth plunged to her death in a dark pit gave differing accounts of her last moments. The most detailed was one Albert Pierrepoint told, several months later and after his resignation as hangman, to a journalist from the *Empire News & Sunday Chronicle* in preparation for a series about his career. The section concerning Ruth's death originally read:

> She had put on a dab of lipstick, but that was all. Even so, I was rather moved to see it. Most men condemned to death take the trouble to shave and comb their hair carefully. But Ruth Ellis's lipstick was a poignant reminder that she was still a woman, though in the condemned cell she had worn spectacles nearly all the time, and let her hair stray loose down her back . . . I put my arm around her shoulder, and said, 'Come with me, luv, I'm not going to hurt you.' I didn't walk in front of her, saying 'Follow me', as I usually do with a man. I led her in, and she walked with me utterly calmly, nor did she flinch at the sight of the apparatus of execution. I lifted up her long, loosely-combed fair hair, but I did it so quickly that I'm not sure if she really felt what I was doing with her hair, for she had glimpsed the white cap in my other hand, over her head, and pouted again. 'Have I got to have that thing on?' I said, 'Yes, luv, I'm sorry,' but I doubt very much if she heard me finish the

sentence, for she was already gone before I'd done speaking. And that was how I intended it.[8]

The article was due to run in March 1956 but the government discovered what was planned and threatened both the newspaper and Albert with prosecution for breaching the Official Secrets Act. The piece was shelved but the editor was determined not to lose his front-page scoop, and replaced it with the headline: 'Ruth Ellis Home Office Gag. Pierrepoint Told: You May Not Reveal Her Last Words.'[9] Albert's censored recollections of that morning read instead:

> In her last moments I was as gentle as I could possibly be with Ruth Ellis. She was paying her price but it was a time for pity not for mistaken sympathy, and the performing of this sad task certainly did not upset me as people have tried to make out. Ruth Ellis died instantly, quicker even than the man she killed.[10]

The series was dropped after a few more instalments.

Almost certainly, either Albert or the journalist to whom he spoke exaggerated his meeting with Ruth on the scaffold. As a consequence, in his autobiography he was forced to address the rumour that he had been forcibly removed from the list of executioners 'because I was about to reveal the last words of Ruth Ellis. She never spoke.'[11] In a 1961 interview for the BBC, he repeated that Ruth had come to him 'in the ordinary way' and stood on the chalk mark on the trapdoors: 'She never spoke to me. I can see her now. Just flicked her eyes and puckered her lips as though she was trying to smile. She was a brave woman.'[12] Afterwards, he recited the same thing whenever he was asked about her death: 'I don't really like talking about Ruth . . . She was a great woman. I have seen some brave men die, but nobody braver than her.'[13] He told Muriel the same during their brief correspondence, adding that Ruth had lifted the corners of her mouth slightly, as if to smile. He later said with even greater authority that Ruth was 'the bravest woman I ever hanged'.[14]

*

Whatever the truth of his encounter with the living Ruth, after she had been declared dead, Albert returned to the pit beneath the gallows to prepare her body for burial. It was a process with which he was long familiar and held no surprises or revulsion for him. While Ruth's body twisted slightly on the rope, her face covered by the white hood, Albert removed the soft leather straps from her wrists and ankles, then carefully set aside all the articles of her clothing. He passed a rope beneath her armpits and, in the chamber above, after attending to the equipment of the gallows, Royston hauled her body upwards. Albert stood squarely on the scaffold, Ruth drooping in his arms, and took off the noose and white hood, then placed her head in his hands, moving it gently from side to side in order to assure himself that her neck had broken as it should, cleanly. It was heavily bruised from the wrench of the rope. He returned to the pit and waited while Royston slowly lowered Ruth's unclothed body down to him, then placed her reverently on a mortuary stretcher.

Until that year, it had been part of Albert's duties to measure how far the neck of the condemned prisoner had stretched after hanging – usually one to two inches – and to record it in the Execution Register. A change in the rules meant that it was no longer necessary, although Albert could see quite clearly the elongation of Ruth's neck caused by the long fall he had calculated for her. His duties done, all that remained was for him to dismantle the trappings of his trade in the chamber above. Then together with Royston, he collected his belongings from the room in which they had spent the previous night and headed through the corridors to leave Holloway.

Outside the prison, at precisely 9.18 a.m., the crowd surged forward as the notice of execution was posted on the gates. A man held up his small daughter to read the declaration: 'We, the undersigned, hereby declare that Judgment of Death was this day executed on Ruth Ellis in Her Majesty's Prison of Holloway in our presence.'[15] People continued to mill about the gates of Holloway for some time. Gladys Langford recorded in her diary: 'I feel sure that if executions were in public there would be as great crowds today as ever there were. People don't change.'[16] Frederic Raphael made a note of the day's main news story in his diary:

> I daresay she was a vulgar little tart . . . but to sentence her to die
> at such and such a time, in *that* way, is to make her into a dying
> goddess. London shuddered in the heat, and so it should.
> Executions are unnatural crimes.[17]

The architect of the unnatural crime was astonished by the size and fury of the crowd that greeted him on his exit: 'When I left Holloway after the execution of Ruth Ellis, the prison was almost besieged by a storming mob,' Albert recalled in his autobiography. 'I needed police protection to get me through. I knew that I would have walked out of Strangeways [where Sarah Lloyd was due to hang until her reprieve] a week earlier into an empty street.'[18] The police escort included Chief Inspector Robert Fabian, then well known to the public through the television series *Fabian of the Yard*. The two men were photographed with unfortunate smirks on their faces at Euston Station, where a pack of pressmen waited. 'I shielded my face from the cameras as I ran for my train,' Albert remembered:

> One young reporter jogged alongside me asking, 'How did it feel to hang a woman, Mr Pierrepoint?' I did not answer. But I could have asked, 'Why weren't you waiting to ask me that question last year, sonny? Wasn't Mrs Christofi a woman, too?'[19]

*

Unusually, pathologist Dr Cedric Keith Simpson's post-mortem report on Ruth was made public. In it he described her as a 28-year-old woman of 'spare' build and 'a healthy subject at the time of death'. He pronounced cause of death as 'injuries to the central nervous system consequent upon judicial hanging' and observed 'little destruction of soft tissues' to the 'soft and bony structures of the neck'.[20] Death had been instantaneous, due to the 'fracture dislocation of the second and third vertebrae'.[21] He noted the contents of her stomach: 'small food residue, and odour of brandy' and under 'Character of the Prisoner's Neck' wrote: 'Thin.'[22]

Ruth's final effects were removed from the condemned cell, which was cleared, cleaned and closed up. A wardress made the last entry in Ruth's hospital case notes: 'Executed. 9 a.m. Pierrepoint. 8'4' – 8'6'. Dist: 2 – 3rd cervical vertebrae. Complete severing of spinal cord. P.M. Mr Keith Simpson – organs shew no sign of disease.'[23]

In her office, the Governor drafted a memo after taking a call from the Home Office that confirmed the apparent reprieve had indeed been a hoax:

In view of the unsatisfactory source of the message, and after consultation with the Under-Sheriff, Mr Gedge, it was decided to carry on with the execution. This was done, and the execution took place at 9.1 a.m. instead of 9 a.m. as arranged.[24]

The inquest into Ruth's death was conducted in the Governor's office by Her Majesty's Coroner for the City of London, James Milner-Helme. Despite detectives Claiden and Davies arriving to identify the body, the coroner decided to send for Ruth's brother Granville, still in Fleet Street. When he presented himself at Holloway, a warder led him into the prison grounds to a spot under an arch where Ruth's body had been laid out on boards and trestles, away from the sun's glare. Prison officials had placed a cross near her head and two candles either side of where she lay. A scarf was draped about her neck to disguise the livid weals of Albert's rope, and her face was pale apart from lipstick and powder. Although Granville appreciated the effort to make his sister look as if she had died a natural death, 'I could see it wasn't so,' he said afterwards.[25]

He turned to the Governor: 'Doesn't she look beautiful?'[26]

Someone touched his shoulder and told him he was a brave man, then the Governor led them all into her office for the inquest, where the coroner persistently referred to Ruth as 'the murderess'.[27] Eventually Granville exploded: 'Can't you think of something bloody well else to say, other than murderess?'[28] Dr Taylor took him out for a glass of water and sat with him until he was calm again.

The inquest did not last long, but the effect upon Granville caused MP Douglas Glover to write to the Home Office on 27 July:

> I supported capital punishment but the next of kin having to identify the body is barbaric. It is surely bad enough for any family to know that one of their members is being hanged, but after the law has taken its course to demand then that the next of kin shall come and see the body seems to be quite dreadful.[29]

He questioned the logic of the coroner ordering a full post-mortem simply to establish that Ruth's hanging had been fatal. The Home Office forwarded his complaint to Milner-Helme, who responded that it was normal practice.

As the day wore on, the temperature climbed quickly into the 80s, with freak storms across the country. Ruth was buried that afternoon in the small cemetery at Holloway, under brilliant blue skies. A Home Office memorandum instructed: 'Burial of the body takes place in the prison graveyard during the dinner hour. The chaplain reads the burial service . . . In some prisons bodies are already buried three deep.'[30] Ruth was placed in a standard prison-issue coffin and lowered into the ground. She shared her grave with four other executed women: Finchley 'baby farmers' Annie Walters and Amelia Sach, Edith Thompson and Styllou Christofi.

*

The day after Ruth's death, the weather broke with such violence that it temporarily ousted her execution and the debate about capital punishment from the front pages. At Ascot, where two days earlier Sir Frank Newsam had been recalled to the Home Office to discuss Ruth's case, torrential rain began drenching the crowds just before 4 p.m. Thunder cracked and three wicked flashes of lightning hurled more than a hundred racegoers into the air. Over forty people were taken to hospital suffering burns, shock and temporary loss of consciousness; two people died on the course, one of whom was a pregnant woman. Among the crowd was Cherry Marshall, who had accompanied a group of models there to be filmed wearing the season's fashions. 'We were all very depressed and we talked a lot about capital punishment as we drove down to the racecourse,' she recalled:

> As they performed for the camera . . . the models were smiling
> . . . but I knew how wretched they were feeling. Suddenly a
> tremendous crack of thunder shattered the crowds and we heard
> cries and screaming . . . I looked up at the sky and froze inside,
> half expecting to see the face of Ruth Ellis above me. Was this
> some kind of retribution, I wondered?[31]

Hundreds of miles away, on the promenade in Blackpool, a billboard outside Louis Tussaud's waxworks exhibition advertised: 'Ruth Ellis Executed, Holloway Gaol, On View Here'. Only 40 minutes after her death, artists in London had begun creating Ruth's effigy for display in the Chamber of Horrors. Dressed in a black evening gown with a gossamer stole, 'Ruth' was placed on stage with a backdrop of floral curtains, as if in an amateur theatrical. It was a terrible likeness and questions were immediately asked about whether the exhibit was in good taste or not. The creators were unrepentant: 'We don't adjudicate on morals . . . it was made from photographs. Many of our experts worked on the job.'[32] It caused outrage in the press, with the *Daily Express* reporting: 'Row Over Ruth Ellis Effigy . . . Ban This Horror', while the *News Chronicle* referred to it as 'the wrong kind of thrill'.[33] The public certainly did not seem to mind; the *Daily Express* again reported on 14 July: 'In four hours last night, more than 3,000 people queued to see the waxworks – twice as many as in a normal day.'[34] The following day there were yet more visitors, 7,000 in all, each paying 1/6. The managing director was delighted: 'This is a record number of visitors to the Chamber of Horrors on a Friday.'[35] Julian Neilson travelled to the resort to plead with the organisers to remove the exhibit, but to no avail: the effigy continued to attract holidaymakers in droves throughout the summer.

Ruth's death was a lead news story for some time. The *Spectator* commented:

It is no longer a matter of surprise that Englishmen deplore bull-fighting but delight in hanging. Hanging has become the national sport . . . Mr Lloyd George, the Home Secretary, has now been responsible for the hanging of two women in the past eight months. This compares with the hanging of twelve women in the previous fifty-four years. Is this increase of something like 1250 per cent the result of an outbreak of feminine terrorism? Of course not. It is merely the consequence of a weak Home Secretary . . . Men who go on hanging women, who should not be hanged, can hardly expect to be held in universal esteem.[36]

Lloyd George wanted to sue after reading the article but was dissuaded by his friend Viscount Kilmuir: 'As a lawyer, an ex-Home Secretary and an old friend I advise you to let it die in its own smell.'[37]

The world's press reacted to Ruth's execution with disgust. In Australia, the *Melbourne Argus* thundered: 'Hanging shames Britain in the eyes of the civilised world', while in France one columnist wrote contemptuously: 'Passion in England, except for cricket and betting, is always regarded as a shameful disease.'[38] The *Evening News* picked up on their ill feeling: 'All the French newspapers today reported the scenes outside Holloway prison and the details of the execution of Ruth Ellis.

Combat said she had been hanged in spite of public opinion. "The strictness of British justice in this case appalled the country."[39] The Ambassador to Sweden, Robert Hankey, warned Harold Macmillan on 19 July: 'The campaign in the press has been exceptionally violent – indeed, I can think of no issue since I arrived in March 1954 which has given rise to comparable criticism of our policy or institutions.'[40]

On 20 July, the *Daily Mirror* insisted: 'The Noose Must Go', declaring that almost 26,000 of its 39,666 readers opposed capital punishment. A Gallup poll conducted that summer was less conclusive: 50 per cent were in favour of the death penalty, 37 per cent against and 13 per cent couldn't make up their minds. A housewife taking part in the poll ventured:

> I think it was dreadful to hang Ruth Ellis. I was ill all the time the trial was on. I could not believe they could hang her, especially a woman. She loved him and did not mean to kill him, it was done on the spur of the moment. I would stop this horrible death penalty.[41]

A 21-year-old odd-job man disagreed: 'I think Ruth Ellis deserved to swing. Women can be as vicious as men. More so, in some cases.'[42]

One of the strongest pieces of journalism was published in the *Lancet* medical journal on 23 July:

> The laws against witchcraft were repealed in this country in 1736; but they had been recognised, long before that, as an ugly piece of humanity, disgracing the statute book. To many of our countrymen today, and to the whole peoples of some European countries, the death penalty seems as grotesque as did the witchcraft laws to 18th century Englishmen ... The children ... have been dealt a most shattering psychological blow ... Let us hope that those Members of Parliament who have launched a new attempt to get the law changed will succeed in freeing us from this recurrent demoralisation.[43]

The *Observer* brought matters closer to home, asking:

> Consider the task of explaining to the late Ruth Ellis's ten-year-old son what has happened. This boy, who is fatherless, has had something

done to him that is so brutal it is difficult to imagine. We should realise that it is we who have done it.[44]

Andre was then on holiday with George Rogers and his wife but eventually he was told what had been done to his mother. He returned to live with his grandparents, who received scores of letters about Ruth's execution on a daily basis. Ruth's mother reflected: 'My Dear Daughter was not half as bad as she seemed. She had a good and loving nature and normally would not hurt anyone ... I am sure when she committed this crime she must have been half demented.'[45]

In December 1955, a Mass Observation Survey questioned how people would react to a five-year trial suspension of the death penalty and found that 34 per cent approved, with women in particular 'influenced towards disapproval of capital punishment by the emotional influence of the case of Ruth Ellis'.[46] Together with publisher Victor Gollancz, writer and political activist Arthur Koestler established a national campaign for abolition and worked on a book about the injustice of the system, having been driven into 'a frenzy' by Ruth's hanging.[47] Sydney Silverman's Death Penalty (Abolition) Bill was introduced in the House of Commons in November 1955; three months later the Commons debate about the Bill was opened by the Home Secretary, who insisted there had been no miscarriages of justice in the past. MP George Rogers protested in anger:

> Mark these words, Mr Speaker: I will make the Home Secretary eat those words before I am much older ... Ruth Ellis had a son. I took that boy into my house to try and save him from the horror of the day of execution. Can you imagine the agony experienced by my wife and children when they had to pretend to that fatherless boy that everything was normal when at the same time his mother was being taken from the condemned cell to be hanged?[48]

That year saw the cinema release of a powerful adaptation of Joan Henry's 1954 novel *Yield to the Night*, the story of a woman sentenced to death for shooting her lover's other, wealthier mistress. Diana Dors played the lead, proving definitively that she was a fine actress and not simply a pin-up girl. In her memoir she recalled:

At the time, everyone thought the film moguls were cashing in on the unfortunate story of the tragic murderess Ruth Ellis, the last woman to be hanged in England, but strangely enough the story had been written two years before, by authoress Joan Henry . . . whatever happens to me for the rest of my career, at least I can always point with pride at *Yield to the Night* and say, 'I did that.'[49]

The film was produced by Kenneth Harper, who had given Vicki Martin her big break in *It Started in Paradise*. A critical success but a box-office flop, *Yield to the Night*'s release in summer 1956 coincided with the Abolition Bill being passed by Parliament. A special screening of the film was held at the National Film Theatre for peers of the realm on the day that the House of Lords were due to debate the Bill, but only six of them troubled to attend. The Bill was subsequently defeated.

Nonetheless, in its first few months the campaign for abolition drew 33,000 members and was supported by the *Spectator*, the *Picture Post* and the *Observer*. In March 1957 the Homicide Act was introduced, leading to a number of significant changes in the legal system and, most crucially, allowing the defence of diminished responsibility. Just over half of the 65 people condemned to death after the introduction of the Homicide Act were reprieved.

Ten years after Ruth's execution, on 8 November 1965, Sydney Silverman's Murder (Abolition of the Death Penalty) Act was passed, with a vote on permanent abolition due within the next five years. The first major case to come before the courts in that time was the Moors Murders, which led to a fierce argument regarding the reinstatement of the death penalty; a great many people were appalled that Ian Brady and Myra Hindley should escape the rope following the sexual torture and murder of children. But the suspension remained and there were no more executions.

In December 1969 capital punishment was permanently abolished in Britain.

On 23 September 1955, the *Warrington Examiner* ran a story on George Ellis, 'the former husband of Mrs Ruth Ellis who was executed earlier this year for shooting her lover'.[1] He had resigned from his dental work and was granted three months' leave with full pay. The reasons were twofold: he was unable to curb his drinking and his psoriasis was worsening, which led to complaints from patients. His home life was equally unhappy: the Lawtons were desperate to adopt Georgina, but he would not allow it. The rows between George and Peter Lawton escalated and they came to blows. George began spending long hours away from home, drinking himself into a stupor.

On 18 June 1958, he was arrested for being 'drunk and incapable' on the street where he lived.[2] From then until the end of July, George lived in various hotels, funded by a £650 settlement he received in a slander case on 1 July. He was in severe difficulties: aside from his uncontrollable drinking, the British Motor Company Limited were suing him for arrears on a hire purchase agreement. The case was adjourned until 25 July, when he was due to appear in court in London. Before then, on 9 July, the *Liverpool Echo* reported:

> Dentist Fined – Drunk Outside House: After being told he was being taken into custody for drunkenness, a dentist was alleged at Stockton Heath yesterday, to have replied, 'You do and I will have the Lord Chief Justice on you – he is a friend of mine.' The man, George Johnson Ellis . . . pleaded guilty to being drunk on June 18 and to conduct likely to cause a breach of the peace.[3]

The next day, George flew out to Jersey and booked into Le Chalet Hotel on the cliffs at Corbiere. A week later he flew back to England, where, according to Muriel's interview with Little Club manager Peter

Nolan, he visited Ruth's former workplace, sober and in a smart suit. Nolan claimed that George wanted to talk about Ruth and gave him £5 to put flowers on her grave, which was impossible, since Ruth was buried in the confines of Holloway Gaol. If George had returned to London in order to attend his court hearing, then he evidently changed his mind, for on 22 July he caught a flight back to Jersey and booked into Le Chalet again.

The hotel manager, John Scherer, told George he could only have the room he wanted until 2 August because it had been booked for other guests. George drank heavily during his stay and the date for his court hearing in London passed without him making any attempt to let the authorities know his whereabouts. On Friday, 1 August, he called Scherer to his room during the day, explaining that he had no money and no cigarettes. Scherer arranged for a packet of cigarettes to be sent to his room but reminded George that he still had not paid anything towards his bill. George assured him there was no need to worry, but the hotel manager telephoned his bank and was warned not to give credit. He then called George's solicitors, who confirmed that their client had no funds at his disposal. Armed with this information, when George asked if he might settle his bill by cashing a cheque, Scherer refused but noticed that he seemed genuinely upset at the thought of leaving the hotel the next day; he told Scherer he felt 'very much at home' there, adding that for the first time in years he felt as if he was being treated 'as a human being'.[4] Later that day, still drinking heavily, George spent a lot of time talking with Mrs Scherer, who told him to 'go back and start afresh'.[5]

Shortly after midnight, George rang for a tray of tea and biscuits to be brought to his room. On Mrs Scherer's instructions the night waiter took them to him; George was then in bed and everything seemed quite normal. But there was no answer the following morning when a chambermaid knocked on the door with his usual cup of tea. She tried the door, but it was locked and she called the receptionist, who went outside with a chair to look through the window. He peered in and saw a shape on the floor. Climbing into the room he found George lying in his pyjamas on an eiderdown next to the bed. The cord of his dressing-gown had been wound around his neck and tied with a knot. Beside his body was a coat hanger. There were no signs of disturbance in the room, or of a struggle having taken place. George's watch had stopped at 7.50 a.m., his bed had been slept in, and it appeared that he had either awoken or lain awake before deciding in the early hours of the morning to kill himself.

The *Jersey Evening Post* reported his death that same day but did not make the connection with Ruth. By the time of the inquest, which was held on 6 August at the General Hospital on Jersey, the local and international press had uncovered the fact that George was the ex-husband of Ruth Ellis. Reporters flocked to the inquest, where James Edward Ellis gave evidence of his brother's 17-year struggle with alcoholism. He explained that he 'only occasionally' saw George, who 'kept everything from me'.[6] Three doctors answered questions about whether self-strangulation was possible; they confirmed that indeed it was and that cause of death was asphyxia due to strangulation.

*

Although Georgina was only four in 1955, she had not forgotten her mother:

> I always thought I'd see her one day. But some other part of me thought she had been killed in a car crash, and that is why they said nothing to me. I used to dream about her. I kept having one dream in particular. I was walking along a road holding my mother's hand. There was a man on a roof shooting at her, killing her.[7]

Georgina was seven when her father committed suicide; the Lawtons told her he had died in a motor accident. 'I did not feel sad at all,' Georgina recalled. 'My first thought was one of relief, knowing that I would face no more of his drunken nights.'[8] She attended his funeral service and years later reflected: 'Perhaps he might have been a good man, had it not been for his drink problem.'[9]

Georgina discovered the truth about her mother soon after her father's death. On a rainy day at home she was rummaging through an old trunk when she found a stack of newspapers about Ruth's execution. Immediately, a memory of the flat above the Little Club came to her. She recalled:

> I didn't cry but I felt an overwhelming sadness for her and was curious to know what her lover had done to make her shoot him . . . I only had vague memories of my mother, from the short time we were together up

until I was two and a half . . . but I always remember her breezing in and being very generous and loving. I can't recall specific incidents, but she always had a bright, warm smile . . . up until I found the newspapers, I had always believed she was going to come back and get me.[10]

Georgina said nothing to the Lawtons about the discovery in the trunk. They succeeded in adopting her and she was happy with them. It was some time before she became curious enough about her mother to seek out further information, but in her early teens she was sent to boarding school: 'I went to the library and read all the books I could about her life, and about how her lover had beaten and rejected her.'[11] She confided in her best friend that she was the daughter of the last woman to be hanged, and within days the school was buzzing with the news. Overnight, it seemed as if everyone changed towards her; she was a curiosity but somehow 'not nice' to know, and came to feel that 'being a murderess's daughter was no good at all'.[12]

After a furious row with her adoptive parents in her teens, Georgina blurted out that she knew about her real mother. Phyllis Lawton then broke her own silence to speak about Ruth, but Georgina 'didn't like the things she said, or the way she said it . . . I knew she was also good, or at least I didn't want or need to hear any of these bad things.'[13] Despite her expensive education, Georgina craved the same life as her mother: 'I wanted London, glamour and modelling. I wanted fast cars, film stars, footballers, racing car drivers . . . I left home to get those things, and I got them.'[14] In 1975 the *News of the World* approached her about Ruth and Georgina decided to 'come clean'. She was photographed by Terry O'Neill, styled in order to resemble her mother more closely. The article, entitled 'My Agony, by the Daughter of Ruth Ellis', focused largely on her affairs with George Best and Richard Harris. Georgina recalled: 'I lost my own identity overnight and became known to the world as "Ruth Ellis's daughter". Some people accused me of cashing in on my mother's memory, which hurt a lot.'[15] She did suggest that she should take the lead role in a film about her mother's life, which was then being mooted, with Angie Bowie tipped to play Ruth, but the film was never made.

Following disclosure in the press, Georgina found her three half-brothers. She and Andre met after a 20-year gap; in her 1996 memoir, Georgina is sympathetic towards him, but less so in an interview she gave to Polly Toynbee for her book about adopted children:

He was a severe depressive who had become addicted to his anti-depressants. [Georgina] met him just once. 'He was a tramp,' she says with distaste. 'I had nothing whatever in common with him.' They sat and talked a little but said nothing of importance to one another.[16]

She also met her half-brothers from her father's first marriage: 'Through the efforts of a journalist friend of theirs, they traced me and we met up . . . We have kept in touch ever since. Both have secured their own niches, Richard in property, and John as a lawyer.'[17]

In 1997 Georgina gave a lengthy interview to *The Independent* to promote a film she had made for the BBC about women who fall for notorious men. She discussed her own relationship history, including her brief liaison with Great Train Robber Charlie Wilson when she was thirty-seven and he was sixty, and two marriages. She had six children, and a variety of careers behind her. She spoke of her desire not to be 'stuck with a boring man – I want someone with a little zest' and of her mother she said: 'I know she loved David Blakely more than she loved me. I do accept that – I've had plenty of time to get used to it.'[18] Later that year, while working as a corporate entertainer, she met the man who would become her third and final husband: Yorkshire sportsman Mike Blackburn. They married at Beverley Register Office in September 1997, with the local press carrying the story on their front pages. Georgina began a new business – hat-making – into which she poured her natural flair for fashion, but the following year she was diagnosed with bladder cancer. An operation left her with numerous complications and infections that kept her largely confined to hospital. A journalist described her:

She was obviously in pain and could barely walk. Yet she was still taking pride in her appearance. A good-looking woman with high cheekbones and forget-me-not blue eyes, she was meticulously made-up with her nails painted fiery red.[19]

Georgina died at Dove House Hospice in Hull on 30 November 2001; she was 50 years old. Her funeral in Cheshire was a vast affair and her widower, Mike Blackburn, still talks of her with love and affection:

She was a wonderful person with so much to live for, full of life and vitality, but whose life was always tinged with sadness and controversy. I knew her as a very dear sound person whom I loved very dearly and would always go out of her way to help anyone. She will be irreplaceable to me.[20]

In one of her last interviews, Georgina admitted that – after a lifetime of insisting her character, her triumphs and her mistakes had nothing to do with the past – she had spent years trying to emulate her mother:

There are amazing parallels between our two lives, to the point where I wondered whether I have lived out vicariously my mother's remaining years. We both craved the bright lights and were determined not to be mediocre . . . I don't feel hatred against the Government of the day who allowed my mum to hang, or to the man who pulled the lever, Albert Pierrepoint. Why put your energy into something so negative?[21]

Of Georgina's children – Ruth's grandchildren – her son Stephen David T. Beard is the most well-known: he took part in MTV's 2007 reality show *Living on the Edge*, and played Archie Carpenter in the Channel 4 soap opera *Hollyoaks*. In 2007, while appearing in *One Flew Over the Cuckoo's Nest* at the Edinburgh Fringe Festival, Stephen was invited to watch *Follow Me*, a play telling the story of Ruth's execution. 'When I went there I had no idea what to expect,' he admitted afterwards:

It was really shocking, not heartbreaking but a bit strange. I was emotionally attached to an actor I had never seen before in my life. I didn't know my grandmother but I didn't want her to be hurt, to be hung [*sic*]. It was like a first meeting, if you like, it was really, really strange.[22]

He compared the experience to a dream: 'It was as if I had been allowed to see my grandmother for an hour and fifteen minutes again, just before the hanging.'[23]

*

After his mother's death when he was ten years old, Andre was enrolled as a boarder at St Michael's College in Hitchin. The Assumptionist priests who taught there wore long black habits and leather belts around their waists that were often used to discipline the pupils, who in turn wore a maroon uniform with the school badge on cap and blazer, displaying the motto: *Quis Ut Deus – Who is alike unto God.* Andre's time at the school occurred during the 'Roger Killeen Years', described on the College website as 'a somewhat turbulent period in the College's sixty-five-year history'.[24] Killeen was the son of a former Royal Ulster Constabulary officer and the favourite of his devout Catholic mother. He arrived at the College in the mid-1940s as a temporary staff member, was appointed senior history teacher in 1950 and the following year became headmaster. According to the website: 'Killeen strove and demanded success for the College. He was not prepared to accept failure.'[25]

The regime was particularly strict. Andre's fellow pupil Bob Ashurst recalls:

> The building itself was stark and unfriendly. Killeen was an extremely unpleasant man. I remember him beating a fifth form boy around the face, berating him in front of the entire school at assembly, then giving him the cane. The offence? Smoking at the back of the bus on the way home from school . . . The very sight of Killeen aroused feelings of tension and fear.[26]

Another pupil, Nic Szeremeta, confirms: 'Killeen conducted a reign of terror. His moods and behaviour were erratic and unpredictable. The culture of violence he created spread to the other monks and pupils. Killeen would conduct public floggings and beatings up at the morning school assemblies.'[27] Not all the pupils felt quite so strongly, and corporal punishment was then the norm, with children elsewhere regularly caned for getting low marks. Jim Hoare, another contemporary of Andre's, cautions: 'I would not wish to exaggerate about St Michael's under Father Roger – he was a bit like a dragon from the clouds, appearing and disappearing. In general, the atmosphere as far as I was concerned was not bad.'[28] Bob Ashurst agrees that Killeen succeeded in raising 'the educational standards of the school to a level that brought it full recognition and status by the educational authorities'.[29]

Killeen enrolled Ruth's son at St Michael's College under the name Andrew Hornby (his grandfather's original surname) and if he and the other priests knew about his background, as they surely must have done, then they kept it to themselves. From the beginning, Andre was regarded as a strange, fragile boy with pale, pinched features under a shock of dark hair. His only real friend was Brian Jacobs, who remembers him as:

> an absolute bundle of nerves. He had two nicknames. 'Double-oh' because of his surname – Hornby, the trains. That was what we usually called him. But because of his peculiarity and his love of stamp-collecting, which he had an absolute passion for, he was also sometimes referred to, though never to his face, as 'the philatelist with the perforated brain'.[30]

It was the boys' mutual interest in stamp-collecting that led to their friendship. 'He taught me a lot about that,' Brian recalls:

> He was hopelessly shortsighted and when we used to look at stamps together he would lift up his glasses and bring his nose right down to the page. He had a very curious laugh, too. He would throw his head right back and give this laugh without moving his face at all. He was such a strange boy – we all thought he was so very odd, but there was certainly no harm in him. He kept himself very much to himself, and I can still see him now, in the trousers that never fitted him and always looking a bit of a mess, walking along the wall during break time, keeping right up close to it, so that he wouldn't make eye contact with anyone. He had a stutter, which I think came purely through his nerves. We walked together around the school field very often but he never said anything about himself as such. How did he get on with Killeen? He just seemed to shrug everything off really. He was no good at sports because he had no co-ordination. None of us were aware of his background. I was his best friend, but even to me he never said anything about his home life or circumstances and I didn't ask.'[31]

After ten years as headmaster, in 1959 Father Killeen left St Michael's College and was replaced by Father Bernard Rickett. In the wake of Killeen's departure from St Michael's, the school was transformed. 'It was like a breath of fresh air through the entire place,' Nic Szeremeta recalls.[32] Before leaving, Killeen drew Bertha Neilson's attention to her grandson's persistent truancy. Despite winning a smattering of awards, including the Junior School History Prize in 1959–60, Andre was unable to settle and frequently did not turn up for classes. He was referred to John Stroud, the Boys' Welfare Officer at County Hall in Hertford, but even his experience with troubled youngsters couldn't convince Andre to return. He was expelled from St Michael's, and his name doesn't appear in the GCE results lists for 1961. Living with his grandparents in Hemel Hempstead, Andre spent much of his time in his bedroom, writing notes by candlelight before sticking them onto the wall. Repeating the habits of his childhood, he often travelled alone and without purpose on buses and trains for hours on end. The doctor prescribed him anti-depressants, which according to his aunt he swallowed like sweets, keeping them in his briefcase and popping one in his mouth as he walked along.

In 1971, when he was in his late 20s, Andre was approached by the Home Office regarding plans to disinter his mother's remains from the small cemetery in Holloway. The entire prison complex had been marked for redevelopment. The Home Office contacted Scotland Yard initially:

> Of the five executed prisoners buried at Holloway, only in the case of Ruth Ellis . . . does there seem to be any possibility that a relative may be both interested and traceable. The purpose of this letter is therefore to seek your help in tracing her relatives.[33]

If none could be found, then Ruth's remains were to be cremated and her ashes interred in a public cemetery.

The press were quick to find out about the plans and were keen to learn which relatives of Ruth's were still alive. Peter Nolan, former manager of Dorothy's Club (previously the Little Club), called the Home Office, introducing himself as 'the one who had taken Ruth's job at the club' and explained that he wanted Ruth to have a 'smart funeral' and a headstone, adding that 'clubland' would provide the necessary funds.[34] He was told that the wishes of relatives would come first, but there were already concerns at the Home Office; a note in the file reads:

> Miss Mason [the Home Office official who first contacted

Scotland Yard about the exhumation] said that Ruth Ellis's son was a schizophrenic and that he had telephoned the Yard from time to time but not with regard to the recent publicity.[35]

A civil servant named Wilson was given the task of locating relatives. He spoke to Ruth's brother Granville, who told him that he did not want to cause trouble but it was his wish that Ruth should be cremated and her ashes given to him so that he might keep them on the mantelpiece. Muriel recalls being visited by Dr Charity Taylor and Principal Officer Griffin; afterwards, she contacted the Home Office herself to give them Andre's details. An internal report at the Home Office notes:

> She said that she had been in touch with her nephew and that he wants to have a proper funeral with a Catholic ceremony. He said that money was no problem and that he had been to the Home Office and everything was arranged. Mrs Jakubait said that her nephew was something of a hippie and that he was known by various names, sometimes Nielson, sometimes Hornby and recently as Mr S.M. Turner. She could not understand where he was getting the money from, as he was usually hard up. She wondered whether Ruth's associates had been in touch with him. Mr Wilson also telephoned Miss Mason at New Scotland Yard. She confirmed that the Yard had information about the son. He had telephoned a few months ago saying he had new evidence concerning the murder of which his mother was convicted.[36]

Wilson did not approach Ruth's mother and was unable to track down Georgina. He spoke to Muriel, who originally hoped to bury Ruth's ashes 'under a rose tree in the grounds of Woking Crematorium'.[37] In his subsequent report, Wilson recorded that Muriel withdrew her request after learning that it 'conflicted with other members of her family' and asked only that her sister's remains should be dealt with 'as decently and quietly as possible'.[38] She had had no contact with Granville for several years. Wilson then turned to Andre, confirming that he was already known to Scotland Yard, and was said to be,

a rather unstable young man who had, in the past, received

treatment for schizophrenia and for drug taking. Andria used several names and several addresses. Until about six months ago, he lived with his grandmother (Mrs Hornby) but had found other accommodation when she entered hospital.[39]

Wilson was doubtful of the 'wisdom of making a direct approach' to Andre but contacted him by telephone and they met at least once. Andre asked whether his mother might be reburied in the same cemetery as David Blakely and told Wilson he had 'affectionate memories of "David"' and 'would like to be able to visit both graves'.[40] In his report, Wilson described Andre as:

a nervous, pale-faced, slightly shabby young man of 26 who looks as though he could do with a good meal. His speech suggests that he is reasonably well educated and for most of the time he expresses himself clearly. He has, or claims to have, a good memory of the events of 1955 and has clearly relived them many times over since then. He believes passionately that his mother should not have been hanged and the execution has clearly shaped the course of his life. He has some respect and affection for his aunt who he would like to associate with his proposed funeral arrangements; but he has neither for his uncle [Granville].[41]

Wilson concluded that Ruth's remains should be passed to her son: 'His personality and situation in life are such that he may need some assistance with the actual arrangements but with a little unofficial encouragement they should be within his compass.'[42] The costs of the funeral were to be met by the Home Office.

The disinterment began on the afternoon of 31 March 1971. The plot where Ruth and her fellow prisoners lay in Holloway's tiny walled cemetery was screened off and partially uncovered by works staff. The plot was then left, screened and guarded, until 10.15 p.m. that night, when employees of the London Necropolis Company Ltd carefully excavated the grave by lamplight. Ruth's remains were transferred from the coffin in which she had lain in Holloway into another for collection by the funeral directors. In the early hours of the morning, while it was still dark, Andre arrived in Amersham, a picturesque market town six miles north-east of the Holy Trinity church in Penn, whose vicar had refused to grant permission for Ruth to be buried near David. A few reporters watched from a distance as Andre stood by the open grave with only the vicar for company as his mother's coffin was laid to rest. The *Daily Sketch* observed:

> There was no marker for the plot. No stone. No card with the flowers. No service. Just Martin [Andre] Neilson muffled in a heavy black overcoat, standing silently by the graveside. As the single bell of St Mary's Church tolled two strokes for the half-hour, he turned and walked away, leaving the foreman of the undertaking firm to place the flowers on the grave.[43]

Andre left two wreaths of red and white carnations and, six months after the funeral, arranged for the grave to be marked by a plain white headstone inscribed *Ruth Hornby 1926–1955*.

He and his half-sister Georgina tried to establish a relationship but without real success. At their first meeting she was disturbed to find:

> a destroyed man, unable to fulfil a useful role in society. He was dishevelled and unkempt but not dirty, his appearance born more of careless indifference than desperation and degradation. He was living in a poky flat in the rundown area of London that encircles Euston Station.[44]

She became alarmed when he mistook her for Ruth:

> He wanted to know where I had been, but the question was always phrased in the short term, as though Ruth had just popped out to the shops a little while earlier. Equally suddenly he would revert to relating to me as his sister. I never felt menaced by him though in any way. He had a gentleness about him that reassured me.[45]

Andre's behaviour was harmlessly erratic; he wore the sweater Georgina gave him almost every day and when she told him she liked Estee Lauder's 'Ashes of Roses' lipstick, he had a box of them sent to her from Harrods. When she last saw him, he was 'unusually lucid . . . not confusing characters or chronology, and he began to talk about Ruth [and] said to me: "You know, Georgie, you inherited all her strengths and I all her weaknesses."'[46]

In 1981, Andre drew up his will, requesting that he should be buried with his mother. He began calling his aunt Muriel late at night, telling her that Ruth had visited him – she had appeared in the corner of the room, holding her arms out to him. On a spring day the following year he caught a train to Amersham and destroyed his mother's headstone. That May, he committed suicide in his dingy flat, washing down Glutethimide pills, a hypnotic sedative used to treat insomnia, with alcohol. Long-term use of the drug was known to lead to delirium, hallucinations, convulsions and fever. He was 37 years old.

Andre's body lay in his flat undiscovered for three weeks. On 17 June another tenant 'noticed flies crawling out from under the door'.[47] The police called on Muriel a fortnight later. In her memoir, she writes graphically of her visit to the flat, which had been sealed by the police and still smelled strongly of Andre's decomposing body. The inquest into his death at the Coroner's Court in Westminster returned a verdict of suicide. Muriel gave evidence: 'He said he was going to die before me. I knew something would happen because of the drugs he was taking. The death of his mother had been devastating.'[48] The coroner described Andre as having suffered severe depression for a lengthy period. *The Times* reported the inquest, referring to him as Claire Andre McCallum.[49] A funeral service was held at St John's Chapel in Woking on 28 June 1982. Andre left £30 in his will, which Muriel spent on flowers for him. Georgina attended the service with her aunt. Although Andre had asked to be buried, Muriel was advised to have his body cremated and, on 6 July, she took his ashes to Amersham, where they were buried in a pocket of earth on his mother's grave while a vicar intoned a prayer.

A few months before his death, Andre had arranged to meet Christmas Humphreys, lead prosecutor at his mother's trial, at the Buddhist Society in London. He taped their conversation, possibly with a view to taking his mother's case to appeal. In reply to Andre's question of whether it was right that Ruth had suffered the death penalty, Humphreys replied that she had known what the result would be when she shot David. Andre broke down during their meeting. 'It's the loss-ness of everything,' he said. 'My mother went off and I was very much bonded to her . . . I had no father . . . I wasn't a fully formed person . . . I never developed past sixteen or seventeen.'[50] Humphreys asked if he would accept help from a psychiatrist and made an appointment with him to speak to Dr Desmond Biddulph, a colleague at the Buddhist Society. Humphreys offered Andre friendship and financial help, but just a few months after their meeting Ruth's son was dead. According to Muriel, Humphreys paid the full cost of Andre's funeral after she wrote to him for assistance; she also claims that the judge at Ruth's trial, Mr Justice Havers, sent money to Andre every year at Christmas. Humphreys himself died in 1983; his former home in St John's Wood is now a Buddhist centre.

*

Muriel is the only surviving immediate relative of Ruth Ellis. Their father, Arthur Neilson as he was then, died in 1967 of lung cancer. Two years later, in spring 1969, his wife Bertha was discovered lying unconscious in a gas-filled room at her home in Hemel Hempstead; she never fully recovered and was admitted to Brookwood Hospital in Woking for psychiatric care. In February 1977, Bertha disappeared from her bed during a bitterly cold night marked by snowfall. She was found the following morning by her two grandsons in a disused pigsty within the hospital grounds. She died two years later, in April 1979.

Betty Neilson, Ruth's younger sister, died in October 1955 at the age of 18; her death certificate recorded 'cardiac failure following asthma'. Of all Ruth's siblings, Betty was the most reserved and had never spoken publicly of her sorrow over her elder sister's death in Holloway. Julian Neilson, Ruth's half-brother, died in 1968. Granville Neilson, the last of Ruth's relatives to see her alive, died in Hertfordshire in 1996.

Muriel separated from her husband Joe Jakubait in the late 1980s and channelled her considerable energies into overturning the murder verdict the courts had meted out to Ruth. In November 2011, she celebrated her 91st birthday.

26

All those whose lives were caught up in Ruth and David's relationship and its terrible end remained deeply affected by it. Ant and Carole Findlater divorced at the end of 1956. They tried to make their marriage work in the aftermath of the shooting; Carole wrote an article on the case which earned them £60 and enabled them to take a holiday away from the endless press interest. There was no question of Ant continuing with the Emperor; HRG asked for the engine to be returned and David's brother sold the car's shell to a racing enthusiast in Sussex. But the holiday could not repair the damage done to the Findlaters' relationship and the couple separated after returning to London. Ant married again in 1959 and emigrated to Menton on the French–Italian border, where he worked as a mechanic once more, but on marine engines. He died in 1996, having returned to live in England with his wife. 'The case broke my parents up,' Francesca confirms:

> My father left when I was two and my mother died when I was thirteen and we never spoke about it. I didn't really know anything until I was at school and some friends picked up one of the books about the case and I think that was when I first became aware of it. My parents did not talk about it at all. They just wanted to get on with their lives.[1]

Clive Gunnell, who witnessed David's shooting, married and moved to the south of England, where he lived until his death, never speaking publicly again of that night in Hampstead. Cliff Davis retired from sports car racing in 1957 to focus on his business. He ran the American Car Centre on the Goldhawk Road in London until the early 1980s and became a tireless charity fundraiser; his annual 'Filth Night' dinners were the centrepiece of his work for various causes. He died in 1986 aged 68. David's friend Archie Scott-Brown was killed in May 1958 at the Sports Car GP in Belgium when his Lister-Jaguar skidded off the rain-drenched track and exploded into flames after hitting bales of straw. Mike Hawthorn, the driver with whom David had had a row at the Steering Wheel Club, and whose career Ruth followed with interest, died the following year in a road accident on the Guildford bypass.

The women in David's life fared better. Faith Roberts, who had an affair with David while he was living with Ruth, emigrated to the south of France after his death and opened a successful hotel there. Mary Dawson, David's former fiancée, married and had children; she never spoke publicly about their relationship but said privately that she would always remember David's 'wonderful sense of humour'.[2]

Buried alongside David in Penn's Holy Trinity churchyard is his brother John, who died in February 1963 after a short illness at the age of 42. Behind them is the shared grave of their mother and stepfather; Annie died in June 1975 at the apartment she shared with her husband in Knightsbridge. Her death notice in *The Times* read: 'Anne Beattie Cook, aged 82 years, very deeply loved and admired wife of Humphrey Wyndham Cook and beloved mother of Derek Blakely and Maureen Fahey, and very much loved grandmother and great-grandmother.' Three years later, Humphrey Wyndham Cook, who had fostered his stepson's interest in racing cars with the best of intentions, died and was buried with his wife.

A simple headstone marks David's grave, carved with the insignia of the Highland Light Infantry, among whose ranks he was fleetingly a member. The inscription reads: 'DAVID MOFFETT DRUMMOND BLAKELY 1929 – 1955'. Above a cross are the words: 'He was great of heart, courtly and courageous.' The line is from Longfellow's poem *The Courtship of Miles Standish*: 'For he was great of heart, magnanimous, courtly, courageous;/Any woman in Plymouth, nay, any woman in England,/Might be happy and proud to be called the wife of Miles Standish!'[3]

Outlasting them all, and with a new lease of life, is the Emperor, the car on which David devoted so much time, energy and probably more love than he ever felt for Ruth Ellis. The Emperor passed through various motor collections and for a while was displayed at the Westridge Museum on the Isle of Wight. In the 1990s it was bought by Nigel Hulme, a vintage car enthusiast from Surrey. He raced the Emperor, complete with a replacement HRG engine, at Silverstone in 1998; among the crowd that day was Frances Findlater, who was photographed sitting in the car on which her father and godfather had worked so enthusiastically. Hulme did not take to the vehicle, however, and after his mechanic died while working on it he sold it in 1999 at the Silverstone Historic Festival for the sum of £30,000. It was bought by a Belgian firm, L.M.B. Racing, who also own one of David's other cars. The two vehicles are garaged together, with the Emperor gloriously restored and in immaculate racing condition, just as David had always dreamed.

*

On 11 December 1955, Morris Conley found himself and his vice racket splashed across the front page of *The People*, courtesy of Duncan Webb. Pretending to be a customer, Webb was invited to meet a girl at the flat above the Little Club where Ruth had lived; all the flats in the building were leased in the name of Mrs Hannah Conley. While Webb and his photographer were waiting for Conley to emerge from the Little Club,

> a thick-set and not too wholesome looking individual approached from behind and punched [the photographer] in the side of the head. He then pulled my photographer's flash light equipment from his pocket and slashed his face with it. A fight ensued. Mr Conley . . . uttered certain threats. He then went into the premises at 37 Brompton Road . . . When he came out he again attacked my photographer. The police arrived. Mr Conley protested. He was searched in a shop doorway, but no further action was taken, except that Conley offered and paid, certain damages to my photographer . . . There was no doubt that the tentacles of this vice ring were far flung.[4]

Following his investigations, Webb sent a copy of *The People* to the Hollywood Club and recounts in his 1956 book *Line Up for Crime* that Conley 'buried his head into his hands and burst into tears. "Vot are dey trying to do to me?" he cried. "Vy do dey persecute me like dis?"'[5] Conley closed down the Hollywood Club, dismissing his staff without notice or pay, together with the Carousel Club and the Little

Club, which Webb referred to as 'an unfortunate address altogether for many people, probably more for the victims of that place than for Conley who used it merely as an establishment of filth and corruption'.[6]

For a while Conley vanished from the murky surface of the pond in which he swam, only to resurface six years later when the vice squad swooped on him. On 10 September 1961 the *News of the World* reported Conley's trial for living off immoral earnings after raiding one of his properties in Paddington. Conley initially admitted running a brothel but changed his story when charged, pleading his innocence. At his trial, the extortionate rents he charged the girls caused as many raised eyebrows as the accusations against him. He quietly disappeared from view afterwards and died in obscurity.

*

Ruth's executioner resigned in January 1956 after a dispute about pay. Albert Pierrepoint had driven from Preston to Strangeways in poor weather to hang Thomas Bancroft, only to be told upon arrival that Bancroft had been reprieved. Unable to return to Preston on account of the weather, Albert had no choice but to stay in a hotel. At first the authorities were unwilling to reimburse him fully and he handed in his resignation. He refused to reconsider despite the authorities agreeing to pay his expenses after all, and within a month he had signed a deal with the *Empire News* to write his memoirs for the sum of £20,000 (more than £400,000 today). In 1961 he was interviewed for a BBC documentary about capital punishment, but otherwise maintained a low profile, running the Rose and Crown pub with his wife until their retirement. Beneath his bed in the Southport bungalow he shared with Anne was the suitcase packed with remnants from his past: his execution diaries, photographs, rope, white hood and the leather straps.

In 1974 his autobiography, *Executioner Pierrepoint*, was published. It ended:

> I now sincerely hope that no man is ever called upon to carry out another execution in my country. I have come to the conclusion that executions solve nothing and are only an antiquated relic of a primitive desire for revenge . . . . All the men and women whom I have faced at that final moment convince me that in what I have done I have not prevented a single murder. And if death

does not work to deter one person it should not be held to deter any.[7]

Five years later, in a meeting engineered by *The Sun*, he came face to face with Muriel at a hotel in Knightsbridge. Afterwards, the two of them visited Ruth's grave, but Muriel refused to shake Albert's hand when he offered it.

In his later years, Albert began suffering from dementia and was admitted to a nursing home where he and Anne shared a room. In 1991 the *News of the World* ran a feature on him, captioning their photograph: 'Twilight Years of a Haunted Hangman . . . The ghost of the gallows has come to haunt Britain's most famous hangman.'[8] Albert died on 10 July 1992 at the age of 87 of bronchopneumonia and Alzheimer's disease.[9]

*

John Bickford, the solicitor Ruth deposed after learning she would not be reprieved, was haunted all his life by the events of 1955. On the day of his former client's execution, he received a letter from journalist Peter Grisewood, who intended to write a book about the case. Bickford replied that he was 'too upset' to see or talk to anyone.[10] Grisewood tried again, declaring that Ruth's defence had been 'badly handled'.[11] Out of the blue, Bickford suggested that rather than simply contributing to the book, he would co-write it, on the understanding that his name did not appear on the cover. When the two men met, Grisewood found the solicitor,

> in a very nervous state, obviously having suffered a great strain. He was unable to remain seated or still for more than a few minutes at a time . . . He told me the case had been a hopeless one and that Ruth Ellis would not help him or herself.[12]

Bickford blamed the Findlaters for David's death and repeated Dr Creditor's allegations.

Grisewood was keen to talk about Desmond but 'Mr Bickford at once became most insistent that he could not discuss that, or allow Mr Cussen to appear in the book.'[13] During a second meeting, according to Grisewood, Bickford 'had too much to drink' and invited him to his office to listen to the tape recordings of Ruth,

Desmond and David, which he said had been given to him by Desmond 'for safety'.[14] Grisewood recalled that Bickford claimed to have,

> *all* Ruth Ellis's clothes in his possession and would have to return them to her family but was arranging to have them photographed first ... Bickford had told me that Mrs Neilson, Ruth Ellis's mother, was hostile to him and had as he put it 'the silly idea that he had not done all he could for her daughter and had been paid by Cussen to protect *him*'.[15]

Grisewood claimed to have severed all contact with Bickford after this meeting. He continued his investigations, however, and came to believe that Bickford and Desmond 'had not recently met but knew each other well'.[16] He vowed that Ruth's parents had spoken to Bickford concerning their suspicion that Desmond had given their daughter the gun, but the solicitor had advised them to say nothing, since it would not affect the outcome of the case. Grisewood eventually shelved the idea of writing a book but joined forces with reporter Duncan Webb in an effort to discover the truth about the origins of the gun. In the meantime, Bickford attempted to get on with his life by leaving his old firm and setting up a practice of his own. He admitted years later that Ruth's dismissal of him 'was the thing that absolutely had a tremendously deep effect on me and, in fact, I can't say it ruined my life but it had such a profound effect as to change my life'.[17] When his business failed, he left London and settled in Sliema on the northeastern coast of Malta, where he tried to forget Ruth Ellis and sought solace in alcohol when he could not.

On 6 March 1972 Bickford wrote to Scotland Yard, requesting an interview with one of the senior CID officers who had worked on Ruth's case. When he received a brief letter informing him that those men had since retired from the force, he departed for London and wrote again in his peculiarly jaunty style to New Scotland Yard:

> Dear Sir
> Re Ruth Ellis dec'd.,
> In reply to your letter of yesterday, I was only expressing a 'pious hope'!
> I am due to return to Malta very shortly and it is just possible that

I may have committed a crime in that, in the eyes of the law, I may have been an accessory after the fact to a crime of murder. I want either to be charged or re-assured, after fifteen years of conscience! I did not know what I ought to have done, but, I am satisfied now, that I ought to do something. Unfortunately, there was nobody, who was prepared to help me in my dilemma.

If the Police prefer to let 'sleeping dogs' lie, that is their affair: but I feel that, after all this time, I must make my gesture. Probably, I should have done it years ago – I just don't know.

Yours faithfully,

John G.A. Bickford.[18]

Within the week, he presented himself at the offices where he was interviewed by Detective Inspector William Pallett. Bickford announced that he had been aware from the very beginning that Desmond Cussen had given his client the murder weapon. Although he claimed to have other facts to corroborate this, he refused to elaborate and didn't want to make a written statement. He then declared that he would be returning to Malta the following week and would think about what he should do. According to DCS Payton's report:

> Mr Bickford's conscience was clearly disturbed by some matter which he believed he had failed to disclose or deal with properly at the time of the Ruth Ellis trial . . . The fact that Ruth Ellis had obtained the gun from Cussen was a line of enquiry previously investigated and dealt with.[19]

A few weeks later, on 11 June 1972, Bickford wrote from Malta again. His letter (Appendix II) formed the statement he had previously refused to make; he wrote at length about Ruth, Desmond and the gun, explaining why he had not revealed what he knew either before or during the trial – namely, that his first duty was to his client, and that by showing his hand, her chances of a manslaughter verdict, and thereafter a reprieve, 'would virtually have vanished'.[20] He admitted that the case 'with all its publicity and the weeks of strain' had had 'a profound effect on me and I have never ceased to brood about it'.[21] He had decided to speak out after listening to Ruth's tape recordings again and realised that he 'ought to have gone to the police and told them what I knew'.[22] He was uncertain as to whether he should be charged with being an accessory after the fact, but,

> after all these years of almost ceaseless brooding . . . wondering
> and worrying, I have had to find the answer for myself. I know
> it will stir up mud and I do not relish the task of being involved,
> but having at least made up my mind, I must leave it up to you
> to do what is right and just.[23]

There was no response to Bickford's letter. Frustrated, and evidently still brooding, he turned up at Scotland Yard on 7 September 1972, where DCS Payton spoke to him and took possession of Ruth's tape recordings. Somewhat mystified as to Bickford's motives, DCS Payton dismissed the tapes as 'merely a lot of meaningless talk'.[24] But Bickford would not let the matter drop. On 23 September, while still in London, he wrote to 'Dear Payton' about 'our mutual friend' (Desmond Cussen), claiming to have discovered a 'plausible motive' for his giving Ruth the gun: Desmond had found out she had lied to him about her relationship with David and 'was playing out some kind of drama in which he appeared to himself to be the "hero"'.[25] Bickford finished: 'If she had been allowed to live, all this might have come out . . . I only regret my subsequent error and hope that there is something I can do to repair the mischief . . . PS: Hi! What about my tape?'[26]

Payton's response was muted. A letter was sent to Bickford, asking him to call at Scotland Yard again when he was next in London, 'bringing with him certain articles mentioned in his statement'.[27] Privately, Payton made a note: 'Much of his letter . . . is theory and does not assist with any facts . . . One thing is abundantly clear, however, and that is his firm belief that only action taken against Cussens will clear his conscience which is so deeply troubled by past events.'[28] Payton suggested that his own report and relevant documents should be forwarded to the Director of Public Prosecutions. Bickford was duly informed in December 1972 that no further action would be taken.

Exactly one year later, the *Sunday People* published Ruth's last statement and a partial transcript of the tape-recorded conversation between Ruth and Desmond. Bickford had sold it to them, possibly in order to put pressure on Desmond, whom he clearly felt should have been questioned more closely if nothing else. The article occupied the entire front page: 'Ruth Ellis Sensation: We Reveal Evidence that Could Have Saved Last Woman to Hang'.[29] The 'evidence' was Ruth's last statement and an interview Bickford granted the newspaper, in which he declared:

> I have made my statement to the Yard in the interests of honour and truth. For 17 years I brooded over the tragedy. From a professional point of view as a solicitor, I think I acted perfectly properly at the time. But now I want the truth to be told before I die . . . The Home Office did not contact me. The police did not come near me. Yet I possessed the evidence they were seeking as the hours were running out for Ruth Ellis . . . One phone call from the Home Office would have been enough to release me from the bond of confidence. I could have given the facts that would have saved Ruth Ellis. I will regret to my dying day that I did not.[30]

Bickford wrote to Muriel a few months before the newspaper article, but she did not receive his letter until several years later. In 1973, he was expelled from Malta after conducting a strenuous campaign against 'local government abuses' and returned to England.[31]

Bickford's last ever interview was given to producer Peter Williams for the Thames Television documentary *The Story of Ruth Ellis*, in 1977. He declared then that by making a statement to Scotland Yard five years earlier:

> whatever else may be said, I've done the duty I owed society . . . nobody could afterwards turn round and say that I had deliberately protected this man for money . . . I didn't want anything to happen to [Cussen], it's too long ago, but I think it was very much a thing where I had been worried about it for years and years.[32]

Ruth's friend Jacqueline Dyer, interviewed for the same documentary, was incensed by Bickford's comment:

> Why did he keep it to himself? It is no good saying it now . . . She might have got ten years in jail . . . the law changed . . . When you kill somebody you can't go and dig them up and say, 'Well look, start again.' She's dead, gone, finished.[33]

John Bickford died of alcoholism in Merton, south-west London, in 1977.

*

When DCI Davies wrote his final report on Ruth's case on 15 July 1955, he referred to Desmond and the subject of the gun, declaring: 'He maintained he had not given it to her and had never seen this revolver.'[34] There the matter ended, although the press sensed there was more to the story than had yet emerged; the *Daily Sketch* queried: 'Is There a Guilty Man?' and asked: 'What are the police doing about this man? Are they going to charge him? If not, why not?'[35] Their questions remained unanswered.

Peter Grisewood and Duncan Webb stepped up their own investigations. Webb interviewed Andre a few months after Ruth's execution and claimed that Andre had told him that on the morning of the shooting, 'Uncle Desmond' had driven them all to Tanza Road and then to Penn to look for David, whom they didn't find. On the journey home, Andre heard Desmond say to his mother: 'I've got one, but it's old and rusty and needs oiling.'[36] In a later account, Webb added that Ruth had remarked beforehand: 'If I had a gun, I would shoot him.'[37] Grisewood's interview with Andre resulted in the same information.

The two journalists pooled their findings into a front-page scoop on 15 January 1956. *The People* headline read: 'Ruth Ellis: Sensational New Evidence'. They did not reveal Desmond's name in their conversations with Andre, but it was blatantly obvious that he had been earmarked as the guilty party. For five consecutive weeks, *The People* ran reports based on their research. On 5 February, the newspaper asked: 'When Was Ruth Given the Murder Gun?'. Webb asserted that she must have been given it when she changed her clothes (from the black suit described by those who saw her leave Egerton Gardens to the grey suit in which she committed the crime and was arrested) – implying that this could only have been done at Desmond's flat, although again he was not named. On the following Sunday, the headline declared: 'Ruth Ellis Lied about the Gun', and the article featured quotes from Ruth's mother, Jacqueline Dyer and Elizabeth Riley.

What intrigued Webb most was Ruth's loyalty to Desmond in the period between her arrest and her statement to Victor Mishcon. He felt certain that an agreement had been made between them, most probably that Ruth would not mention his name in return for Desmond's assurance that he would take care of Andre if she were to hang. Ruth's brother Granville didn't feel this was the case; he believed that the pact had simply been for Desmond to give Ruth the gun as she asked. Grisewood went further: he claimed that Desmond,

> promised to look after Andre. After she was released he said he would marry her and they would go to Canada ... When she saw how Bickford and Cussen had tricked her, she dismissed Bickford and sent for Mr Mishcon and told the truth.[38]

Grisewood stated that Desmond then bribed Bickford into covering for him. But if this were true, why didn't Ruth say as much in her statement to Mishcon? After all, she had absolutely nothing to lose at that stage.

Webb presented his and Grisewood's findings to the Home Office. He recalled that the reply he received was to the effect that 'Mr Lloyd George did not want to read the documents, or any of the evidence I had collected.'[39] In fact, a Home Office official considered the journalists' observations carefully, positing in an internal letter:

> It might be possible to prove that Cussen and Ruth Ellis were together in Cussen's flat in the evening, and they drove together to the neighbourhood of the crime ... but on public grounds there is a good deal to be said for not re-opening the case.[40]

On that basis, the Webb and Grisewood papers were sent to the Director of Public Prosecutions, who conducted an inquiry into Desmond Cussen's alleged supplying of Ruth with the gun and his movements that Easter Sunday. Ultimately, the decision was taken to shelve the investigation because there seemed little sense in pursuing the case 'given that Ellis is no longer available as a witness [and] there is no evidence to prove that Cussen supplied her with the gun'.[41] Perhaps in an effort to prevent further outcry, the Home Office simply told Duncan Webb in a letter dated 15 March 1956 that 'the Secretary of State has considered this memorandum but has found no grounds for further action on his part and he does not, therefore, desire to take advantage of your offer to make the documents available to him'.[42]

Angered by the outcome, in his 1956 book *Line Up for Crime*,

Webb referred to Andre's account of Easter Sunday and stated categorically that he had been able to prove Desmond 'conspired with Ruth Ellis to murder Blakely. He induced her to do it. I was able to obtain the necessary corroborative evidence to prove this. Furthermore, I was able to prove that an alibi this monster made to the police was no alibi at all. It was a lie.'[43] He ended the book with a pledge to tell Andre the truth about his mother's death and a challenge to Lloyd George 'to justify the wanton killing of Ruth Ellis'.[44] Two years later, at the age of forty-one, Webb died of food poisoning while in America.

*

The man at the heart of the controversy, Desmond Cussen, was able to live anonymously for several years. He left Goodwood Court in 1957, first to live-in rooms at the Lanterns club in Craven Road, and then at the Atlantic Hotel, where he remained the loner he had always been, paid his rent on time, went out to work and each evening had a large whisky in the bar without ever really seeming to get to know anyone else. Robert Hancock contacted him again during the writing of *Ruth Ellis: The Last Woman to be Hanged* and persuaded him to agree to an informal interview. Over a drink or two, Hancock asked about the gun. Desmond replied hesitantly:

> If I were writing your book I'd say the man who gave her the gun
> never thought she'd use it . . . I think you should say that Ruth
> told him that she knew someone who would shoot David for her
> but she had to get a gun for him.[45]

Like Webb before him, Hancock did not name Desmond in his book, but he was transparently the anonymous 'besotted' man who gave Ruth the revolver.

In 1964 Desmond sold his shares in the family business for £10,000 and emigrated to Australia, where his mother had already settled following his father's death. He joined a Sydney trucking company initially, then set up his own second-hand car dealership, but it was closed down following the discovery that he had failed to obtain the correct trading licence. In 1967 he embarked on a countrywide trip across Australia and decided to settle in Perth. For three years, he compiled feasibility studies for a company of estate agents, but was not a success and fared no better speculating on stocks and shares. He moved to Stirling for a brief time but eventually returned to Perth, where he became a florist, using the last of his money to open a shop, Chez Fleur.

Desmond had no knowledge of Bickford's desire to 'come clean' to Scotland Yard in 1972. In one letter to the authorities, Bickford wrote:

> I cannot quite understand why [Desmond] was not charged with unlawful possession – except that, for some reason, he was called for the prosecution . . . He took precautions to exculpate himself before the event took place. He was quick-witted and intelligent – hence the way in which he apparently satisfactorily accounted to the Police for all his weapons. A man as intelligent as that must have known that [Ruth] had no possibility of getting away with her part in it. Why did he, professedly her protector, place her in such a position? . . . She out of loyalty was, until the end, prepared to protect him. She thought him to be her most loyal friend and it was only when he ceased to visit her, after her conviction, that she became suspicious of him.[46]

But the Director of Public Prosecutions dismissed Bickford's allegations.

In 1973, when the *Sunday People* published extracts from Ruth's tape recordings, they also tracked Desmond down to his 'shabby seaside flat' and presented him with Bickford's statement, which he read with 'trembling fingers' before murmuring, 'I won't say she's a liar. But funny things go through people's minds at the twelfth hour.'[47] Asked if Ruth deserved to hang, Desmond replied: 'No. But she was hanged according to the law at the time.'[48] Questioned whether he had given Ruth the gun, he thought a moment before replying: 'Whatever I say, it won't bring it back, will it? No, I don't want to say anything about guns. I have nothing to say.'[49]

Three years later, Laurence Marks located Desmond for the purposes of the Thames TV documentary. He admits his telephone call must have come as 'a horrific surprise'.[50] Marks gave Desmond the chance to think about whether he was willing to participate in the documentary, but pointed out that it was time to tell the truth at last. 'He was a sad, good man,' Marks reflects:

> Unlucky in love and in success. He was very much a product of his time. He never forgot Ruth – he really did love her. I think

it's obvious he gave her the gun. Why? To get Blakely out of the way. I'm sure he thought Ruth would get off. He knew what he did was wrong. His intentions – apart from that one – were always honourable.[51]

The interview with Desmond Cussen in the 1977 documentary makes for extremely uncomfortable viewing. He struggles with every question, repeatedly quells irritation and gives the impression of a man who has agreed to be interviewed against his better judgement. It was not a good time for Desmond: his business was on the verge of bankruptcy and he complained of 'worms in the carnations this autumn'.[52] After watching a tape of Bickford speaking to producer Peter Williams, he declared: 'Let me state very clearly I did not give Ruth the gun. Nor on that occasion did I drive her up to Hampstead.'[53] Asked if he was under Ruth's influence, he replied, 'It could have been I wanted to help her. Not to the point of giving her a gun if that's what you're getting at. That's ludicrous.'[54] He said he could not remember where he was on the night of the shooting ('I must have been at home') and realised he had lost Ruth forever 'when she went and killed him'.[55] He regarded Ruth's final statement to Mishcon as 'a complete desperate effort to get herself a stay of execution or something like that . . . I, in those days, obviously acted as a bloody fool but what I did I did with the best of intentions.'[56] Asked if Ruth was the only woman for him, he paused, then replied: 'I thought so at the time. I did meet somebody else since then . . . She unfortunately died of cancer . . . I was beginning to become very fond of her as well and there is no doubt she was of me.'[57] Life is hard, producer Peter Williams commented. Desmond nodded slowly, 'Yes. Some find it easy, some find it hard.'[58]

In the years after his last known interview, Desmond Cussen closed down his floristry business and moved to Parry House, a retirement village on the Australian Air Force Memorial Estate at Bull Creek, about 12 miles south of Perth. He used his bathroom as a home brewery and became a dedicated alcoholic. On 24 April 1991, he suffered a fall at his flat. The alarm was raised by a visiting neighbour, who saw him lying on the floor and called a doctor. Desmond was admitted to hospital and found to have a fracture-dislocation of the neck. He contracted pneumonia and died on 8 May 1991 after multiple organ failure, taking the secret of whether or not he truly gave Ruth the revolver to his grave.

Epilogue

In 1998 Muriel Jakubait instructed lawyers to appeal against her sister's conviction for murder. Georgina supported the bid, and after some discussion it was decided it should be brought in her name. Following Georgina's death in 2001, the appeal reverted to Muriel. Evidence was then presented to the Criminal Cases Review Commission that Ruth had been badly served by her defence team, that Desmond Cussen incited her to commit the crime, that Ruth had been sexually abused by her father, was physically abused by George Ellis and was suffering depression following a miscarriage at the time of the shooting. It was further alleged that she was a victim of post-traumatic stress disorder, although the condition was not recognised in 1955. On 8 February 2002, the Criminal Cases Review Commission referred the case to the Court of Appeal. Ruth's family were potentially eligible for compensation if the original verdict were overturned. Muriel told the press that she was not interested in financial gain, 'though if there is any money, I don't see why I shouldn't get my share'.[1]

Amid a great deal of press interest, the case was heard at the Court of Appeal on 16 and 17 September 2003 before Lord Justice Kay, Mr Justice Silber and Mr Justice Leveson. Representing Ruth was Michael Mansfield QC, a socialist and 'radical lawyer' known for taking on particularly controversial cases. Mansfield argued that Ruth was suffering from 'battered woman syndrome' when she committed her crime, again a condition not accepted as a defence until 45 years after the shooting.[2] Mansfield asserted that all those in the legal profession who were involved in Ruth's trial had been 'labouring under a misconception of the law' in believing that she must have been seen to have acted in the heat of the moment in order to establish provocation; Mansfield claimed that in fact they had needed to prove her intention to kill arose from a 'loss of control and provocative conduct'.[3] He argued that 'cumulative provocation' was to blame and that this should have been considered as a defence.[4]

Presenting a much fuller and more complex picture of Ruth's life with David before the shooting, Mansfield asserted that this was therefore a case of manslaughter rather than murder. For the first time, a court heard that Ruth had intended to kill herself on the night she shot David but was unable to do so. A statement was also read from a retired midwife in Australia, Moreen Gleeson, who had contacted the Criminal Cases Review Commission in 1999. Gleeson claimed that, while living in Hampstead in 1955, she had encountered Ruth on the night of the shooting, some time prior to the event. Ruth was 'stressed and weeping' on the street and said that her boyfriend was with another woman.[5] Gleeson recalled Ruth mentioning that she had a gun, whereupon a 'bulky man with a proprietary air' appeared and stood 'possessively' over Ruth.[6] Gleeson was not present in court; after making her statement to this effect, she was no longer in contact with Muriel's legal team and her whereabouts were unknown.[7]

Appearing on behalf of the Crown was Mr David Perry, who argued that the defence of diminished responsibility was not recognised at the time of Ruth's trial and therefore could not be retrospectively applied; the defence of provocation as it stood then had indeed required a sudden loss of self-control. Ruth's response to the only provocation under those terms – that is, David's failure to contact her on Easter Sunday – was 'wholly disproportionate'.[8]

On 8 December 2003 Lord Justice Kay dismissed the appeal as 'without merit' and declared that Ruth had been properly convicted at her trial in 1955.[9] He stated:

> Under the law at the date of the trial, the judge was right to withdraw the defence of provocation from the jury and the appeal must fail. If her crime were committed today, we think it likely that there would have been an issue of diminished responsibility for the jury to decide. But we are in no position to judge what the jury's response to such an issue might be.[10]

He was highly critical that the case had been considered at all, adding with clear irritation:

If we had not been obliged to consider her case, we would perhaps in the time available have dealt with eight to 12 other cases, the majority of which would have involved people who were said to be wrongly in custody. Parliament may wish to consider whether going back many years into history to re-examine a case of this kind is a use that ought to be made of the limited resources available.[11]

He ended:

We have to question whether this exercise of considering an appeal so long after the event, when Mrs Ellis herself had consciously and deliberately chosen not to appeal at the time, is a sensible use of the limited resources of the court of appeal. On any view, Mrs Ellis had committed a serious criminal offence.[12]

A devastated Muriel told the press:

I can't believe it after all these years. What is so different about Ruth than anyone else? The whole thing seems very unfair and I am never going to give up over this until I am taken from this earth. Ruth always said she hoped the truth would come out one day.[13]

Mike Blackburn, Georgina's widower, agrees: 'I am just glad that Georgina didn't know what the courts decided. It would have broken her heart.'[14]

*

From a modern-day perspective, the case of Ruth Ellis is beginning to be read as a lesson in female morality and the shifting social landscape. Undoubtedly, her trial occurred in a time when:

women, having been shooed back into domesticity after the war, were being portrayed in advertisements and on the radio as the core of the modern nuclear family. There had been a general outcry against the collapse of morals due to the pressures of war, and calls had gone up for the re-establishment of 'traditional values' – always bad news for women. Ruth Ellis served as a perfect example of the consequences of female venality, and the double standard relating to sexual behaviour was never questioned.[15]

Past discussions implied that Ruth was to blame for the beatings she took from the men in her life. Writer Robert Hancock declares that it was a pity George and David could not have discussed how Ruth ('a woman who never knew how to shut up') behaved once she had a ring, or the prospect of a ring, on her finger. It was this, Hancock believed, which 'turned Ruth from a woman with whom it was tolerably easy to live with into a shrew'.[16] Even the usually redoubtable Marks and Van den Burgh questioned what it was about Ruth that 'made her invite violence . . . it could be that she felt guilt and invited expiation by provoking physical attack'.[17] Muriel, too, is on record as stating:

> Ruth had a dreadful time with men, she took so many beatings. Every man that Ruth ever had belted her, God knows why and what for. I asked her once, 'Ruthie, whatever do you do to cause it?' She told me she never did anything, she didn't understand it. She didn't ask for all that beating up. It started with our father, he was a terribly cruel man. And I think it had a terrible effect on her.[18]

Beatings were what Ruth had come to expect; they were the unwelcome but seemingly inevitable norm.

The other question which placed the onus on Ruth was why she chose to stay with David, given the abuse within their relationship. Perhaps for the same reasons as countless other women in her situation then and now: David promised to reform and she still loved him enough to want to believe him; because he continued to threaten her; because she had no other real refuge (the only alternative, Desmond, was not without complications); because David had succeeded in separating her from family, friends and colleagues by accusing her of sleeping with everyone she met or loving them more than she loved him; and because she no longer knew who she was or what would become of her. David was controlling and possessive, refusing to help her with money when he could have done so, and he held onto the keys to the flat he shared with her even when she asked for them to be returned. Whether or not he wanted Ruth no longer mattered; on one level he saw her as his property. An abusive relationship is a trap that often does not appear deadly until it is too late. When David left her on Good Friday, she expected him to return at some point; after her arrest and in court, Ruth attempted to explain that she had not killed him because he had abandoned her, but because he would come back eventually and she could see no end to the cycle of humiliation. With this in mind, today might we ask instead: why didn't *he* let her go?

*

The last House of Commons vote on the reinstatement of the death penalty was in 1994; it was defeated by 403 votes to 159. On 11 October 1997, Britain's then Prime Minister Tony Blair signed the Council of Europe Declaration calling for the universal abolition of the death penalty. But in July 2011, with the launch of the government's new e-petition site on which any petition securing 100,000 signatures would be eligible for debate in the House of Commons, the issue was once again to the fore. Blogger Guido Fawkes submitted a petition to bring back the death penalty for 'the murder of children and police officers when killed in the line of duty'.[19] The campaign received a great deal of attention in the press and on television, where almost every lengthy discussion about it mentioned Ruth's name. The petition closed on 4 February 2012, having gained 26,349 signatures, far less than needed to raise the matter in Parliament.

Writer Laurence Marks reflects:

> People talk about Evans–Bentley–Ellis as the last 100-metre dash to abolition but that's not true. Evans and Bentley were innocent – they didn't kill anyone. Ruth Ellis set out to end David Blakely's life and she did just that. She is only included on that list and important to it because of her gender.[20]

Nonetheless, Ruth's case gave an added incentive to the campaign for abolition and equally importantly it ushered in the defence of diminished responsibility – too late for her but not for others. In his book, *The Art of Hanging*, John Deane Potter grudgingly draws the same conclusion: 'Hysterical, immoral Ruth Ellis served her pitiful purpose.'[21] Women in court were dealt a far rawer deal by the justice system than men, and that remains the case today, as barrister Helena Kennedy demonstrates to devastating effect in *Eve Was Framed: Women and British Justice*. The situation is no better in the legal seats than in the dock; even now only 7 per cent of the judiciary are women.

Perhaps this then, is the real reason why the female figure of Justice standing atop the Old Bailey where Ruth was sentenced to death wears a blindfold; less to represent fairness and more because she is unable to look at 'what male Law does in her name'.[22]

VI

Worms in the Carnations

Appendices

Appendix I

In 2005, Muriel Jakubait's memoir *Ruth Ellis: My Sister's Secret Life* was published. Ghostwritten by Monica Weller, the narrative is intricately weaved with a complex conspiracy theory in which Desmond Cussen, a probable MI5 agent, killed David Blakely and framed Ruth Ellis for the murder, thereby neatly disposing of the two lovers whose knowledge about the Burgess and Maclean spying scandal rendered them a threat to the Establishment; the uproar over Ruth's execution also conveniently deflected public attention from the same.

The basic premise of the theory is as follows: from early on in her career as a nightclub hostess, Ruth stumbled into a web of spies; Stephen Ward, a suspected double agent, was Ruth's lover and manipulated her at the behest of the intelligence services; Ruth's marriage to George Ellis was one of convenience, providing a cover for *his* spying activities; David Blakely and Desmond Cussen knew each other long before it was publicly acknowledged and they too were spies; David was a homosexual, which left him vulnerable to blackmail; by 1955, after amassing certain information by virtue of the circles in which she moved, Ruth had become a danger to MI5; Desmond deliberately engineered a situation whereby Ruth was coerced into wanting to kill David, who was an equal threat to the Establishment; Desmond drove Ruth to Hampstead that Easter Sunday evening, placed a gun in her hand and sent her in search of David; the witnesses outside the Magdala were tricked into thinking they had seen Ruth kill her lover while in fact it was Desmond, hidden from view, who fired the fatal shots; thereafter the police and judiciary skimmed over Desmond's involvement, aided by the press, who were infiltrated by the intelligence services; Ruth was expediently condemned to death without ever revealing the truth; and, finally, the revolver displayed in New Scotland Yard's Crime Museum is not the murder weapon it is purported to be.

There are a number of immediate difficulties with this theory, foremost being the fact that it is based primarily on the authors' assumptions, speculations and hearsay. There is little tangible evidence to support their ideas and when definitive statements are made, these are undermined by the lack of identifiable sources. Very often we read: 'I believe', 'I suspect', 'It could have been that', 'I can only assume', 'I'll have to assume', 'My intuition told me', 'It suggests to me', 'I'd say', 'It implied' . . . One or two such remarks are within the bounds of reason, but to rely on them weakens the infrastructure of the theory.

Material that would otherwise detract from their premise or for which there is a simple, given explanation is regarded as suspect. This includes the very well-recorded suicide of George Ellis on the island of Jersey in 1958; the authors believe his death may have been faked by the Secret Services. Unfortunately, they do not elaborate on why this may have been the case, nor explain how a range of people – the hotel staff, the police on the island, the coroner, etc. – were either hoodwinked or persuaded to collude in the matter. The idea is dropped into the story uncorroborated. Elsewhere, their reference to Ruth being seen walking past the School of Navigation in Warsash during her marriage to George Ellis is described as a 'diversion' and Ruth herself 'a cover', but for what or who they do not divulge.[1] Similarly, the authors claim that Desmond paid the rent at Egerton Gardens up until 11 April, the day after the shooting, with the implication that he paid well in advance because he knew there would be no need to make further payments beyond that date. Mrs Winstanley's police statements show this wasn't necessarily the case: 'When the accused took the room in February, it was for an indefinite period.'[2] The last date covered by the rent that had already been paid was indeed 11 April, but how often the rent had been paid is unclear; whether it was a lump sum or weekly was not made explicit at the time.

Occasionally the authors confuse coincidence for evidence – for example, the baffling notion that spy Donald Maclean taking the 706 Green Line bus past George Ellis's home might be relevant, or that Maclean's family lived in Penn and he is buried in the same churchyard as David. The authors further assert that David was 'placed' in Penn, again without telling us how the Establishment were able to convince his family that they should make the village their permanent home solely in order for David to continue his alleged covert activities.

As the conspiracy builds, straightforward matters are given an ominous edge – for example, George's use of 16 Soho Square ('prostitute land') in London as an alternative address.[3] This was, in fact, the offices of his solicitor, Messrs Garber, Vowles & Co., and there is nothing untoward about his referring people to them. Occasionally the authors contradict themselves: on one page we read that nobody recalls Ruth being 'knocked about' by George and again we are told that such stories were created to provide 'a diversion', but several pages later we are informed that George did indeed mistreat Ruth during their marriage.[4] Likewise, the authors state that Granville's appearance at Goodwood Court with an unnamed journalist on the night before Ruth's execution gave Desmond the chance to flee while police were searching for him, but elsewhere they question how Desmond knew to leave, and suggest that he was watching Stephen Ward to determine when it was wise to disappear.

The authors are irrefutably mistaken on at least two issues relevant to the conspiracy. Desmond told detectives that he couldn't have driven Ruth to Hampstead in a taxi cab on the night of the shooting because he had already disposed of the vehicle to his brother. The authors twice state that Desmond was an only child, but he was not; as we know, he did indeed have a younger brother who lived in Windsor at that time. Whether he was being truthful about passing the taxi on to William is another matter. The authors also query whether Desmond later used 'Harry Harris' as an assumed name, noting that – like Desmond – 'Harry Harris' stayed at the Lanterns club in Bayswater, and was also among those listed in the acknowledgements of Marks and Van den Bergh's *Ruth Ellis: A Case of Diminished Responsibility?*. Laurence Marks explains: 'Harry Harris was a reporter who helped us with our research for the book. He is still a very respected sports writer and has nothing to do with Desmond Cussen.'[5]

At the crux of the theory is Ruth's alleged relationship with Stephen Ward. Muriel Jakubait and Monica Weller were not the first people to discern that the two moved in similar circles. Eighteen years before the publication of *Ruth Ellis: My Sister's Secret Life*, two books highlighted the fact: Phillip Knightley and Caroline Kennedy's *An*

Affair of State: The Profumo Case and the Framing of Stephen Ward
(1987) and Anthony Summers and Stephen Dorril's *Honeytrap: The
Secret Worlds of Stephen Ward* (1987). Both note that Ruth and David
frequented at least one club that was a regular haunt of Ward's (the
Steering Wheel Club), and both observe that Ward's prototype
Pygmalion project happened to be Ruth's best friend Vicki Martin.

Whether theirs was a passing acquaintance or something more
substantial is the question. Given their mutual bond with Vicki and the
familiarity of London's clubland – a small world where the same faces
constantly appeared at different bars, which were indeed a breeding
ground for vice, gangsters and spies – it is safe to assume that Ruth and
Ward met or at least knew of each other. However, Muriel Jakubait and
Monica Weller contend that the two were lovers during the late 1940s.
They propose that Ruth and Ward made up a foursome at the White
Hart pub in Brasted at that time, revealing that the other couple were
Ruth's 'best friend' of the period, actress Deborah Kerr and her then
husband Anthony Bartley, a former Battle of Britain pilot.

These are startling revelations. However, apart from the hotel's
chef, no one is able to confirm a friendship between Kerr and Ruth.
The authors admit that over several months they showed photographs
of Ruth, Kerr and Bartley to people connected with the hotel but
nobody recognised Ruth. Nor is she mentioned in any of the
voluminous writings about Deborah Kerr; this is also true of the latest
biography of the actress, *Deborah Kerr* by Michelangelo Capua
(McFarland & Co., 2010). At my request, Capua carefully checked
his archives 'but I did not find any reference or relation between
Deborah and Ruth Ellis'.[6] Furthermore, Bartley penned a chronicle of
his years as one of 'the Few', recalling in detail his days at the White
Hart. He discusses those whom he knew there, famous and otherwise,
but nowhere does he allude to Ruth, which would seem a substantial
oversight given what we are told in Muriel's memoir.

Regarding an affair between Ruth and Ward, again no one is able
to corroborate this idea apart from the former White Hart chef. The
authors refer to a conversation with Desmond Cussen's accountant in
which he mentioned Ruth's 'friendship' with Ward, but they state that
they cannot name the accountant and do not quote him directly. The
authors do quote from a letter written by Deborah Kerr's assistant
Faith Yates in which she informed them that Miss Kerr (who had been
suffering from Parkinson's disease for many years) did recall Ruth and

Ward but not in any detail. However, she did not qualify the context in which Kerr remembered them and pointed out that Kerr and Bartley emigrated to America in 1946 and did not return to England. This presents a further conundrum; the White Hart chef claimed to recall the foursome regularly visiting the pub 'towards the end of the 1940s', but clearly this was impossible, given that Kerr and Bartley had long since left for America.[7]

As we know, Muriel Jakubait and Monica Weller believe Ruth's uncredited role in *Lady Godiva Rides Again* was won for her by Ward, but the section of the book which deals with the film is peppered with conjecture: 'Ward probably promised . . . Ruth must have known Ward . . . Her part in the film must have been planned . . . She probably met him.'[8] Diana Dors only once refers to Ward during the making of the film and never mentions a relationship with Ruth, despite penning several memoirs, giving innumerable interviews and being a ubiquitous chat show participant. While it is true that Ward set his girls up in flats, the suggestion that this is how Ruth came by her flat in Tooting Bec is without merit; when Vicki Martin met Ward, she was already living with Ruth in that same flat and told him that she had to find somewhere else because Ruth was moving out.

Laurence Marks, one of the authors of *Ruth Ellis: A Case of Diminished Responsibility?*, is unambiguous in his response to whether or not Ruth was one of Ward's 'stable':

> It's nonsense. Ruth wasn't Ward's type at all. She wasn't young enough or attractive enough for him or his friends. She was too worldly by far, and she had responsibilities – a real job and two children, which wouldn't have appealed to him one bit.[9]

Peta Steel, the daughter of Marks' co-author Tony Van den Bergh, states:

> My father met Stephen Ward a couple of times and he would certainly have known if Ward was 'working' Ruth. It's certainly true that everybody knew each other in that milieu, so their paths may well have crossed but nothing more, absolutely not.[10]

Someone far closer to Ward is equally forthright in disputing the idea of an affair with Ruth: Christine Keeler. Douglas Thompson, who co-wrote Christine's memoirs, canvassed her opinion for the purposes of this book:

> Christine doesn't remember Stephen ever talking about Ruth, although he certainly talked about Vicki Martin. She thinks it's very possible that they met, since Stephen knew everyone there was to know in London, but he never spoke about Ruth. It seems impossible that he would have kept it to himself, given what he did tell Christine about the people he knew. So I would give that idea a definite thumbs-down.[11]

We turn next to the more pressing matter of who actually killed David Blakely. Muriel Jakubait and Monica Weller believe that Desmond timed his and Ruth's arrival at Tanza Road on Easter Sunday evening to occur before David and Clive left for the Magdala, although we are not told how he was able to ensure the two men would visit the pub that night. They ask why Ruth wasn't questioned at her trial about her decision to make the 'long walk' of approximately twelve minutes to the Magdala instead of taking a taxi; but it is in fact a very short walk from 29 Tanza Road to the pub at the foot of South Hill Park – six minutes at most, walking at a fairly leisurely pace.

The authors maintain that, once outside the pub, Ruth only 'appeared' to fire at David when he emerged and that it was actually Desmond, concealed in some bushes opposite the Magdala, who fired the fatal bullets. They assert that the five witnesses standing so nearby – Clive Gunnell by the Vanguard, Gladys Kensington Yule and her husband at the junction of South Hill Park and Parliament Hill (dangerously close to where Desmond is alleged to have hidden), David James Lusty and George McLaughlin Stephen outside Hanshaw's newsagents, adjacent to the Magdala – could not possibly have seen what they claimed in their police statements: Ruth shooting David at close range. Their assertion is based largely on the trajectory of the 'bullet holes' in the curving wall of the Magdala, describing these as being about 20 ft to the left of the main door and about 12 in. apart. The authors then ask a very pertinent question in relation to the bullet holes: why were they not photographed by police in 1955?

The answer is very simple: the 'bullet holes' were not there in 1955. Because, in fact, they are not bullet holes at all. Four of them are marks made by a plaque that was once attached to the wall of the

Magdala describing the crime; they are nothing more sinister than the symmetrical holes where the screws held the plaque in place. The other marks on the wall – more convincing 'bullet holes' – were chipped into the tiles for dramatic effect by the son of a former landlord who shrewdly calculated that 'evidence' of the shooting would bring extra publicity and business their way. The present management of the Magdala confirmed this to be the case.

Muriel Jakubait and Monica Weller contend that, immediately after the shooting, Desmond escaped to his taxi parked on Parliament Hill, but instead of driving off he stopped outside the Magdala to ferry the injured Mrs Yule and her husband to hospital. While the Yules' cab driver was never traced, if we allow for Desmond fitting the role, then it is reasonable to assume that Mrs Yule might have recognised him from the many photographs of Ruth's 'alternative lover' that appeared in the press before the trial at the Old Bailey. We know that she took an interest in the coverage of the case and it seems improbable that neither she nor her husband would have spotted the likeness, especially since there was an argument with the cab driver, who was perturbed by the thought of blood spoiling his taxi.

Regarding the murder weapon itself, the authors cast doubt on the validity of the gun in the Crime Museum primarily because it appeared to be in good condition when they were permitted to inspect it. But the fault that showed up during testing in the police laboratory after Ruth's arrest is an internal one that can only be detected either by taking the gun apart or attempting to fire it again, at which point the barrel will fail to revolve correctly. Given this defect, the authors question why the gun did not break on the night of the shooting, which is to ignore the arbitrary nature of so much else, in the same way that David might have lived had he chosen to remain at Tanza Road that night instead of heading to the Magdala.

The authors also insist that it is crucial to know the distance at which the gun was fired; this, and their other point about the absence of fingerprinting, is valid, although police felt that the latter was not necessary in view of the weight of evidence placing Ruth at the scene of the crime with the gun in her hands. However, the statements in the National Archives tell us that Ruth was standing immediately outside the Magdala with her back to the wall and therefore within a few feet of David as he came out of the well-lit pub, and the last shot, as forensics expert Lewis Charles Nickolls testified, was fired at a distance of less than 3 in. from David's body as evidenced by the circle of powder fouling around the bullet hole. It should also be borne in mind that the bullets recovered from David's body were confirmed as having been fired from the gun PC Thompson took from Ruth. In other words, if the marksman theory had any validity, there would have been two sets of bullets or the ones found in David's wounds (the bullet in his tongue having been identified as the most fatal) would not have been a match for the gun that Ruth was holding.

The authors also believe that Ruth was physically incapable of shooting anyone due to several factors, the first being that the gun would have been impossibly large in her hands. I have held the gun in the Crime Museum; it is fairly compact, with a little heaviness on first handling that soon becomes comfortable and not at all difficult to manage. The authors point out that one of Ruth's hands was gnarled as a result of the arthritis she suffered during her teenage years, that she had poor eyesight and was small in stature. Nonetheless, Ruth's hospital case notes from Holloway disclose that it was her *left* hand that showed the effects of her illness – and she was right-handed. She wore her despised spectacles that night, indicating that she was determined to be able to see her target as clearly as possible, plus the street lamps were lit, the lights above the door of the Magdala were illuminated – and we know that Desmond may well have tutored her in firing the gun. With reference to her diminutiveness, I am only one inch taller than Ruth Ellis and have quite small hands – the gun was not difficult for me to handle in that sense. Crime Museum curator Paul Bickley also explains:

> We have many women officers who are fairly small in stature and they are capable of handling much larger guns than this – don't forget too, what high emotion can do to a person's strength, making them more able to do things that perhaps they could not normally manage.[12]

Ultimately, although Muriel Jakubait and Monica Weller ask a number of highly relevant questions and are not the first to speculate that Desmond Cussen played a far greater role in the shooting than was believed, there are many weak spots in their theory. Not least of these is their certainty that virtually all those involved – from the reporters on the case to Muriel's own parents – actively colluded with

Desmond to save him from exposure, thereby sending Ruth to the gallows. As we have seen, there is often a simple explanation for the issues that they regard with suspicion – for instance, their sensing 'skullduggery' in the handling of the evidence and statements put before the court in 1955, when in fact such sifting, editing and modification is a matter of everyday legal procedure in how a case is presented for a jury's consideration.[13]

Was Ruth Ellis a pawn in a powerful game of spies? 'There's not a whisper of truth to that,' responds Laurence Marks:

> It's just nonsense. The hand that pulled the trigger outside the Magdala on Easter Sunday 1955 belonged to Ruth. Desmond probably gave her the gun and taught her how to fire it because he wanted David out of the way and hoped that the courts would be lenient with her. That's the real story, however difficult it is for Muriel, particularly, to accept.[14]

Peta Steel agrees:

> Their theory isn't completely implausible given the circles in which the characters mixed – for instance, my own father was a Marxist and he was also approached for the sort of intelligence work discussed in Muriel's book. He went straight to the authorities and told them everything. But if Desmond Cussen was the real assassin then my father and Laurence would have uncovered it years ago. They both had so many contacts and knew everyone there was to know concerned with Ruth's story.[15]

Victoria Blake, author of *Ruth Ellis* in the National Archives' Crime Archives series, comments that Bickford's version of events as told to Scotland Yard in 1972 rings true,

> unlike theories which have recently tried to portray Cussen as the villain of the piece. The most recent of these is laid out in Muriel Jakubait's book *Ruth Ellis: My Sister's Secret Life* . . . the theory outlined seems utterly implausible . . . Attempts to portray Cussen as some sort of evil Svengali figure who brainwashed Ruth into killing are equally unconvincing. They presuppose that Cussen was so eager to kill David that he was

willing to sacrifice Ruth in the process. That makes no
psychological sense at all. Cussen doted on Ruth and was eager
to do whatever she wanted.[16]

But that eagerness *might* also have included providing her with a gun,
if Ruth herself and Bickford are to be believed. We have Bickford's
statement that Ruth was so persistent about wanting a gun and
Desmond was 'so much in love with her that he eventually gave way'.[17]
But Desmond must have known that in giving Ruth the gun, his
actions could very well result in her death too. Did he truly believe
that she would be spared if she were presented to the court as a woman
driven insane with jealousy? Was he so enthralled that he would do
anything she asked, even if it meant putting her life – and perhaps his
own – at risk? It is curious that acres of print have been devoted to
Ruth's state of mind prior to the murder and yet very little said about
Desmond's own mental health. Certainly, his behaviour immediately
before the shooting was as erratic as Ruth's own and, despite his
protestations, he did nothing to help her to look at matters rationally.
He remained devoted to her until the day of the Old Bailey verdict;
thereafter he vanished from her life, presumably in order to begin a
new one of his own and to put all that had happened since he set foot
in the Little Club two years earlier firmly in the past.

But there is one clue: a search in the archives of Smith & Wesson
reveals that the gun recovered from the shooting outside the Magdala
– serial number 719573 – was

> shipped from our factory on December 1, 1940 and delivered to the
> Director General of Directorate of War Supplies, Cape Town, South
> Africa. The records indicate that this shipment was for 1600 units. We
> have no information concerning the distribution of these revolvers in
> South Africa.[18]

Thus, the revolver was dispatched under the terms of the 'Lease-Lend'
programme, which saw many thousands of guns sent to overseas
troops. And among those young British men stationed in South Africa
during the war was one Desmond Edward Cussen, training as an RAF
pilot. All things considered, it is distinctly plausible that Desmond
brought his service revolver home with him and handed it to Ruth
when she asked for it, either doubting that she would go through with

her wish to kill David, or else believing, like Ruth, that there was no other way out of the tangled situation in which they found themselves. But David, whatever his faults, did not deserve to die at the age of only 25.

Muriel's book is suffused with genuine grief about the death of her sister and it is clear that the theory within its pages arises from an abiding sense of injustice. But the facts remain: Ruth Ellis *did* kill David Blakely on Easter Sunday 1955 and although she declared herself 'quite happy' afterwards to join him, her death on the scaffold was undoubtedly a stain on English law, for is there ever a fine day for a hanging?

Appendix II

On 11 June 1972, John Bickford, former solicitor for Ruth Ellis, made the following statement in writing to Scotland Yard:

I, John George Arscott Bickford of 18/1 Locker Street, Qui-Si-Sana, Sliema, Malta GC, retired solicitor, having been duly cautioned, make this statement of my own free will :-

1. Ruth Ellis murdered David Blakely at about 9.30 p.m. on Easter Sunday evening, the 10th April 1955, by shooting him with a .38 Smith & Wesson revolver, outside the Magdala Public House in Hampstead. She was, thereupon arrested and later charged with murder. She was arrested by a Police Officer, who was off duty in civilian clothes, and it was to him that she surrendered the then empty gun.

2. The following day I was asked by the housekeeper of the block of apartments in Egerton Gardens, where Ruth Ellis had been living, to go and see Ruth Ellis at Holloway Prison and to ask whether there was anything she needed, or if she wanted help of any kind.

3. That evening I called at Holloway but was told that Ruth Ellis was under sedation, so I arranged to call the following morning, I think at about 10.30 a.m., which I did. I saw Ruth Ellis.

4. She was grateful for the offer of assistance and, having asked me to deal with certain domestic matters, she also said that she wished me to convey a message to a man called Desmond

Cussens, whose address 'Goodwood Court' she gave me and I think, also, his telephone number.

5. The message she wished me to convey was to the effect that she had told the police that she had got the gun some time previously from a man she met at the Little Club, Knightsbridge, who offered it as security for a loan. I wrote a note in red ink, which I subsequently destroyed. I arranged to see her the following morning.

6. I then went to see her mother – a Mrs Nealson [*sic*], at a house in Hendon, where she was the housekeeper. Having conveyed the message from Ruth Ellis to her mother and collected certain domestic articles, I contacted Cussens by telephone and I think I met him at his flat.

7. It appeared that he knew Ruth Ellis very well, he helped me to collect her things and was most co-operative. I gave him the message and it was, to me, obvious from his manner that he wished to say a great deal more; but since I was merely carrying out Mrs Ellis's various requests, I did not encourage him to talk about the case, partly because I knew very little about it then.

8. I returned to see Mrs Ellis the following day and reported on the result of my errands. She told me then that she thought she was guilty and just wanted to get the whole thing over with, so that she could die and join David Blakely. I talked about her responsibility to her children and so on, and urged her to make an effort. She made it quite plain that she was quite prepared to die; but wanted her story told so that her friends and relations would know why she had done what she did.

9. I asked her if she had a solicitor, and she said that, as regards her divorce from George Ellis, she had instructed Messrs Victor Mishcon & Co. I asked her if she would like me to get in touch with them, but she said she would prefer me to act. I said I could not do that without first contacting Messrs Victor Mishcon which, in fact, I did, and they made it clear that they would be

happy for my firm Messrs Cardew-Smith & Ross of which I was then a partner to act.

10. I went back to Mrs Ellis and she said that she would like to be represented. We then discussed the case in all its aspects in a general sort of way. She was most anxious that nobody else should be involved, she did not then want to defend herself but she wanted to tell her story.

11. Having obtained a picture of sorts and various names and addresses, I left her, and started contacting and visiting various people, including in particular, Desmond Cussens.

12. I think it was on the same day, which would have been Wednesday 13 April 1955, when I saw him at his flat. It appeared that he was intimately concerned with both Ruth Ellis and David Blakely and knew as much as anybody of the association and was quite clearly on the side of Ruth Ellis. So much that, having been assured by me that I only had Ruth Ellis's interests at heart, he told me of the part which he had played in the affair.

13. Amongst other things, he told me that he had supplied her with the revolver. He said that he had cleaned and oiled it. He wiped the bullets and loaded it. He showed her how it worked, his explanation being that she knew that he had a collection of three or four guns, she was so beside herself and so persistent and he was so much in love with her that he, eventually, gave way.

14. Throughout Good Friday and Saturday, she had been in constant touch with him and he had driven her wherever she wished to go, in search of Blakely.

15. She was quite beside herself with grief, jealousy, frustration and, consequently, anger. From recollection and without reference to papers, I feel sure he told me that it was on Easter Sunday morning at his flat that he prepared and gave her the gun.

16. Probably about midday or in the early afternoon, Mrs Ellis

and Cussens, together with her young son Andrew or 'Andy' as she called him, aged then between 10 and 13, I can check this if necessary, drove to Penn Buckinghamshire in search of Blakely. They did not find him and started off on the return journey. On the way back, I think near Gerrards Cross, they stopped by a wood and Ruth Ellis got out of the car and fired at a tree. It is just possible that the son may recollect this. They continued on their way and when going over one of the bridges over the Thames, I am not at the moment certain which one he said it was, Cussens stopped the car and having previously reloaded the gun with another bullet to replace the one which had been fired, he threw the remaining spare bullets and the cleaning materials, which he had used, into the Thames.

17. They drove back to Mrs Ellis' flat in Egerton Gardens and I seem to recollect that he said he left her there with the boy. Whether he waited or not, I cannot now say, but she put Andy to bed, took the gun in her handbag and was driven to Tanza Road by Desmond Cussens, where he left her and drove back home.

18. After Ruth Ellis had shot David Blakely, she was arrested and kept in custody. Cussens went to see her daily until she was convicted, when he ceased his visits.

19. The next day, when I saw Ruth Ellis, I told her this and she admitted that it was true, but told me that, in no circumstances was he or anybody else to be involved. She said that she had over-persuaded him, because she knew he loved her.

20. My first duty was to my Client. I found myself in a quandary, because if evidence had been available that she had been acting in concert with someone else, in the circumstances which I have now disclosed, her chances of an alternative verdict of manslaughter on the possible grounds of lack of premeditation were virtually nil, and likewise, her then very feasible chance of a reprieve, would virtually have vanished.

21. I therefore decided, in the interests of my client and, having

regard to the professionally confidential relationship, which then existed, that it was my duty to withhold this information and to recommend Cussen to go to another solicitor, which he did.

22. In the events which happened, Ruth Ellis was convicted and the application for reprieve was refused. By then she seemed to have acquired a will to live because, when I saw her on the day her reprieve was refused, she accused me of deliberately throwing away her case and of having accepted a bribe from Cussens to ensure that she was hanged and that he got away free. She dismissed me and asked me to contact Messrs Victor Mishcon, which I did.

23. Mr Victor Mishcon saw me in my office with his Managing Clerk the following morning. He asked me if there was anything I could possibly think of, which might save her life. I said that I, personally, could think of nothing; but I added that, although I thought it would do more harm than good, he might care to ask her where she got the gun. I have reason to believe that he did so and that she subsequently made a statement, which does not, in fact, exactly accord with the statement which I have made above.

24. This case with all its publicity and the weeks of strain under which I had been labouring had a profound effect on me and I have never ceased to brood about it. I kept wondering, among other things, what my duty was, after Ruth Ellis had been executed. I succumbed to the temptation to 'let sleeping dogs lie'. I put hypothetical questions to lawyers and others without getting any satisfactory answers, but I have never stopped thinking about it.

25. It was only recently, in older age, when I was listening to a copy of a tape recording, which Desmond Cussens had given me, that I realised what I ought to have done.

26. To me, it has always been clear that, whilst I was acting for Ruth Ellis, the bond of professional confidence was such that I was not under any obligation to disclose anything, which might be to the detriment of my client, even though it was in the

interests of Justice, but once she, herself, had disclosed it, not only to her other lawyer but to her relations and certainly, after she was dead and her own instructions could not be sought, I ought to have gone to the police and told them what I knew. It is therefore for consideration as to whether or not a charge ought to legitimately be brought against me for being an accessory after the fact. I am, of course, most conscious of this.

27. If she had not been given this fully loaded gun, there might have been a chance for her passions to cool and the crime might never have been committed.

28. On reflection, after all these years of almost ceaseless brooding, I have come to the conclusion that Desmond Cussens was as much, if not more responsible, for the murder than Ruth Ellis, and since he has had nearly 17 years of extra life and is now in no danger of being hanged, it is my personal desire to vindicate myself of the last gross insult, which Ruth Ellis uttered against me in front of a Prison Wardress.

29. There is just one more point, Cussen no doubt thought at the time that he was speaking to me in confidence, but my answer to that is (i) that I am not at liberty to withhold confidences from my client and she has released me from it by making it public and (ii) that, in any event, I should not have kept a confidence of such a character once I was released from my duty to my client. And so, after all these years of wondering and worrying, I have had to find the answer for myself. I know it will stir up mud and I do not relish the task of being involved, but having at least made up my mind, I must leave it up to you to do what is right and just.

Signed: John Bickford.[19]

Notes

Preface

1. Bresler, Fenton, *Reprieve: A Study of a System* (London: Harrap, 1965), p.241.
2. Edward Henry, email to Laurence Marks, 24 February 2012.

Chapter 1

1. *The Times*, 'Teachers' Comment on Execution: School near Prison in a Ferment', 14 July 1955.
2. Diary of Gladys Langford, 1890–1972; archives of Islington Local History Centre.
3. *Daily Mirror*, 'Cassandra Talks to YOU About – The Woman Who Hangs This Morning', 13 July 1955.
4. Weis, Rene, *Criminal Justice: The True Story of Edith Thompson* (London: Penguin, 1988), p.265.
5. Photograph, Mirrorpix, 12 July 1955.
6. *The Independent*, 'Obituary: Lady Taylor', Daniel Yates, 7 January 1998.
7. *Ibid.*
8. PCOM 9/2084.
9. *Ibid.*
10. A London Childhood: 13 July 1955, Martin Day, St Margaret's Community website: www.stmgrts.org.uk.
11. Pierrepoint, Albert, *Executioner Pierrepoint: An Autobiography* (Cranbrook: Eric Dobby, 2005), pp.173–5. The original memorandum uses 'he' as a prefix; the female has been substituted here for reasons of clarity.
12. *Daily Mirror*, 'I Will Always Be Haunted by Look Ruth Ellis Gave Me', Ruki Sayid, 1999.
13. Galilee refers several times to a green screen; usually the door to the execution chamber was concealed by a wardrobe on castors, which may have been the case here, but to avoid confusion, Galilee's description is used throughout the text.

14. *Daily Mirror*, 'I Will Always Be Haunted by Look Ruth Ellis Gave Me', Ruki Sayid, 1999.
15. Goodman, Jonathan and Pringle, Patrick (eds), *The Trial of Ruth Ellis* (Newton Abbot: David & Charles, 1974), p.71.
16. *Daily Mirror*, 'I Will Always Be Haunted by Look Ruth Ellis Gave Me', Ruki Sayid, 1999.
17. Weis, *Criminal Justice*, p.304.
18. Jakubait, Muriel with Weller, Monica, *Ruth Ellis: My Sister's Secret Life* (London: Constable & Robinson, 2005), p.231.
19. *Ibid*.
20. *Ibid*., pp.231–2.
21. *Daily Mirror*, 'I Will Always Be Haunted by Look Ruth Ellis Gave Me', Ruki Sayid, 1999.
22. PCOM 9/2084.
23. CRIM 8/24.
24. Pierrepoint, *Executioner Pierrepoint*, p.131. Details of how an execution was carried out can be found in Pierrepoint's autobiography; I have drawn on this, other accounts listed in the bibliography and also Home Office memorandums to paint as comprehensive a picture as possible. Pierrepoint gave several accounts of Ruth's last moments and these are discussed elsewhere in the text.
25. *Daily Mirror*, 'I Will Always Be Haunted by Look Ruth Ellis Gave Me', Ruki Sayid, 1999.
26. *Ibid*.
27. *The Story of Ruth Ellis*, Thames Television documentary, 1977.
28. *Evening News*, 14 July 1955. No further details.
29. *The Times*, 14 July 1955. No further details.
30. Goodman and Pringle, *The Trial of Ruth Ellis*, p.73.
31. A London Childhood: 13 July 1955, Martin Day, St Margaret's Community website: www.stmgrts.org.uk.

Chapter 2

1. *Woman's Sunday Mirror*, 'My Love and Hate', Ruth Ellis, 26 June 1955.
2. Hancock, Robert, *Ruth Ellis: The Last Woman to be Hanged* (London: Weidenfeld & Nicolson, 1963), p.1.
3. Entry for Droylsden in Wilson, Revd John Marius, *The Imperial Gazetteer of England and Wales* (London and Edinburgh: A Fullarton & Co., 1872); a copy is available online at www.visionofbritain.org.uk.
4. Arthur's service records show that he did not join the army at 16 and nor did his mother buy him out, as is claimed in Jakubait with Weller, *Ruth Ellis: My Sister's Secret Life*. There are discrepancies in the family history in the book: Muriel's grandfather was Walter William Hornby, not

Charles Hornby; Walter died in 1917, not shortly after Muriel's birth; Arthur did not have a sister named Elizabeth but an aunt, Jane Elizabeth, who was a teacher. Jane died in Prestwich in 1920.

5. In Jakubait with Weller, *Ruth Ellis: My Sister's Secret Life*, ghostwriter Monica Weller cites Ruth's mother's surname as Cothals but official documents record it as 'Goethals', and therefore that surname has been employed here.

6. *Manchester Guardian*, 'The Belgian Refugees', 11 December 1914.

7. Although Muriel later recalled her father changing his surname after she was born in 1920, the registers show that all the children except Julius bore the surname Hornby.

8. Goodman and Pringle (eds), *The Trial of Ruth Ellis*, pp.13–14.

9. Not the Theatre Royal as stated in Jakubait with Weller, *Ruth Ellis: My Sister's Secret Life*.

10. HO291/236.

11. *The Independent*, 'I Intended to Kill Him', Catherine Pepinster, 21 September 2003.

12. Tony Cox, email to author, December 2011.

13. The hospital closed in the late 1990s and was bought by property developers. Today, hardly anything of the old building remains.

14. Huggett, Renee and Berry, Paul, *Daughters of Cain* (London: Pan, 1960), p. 266.

15. *Woman's Sunday Mirror*, 'My Love and Hate', Ruth Ellis, 26 June 1955.

16. Jakubait with Weller, *Ruth Ellis: My Sister's Secret Life*, p.33.

17. *Ibid.*, p.34.

18. *Mail on Sunday*, 'The Real Ruth?', Alice Fowler, 14 October 2001.

19. *Woman's Sunday Mirror*, 'My Love and Hate', Ruth Ellis, 26 June 1955.

Chapter 3

1. *Sunday Dispatch*, 'The Woman Who Wants to Die!', Godfrey Winn, 26 June 1955.

2. PCOM 9/2084.

3. *Woman's Sunday Mirror*, 'My Love and Hate', Ruth Ellis, 26 June 1955.

4. Marks, Laurence and Van den Bergh, Tony, *Ruth Ellis: A Case of Diminished Responsibility?* (London: Penguin, 1977), p.15.

5. *Ibid.*

6. *Woman's Sunday Mirror*, 'My Love and Hate', Ruth Ellis, 26 June 1955.

7. *Empire News*, 'My Sister Ruth Has Lost the Will to Live', Granville Neilson, 26 June 1955.

8. *Ibid.*

9. PCOM 9/2084.

10. *Ibid.*

11. *Woman's Sunday Mirror*, 'My Love and Hate', Ruth Ellis, 26 June 1955.
12. *Empire News*, 'My Sister Ruth Has Lost the Will to Live', Granville Neilson, 26 June 1955.
13. *Woman's Sunday Mirror*, 'My Love and Hate', Ruth Ellis, 26 June 1955.
14. A very different story of how they first met is told in the *Woman's Sunday Mirror*: 'My first serious date became my first love, my first taste of ecstasy and my first experience of absolute and bitter misery. I worked with a woman friend at the Lyceum. She was several years older than I and I knew she went to dances and parties with servicemen. One day she said, "I've got a date with a Canadian tonight . . ." We met at the Lyceum, I was excited, happy and looking my best. I liked my boy, Mac, from the start . . . Mac loved me devotedly, and when he was with his unit he would write not once but often twice a day . . . Then one raw November morning the telegram came. Mac was dead.' Muriel is adamant that this is inaccurate, and the conclusion of this part of Ruth's story is undoubtedly false.
15. *Woman's Sunday Mirror*, 'My Love and Hate', Ruth Ellis, 26 June 1955.
16. *Ibid.*
17. PCOM 9/2084.

Chapter 4

1. *Sunday Graphic*, 'The Downfall of My Sister Ruth', Granville Neilson, 26 June 1955.
2. *Woman's Sunday Mirror*, 'My Love and Hate', Ruth Ellis, 26 June 1955.
3. Muriel states that the flowers were roses, but all other sources name them as carnations.
4. Although Ruth's other biographers place her either at the Streatham Locarno or the Lyceum on the Strand during the war years, Muriel is adamant that she continued working at Lyons after giving birth to Andre and switched to the Locarno around 1946. In this instance, I have chosen to follow Muriel's lead, since she did the bulk of babysitting for Ruth in the first couple of years after Andre was born.
5. Authors Goodman and Pringle, and Robert Hancock, claim that Ruth worked at the Lyceum Dancehall in the Strand, but other sources, including the more reliable Marks and Van den Bergh, are firm that it was Streatham Locarno.
6. *Daily Mail*, 'Britain 1947: Poverty, Queues, Rationing – and Resilience', Tony Rennell, 20 November 2007.
7. *Woman's Sunday Mirror*, 'My Love and Hate', Ruth Ellis, 26 June 1955.
8. Dors, Diana, *Dors by Diana* (London: Futura, 1981), p.44.
9. *Woman's Sunday Mirror*, 'My Love and Hate', Ruth Ellis, 26 June 1955.
10. PCOM 9/2084. There are discrepancies in both the published and

unpublished sources on Ruth's life in the immediate aftermath of the war. The Holloway prison doctor noted that Ruth was 17 when she began working for Morris Conley. If that were true, then Ruth would have been working as a hostess in the Court Club before she gave birth to Andre. All other sources agree that she began working for Conley after the war; Robert Hancock states that she began working for Conley in 1946, which is much more likely – she was then 19.

11. *Ibid.*

12. *The People*, Duncan Webb, 11 December 1955.

13. *Ibid.*

14. *The Times*, 'Amusement Arcades Criticised: Magistrate on "Plague Spots"', 18 August 1939.

15. Marks and Van den Bergh, *Ruth Ellis: A Case of Diminished Responsibility?*, p.24.

16. Linnane, Fergus, *London's Underworld: Three Centuries of Vice and Crime* (London: Robson, 2003), p.129.

17. Glinert, Ed, *West End Chronicles: 300 Years of Glamour and Excess in the Heart of London* (London: Penguin, 2007), p.219.

18. Webb, Duncan, *Line Up for Crime* (London: Frederick Muller, 1956), pp.209–10.

19. *Ibid.*

20. Summers, Anthony and Dorril, Stephen, *Honeytrap: The Secret Worlds of Stephen Ward* (London: Weidenfeld & Nicolson, 1987), pp.32–3.

Chapter 5

1. Knightley, Phillip and Kennedy, Caroline, *An Affair of State: The Profumo Case and the Framing of Stephen Ward* (London: Jonathan Cape, 1987), p.37.

2. Parker, Tony, *The Plough Boy* (London: Arrow, 1965), p.23.

3. Lewis, Peter, *The Fifties* (London: William Heinemann, 1978), p.42.

4. Kynaston, David, *Family Britain, 1951–1957* (London: Bloomsbury, 2009), p.572.

5. *Ibid.*, p.570.

6. *Ibid.*, p.566.

7. *Ibid.*

8. *Ibid.*, p.551.

9. *Ibid.*, p.558.

10. Lewis, *The Fifties*, pp.42–3.

11. *Woman's Sunday Mirror*, 'My Love and Hate', Ruth Ellis, 26 June 1955.

12. Knightley and Kennedy, *An Affair of State*, p.38.

13. *Ibid.*

14. Summers and Dorril, *Honeytrap*, pp.32–3.

15. *Ibid.*, p.4.
16. *Ibid.*, p.34.
17. Knightley and Kennedy, *An Affair of State*, p.38.

Chapter 6

1. South London and Maudsley NHS Trust.
2. *Ibid.*
3. HO291/237.
4. *Ibid.*
5. In another version of events, not one but three men beat up George after encountering him outside the club.
6. HO291/237.
7. *Ibid.*
8. *Ibid.*
9. Kynaston, *Family Britain*, p.215.
10. HO291/237.
11. *Ibid.*
12. *Ibid.*
13. *Ibid.*
14. *Ibid.* Muriel disputes this and other accounts of Ruth and George living well and for some time in Newquay; she states that the couple stayed at the Hotel Bristol in Newquay, owned by the Young family since 1927. But Mrs Young also claims that the Ellis family came to them every year, while in fact George's father died in 1936 and wasn't a dentist as she thought.
15. Knightley and Kennedy, *An Affair of State*, p.39.
16. *Ibid.*
17. *Woman's Sunday Mirror*, 'My Love and Hate', Ruth Ellis, 26 June 1955.
18. *Ibid.*
19. South London and Maudsley NHS Trust.
20. *Ibid.*
21. *Ibid.*
22. PCOM 9/2084.
23. South London and Maudsley NHS Trust.
24. *Ibid.*
25. *Ibid.*
26. Ellis, Georgina and Taylor, Rod, *Ruth Ellis, My Mother: Memoirs of a Murderer's Daughter* (London: Smith Gryphon, 1995), p.42.
27. HO 291/237.
28. *Ibid.*

Chapter 7

1. Dors, *Dors by Diana*, pp.105–6.

2. Paul Sullivan, email to author, December 2011. The official Diana Dors website can be found at: www.dianadors.co.uk.

3. *Folkestone Herald*, 'Beauty Queens Invade Folkestone', 12 May 1951.

4. Collins, Joan, *Past Imperfect* (London: WH Allen & Co., 1985), p.21.

5. South London and Maudsley NHS Trust.

6. *Ibid.*

7. *Ibid.*

8. *Ibid.*

9. *Ibid.*

10. *Ibid.*

11. *The Story of Ruth Ellis*, Thames Television documentary, 1977.

12. Hancock, *Ruth Ellis: The Last Woman to be Hanged*, p.36.

13. *Ibid.*

14. Marks and Van den Bergh, *Ruth Ellis: A Case of Diminished Responsibility?*, p.43.

15. Kynaston, *Family Britain*, p.6.

16. Sage, Lorna, *Bad Blood* (London: Fourth Estate 2000), p.102.

17. PCOM 9/2084.

18. *Ibid.*

19. *Woman's Sunday Mirror*, 'My Love and Hate', Ruth Ellis, 26 June 1955.

20. Ellis and Taylor, *Ruth Ellis, My Mother: Memoirs of a Murderer's Daughter*, p.49.

21. South London and Maudsley NHS Trust.

22. HO 291/237.

23. *Woman's Sunday Mirror*, 'My Love and Hate', Ruth Ellis, 26 June 1955.

24. Hancock, *Ruth Ellis: The Last Woman to be Hanged*, p.39.

25. Kynaston, *Family Britain*, p.104.

26. Knightley and Kennedy, *An Affair of State*, p.39.

Chapter 8

1. *Daily Mirror*, 27 January 1953, newspaper clipping. No further information available.

2. Kynaston, *Family Britain*, p.262.

3. *Woman's Sunday Mirror*, 'My Love and Hate', Ruth Ellis, 26 June 1955.

4. Hancock, *Ruth Ellis: The Last Woman to be Hanged*, pp.40–1.

5. *Ibid.*, p.41.

6. *1956 BARC Yearbook*, advertisement (London: British Autombile Racing Club, 1956).

7. Olivia Temple, email to author, December 2011.

8. Knightley and Kennedy, *An Affair of State*, pp.39–40.

9. *Ibid.*, p.41.

10. Previous authors haven't been able to agree on an approximate date for when Ruth Ellis met David Blakely. Goodman and Pringle believe it was probably after her 27th birthday, which was celebrated at Carroll's, but David sent her a telegram for the occasion, which makes it clear they were already on friendly if not intimate terms. At her trial Ruth insisted it was August 1953 when she was made manageress of the Little Club and she had no reason to lie. Muriel is keen to dispute the accepted version of how Ruth and David met. She spoke to Sylvia Smith, who worked at the now defunct House at Home pub in Westerham in the early 1950s; Smith told Muriel that Ruth Ellis and David Blakely frequented the pub between 1951 and 1953 and may even have rented a cottage in the area. This seems highly unlikely given all the evidence to the contrary, including Ruth's own recollections and her statements to the police.
11. *Woman's Sunday Mirror*, 'My Love and Hate', Ruth Ellis, 26 June 1955.
12. *Ibid.*
13. HO291/237.
14. PCOM 9/2084.
15. *The Story of Ruth Ellis*, Thames Television documentary, 1977. There is a slightly different version of this story in Marks and Van den Burgh, *Ruth Ellis: A Case of Diminished Responsibility?* and in Jakubait with Weller, *Ruth Ellis: My Sister's Secret Life*.
16. *Murder Casebook: Investigations into the Ultimate Crime: Issue 11: Crimes of Passion* (London: Marshall Cavendish), p.372.
17. Ellis and Taylor, *Ruth Ellis, My Mother: Memoirs of a Murderer's Daughter*, p.50.
18. Toynbee, Polly, *Lost Children: The Story of Adopted Children Searching for their Mothers* (London: Hutchinson, 1985), p.96.
19. *Woman's Sunday Mirror*, 'My Love and Hate', Ruth Ellis, 26 June 1955.
20. *Ibid.*
21. *Ibid.*
22. *Ibid.*

Chapter 9

1. HO 291/237.
2. *Sheffield Independent*, 'Murder Charge Against Sheffield Doctor Fails: Defence Evidence Not Called', 22 February 1934.
3. *Ibid.*
4. *Sheffield Star*, 'Charges Against a Doctor', 21 February 1934.
5. Sheffield newspaper clipping; no further information available.
6. *Ibid.*
7. *Ibid.*
8. *Ibid.*

9. *Sheffield Independent*, 'Drug Which Leaves No Trace: Story in Charge Against Doctor: Alleged Visits to Girl: Diary and Phial Found After Death', 21 February 1934.

10. *Ibid.*

11. *Sheffield Daily Telegraph*, 'Doctor and Drug: Further Charge in Sheffield Case', 21 February 1934.

12. *Sheffield Independent*, untitled article, 13 February 1934.

13. *Sheffield Independent*, 'Drug Which Leaves No Trace: Story in Charge Against Doctor: Alleged Visits to Girl: Diary and Phial Found After Death', 21 February 1934.

14. *Sheffield Independent*, untitled article, 13 February 1934.

15. *Sheffield Independent*, 'Drug Which Leaves No Trace: Story in Charge Against Doctor: Alleged Visits to Girl: Diary and Phial Found After Death', 21 February 1934.

16. *Ibid.*

17. Bentley, David, *The Sheffield Murders 1865–1965* (Sheffield: ALD Design & Print, 2003), Kindle edition; no page numbers.

18. *Sheffield Independent*, 'Murder Charge Against Sheffield Doctor Fails: Defence Evidence Not Called', 22 February 1934.

19. *Daily Mail*, 'The Paedophile Headmaster, His Sadistic Wife and the Schooldays that Scarred Me Forever', A.N. Wilson, 11 June 2011.

20. *Ibid.*

21. *Ibid.*

22. *Ibid.*

23. David Blakely, Shrewsbury School Report Summary Sheet.

24. *Ibid.*

25. *Ibid.*

26. *Ibid.*

27. *Ibid.*

28. *Ibid.*

29. *Ibid.*

30. *Ibid.*

31. *Ibid.*

32. *Ibid.*

33. *Ibid.*

34. *Lewiston Daily Sun*, quoted on the *Queen Mary* website, 5 February 2010, www.queenmarystory.com/2010_02_01_archive.html.

35. HO 291/237.

36. Beauman, Nicola, *The Other Elizabeth Taylor* (London: Persephone Books, 2009) p.278.

37. Hancock, Robert, *Ruth Ellis: The Last Woman to be Hanged* (London: Weidenfeld & Nicolson, 1963), p.50.

38. HO 291/238.

Chapter 10

1. Muriel believes that the Findlaters met David while he was in the military and that they made up a foursome with David's sister, but Maureen departed for a new life in America in 1945 and David did not leave Shrewsbury School until 1947. The meeting occurred, as previous writers state, a few years later when the Findlaters were trying to sell their car. Maureen would sometimes join her brother and the Findlaters for nights out when she was home from America and staying at Culross Street.
2. HO 291/238.
3. *Ibid.*
4. Marks and Van den Bergh, *Ruth Ellis: A Case of Diminished Responsibility?*, p.53.
5. HO 291/238.
6. Marks and Van den Bergh, *Ruth Ellis: A Case of Diminished Responsibility?*, p.54.
7. Muriel claims that the house in Penn was rented from 1949 and that David's mother and stepfather changed its name to Albi, although it reverted to its former name when they left. She also states that a neighbour recalls David's siblings living at the house, but she is mistaken on this point; David's brothers and sister lived elsewhere.
8. Beauman, *The Other Elizabeth Taylor*, p.182.
9. Taylor, Elizabeth, *In a Summer Season* (London: Virago Press, 1983), p.23.
10. Beauman, *The Other Elizabeth Taylor*, p.279.
11. Police papers refer to him as Borti; in her book Muriel refers to him as Bortolotti.
12. MEPO 2/9888.
13. *The Story of Ruth Ellis*, Thames Television documentary, 1977.
14. Edwards, Robert, *Archie and the Listers* (Somerset: Patrick Stephens, 1995), p.50.
15. Marks and Van den Bergh, *Ruth Ellis: A Case of Diminished Responsibility?*, p.68.
16. MEPO 2/9888. Muriel claims that they had known each other far longer; she spoke to an 89-year-old retired Leatherhead dentist who told her that Cussen and Blakely were members of the Paddock Club in Ashtead, Surrey. There is no record of this elsewhere.
17. Marks and Van den Bergh, *Ruth Ellis: A Case of Diminished Responsibility?*, p.64.
18. *Ibid.*, p.66.
19. *Ibid.*

415

20. *Woman's Sunday Mirror*, 'My Love and Hate', Ruth Ellis, 3 July 1955.
21. MEPO 2/9888.
22. *Murder Casebook: Investigations into the Ultimate Crime: Issue 11: Crimes of Passion*, p.371.
23. *Daily Dispatch*, The 6 White Carnations – and the 1 Red, James Reid, 26 June 1955.
24. Hancock, *Ruth Ellis: The Last Woman to be Hanged*, p.56.
25. Beauman, *The Other Elizabeth Taylor*, p.281.
26. *Ibid.*
27. *The Times*, Announcements, 13 November 1953.
28. HO 291/237.
29. *Ibid.*
30. HO 291/238.
31. Marks and Van den Bergh, *Ruth Ellis: A Case of Diminished Responsibility?*, p.66.
32. Goodman and Pringle (eds), *The Trial of Ruth Ellis*, p.19.
33. *Woman's Sunday Mirror*, 'My Love and Hate', Ruth Ellis, 3 July 1955.
34. *Ibid.*
35. *Ibid.*
36. HO 291/237.
37. Muriel recalls it being shortly before Ruth's execution that Georgina was taken from her; she claims Georgina's recollection of events is wrong, since Ruth's daughter was resolute that she was taken away by her father much earlier. But in late 1954 Ruth was using Georgina's whereabouts in Warrington as an excuse to Cussen when she spent the night with David, and in June 1955 Ruth told prison staff that Georgina was in the care of her husband, although she retained legal custody of her daughter.
38. Ellis and Taylor, *Ruth Ellis, My Mother: Memoirs of a Murderer's Daughter*, p.52.
39. *Ibid.*, p.39.
40. *Ibid.*, p.54.
41. HO 291/238.
42. HO 291/237.
43. Goodman and Pringle, *The Trial of Ruth Ellis*, p.20.

Chapter 11

1. MEPO 2/9888.
2. CRIM 8/24.
3. Hancock, *Ruth Ellis: The Last Woman to be Hanged*, p.68.
4. *Ibid.*, p.74.
5. *Woman's Sunday Mirror*, 'My Love and Hate', Ruth Ellis, 3 July 1955.
6. Hancock, *Ruth Ellis: The Last Woman to be Hanged*, pp.76–7.

7. *Woman's Sunday Mirror*, 'My Love and Hate', Ruth Ellis, 3 July 1955.

8. HO 291/237.

9. *Ibid.*

10. *Autosport* Bulletin, 1954 clipping. No further information.

11. HO 291/238.

12. HO 291/235.

13. *Ibid.*

14. MEPO 26/145.

15. *The Story of Ruth Ellis*, Thames Television documentary, 1977.

16. HO 291/237.

17. *Ibid.*

18. *Ibid.*

19. *Ibid.*

20. *Ibid.*

21. *Ibid.*

22. *The Story of Ruth Ellis*, Thames Television documentary, 1977.

23. HO 291/237.

24. *Woman's Sunday Mirror*, 'My Love and Hate', Ruth Ellis, 10 July 1955.

25. HO 291/237.

26. *Woman's Sunday Mirror*, 'My Love and Hate', Ruth Ellis, 10 July 1955.

27. *Ibid.*

28. *Ibid.*

29. *Ibid.*

30. *Ibid.*

31. *Ibid.*

32. *Ibid.*

33. *Ibid.*

34. HO 291/237.

35. HO 291/238.

36. *Ibid.*

37. HO 291/237.

38. *Ibid.*

39. *Ibid.*

40. MEPO 2/9888.

41. HO 291/237.

42. MEPO 2/9888.

43. Marks and Van den Bergh, *Ruth Ellis: A Case of Diminished Responsibility?*, p.200.

44. CRIM 8/24. In her book, Muriel admits she is puzzled why Ruth spent nights with David at the Rodney Hotel in Kensington 'when she had a room at Egerton Gardens', but their last night at the hotel was 4 February; they moved into Egerton Gardens a few days later.

45. *Woman's Sunday Mirror*, 'My Love and Hate', Ruth Ellis, 10 July 1955.
46. Hancock, *Ruth Ellis: The Last Woman to be Hanged*, p.91.
47. *Ibid.*
48. *Woman's Sunday Mirror*, 'My Love and Hate', Ruth Ellis, 10 July 1955.
49. HO 291/238.
50. *The Story of Ruth Ellis*, Thames Television documentary, 1977.
51. MEPO 2/9888.
52. HO 291/237.
53. MEPO 2/9888.
54. *Autosport* Bulletin, 1954 clipping. No further information.
55. MEPO 26/145.
56. *Ibid.*
57. *The Story of Ruth Ellis*, Thames Television documentary, 1977.
58. MEPO 26/145.
59. *Ibid.*
60. *The Story of Ruth Ellis*, Thames Television documentary, 1977.
61. Knightley and Kennedy, *An Affair of State*, p.41.

Chapter 12

1. CRIM 8/24.
2. MEPO 2/9888.
3. Goodman and Pringle, *The Trial of Ruth Ellis*, p.22.
4. HO 291/237.
5. *Ibid.*
6. DPP2/2430/1.
7. MEPO 2/9888.
8. DPP2/2430/1.
9. Marks and Van den Bergh, *Ruth Ellis: A Case of Diminished Responsibility?*, p.89.
10. Knightley and Kennedy, *An Affair of State*, pp.41–2.
11. Summers and Dorril, *Honeytrap*, p.34.
12. PCOM 9/2084.
13. Hancock, *Ruth Ellis: The Last Woman to be Hanged*, p.94.
14. *The Story of Ruth Ellis*, Thames Television documentary, 1977.
15. *Ibid.*
16. Kynaston, *Family Britain*, p.136.
17. *Ibid.*, p.83.
18. *Ibid.*, p.346.
19. DPP2/2430/1.
20. *Ibid.*
21. *Ibid.*
22. *News Chronicle*, 'Another Boom Year Is Here', 3 January 1955.

23. DPP2/2430/1.
24. *Woman's Sunday Mirror*, 'My Love and Hate', Ruth Ellis, 10 July 1955.
25. HO 291/237.
26. *Ibid.*
27. Goodman and Pringle, *The Trial of Ruth Ellis*, p.22.
28. MEPO 2/9888.
29. *Ibid.*
30. HO 291/237.
31. *Ibid.*
32. *Ibid.*
33. *Ibid.*
34. *Ibid.*
35. DPP2/2430/1.
36. MEPO 2/9888.
37. HO 291/237.
38. *Woman's Sunday Mirror*, 'My Love and Hate', Ruth Ellis, 10 July 1955.
39. MEPO 2/9888.
40. *Ibid.*
41. Hancock, *Ruth Ellis: The Last Woman to be Hanged*, p.102.
42. CRIM 8/24.
43. DPP2/2430/1.
44. Marks and Van den Bergh, *Ruth Ellis: A Case of Diminished Responsibility?*, p.91.
45. *Ibid.*, p.45.
46. Hancock, *Ruth Ellis: The Last Woman to be Hanged*, p.102.
47. MEPO 2/9888.
48. *Ibid.*
49. DPP2/2430/1.
50. MEPO 2/9888.
51. DPP2/2430/1.
52. *Ibid.*
53. MEPO 2/9888.
54. DPP2/2430/1.
55. *Ibid.*
56. *Ibid.*
57. HO 291/237.
58. DPP2/2430/1.
59. HO 291/237.
60. *Ibid.*
61. *Ibid.*
62. *Ibid.*
63. Hancock, *Ruth Ellis: The Last Woman to be Hanged*, p.105.

64. HO 291/237.
65. *Ibid.*
66. *Ibid.*
67. *Ibid.*
68. *Ibid.*
69. *Ibid.*
70. MEPO 2/9888.
71. HO 291/237.
72. *Ibid.*
73. *Ibid.*
74. *Ibid.*
75. DPP2/2430/1.
76. *Ibid.*
77. HO 291/237.
78. Webb, *Line Up for Crime*, pp.208–9.

Chapter 13

1. Marshall, Cherry, *The Cat-Walk* (London: Hutchinson, 1978), p.65.
2. *Ibid.*, pp.71–3.
3. HO 291/237.
4. Marshall, *The Cat-Walk*, pp.71–3.
5. HO 291/237.
6. MEPO 2/9888.
7. HO 291/238.
8. HO 291/237.
9. PCOM 9/2084.
10. HO 291/235.
11. HO 291/237.
12. PCOM 9/2084.
13. *Ibid.*
14. HO 291/237.
15. *Ibid.*
16. MEPO 26/145.
17. HO291/236.
18. *Ibid.*
19. HO 291/237.
20. *Ibid.*
21. *Lilliput*, 'Building a 130mph Special', April 1955 (London: Hulton, 1955).
22. HO 291/237.
23. *Ibid.*
24. PCOM 9/2084.
25. Hancock, *Ruth Ellis: The Last Woman to be Hanged*, p.112.

26. HO 291/235.
27. HO 291/237.
28. Ellis and Taylor, *Ruth Ellis, My Mother: Memoirs of a Murderer's Daughter*, p.128.
29. HO 291/237.
30. HO 291/235.
31. *Ibid.*
32. *Ibid.*
33. *Ibid.*
34. *Ibid.*
35. MEPO 26/145.
36. *Ibid.*
37. *Ibid.*
38. *Ibid.*
39. *Ibid.*
40. HO 291/235.
41. HO 291/237.
42. MEPO 26/145.
43. MEPO 2/9888.
44. HO 291/235.
45. HO 291/237.
46. DPP2/2430/1.
47. MEPO 2/9888.
48. HO 291/237.
49. *Woman's Sunday Mirror*, 'My Love and Hate', Ruth Ellis, 17 July 1955.
50. HO 291/237.
51. HO 291/235.
52. The Findlaters later stated that the laughter had probably belonged to their psychologist friend Charlotte, who was a compulsive giggler.
53. HO 291/235.
54. HO 291/237.
55. Hancock, *Ruth Ellis: The Last Woman to be Hanged*, p.137.

Chapter 14

1. *Woman's Sunday Mirror*, 'My Love and Hate', Ruth Ellis, 17 July 1955.
2. HO 291/237.
3. *Ibid.*
4. *Woman's Sunday Mirror*, 'My Love and Hate', Ruth Ellis, 17 July 1955.
5. Marks and Van den Bergh, *Ruth Ellis: A Case of Diminished Responsibility?*, p.74.
6. HO 291/235.

7. HO 291/237.
8. HO 291/235.
9. MEPO 2/9888.
10. HO 291/238.
11. *Ibid.*
12. HO 291/235.
13. HO 291/237.
14. *Ibid.*
15. *The Story of Ruth Ellis*, Thames Television documentary, 1977.
16. DPP2/2430/1.
17. *The Story of Ruth Ellis*, Thames Television documentary, 1977.
18. HO 291/237.
19. *Ibid.*
20. CRIM 8/24.
21. *Ibid.*
22. DPP2/2430/1.
23. HO 291/237.
24. CRIM 8/24.
25. *Ibid.*
26. *The Story of Ruth Ellis*, Thames Television documentary, 1977.
27. CRIM 8/24.
28. Marks and Van den Bergh, *Ruth Ellis: A Case of Diminished Responsibility?*, p.114.
29. CRIM 8/24.
30. PCOM 9/2084.
31. *The Story of Ruth Ellis*, Thames Television documentary, 1977.
32. HO 291/237.
33. CRIM 8/24.
34. DPP2/2430/1.
35. CRIM 8/24.
36. DPP2/2430/1.
37. CRIM 8/24.
38. *Ibid.*
39. DPP2/2430/1.
40. *The Story of Ruth Ellis*, Thames Television documentary, 1977.
41. *Ibid.*
42. HO 291/237.
43. CRIM 8/24.
44. DPP2/2430/1.
45. PCOM 9/2084.
46. HO 291/237.
47. *Ibid.*

48. *Post & Weekly News*, 'Frances Switched from Clippie to Copper', Keith Whitford, 27 February 2003.
49. PCOM 9/2084.
50. CRIM 8/24.
51. *Ibid.*
52. CRIM 8/24.
53. *Ibid.*

Chapter 15

1. *Scotland Yard – The Black Museum*, Central Television documentary, 1988.
2. HO 291/237.
3. DPP2/2430/1.
4. HO 291/237.
5. MEPO 2/9888.
6. HO 291/237.
7. CRIM 8/24.
8. HO 291/237.
9. HO 291/235.
10. Kennedy, Helena, *Eve Was Framed: Women and British Justice* (London: Vintage, 2005), p.239.
11. Hancock, *Ruth Ellis: The Last Woman to be Hanged*, p.14.
12. Marks and Van den Bergh, *Ruth Ellis: A Case of Diminished Responsibility?*, p.94.
13. *Woman's Sunday Mirror*, 'My Love and Hate', Ruth Ellis, 17 July 1955.
14. CRIM 8/24.
15. *Ibid.*
16. *Ibid.*
17. *Ibid.*
18. *Ibid.*
19. MEPO 2/9888.
20. *Ibid.*
21. CRIM 8/24.
22. *Ibid.*
23. *Ibid.*
24. *Ibid.*
25. *Ibid.*
26. *Post & Weekly News*, 'Frances Switched from Clippie to Copper', Keith Whitford, 27 February 2003.
27. *Ibid.*
28. *Woman's Sunday Mirror*, 'My Love and Hate', Ruth Ellis, 17 July 1955.

29. Hancock, *Ruth Ellis: The Last Woman to be Hanged*, p.133.
30. *Manchester Guardian*, 'Man Shot Outside Public House', 11 April 1955.
31. A memo in the National Archives offers a slightly amended version of this: while at the pub, Howell suggested that she write to Ruth recommending Bickford, whose fees the paper would then meet (HO291/238).
32. This differs from the account given in Goodman and Pringle (eds), *The Trial of Ruth Ellis*, and in Cussen's official police statement.
33. MEPO 2/9888.
34. *Ibid.*
35. *Ibid.*
36. *Ibid.*
37. CRIM 8/24.

Chapter 16

1. Camp, John, *Holloway Prison: The Place and the People* (London: David & Charles, 1974), p.21.
2. Henry, Joan, *Who Lie in Gaol* (London: Victor Gollancz, 1952), pp.64–5.
3. PCOM 9/2084.
4. *Ibid.*
5. *Ibid.*
6. *Ibid.*
7. *Ibid.*
8. *Ibid.*
9. *Ibid.*
10. *Ibid.*
11. *Ibid.*
12. Marks and Van den Bergh, *Ruth Ellis: A Case of Diminished Responsibility?*, pp.122–3.
13. Goodman and Pringle, *The Trial of Ruth Ellis*, p.40.
14. *The Story of Ruth Ellis*, Thames Television documentary, 1977.
15. MEPO 26/145.
16. Goodman and Pringle, *The Trial of Ruth Ellis*, pp.36–7.
17. Henry, *Who Lie in Gaol*, p.93.
18. *Ibid.*, p.41.
19. *Ibid.*, p.44.
20. *Manchester Guardian*, 'Remanded on Murder Charge', 12 April 1955.
21. There is some confusion in Bickford's accounts regarding the date of his first meeting with Desmond Cussen. However, he is clear that Desmond spoke to him about the gun on 13 April 1955.
22. *The Story of Ruth Ellis*, Thames Television documentary, 1977.
23. MEPO 26/145.

24. *The Story of Ruth Ellis*, Thames Television documentary, 1977.
25. MEPO 26/145.
26. Goodman and Pringle, *The Trial of Ruth Ellis*, p.51.
27. MEPO 26/145.
28. *Ibid.*
29. *Ibid.*
30. *Ibid.*
31. *Ibid.*
32. PCOM 9/2084.
33. *Ibid.*
34. DPP2/2430/1.
35. PCOM 9/2084.
36. *Sunday Dispatch*, 'The Woman Who Wants to Die!', Godfrey Winn, 26 June 1955.
37. *Empire News*, 'Ruth Ellis: Calm and Pale at the Last Goodbye', Jacqueline Dyer, 17 July 1955.
38. *Ibid.*
39. DPP2/2430/1.
40. *Ibid.*
41. DPP2/2430/1.
42. PCOM 9/2084.
43. *Ibid.*
44. *Ibid.*
45. *Scotland Yard – The Black Museum*, Central Television documentary, 1988.
46. HO 291/237.
47. PCOM 9/2084.
48. *The Story of Ruth Ellis*, Thames Television documentary, 1977.

Chapter 17

1. DPP2/2430/1.
2. *Ibid.*
3. *Ibid.*
4. *Ibid.*
5. *Ibid.*
6. *Ibid.*
7. *Ibid.*
8. *Ibid.*
9. MEPO 2/9888.
10. DPP2/2430/1.
11. MEPO 2/9888.
12. DPP2/2430/1.
13. PCOM 9/2084.

14. *Ibid.*
15. *Ibid.*
16. *Ibid.*
17. PCOM 9/2084.
18. *Daily Mail*, 22 April 1955, newspaper clipping. No further information available.
19. *Ibid.*
20. *Ibid.*
21. Beauman, *The Other Elizabeth Taylor*, p.281.
22. *Ibid.*
23. *Ibid.*
24. *Ibid*, p.282.
25. *Woman's Sunday Mirror*, 'My Love and Hate', Ruth Ellis, 17 July 1955.
26. PCOM 9/2084.
27. *Ibid.*
28. *Ibid.*
29. MEPO 2/9888.
30. DPP2/2430/1.
31. *Ibid.*
32. *Ibid.*
33. *Ibid.*
34. *Ibid.*
35. Simpson, Professor Keith, *Forty Years of Murder* (London: Grafton, 1980), p.154.
36. MEPO 2/9888.
37. CRIM 8/24.
38. MEPO 2/9888.
39. PCOM 9/2084.
40. HO 291/237.
41. *Ibid.*
42. *Ibid.*
43. *Ibid.*
44. *Daily Sketch*, 'Blonde Model for Trial Accused of Shooting Race Driver', 29 April 1955.
45. *Ibid.*
46. Goodman and Pringle, *The Trial of Ruth Ellis*, p.48.
47. MEPO 2/9888.
48. PCOM 9/2084.
49. *Ibid.*
50. *Ibid.*
51. *Ibid.*
52. *Ibid.*

53. Marshall, *The Cat-Walk*, pp.73–5.
54. PCOM 9/2084.
55. *Ibid.*
56. *Ibid.*
57. *Ibid.*
58. *Ibid.*
59. *Ibid.*
60. *Ibid.*
61. CRIM 8/24.
62. PCOM 9/2084.
63. *Ibid.*
64. *Western Mail*, 'Ellis Letter Goes Under the Hammer,' Simon Evans, 3 November 2004.
65. *Ibid.*
66. PCOM 9/2084.
67. Not Rawlinson, as stated in Robert Hancock's biography.
68. Holton, Richard and Shute, Stephen, 'Self-Control in the Modern Provocation Defence', *Oxford Journal Legal Studies, Vol 27, Issue 1* (Oxford: Oxford University Press, 2007), pp.49–73.
69. The Café de Paris, the Trial of Elvira Barney and the Death of Snakehips Johnson, www.nickelinthemachine.com/2010/02/sample-post.html/knightsbridge/
70. *Ibid.*
71. Kennedy, *Eve Was Framed*, pp.199–200.
72. *Ibid.*, p.6.
73. *Ibid.*
74. Rawlinson, Peter, *A Price Too High: An Autobiography* (London: Weidenfeld & Nicolson, 1989), p.60.
75. *Ibid.*
76. Humphreys, Christmas, *Both Sides of the Circle* (London: George Allen & Unwin, 1978), pp.76–7.
77. *Ibid.*, p.171.

Chapter 18

1. Rawlinson, *A Price Too High*, pp.60–1.
2. *Ibid.*
3. *Ibid.*
4. *Ibid.*
5. PCOM 9/2084.
6. *Ibid.*
7. *Ibid.*
8. *Ibid.*

9. *Ibid.*
10. *Ibid.*
11. *Ibid.*
12. *Ibid.*
13. *Ibid.*
14. *The Empire News*, 'My Sister Ruth Has Lost the Will to Live', Granville Neilson, 26 June 1955.
15. PCOM 9/2084.
16. *Ibid.*
17. *Ibid.*
18. *Ibid.*
19. *Ibid.*
20. *Ibid.*
21. *Ibid.*
22. CRIM 8/24.
23. PCOM 9/2084.
24. CRIM 8/24.
25. *Ibid.*
26. PCOM 9/2084.
27. *Ibid.*
28. *Sunday Dispatch*, 'The Woman Who Wants to Die!', Godfrey Winn, 26 June 1955.
29. PCOM 9/2084.
30. *Ibid.*
31. *Ibid.*
32. *Ibid.*
33. *Ibid.*
34. CRIM 8/24.
35. PCOM 9/2084.
36. *Ibid.*
37. *Ibid.*
38. *Ibid.*
39. *Ibid.*
40. *Ibid.*
41. *Ibid.*
42. *Ibid.*
43. *Ibid.*
44. *Ibid.*
45. *Ibid.*
46. HO 291/237.
47. *Daily Dispatch*, 'The 6 White Carnations – and the 1 Red', James Reid, 26 June 1955.

48. PCOM 9/2084.
49. *Ibid.*
50. HO 291/238.
51. *Ibid.*

Chapter 19

1. Webb, *Line Up for Crime*, p.218.
2. HO 291/237.
3. Henry, *Who Lie in Gaol*, p.14.
4. *The Guardian*, 'The Trial of *Lady Chatterley's Lover*', Geoffrey Robertson QC, 22 October 2010.
5. His son Michael became Attorney-General and then Lord Chancellor, and his daughter Elizabeth would be appointed the first female Lord Justice of Appeal.
6. *The Story of Ruth Ellis*, Thames Television documentary, 1977.
7. HO 291/235.
8. *Ibid.*
9. Klein, Leonora, *A Very English Hangman: The Life and Times of Albert Pierrepoint* (London: Corvo, 2006), pp.154–6.
10. HO 291/235.
11. *Ibid.*
12. *Ibid.*
13. *Ibid.*
14. *Ibid.*
15. *Ibid.*
16. Goodman and Pringle, *The Trial of Ruth Ellis*, p.52.
17. HO 291/235.
18. *Ibid.*
19. *Ibid.*
20. *Ibid.*
21. *Ibid.*
22. Klein, *A Very English Hangman*, p.161.
23. HO 291/235.
24. *Ibid.*
25. *Ibid.*
26. *Ibid.*
27. *Ibid.*
28. *Ibid.*
29. *Ibid.*
30. *Ibid.*
31. HO 291/237.
32. *The Story of Ruth Ellis*, Thames Television documentary, 1977.

33. Klein, *A Very English Hangman*, p.165.
34. *The Story of Ruth Ellis*, Thames Television documentary, 1977.
35. HO 291/237.
36. *The Story of Ruth Ellis*, Thames Television documentary, 1977.
37. *Ibid.*
38. MEPO 26/145.
39. *Ibid.*
40. *The Story of Ruth Ellis*, Thames Television documentary, 1977.
41. Marks and Van den Bergh, *Ruth Ellis: A Case of Diminished Responsibility?*, p.141.
42. HO 291/235.
43. *Ibid.*
44. *Ibid.*
45. *Ibid.*
46. *Ibid.*
47. Kennedy, *Eve Was Framed*, p.203.
48. HO 291/237.
49. HO 291/235.
50. *The Story of Ruth Ellis*, Thames Television documentary, 1977.
51. HO 291/235.
52. *Ibid.*
53. *Ibid.*
54. *Ibid.*
55. *Ibid.*
56. *Ibid.*
57. Kennedy, *Eve Was Framed*, p.269.
58. HO 291/235.
59. *Ibid.*
60. *Ibid.*
61. *Ibid.*
62. HO291/237.
63. HO 291/235.
64. *Ibid.*
65. *Ibid.*
66. *Ibid.*
67. *Ibid.*
68. *Ibid.*
69. Goodman and Pringle, *The Trial of Ruth Ellis*, p.53.
70. Webb, *Line Up for Crime*, p.231.
71. *The Story of Ruth Ellis*, Thames Television documentary, 1977.
72. HO 291/235.
73. *Ibid.*

74. *Ibid.*

Chapter 20

1. HO 291/235.
2. *Ibid.*
3. *Ibid.*
4. *Ibid.*
5. *Ibid.*
6. *Ibid.*
7. *Ibid.*
8. *Ibid.*
9. *Ibid.*
10. *Ibid.*
11. Marks and Van den Bergh, *Ruth Ellis: A Case of Diminished Responsibility?*, p.158.
12. Kennedy, *Eve Was Framed*, p.20.
13. HO 291/235.
14. *Ibid.*
15. *Ibid.*
16. *The Story of Ruth Ellis*, Thames Television documentary, 1977.
17. HO 291/235.
18. Kennedy, *Eve Was Framed*, pp.203–4.
19. Klein, *A Very English Hangman*, pp.182–3.
20. Rawlinson, *A Price Too High*, p.60.
21. Kennedy, *Eve Was Framed*, pp.209–10.
22. *Ibid.*, pp.33–4.
23. HO 291/235.
24. *Ibid.*
25. *Ibid.*
26. *Ibid.*
27. *Ibid.*
28. *Ibid.*
29. *Ibid.*
30. *Ibid.*
31. *The Story of Ruth Ellis*, Thames Television documentary, 1977.
32. HO 291/235.
33. The wording was modified in 1948. Until then, the sentence was passed using the term 'hanged by the neck until you be dead'. See Clark, Richard, *Capital Punishment in Britain* (Sittingbourne: Ian Allan, 2009), p.220.
34. HO 291/235.
35. HO 291/237.

Chapter 21

1. Clark, Richard, *Women and the Noose: A History of Female Execution* (Gloucester: Tempus, 2007), p.129.
2. Pierrepoint, *Executioner Pierrepoint: An Autobiography*, p.122.
3. Bresler, Fenton, *Reprieve: A Study of a System* (London: Harrap, 1965), p.240.
4. Huggett, Renee and Berry, Paul, *Daughters of Cain* (London: Pan, 1960), p.291.
5. Henry, *Who Lie in Gaol*, pp.83–4.
6. *Northumberland Gazette*, 'Haunted By Her Memories', 8 August 2005.
7. *Ibid.*
8. *Ibid.*
9. *Ibid.*
10. Bresler, *Reprieve*, p.245.
11. *Daily Mail*, 'Model Smiles at Murder Verdict', 22 June 1955.
12. PCOM 9/2084.
13. HO 291/236.
14. *Reynolds News*, 'The Little Club', John Knight, 26 June 1955.
15. HO 291/237.
16. *Ibid.*
17. *Ibid.*
18. Marks and Van den Bergh, *Ruth Ellis: A Case of Diminished Responsibility?*, p.169.
19. Goodman and Pringle, *The Trial of Ruth Ellis*, p.57.
20. *Ibid.*
21. Marks and Van den Bergh, *Ruth Ellis: A Case of Diminished Responsibility?*, pp.168–9.
22. PCOM 9/2084.
23. *Ibid.*
24. *Ibid.*
25. *Ibid.*

Chapter 22

1. HO 291/237.
2. *Ibid.*
3. *Ibid.*
4. *Ibid.*
5. *Ibid.*
6. *Ibid.*
7. Marshall, *The Cat-Walk*, pp.73–5.
8. HO 291/236.
9. *Ibid.*

10. *Ibid.*
11. *Ibid.*
12. *Ibid.*
13. *Ibid.*
14. Wilson, Jacqueline, *Jacky Daydream* (London: Yearling, 2008), p.176.
15. Koestler, Arthur and Rolph, C.H., *Hanged by the Neck* (London: Penguin, 1961), p.92.
16. MEPO 26/145.
17. *Ibid.*
18. *Ibid.*
19. MEPO 2/9888.
20. *Ibid.*
21. *Ibid.*
22. *Ibid.*
23. *Ibid.*
24. *Ibid.*
25. *Ibid.*
26. *Ibid.*
27. *Ibid.*
28. *Evening Standard*, 'Letters', 2 July 1955.
29. *Ibid.*
30. *Ibid.*
31. PCOM 9/2084.
32. MEPO 2/9888.
33. *Ibid.*
34. HO 291/238.
35. Edwards, *Archie and the Listers*, p.83.
36. HO 291/237.
37. Diary of Gladys Langford, 1890–1972; archives of Islington Local History Centre.
38. HO 291/238.
39. *Ibid.*
40. PCOM 9/2084.
41. HO 291/238.
42. *Ibid.*
43. MEPO 26/145.
44. *Ibid.*
45. *Daily Mail*, 3 November 1955, newspaper clipping. No further information available.
46. De Blank, Bartha, *Joost de Blank: A Personal Memoir* (Ipswich: Boydell Press, 1977), p.86.
47. Hansard, 8 December 1955, vol. 547 c536.

48. *Ibid.*
49. HO 291/238.
50. *Ibid.*
51. HP 291/236.
52. HO 291/235.
53. *Ibid.*
54. Bresler, *Reprieve*, p.250.
55. *Ibid.*, p.251.
56. HO 291/237.
57. HO 291/235.
58. Pierrepoint, *Executioner Pierrepoint*, p.84.
59. *Ibid.*, p.99.
60. *Ibid.*, p.207.
61. *Ibid.*, pp.208–9.
62. Marks and Van den Bergh, *Ruth Ellis: A Case of Diminished Responsibility?*, p.176.
63. HO 291/235.

Chapter 23

1. Goodman and Pringle, *The Trial of Ruth Ellis*, p.55.
2. *The Story of Ruth Ellis*, Thames Television documentary, 1977.
3. MEPO 26/145.
4. *The Story of Ruth Ellis*, Thames Television documentary, 1977.
5. PCOM 9/2084.
6. Goodman and Pringle, *The Trial of Ruth Ellis*, p.63.
7. PCOM 9/2084.
8. *Empire News*, 'Ruth Ellis: Calm and Pale at the Last Goodbye', Jacqueline Dyer, 17 July 1955.
9. *Daily Mail*, 'Was This Man the Evil Force that Turned Ruth Ellis into a Murderer?', Angela Mollard, 25 November 1999.
10. *Guardian*, 'My Sister Ruth', Clare Dyer, 12 September 2003.
11. *Daily Mail*, 'Was This Man the Evil Force that Turned Ruth Ellis into a Murderer?', Angela Mollard, 25 November 1999.
12. *The Story of Ruth Ellis*, Thames Television documentary, 1977.
13. *Ibid.*
14. *Ibid.*
15. *Ibid.*
16. Bresler, *Reprieve*, p.247.
17. *Ibid.*
18. *The Story of Ruth Ellis*, Thames Television documentary, 1977. Ruth's will has not been found; Lord Mishcon replied to Muriel's 2002 letter about the matter by stating that any papers in his office relating to Ruth

would have been destroyed. However, according to solicitor Bruce MacGregor, the Principal Registry only has a formal record of a will once a will has been proved and a grant of probate issued. It's therefore likely that Ruth made a will but that the will was not formally proved. The small estates limit in 1955 was £5,000; thus, if her estate comprised personal possessions only, it is very likely that there was no need to extract a grant of probate or to carry out the small estates procedure.

19. *The Story of Ruth Ellis*, Thames Television documentary, 1977.

20. Goodman and Pringle, *The Trial of Ruth Ellis*, p.64.

21. *Ibid*.

22. Goodman and Pringle, *The Trial of Ruth Ellis*, p.65.

23. PCOM 9/2084.

24. MEPO 2/9888.

25. HO 291/237.

26. Goodman and Pringle, *The Trial of Ruth Ellis*, p.66.

27. *Empire News*, 'Ruth Ellis: Calm and Pale at the Last Goodbye', Jacqueline Dyer, 17 July 1955.

28. *Ibid*.

29. *Ibid*.

30. *Ibid*.

31. *The Story of Ruth Ellis*, Thames Television documentary, 1977.

32. *Daily Mail*, 'Police Hunt After Death Cell Talk', 13 July 1955.

33. Bresler, *Reprieve*, p.249.

34. MEPO 2/9888.

35. HO 291/237.

36. A London Childhood: 13 July 1955, Martin Day, St Margaret's Community website: www.stmgrts.org.uk.

37. HO 291/271.

38. *Ibid*.

39. HO 291/238.

40. *Daily Mail*, 'Police Hunt After Death Cell Talk', 13 July 1955.

41. *Ibid*.

42. *Sunday Dispatch*, 'The Five Ages of Ruth Ellis by Her Parents', 17 July 1955.

43. Pierrepoint, *Executioner Pierrepoint*, p.182.

44. *The Story of Ruth Ellis*, Thames Television documentary, 1977.

45. There is no truth in the statement made by Muriel Jakubait that Pierrepoint interviewed Ruth first in order to ascertain her weight; as we have seen, the execution process was shrouded in secrecy. Nor were Ruth's ankles tied together with rope as is stated in the book (they were bound by a strap), and there were certainly no windows in the execution chamber.

46. Evelyn Galilee was transferred from Holloway soon after the execution but eventually left the prison system and became a nurse. She died in a nursing home in County Durham in June 2011 at the age of 84. One of her most precious possessions had been the gas cigarette lighter bequeathed to her by Ruth.

47. *The Times*, 'Crowds Demand to See Mrs Ellis: Police Reinforcements Outside Prison', 13 July 1955.

48. HO 291/237.

49. HO 291/271.

50. *Ibid.*

51. Goodman and Pringle, *The Trial of Ruth Ellis*, p.70.

52. HO 291/237.

53. Pierrepoint, *Executioner Pierrepoint*, pp.173–5.

54. PCOM 9/2084.

55. *Ibid.*

56. Huggett and Berry, *Daughters of Cain*, p.287.

57. MEPO 2/9888.

58. Marks and Van den Bergh, *Ruth Ellis: A Case of Diminished Responsibility?*, p182.

59. Bresler, *Reprieve*, p.250.

60. *Ibid.*

61. Goodman and Pringle, *The Trial of Ruth Ellis*, p.73.

62. HO 291/237.

63. Klein, *A Very English Hangman*, p.169.

64. *Ruth Ellis – A Life for a Life*, BBC documentary, 1999.

Chapter 24

1. Marks and Van den Bergh, *Ruth Ellis: A Case of Diminished Responsibility?*, p.186.

2. *Post & Weekly News*, 'Frances Switched from Clippie to Copper', Keith Whitford, 27 February 2003.

3. *Ibid.*

4. Marks and Van den Bergh, *Ruth Ellis: A Case of Diminished Responsibility?*, p.186.

5. Rawlinson, *A Price Too High: An Autobiography*, pp.60–1.

6. Marshall, *The Cat-Walk*, pp.75–6.

7. Marks and Van den Bergh, *Ruth Ellis: A Case of Diminished Responsibility?*, p.186.

8. PCOM 9/1773 and PCOM 9/2024.

9. *Ibid.*

10. *Ibid.*

11. Pierrepoint, *Executioner Pierrepoint: An Autobiography*, p.210.

12. *The Story of Ruth Ellis*, Thames Television documentary, 1977.
13. Marriner, Brian, *Crime of the Heart: 18 Shocking True Stories of the People who Killed for Love* (London: Arrow, 1994), p.222.
14. Marks and Van den Bergh, *Ruth Ellis: A Case of Diminished Responsibility?*, p.185.
15. Mirrorpix image.
16. Diary of Gladys Langford, 1890–1972; archives of Islington Local History Centre.
17. Kynaston, *Family Britain, 1951–1957*, p.494.
18. Pierrepoint, *Executioner Pierrepoint*, pp.208–9.
19. *Ibid.*
20. PCOM 9/2084.
21. *Ibid.*
22. *Ibid.*
23. *Ibid.*
24. *Ibid.*
25. Marks and Van den Bergh, *Ruth Ellis: A Case of Diminished Responsibility?*, pp.186–7.
26. *Ibid.*
27. *Ibid.*
28. *Ibid.*
29. HO 291/237.
30. Pierrepoint, *Executioner Pierrepoint*, pp.173–5.
31. Marshall, *The Cat-Walk*, pp.75–6.
32. *Daily Herald*, 'A Chamber of Horrors Has a New "Member"', 16 July 1955.
33. HO 291/237.
34. *Ibid.*
35. *Ibid.*
36. LCO 2/5573.
37. *Ibid.*
38. HO 291/237.
39. *Ibid.*
40. FO 371/116897.
41. Mass-Observations Archive (Special Collections, University of Sussex).
42. *Ibid.*
43. *Lancet* (medical journal), 'The Death Penalty', 23 July 1955.
44. HO 291/237.
45. *Ibid.*
46. Mass-Observations Archive (Special Collections, University of Sussex).
47. Klein, *A Very English Hangman*, pp.177–8.
48. PCOM 9/2024.

49. Dors, Diana, *For Adults Only* (London: Star, 1978), pp.251–3.

Chapter 25

1. *Warrington Examiner*, 23 September 1955, newspaper clipping. No further information available.
2. *Jersey Evening Post*, 'Witnesses Tell of Money Troubles and Drinking: At Inquest on Former Husband of Ruth Ellis', 6 August 1958.
3. *Liverpool Echo*, 'Dentist Fined', 9 July 1958.
4. *Jersey Evening Post*, 'Witnesses Tell of Money Troubles and Drinking: At Inquest on Former Husband of Ruth Ellis', 6 August 1958.
5. *Ibid.*
6. *Ibid.*
7. Toynbee, *Lost Children*, p.99.
8. Ellis and Taylor, *Ruth Ellis, My Mother: Memoirs of a Murderer's Daughter*, p.57.
9. Toynbee, *Lost Children*, p.98.
10. *Daily Mirror*, 'The Price We Pay for Our Parents' Crimes', 1 May 1999.
11. *Ibid.*
12. Toynbee, *Lost Children*, p.102.
13. *Ibid.*, pp.102–3.
14. *Ibid.*, p.103.
15. *Daily Mirror*, 'The Price We Pay for our Parents' Crimes', 1 May 1999.
16. Toynbee, *Lost Children*, p.104.
17. Ellis and Taylor, *Ruth Ellis, My Mother: Memoirs of a Murderer's Daughter*, pp.39–40.
18. *The Independent*, 'In the Good-Time Gang', Emma Cook, 25 July 1997.
19. *Daily Mail*, 'Life in the Hangman's Shadow', Angela Levin, 10 March 2001.
20. *Yorkshire Post*, 'Ruth Ellis's Daughter Dies from Cancer', 2 December 2001.
21. *Daily Mirror*, 'The Price We Pay for our Parents' Crimes', 1 May 1999.
22. *The Scotsman*, 'Ruth Ellis Execution Drama Hit Me Hard', Tim Cornwell, 17 August 2007.
23. *Ibid.*
24. www.stmichaelshitchin.fsnet.co.uk.
25. *Ibid.*
26. Bob Ashurst, email to author, 16 December 2011.
27. Nic Szeremeta, email to author, 14 December 2011.
28. Jim Hoare, email to author, 14 December 2011.
29. Bob Ashurst, email to author, 16 December 2011.

30. Brian Jacobs, interview with author, 26 January 2012.
31. *Ibid.*
32. Nic Szeremeta, email to author, 14 December 2011.
33. MEPO 26/145.
34. HO 282/58.
35. *Ibid.*
36. *Ibid.*
37. *Ibid.*
38. *Ibid.*
39. *Ibid.*
40. *Ibid.*
41. *Ibid.*
42. *Ibid.*
43. *Ibid.*
44. Ellis and Taylor, *Ruth Ellis, My Mother: Memoirs of a Murderer's Daughter*, p.77.
45. *Ibid.*, pp.78–9.
46. *Ibid.*
47. *Ibid.*
48. *The Times*, 'Son of Ruth Ellis Took His Own Life', 20 July 1982.
49. *Ibid.*
50. Jakubait with Weller, *Ruth Ellis: My Sister's Secret Life*, p.269.

Chapter 26

1. Francesca Findlater, interview with author, 13 December 2011.
2. Beauman, *The Other Elizabeth Taylor*, p.280.
3. classiclit.about.com/library/bl-etexts/hwlongfellow/bl-hwl-miless.htm.
4. Webb, Duncan, *Line Up for Crime* (London: Frederick Muller, 1956), pp.158–9.
5. *Ibid.*, pp.163–4.
6. *Ibid.*
7. Pierrepoint, *Executioner Pierrepoint*, pp.210–11.
8. Klein, *A Very English Hangman*, p.228.
9. Anne Pierrepoint died five years after her husband, aged ninety-three. Royston Rickard, who served as Albert's assistant at Ruth's hanging, died in 1999.
10. HO 291/238.
11. *Ibid.*
12. *Ibid.*
13. *Ibid.*
14. *Ibid.*
15. *Ibid.*

16. *Ibid.*
17. Marks and Van den Bergh, *Ruth Ellis: A Case of Diminished Responsibility?*, p.176.
18. MEPO 26/145.
19. *Ibid.*
20. *Ibid.*
21. *Ibid.*
22. *Ibid.*
23. *Ibid.*
24. *Ibid.*
25. *Ibid.*
26. *Ibid.*
27. *Ibid.*
28. *Ibid.*
29. *Ibid.*
30. After reading the article, Granville Neilson asked detectives to visit him at his home in Hemel Hempstead; he wanted to discuss the tape recordings and whether they might have helped Ruth at her trial. Detective Inspector Pallett concluded: 'I formed the impression that Mr Neilson was only interested in this matter from a financial point of view. In fact he did say to me, "Everyone is making money out of this affair except me." He told me he had written to the *Sunday People* newspaper and from their reply it would seem that he had offered to supply them with certain material for monetary reward.' MEPO 26/145.
31. Hancock, *Ruth Ellis: The Last Woman to be Hanged*, p.204.
32. *The Story of Ruth Ellis*, Thames Television documentary, 1977.
33. *Ibid.*
34. MEPO 2/9888.
35. *Daily Sketch*, 'Is There a Guilty Man?', 14 July 1955.
36. HO 291/238.
37. *Ibid.*
38. *Ibid.*
39. Webb, *Line Up for Crime*, p.233.
40. *The Guardian*, 'Ruth Ellis: The Other Confession', Alan Travis, 19 January 1999.
41. *Ibid.*
42. HO 291/238.
43. Webb, *Line Up for Crime*, p.233.
44. *Ibid.*, p.233.
45. Hancock, *Ruth Ellis: The Last Woman to be Hanged*, p.193.
46. MEPO 26/145.

47. *Ibid.*
48. *Ibid.*
49. *Ibid.*
50. Laurence Marks, author interview, January 2012.
51. *Ibid.*
52. *The Story of Ruth Ellis*, Thames Television documentary, 1977.
53. *Ibid.*
54. *Ibid.*
55. *Ibid.*
56. *Ibid.*
57. *Ibid.*
58. *Ibid.*

Epilogue
1. *The Guardian*, 'My Sister Ruth', Clare Dyer, 12 September 2003.
2. *The Guardian*, 'Ruth Ellis was "Battered Woman"', 16 September 2003.
3. *Ibid.*
4. www.capitalpunishmentuk.org/ruth.html.
5. *The Guardian*, 'Ruth Ellis "was in a state of frenzy"', Angelique Chrisafis, 18 September 2003.
6. *Ibid.*
7. *The Independent*, 'Revealed: The New Evidence that Shows Ruth Ellis Should Never Have Hanged. Will the Judges Agree?', Jason Bennetto, 15 September 2003.
8. news.bbc.co.uk/1/hi/england/london/3116722.stm.
9. *The Guardian*, 'Ruth Ellis Murder Verdict Upheld', Clare Dyer, 9 December 2003.
10. *Ibid.*
11. *Daily Telegraph*, Sir John William Kay PC, Obituary, 7 July 2004.
12. *The Guardian*, 'Ruth Ellis Murder Verdict Upheld', Clare Dyer, 9 December 2003.
13. *The Independent*, 'Judges Throw Out "Time-Wasting" Ellis Murder Appeal', Jason Bennetto, 9 December 2003.
14. Mike Blackburn, author interview, January 2012.
15. Kennedy, *Eve Was Framed*, p.269.
16. Hancock, *Ruth Ellis: The Last Woman to be Hanged*, p.79.
17. Marks and Van den Bergh, *Ruth Ellis: A Case of Diminished Responsibility?*, p.41.
18. *The Independent*, 'Why My Sister Ruth Must Rest in Peace', Sean O'Neill, 13 September 2003.
19. www.Order-Order.com.
20. Laurence Marks, author interview, January 2012.

21. Potter, John Deane, *The Art of Hanging* (New York: A.S. Barnes & Co., 1969), p.194.
22. Jones, Ann, *Women Who Kill* (London: Victor Gollancz, 1991), p.369.

Appendix I
1. Jakubait with Weller, *Ruth Ellis: My Sister's Secret Life*, p.71.
2. CRIM 8/24.
3. Jakubait with Weller, *Ruth Ellis: My Sister's Secret Life*, pp.62–3.
4. *Ibid.*, p.72.
5. Laurence Marks, author interview, January 2012.
6. Michelangelo Capua, email to author, 15 December 2011.
7. Jakubait with Weller, *Ruth Ellis: My Sister's Secret Life*, p.59.
8. *Ibid.*, pp.79–80.
9. Laurence Marks, author interview, January 2012.
10. Peta Steel, author interview, 5 December 2011.
11. Douglas Thompson, author interview, December 2011.
12. Paul Bickley, author interview, 12 March 2012.
13. There is one strange line in Jacqueline's story in the *Empire News*: 'There is a man who could have helped [the spiralling situation with David and Ruth]. Instead he led David into wrong paths, paths Ruth feared.' No further explanation was given.
14. Laurence Marks, author interview, January 2012.
15. Peta Steel, author interview, 5 December 2011.
16. Blake, Victoria, *Crime Archive: Ruth Ellis* (London: National Archives, 2008), p.103.
17. MEPO 26/145.
18. Smith & Wesson historian Roy G. Jinks, letter to author, 19 April 2012.

Appendix II
1. MEPO 26/145.

Bibliography

Ruth Ellis

Blake, Victoria, *Crime Archive: Ruth Ellis* (London: National Archives, 2008)

Ellis, Georgie and Taylor, Rod, *Ruth Ellis, My Mother: Memoirs of a Murderer's Daughter* (London: Smith Gryphon, 1995)

Goodman, Jonathan and Pringle, Patrick (eds), *The Trial of Ruth Ellis* (Newton Abbot: David & Charles, 1974)

Hancock, Robert, *Ruth Ellis: The Last Woman to be Hanged* (London: Weidenfeld & Nicolson, 1963, and London: Orion, 2000)

Jakubait, Muriel with Weller, Monica, *Ruth Ellis: My Sister's Secret Life* (London: Constable & Robinson, 2005)

Marks, Laurence and Van den Bergh, Tony, *Ruth Ellis: A Case of Diminished Responsibility?* (London: Penguin, 1977)

Miscellaneous

Beauman, Nicola, *The Other Elizabeth Taylor* (London: Persephone Books, 2009)

Bentley, David, *The Sheffield Murders 1865–1965* (Sheffield: ALD Design & Print, 2003)

Bresler, Fenton, *Reprieve: A Study of a System* (London: Harrap, 1965)

Camp, John, *Holloway Prison: The Place and the People* (London: David & Charles, 1974)

Clark, Richard, *Capital Punishment in Britain* (Surrey: Ian Allan, 2009)

Clark, Richard, *Women and the Noose: A History of Female Execution* (Gloucester: Tempus, 2007)

De Blank, Bartha, *Joost de Blank: A Personal Memoir* (Ipswich: Boydell Press, 1977)

Dors, Diana, *Dors by Diana* (London: Futura, 1981)

Dors, Diana, *For Adults Only* (London: Star, 1978)

Edwards, Robert, *Archie and the Listers* (Somerset: Patrick Stephens, 1995)

Ellis, John, *Diary of a Hangman* (London: Forum Press, 1996)

Everett, Rupert, *Red Carpets and other Banana Skins* (London: Abacus 2007)

Fielding, Stephen, *The Executioner's Bible* (London: John Blake, 2008)

Glinert, Ed, *West End Chronicles: 300 Years of Glamour and Excess in the Heart of London* (London: Penguin, 2007)

Henry, Joan, *Who Lie in Gaol* (London: Victor Gollancz, 1952)

Huggett, Renee and Berry, Paul, *Daughters of Cain* (London: Pan, 1960)

Humphreys, Christmas, *Both Sides of the Circle* (London: George Allen & Unwin, 1978)

Jesse, F. Tennyson, *A Pin to See the Peepshow* (London: Virago, 1994)

Jones, Ann, *Women Who Kill* (London: Victor Gollancz, 1991)

Keeler, Christine and Thompson, Douglas, *Christine Keeler: The Truth at Last* (London: Sidgwick & Jackson, 2001)

Kennedy, Helena, *Eve Was Framed: Women and British Justice* (London: Vintage, 2005)

Kennedy, Ludovic, *The Trial of Stephen Ward* (London: Victor Gollancz, 1987)

Klein, Leonora, *A Very English Hangman: The Life and Times of Albert Pierrepoint* (London: Corvo, 2006)

Knightley, Phillip and Kennedy, Caroline, *An Affair of State: The Profumo Case and the Framing of Stephen Ward* (London: Jonathan Cape, 1987)

Koestler, Arthur and Rolph, C.H., *Hanged by the Neck* (London: Penguin, 1961)

Kynaston, David, *Austerity Britain, 1945–1957* (London: Bloomsbury, 2008)

Kynaston, David, *Family Britain, 1951–1957* (London: Bloomsbury, 2009)

Lewis, Peter, *The Fifties* (London: William Heinemann, 1978)

Linnane, Fergus, *London's Underworld: Three Centuries of Vice and Crime* (London: Robson, 2003)

Lord, Graham, *Joan Collins: The Biography of an Icon* (London: Orion, 2007)

Mansfield, Michael, *Memoirs of a Radical Lawyer* (London: Bloomsbury, 2009)

Marshall, Cherry, *The Cat-Walk* (London: Hutchinson, 1978)

Parker, Tony, *The Plough Boy* (London: Arrow, 1965)

Pierrepoint, Albert, *Executioner Pierrepoint: An Autobiography* (Cranbrook: Eric Dobby, 2005)

Potter, John Deane, *The Art of Hanging* (New York: A.S. Barnes & Co., 1969)

Ramsey, Winston G., *Scenes of Murder Then and Now* (Essex: After the Battle, 2012)

Rawlinson, Peter, *A Price Too High: An Autobiography* (London: Weidenfeld & Nicolson, 1989)

Sage, Lorna, *Bad Blood* (London: Fourth Estate, 2000)

Simpson, Professor Keith, *Forty Years of Murder* (London: Grafton, 1980)

Skinner, Keith and Moss, Alan, *The Scotland Yard Files: Milestones in Crime Detection* (London: National Archives, 2006)

Summers, Anthony and Dorril, Stephen, *Honeytrap: The Secret Worlds of Stephen Ward* (London: Weidenfeld & Nicolson, 1987)

Toynbee, Polly, *Lost Children: The Story of Adopted Children Searching for their Mothers* (London: Hutchinson, 1985)

Webb, Duncan, *Line Up for Crime* (London: Frederick Muller, 1956)

Weis, Rene, *Criminal Justice: The True Story of Edith Thompson* (London: Penguin, 1988)

Whistler, Theresa, *The Life of Walter De La Mare* (London: Gerald Duckworth & Co., 2003)

Wilson, Jacqueline, *Jacky Daydream* (London: Yearling, 2008)

Carol Ann Lee is a bestselling author of true crime and historical biography, but has also written novels and books for children. Her passion for storytelling began at a very early age; she was eight years old when she first read *The Diary of Anne Frank* and knew then that she wanted to write about the world's most famous diarist. Twenty years later, Carol's first book, *Roses From The Earth: The Biography of Anne Frank* was published, followed by *The Hidden Life of Otto Frank*, and three books for children about the Holocaust. She is best known for true crime, including *One of Your Own: The Life and Death of Myra Hindley* and *Evil Relations: The Man Who Bore Witness Against the Moors Murderers*, the latter of which was shortlisted for the CWA Non-Fiction Dagger, Britain's leading award for crime non-fiction. Carol's biography of Ruth Ellis, *A Fine Day for a Hanging*, was also shortlisted for the CWA Non-Fiction Dagger and is the inspiration for Silverprint's drama for ITV *A Cruel Love*. Carol's recent books include *Somebody's Mother, Somebody's Daughter: True Stories from the Victims and Survivors of the Yorkshire Ripper*, *A Passion for Poison: The Extraordinary Crimes of Graham Young* and *Something Wicked: The Lives, Crimes and Deaths of the Pendle Witches*. Known for her thorough research and compelling narratives, Carol continues to captivate readers with her explorations of history's darkest corners.